Communications in Computer and Information Science 2319

Series Editors

Rationale
The CCIS series is devoted to the publication of proceedings of computer science conferences. Its aim is to efficiently disseminate original research results in informatics in printed and electronic form. While the focus is on publication of peer-reviewed full papers presenting mature work, inclusion of reviewed short papers reporting on work in progress is welcome, too. Besides globally relevant meetings with internationally representative program committees guaranteeing a strict peer-reviewing and paper selection process, conferences run by societies or of high regional or national relevance are also considered for publication.

Topics
The topical scope of CCIS spans the entire spectrum of informatics ranging from foundational topics in the theory of computing to information and communications science and technology and a broad variety of interdisciplinary application fields.

Information for Volume Editors and Authors
Publication in CCIS is free of charge. No royalties are paid, however, we offer registered conference participants temporary free access to the online version of the conference proceedings on SpringerLink (http://link.springer.com) by means of an http referrer from the conference website and/or a number of complimentary printed copies, as specified in the official acceptance email of the event.

CCIS proceedings can be published in time for distribution at conferences or as post-proceedings, and delivered in the form of printed books and/or electronically as USBs and/or e-content licenses for accessing proceedings at SpringerLink. Furthermore, CCIS proceedings are included in the CCIS electronic book series hosted in the SpringerLink digital library at http://link.springer.com/bookseries/7899. Conferences publishing in CCIS are allowed to use Online Conference Service (OCS) for managing the whole proceedings lifecycle (from submission and reviewing to preparing for publication) free of charge.

Publication process
The language of publication is exclusively English. Authors publishing in CCIS have to sign the Springer CCIS copyright transfer form, however, they are free to use their material published in CCIS for substantially changed, more elaborate subsequent publications elsewhere. For the preparation of the camera-ready papers/files, authors have to strictly adhere to the Springer CCIS Authors' Instructions and are strongly encouraged to use the CCIS LaTeX style files or templates.

Abstracting/Indexing
CCIS is abstracted/indexed in DBLP, Google Scholar, EI-Compendex, Mathematical Reviews, SCImago, Scopus. CCIS volumes are also submitted for the inclusion in ISI Proceedings.

How to start
To start the evaluation of your proposal for inclusion in the CCIS series, please send an e-mail to ccis@springer.com.

Constantine Stephanidis · Margherita Antona ·
Stavroula Ntoa · Gavriel Salvendy
Editors

HCI International 2024 – Late Breaking Posters

26th International Conference, HCII 2024
Washington, DC, USA, June 29 – July 4, 2024
Proceedings, Part I

Springer

Editors
Constantine Stephanidis
University of Crete and Foundation for Research and Technology – Hellas (FORTH)
Heraklion, Crete, Greece

Margherita Antona
Foundation for Research and Technology – Hellas (FORTH)
Heraklion, Crete, Greece

Stavroula Ntoa
Foundation for Research and Technology – Hellas (FORTH)
Heraklion, Crete, Greece

Gavriel Salvendy
University of Central Florida
Orlando, FL, USA

ISSN 1865-0929 ISSN 1865-0937 (electronic)
Communications in Computer and Information Science
ISBN 978-3-031-78515-3 ISBN 978-3-031-78516-0 (eBook)
https://doi.org/10.1007/978-3-031-78516-0

This Springer imprint is published by the registered company Springer Nature Switzerland AG
The registered company address is: Gewerbestrasse 11, 6330 Cham, Switzerland

Foreword

This year we celebrate 40 years since the establishment of the HCI International (HCII) Conference, which has been a hub for presenting groundbreaking research and novel ideas and collaboration for people from all over the world.

The HCII conference was founded in 1984 by Prof. Gavriel Salvendy (Purdue University, USA, Tsinghua University, P.R. China, and University of Central Florida, USA) and the first event of the series, "1st USA-Japan Conference on Human-Computer Interaction", was held in Honolulu, Hawaii, USA, 18–20 August. Since then, HCI International is held jointly with several Thematic Areas and Affiliated Conferences, with each one under the auspices of a distinguished international Program Board and under one management and one registration. Twenty-six HCI International Conferences have been organized so far (every two years until 2013, and annually thereafter).

Over the years, this conference has served as a platform for scholars, researchers, industry experts and students to exchange ideas, connect, and address challenges in the ever-evolving HCI field. Throughout these 40 years, the conference has evolved itself, adapting to new technologies and emerging trends, while staying committed to its core mission of advancing knowledge and driving change.

As we celebrate this milestone anniversary, we reflect on the contributions of its founding members and appreciate the commitment of its current and past Affiliated Conference Program Board Chairs and members. We are also thankful to all past conference attendees who have shaped this community into what it is today.

The 26th International Conference on Human-Computer Interaction, HCI International 2024 (HCII 2024), was held as a 'hybrid' event at the Washington Hilton Hotel, Washington, DC, USA, during 29 June – 4 July 2024. It incorporated the 21 thematic areas and affiliated conferences listed below.

A total of 5108 individuals from academia, research institutes, industry, and government agencies from 85 countries submitted contributions, and 1271 papers and 309 posters were included in the volumes of the proceedings that were published just before the start of the conference. Additionally, 222 papers and 104 posters were included in the volumes of the proceedings published after the conference, as "Late Breaking Work". The contributions thoroughly cover the entire field of human-computer interaction, addressing major advances in knowledge and effective use of computers in a variety of application areas. These papers provide academics, researchers, engineers, scientists, practitioners and students with state-of-the-art information on the most recent advances in HCI. The volumes constituting the full set of the HCII 2024 conference proceedings are listed on the following pages.

I would like to thank the Program Board Chairs and the members of the Program Boards of all thematic areas and affiliated conferences for their contribution towards the high scientific quality and overall success of the HCI International 2024 conference. Their manifold support in terms of paper reviewing (single-blind review process, with a minimum of two reviews per submission), session organization and their willingness to act as goodwill ambassadors for the conference is most highly appreciated.

This conference would not have been possible without the continuous and unwavering support and advice of Gavriel Salvendy, founder, General Chair Emeritus, and Scientific Advisor. For his outstanding efforts, I would like to express my sincere appreciation to Abbas Moallem, Communications Chair and Editor of HCI International News.

September 2024 Constantine Stephanidis

HCI International 2024 Thematic Areas and Affiliated Conferences

- HCI: Human-Computer Interaction Thematic Area
- HIMI: Human Interface and the Management of Information Thematic Area
- EPCE: 21st International Conference on Engineering Psychology and Cognitive Ergonomics
- AC: 18th International Conference on Augmented Cognition
- UAHCI: 18th International Conference on Universal Access in Human-Computer Interaction
- CCD: 16th International Conference on Cross-Cultural Design
- SCSM: 16th International Conference on Social Computing and Social Media
- VAMR: 16th International Conference on Virtual, Augmented and Mixed Reality
- DHM: 15th International Conference on Digital Human Modeling & Applications in Health, Safety, Ergonomics & Risk Management
- DUXU: 13th International Conference on Design, User Experience and Usability
- C&C: 12th International Conference on Culture and Computing
- DAPI: 12th International Conference on Distributed, Ambient and Pervasive Interactions
- HCIBGO: 11th International Conference on HCI in Business, Government and Organizations
- LCT: 11th International Conference on Learning and Collaboration Technologies
- ITAP: 10th International Conference on Human Aspects of IT for the Aged Population
- AIS: 6th International Conference on Adaptive Instructional Systems
- HCI-CPT: 6th International Conference on HCI for Cybersecurity, Privacy and Trust
- HCI-Games: 6th International Conference on HCI in Games
- MobiTAS: 6th International Conference on HCI in Mobility, Transport and Automotive Systems
- AI-HCI: 5th International Conference on Artificial Intelligence in HCI
- MOBILE: 5th International Conference on Human-Centered Design, Operation and Evaluation of Mobile Communications

Conference Proceedings – Full List of Volumes

1. LNCS 14684, Human-Computer Interaction: Part I, edited by Masaaki Kurosu and Ayako Hashizume
2. LNCS 14685, Human-Computer Interaction: Part II, edited by Masaaki Kurosu and Ayako Hashizume
3. LNCS 14686, Human-Computer Interaction: Part III, edited by Masaaki Kurosu and Ayako Hashizume
4. LNCS 14687, Human-Computer Interaction: Part IV, edited by Masaaki Kurosu and Ayako Hashizume
5. LNCS 14688, Human-Computer Interaction: Part V, edited by Masaaki Kurosu and Ayako Hashizume
6. LNCS 14689, Human Interface and the Management of Information: Part I, edited by Hirohiko Mori and Yumi Asahi
7. LNCS 14690, Human Interface and the Management of Information: Part II, edited by Hirohiko Mori and Yumi Asahi
8. LNCS 14691, Human Interface and the Management of Information: Part III, edited by Hirohiko Mori and Yumi Asahi
9. LNAI 14692, Engineering Psychology and Cognitive Ergonomics: Part I, edited by Don Harris and Wen-Chin Li
10. LNAI 14693, Engineering Psychology and Cognitive Ergonomics: Part II, edited by Don Harris and Wen-Chin Li
11. LNAI 14694, Augmented Cognition: Part I, edited by Dylan D. Schmorrow and Cali M. Fidopiastis
12. LNAI 14695, Augmented Cognition: Part II, edited by Dylan D. Schmorrow and Cali M. Fidopiastis
13. LNCS 14696, Universal Access in Human-Computer Interaction: Part I, edited by Margherita Antona and Constantine Stephanidis
14. LNCS 14697, Universal Access in Human-Computer Interaction: Part II, edited by Margherita Antona and Constantine Stephanidis
15. LNCS 14698, Universal Access in Human-Computer Interaction: Part III, edited by Margherita Antona and Constantine Stephanidis
16. LNCS 14699, Cross-Cultural Design: Part I, edited by Pei-Luen Patrick Rau
17. LNCS 14700, Cross-Cultural Design: Part II, edited by Pei-Luen Patrick Rau
18. LNCS 14701, Cross-Cultural Design: Part III, edited by Pei-Luen Patrick Rau
19. LNCS 14702, Cross-Cultural Design: Part IV, edited by Pei-Luen Patrick Rau
20. LNCS 14703, Social Computing and Social Media: Part I, edited by Adela Coman and Simona Vasilache
21. LNCS 14704, Social Computing and Social Media: Part II, edited by Adela Coman and Simona Vasilache
22. LNCS 14705, Social Computing and Social Media: Part III, edited by Adela Coman and Simona Vasilache

23. LNCS 14706, Virtual, Augmented and Mixed Reality: Part I, edited by Jessie Y.C. Chen and Gino Fragomeni
24. LNCS 14707, Virtual, Augmented and Mixed Reality: Part II, edited by Jessie Y.C. Chen and Gino Fragomeni
25. LNCS 14708, Virtual, Augmented and Mixed Reality: Part III, edited by Jessie Y.C. Chen and Gino Fragomeni
26. LNCS 14709, Digital Human Modeling and Applications in Health, Safety, Ergonomics and Risk Management: Part I, edited by Vincent G. Duffy
27. LNCS 14710, Digital Human Modeling and Applications in Health, Safety, Ergonomics and Risk Management: Part II, edited by Vincent G. Duffy
28. LNCS 14711, Digital Human Modeling and Applications in Health, Safety, Ergonomics and Risk Management: Part III, edited by Vincent G. Duffy
29. LNCS 14712, Design, User Experience, and Usability: Part I, edited by Aaron Marcus, Elizabeth Rosenzweig and Marcelo M. Soares
30. LNCS 14713, Design, User Experience, and Usability: Part II, edited by Aaron Marcus, Elizabeth Rosenzweig and Marcelo M. Soares
31. LNCS 14714, Design, User Experience, and Usability: Part III, edited by Aaron Marcus, Elizabeth Rosenzweig and Marcelo M. Soares
32. LNCS 14715, Design, User Experience, and Usability: Part IV, edited by Aaron Marcus, Elizabeth Rosenzweig and Marcelo M. Soares
33. LNCS 14716, Design, User Experience, and Usability: Part V, edited by Aaron Marcus, Elizabeth Rosenzweig and Marcelo M. Soares
34. LNCS 14717, Culture and Computing, edited by Matthias Rauterberg
35. LNCS 14718, Distributed, Ambient and Pervasive Interactions: Part I, edited by Norbert A. Streitz and Shin'ichi Konomi
36. LNCS 14719, Distributed, Ambient and Pervasive Interactions: Part II, edited by Norbert A. Streitz and Shin'ichi Konomi
37. LNCS 14720, HCI in Business, Government and Organizations: Part I, edited by Fiona Fui-Hoon Nah and Keng Leng Siau
38. LNCS 14721, HCI in Business, Government and Organizations: Part II, edited by Fiona Fui-Hoon Nah and Keng Leng Siau
39. LNCS 14722, Learning and Collaboration Technologies: Part I, edited by Panayiotis Zaphiris and Andri Ioannou
40. LNCS 14723, Learning and Collaboration Technologies: Part II, edited by Panayiotis Zaphiris and Andri Ioannou
41. LNCS 14724, Learning and Collaboration Technologies: Part III, edited by Panayiotis Zaphiris and Andri Ioannou
42. LNCS 14725, Human Aspects of IT for the Aged Population: Part I, edited by Qin Gao and Jia Zhou
43. LNCS 14726, Human Aspects of IT for the Aged Population: Part II, edited by Qin Gao and Jia Zhou
44. LNCS 14727, Adaptive Instructional System, edited by Robert A. Sottilare and Jessica Schwarz
45. LNCS 14728, HCI for Cybersecurity, Privacy and Trust: Part I, edited by Abbas Moallem
46. LNCS 14729, HCI for Cybersecurity, Privacy and Trust: Part II, edited by Abbas Moallem

47. LNCS 14730, HCI in Games: Part I, edited by Xiaowen Fang
48. LNCS 14731, HCI in Games: Part II, edited by Xiaowen Fang
49. LNCS 14732, HCI in Mobility, Transport and Automotive Systems: Part I, edited by Heidi Krömker
50. LNCS 14733, HCI in Mobility, Transport and Automotive Systems: Part II, edited by Heidi Krömker
51. LNAI 14734, Artificial Intelligence in HCI: Part I, edited by Helmut Degen and Stavroula Ntoa
52. LNAI 14735, Artificial Intelligence in HCI: Part II, edited by Helmut Degen and Stavroula Ntoa
53. LNAI 14736, Artificial Intelligence in HCI: Part III, edited by Helmut Degen and Stavroula Ntoa
54. LNCS 14737, Human-Centered Design, Operation and Evaluation of Mobile Communications: Part I, edited by June Wei and George Margetis
55. LNCS 14738, Human-Centered Design, Operation and Evaluation of Mobile Communications: Part II, edited by June Wei and George Margetis
56. CCIS 2114, HCI International 2024 Posters: Part I, edited by Constantine Stephanidis, Margherita Antona, Stavroula Ntoa and Gavriel Salvendy
57. CCIS 2115, HCI International 2024 Posters: Part II, edited by Constantine Stephanidis, Margherita Antona, Stavroula Ntoa and Gavriel Salvendy
58. CCIS 2116, HCI International 2024 Posters: Part III, edited by Constantine Stephanidis, Margherita Antona, Stavroula Ntoa and Gavriel Salvendy
59. CCIS 2117, HCI International 2024 Posters: Part IV, edited by Constantine Stephanidis, Margherita Antona, Stavroula Ntoa and Gavriel Salvendy
60. CCIS 2118, HCI International 2024 Posters: Part V, edited by Constantine Stephanidis, Margherita Antona, Stavroula Ntoa and Gavriel Salvendy
61. CCIS 2119, HCI International 2024 Posters: Part VI, edited by Constantine Stephanidis, Margherita Antona, Stavroula Ntoa and Gavriel Salvendy
62. CCIS 2120, HCI International 2024 Posters: Part VII, edited by Constantine Stephanidis, Margherita Antona, Stavroula Ntoa and Gavriel Salvendy
63. LNCS 15374, HCI International 2024 - Late Breaking Papers: Part I, edited by Masaaki Kurosu, Ayako Hashizume, Hirohiko Mori, Yumi Asahi, Dylan D. Schmorrow and Cali M. Fidopiastis
64. LNCS 15375, HCI International 2024 - Late Breaking Papers: Part II, edited by Adela Coman, Simona Vasilache, Fiona Fui-Hoon Nah, Keng Leng Siau, June Wei and George Margetis
65. LNCS 15376, HCI International 2024 - Late Breaking Papers: Part III, edited by Vincent G. Duffy
66. LNCS 15377, HCI International 2024 - Late Breaking Papers: Part IV, edited by Jessie Y.C. Chen, Gino Fragomeni, Norbert A. Streitz, Shin'ichi Konomi and Xiaowen Fang
67. LNCS 15378, HCI International 2024 - Late Breaking Papers: Part V, edited by Panayiotis Zaphiris, Andri Ioannou, Robert A. Sottilare, Jessica Schwarz and Matthias Rauterberg
68. LNCS 15379, HCI International 2024 - Late Breaking Papers: Part VI, edited by Margherita Antona, Constantine Stephanidis, Qin Gao and Jia Zhou

69. LNCS 15380, HCI International 2024 - Late Breaking Papers: Part VII, edited by Aaron Marcus, Elizabeth Rosenzweig, Marcelo M. Soares, Pei-Luen Patrick Rau and Abbas Moallem
70. LNCS 15381, HCI International 2024 - Late Breaking Papers: Part VIII, edited by Don Harris, Wen-Chin Li and Heidi Krömker
71. LNCS 15382, HCI International 2024 - Late Breaking Papers: Part IX, edited by Helmut Degen and Stavroula Ntoa
72. CCIS 2319, HCI International 2024 - Late Breaking Posters: Part I, edited by Constantine Stephanidis, Margherita Antona, Stavroula Ntoa and Gavriel Salvendy
73. CCIS 2320, HCI International 2024 - Late Breaking Posters: Part II, edited by Constantine Stephanidis, Margherita Antona, Stavroula Ntoa and Gavriel Salvendy
74. CCIS 2321, HCI International 2024 - Late Breaking Posters: Part III, edited by Constantine Stephanidis, Margherita Antona, Stavroula Ntoa and Gavriel Salvendy

https://2024.hci.international/proceedings

26th International Conference on Human-Computer Interaction (HCII 2024)

The full list with the Program Board Chairs and the members of the Program Boards of all thematic areas and affiliated conferences of HCII2024 is available online at:

http://www.hci.international/board-members-2024.php

HCI International 2025 Conference

The 27th International Conference on Human-Computer Interaction, HCI International 2025, will be held jointly with the affiliated conferences at the Swedish Exhibition & Congress Centre and Gothia Towers Hotel, Gothenburg, Sweden, June 22–27, 2025. It will cover a broad spectrum of themes related to Human-Computer Interaction, including theoretical issues, methods, tools, processes, and case studies in HCI design, as well as novel interaction techniques, interfaces, and applications. The proceedings will be published by Springer. More information is available on the conference website: https://2025.hci.international/.

General Chair
Prof. Constantine Stephanidis
University of Crete and ICS-FORTH
Heraklion, Crete, Greece
Email: general_chair@2025.hci.international

https://2025.hci.international/

Contents – Part I

User Interface and Interaction Design

Human Perceptions of Novel Visual and Non-Visual Explanations in High-Stakes Decision-Making Domains ... 3
Edwina Borteley Abam, Helena Webb, Liz Dowthwaite, and Isaac Triguero

Optimizing E-Commerce Warehouse Item Placement: A Three-Pronged Approach ... 14
Aakash Bhatt, Matthew Jurado, and Amith Tarigonda

Towards the Control of Smart Devices Using a GUI-Free EOG-Based HMI System ... 25
Tracey Camilleri, Nathaniel Barbara, Matthew Mifsud, Salah Ad-Din Al Youbi, and Kenneth Camilleri

Cognitive Dynamics of Theory of Mind in Collaborative Problem-Solving: A Framework for Understanding Teamwork in Complex Environments ... 35
Fiona Duruaku, Stephen M. Fiore, and Florian G. Jentsch

Color Design for Pet App Based on Emotional Human-Computer Interaction ... 51
Xuan Gao and Qian Ji

Integrating User Perspectives: A Framework for Ad-Hoc Privacy Preference Implementation in Information Systems ... 60
Mandy Goram

Research on Emotional Image of Custom Fonts in Chinese Enterprises Based on Kansei Engineering ... 70
Shua-Hua Jin and Xiang Liu

Designing Warmth: Enhancing School Belonging and Identity Through Student-Generated Photographic Content ... 86
Jie Ling, Li Li, and Li Ou Yang

A Help System for Optimizing Complex Ordering Configurations Based on Cognitive Decision Model ... 97
Yuanyuan Liu and Ying Xia

Human-Centered Organizational Renewal: Transformative Design Science in Action 102
Jessica Lowry

How Might We Improve HCI on a Platform Designed to Improve Interagency Collaboration? 113
Beth A. Martin, Basil White, and Jason Traquair

From Designer to Imagineer: Personal Fabrication Embedded in Designer's 3D Printing Practice 118
Jue Ren and Leirah Wang

Investigating the Relationship between Anthropomorphic Expressions and Preferences Based on Kansei Design 128
Haruki Tanaka and Kang Namgyu

Optimization of SSVEP-BCI Interface Design - a Study Based on Visual Comfort 138
Mu Tong and Yun Lin

Competency-Driven Strategies for Sustainable Professional Growth 145
Florence Williams

Usability and User Experience Evaluation

Study on Motion Sickness Cases in Multiple Driving Simulator Studies 157
ISol Bae, Bogyu Choi, and Ji Hyun Yang

Conducting Usability Testing with Tweens on Mobile AR Platforms 165
Hanah I. S. Correa, Marcos Silbermann, and Mariana Lopes

Immersive Test Study to Evaluate XR Device Performance and Usability 177
Anderson V. C. de Oliveira, Pio H. Ordozgoith F. S., Hanah I. S. Correa, and Renato A. O. Andrade

Automated Evaluation of Metrics for Immersive Test Using Reinforcement Learning 188
Roberto G. Estrada L., Anderson V. C. de Oliveira, Agustin Alejandro Ortiz Diaz, Jeferson B. da Costa, and Emerson S. Domingos

Exploring the Effectiveness of Augmented and Virtual Reality for Visualizing Complex Lighting Simulation Data Structures and Evaluating User Experience 198
Elham Mohammadrezaei, Fatemeh Sarshartehrani, Majid Behravan, and Denis Gračanin

Why Social Media Users Are Hesitant to Embrace the Metaverse: Technology Acceptance, Perceived Risks and Mitigations 206
Haoran Qiu, Dion Hoe-Lian Goh, Albert Ong, Shiming Jin, and Shuyu Wang

Moving Beyond SUS and Other Lazy Metrics: Redefining Usability of Cloud Solutions 215
Vanshika Sanghi, Sparshad Kasote, and Santhosh Rao

Innovative Technologies and Human-Centered Solutions

Social Behaviors on Sharing Expenses in Saudi Arabia 229
Saif Alshammari and Munira Alenzi

"Cerésbox: Development of an Innovative Platform for the Commercialization of Green Products Through 4.0 Technologies" 237
Heidy Bravo and Jairo Narváez

Versatile Video Coding (VVC) Applied to Mobile Screen Content 244
Anderson V. C. de Oliveira, Paulo S. S. Farias, and Emerson S. Domingos

Exploiting American Patriotism in Influence Operations 253
April Edwards, Peter Antonaros, Meyer Levy, and Dana Weinberg

Effect of a Movement Imagery-Based Fashion Model Walking Program Using Kinect on EEG Activity and Cognitive Function 263
SungHee Hong, SunHee Park, and SunOk Jung

Habit Instigation vs Execution Related Behavior Change Techniques (BCT) in Mobile Intervention for Physical Activity: A Systematic Review and a z-curve Analysis 272
Hyun Seon Kim and Alison L. Phillips

Development of a Virtual Human Based Interactive Kiosk 276
Jae-Hwi Kwon and Chang Joo Lim

Revitalizing Community Identity Through Interactive Art Installations: A Case Study of Gan Zhu Tan Hydropower Station in Zuotan Village 281
Jie Ling, Ran Wang, and Li Ou Yang

Offline Indoor Navigation via QR Codes 292
Robert Modic, Matevž Ogrinc, Andraž Simčič, Bojan Blažica, and Drago Torkar

Government Management and Inventory System 297
Jose Ricardo Mondragon Regalado, Grimaldo Heredia Pérez, Jaime Mundaca Araujo, Alexander Huaman Monteza, Willam Suárez Peña, Nancy Saldaña Mendoza, Orestes Daniel Adrianzén Guerrero, John Smith Rodríguez Estacio, and Wesley Olano Chuquihuanga

Movement Characteristics During Directional Change in Wheelchair Badminton 303
Hiroyuki Ohshima, Akinori Sasaki, Hitoshi Ishido, and Shigenobu Shimada

Contrastive Learning with Multi-level Embeddings for Speech-Based Emotion Recognition 312
Mei Si

BrailleÉcran: A Tangible Braille Approach for Smartphone Text Entry 322
Fabrizzio Soares, Joyce Siqueira, Mateus M. Luna, Emilia A. Nogueira, Lillian Cristina dos Santos, Juliana G. Faria, Juliana Paula Felix, Joao Soares de Oliveira Neto, Afonso U. Fonseca, and Thamer Horbylon Nascimento

ChatGPT, Machine Learning and AI Killed My Password. Building Next Generation Authentication Systems 332
Afamefuna P. Umejiaku and Victor Sheng

Cognitive Conflict Classification Depending on Background Auditive Environment Using Support Vector Machine Based on Near-Infrared Hemoencephalography 341
Kota Yokoyama, Keiichi Zempo, and Sandra Puentes

Author Index 355

Contents – Part II

Innovations in Extended Reality

A Study on the Application of Game Techniques to Increase Virtual Human Immersion 3
Mu Seong Choi and Chang Joo Lim

Architecting Social VR: Exploring Encounter and Serendipitous Interactions in Virtual Public Spaces 10
Yihao He

Meta Arm—VR Control Device for Forearm Amputees 17
Ziqiang He and Ke Jiang

Enhancing Visual Cognition Through Virtual Reality (VR): A Case Study of Zhongkai University of Agriculture and Engineering 23
Jie Ling, Zihong Wu, Wenxi Wei, Rui Liu, Shunda Huang, Qiguang Luo, and Li Ou Yang

Beyond Illusions: Diminished Reality's Potential, Pitfalls, and Ethical Reflections 34
Katlin T. Moffis, Yves Valentin, and HeeSun Choi

Process of Identifying and Conceptualizing Gestures for Creating Experiences of Use in Mixed Reality (XR) 43
Alef Santos, Najara Paixão, and Marcos Silbermann

Marker-Based Real Time Motion Tracking for Sense of Virtual Body Ownership in Virtual Reality 54
Linfeng Wu and Karen B. Chen

How to Tell a Good Story with VR: A Research of Narrative Approaches to VR Film 60
Wangxuyu Xu

Research on Desensitization Training Path for Space Motion Sickness Based on Mixed Reality 69
Jin Zhu, Chenxi Tai, Yunjia Chen, Longfei Zhou, and Junjie Zhang

Smart Systems and Intelligent Design

ParkWise: Smart Augmented Reality Parking Simulation Planner 81
Lian Zeyad Alhedaithy, Yasmin Fahad Alsharif, Mashael Sulaiman Alyahya, Afnan Hafiz Rahman, Mohamed Bahloul, and Hoda Elsayed

Intelligent Speaker Design Based on Emotional Design Concept 91
Yingyu Chen and Yi Li

User Interface Design for Managing Emergencies in SAE Level 4 Automated Vehicles 100
Bogyu Choi and Ji Hyun Yang

Estimation of Standard Times of Manual Activities with IoT Tools 108
Hernán Espejo-Viñán, Lloyd Molina, Carlos Ramírez, and José Andagama

Users' Seamless Guidance in Shared Automated Mobility On-Demand Through Emoji Companions 115
Fabian Hub, Thorben Brandt, and Michael Oehl

Development of an Intelligent Olive Fruit Fly (B. Oleae) Trap for Remote Pest Monitoring 124
George Kapnas, Maria Doxastaki, Manousos Bouloukakis, Christos Stratakis, Nikolaos Menelaos Stivaktakis, Theodoros Evdaimon, Maria Korozi, Asterios Leonidis, and Constantine Stephanidis

Enhancing Driver Takeover Quality in Conditional Automated Driving Optimizing HMI Expression During Takeover Process 133
Yang Liu

Optimization of the Solvent Based Paint Manufacturing Process Through Automation and Quality Control to Meet Industry Standards 143
David Naranjo-Pullupaxi, Blanca Topon - Visarrea, Christian Iza, Fabian Sarmiento, and Israel Pozo

Accurate Automation in Nutrient Solution Dosage for Pressurized Irrigation Systems 152
Fabian Sarmiento-Ortiz, Blanca Topon - Visarrea, and Christian Iza

Household Dehumidifier Based on AHP and QFD 161
Yanmin Xue and Shuting Huang

AI and Design for Human-Centric Applications

Plan Future Graph Visualization and Improvement ... 177
Bryan L. Croft

Harmonizing AI and Human Values: The Ubuntu Approach to Super Alignment in OpenAI's Initiatives ... 186
George Frempong and Raavee Kadam

Generation of Listener's Facial Response Using Cross-Modal Mapping of Speaker's Expression ... 194
Ayaka Fujii and Ken Fukuda

Multi-agent AI: Collaborative Design with Multiple AI Tools in Interior Design Workflow ... 202
Xiaomei Li, Pengfei Wu, Ziming He, Jinling Li, and Ling Fan

A Computational Aesthetic Measurement Framework for AI Design - a Case Study of Office Space Design ... 212
Xiaomei Li, Ziming He, Pengfei Wu, Jinling Li, and Ling Fan

Integrating Generative AI into Visual Perception Therapy for Children with Developmental Delays: An Empirical Eye-Tracking Study ... 221
Bo Liu and Yang-cheng Lin

Goal-Driven XAI: The Normative Value of the Ladder of Regret in Human-Centered AI ... 233
Rosa E. Martín-Peña

Travai: Customized Travel Planning Program Using LLM ... 244
Seohyun Oh, Jihee Lim, Soojin Cheon, Eun Heo, and Yangkyu Lim

Researching Character Design with Generative AI: –Focusing on Creating Five Probiotic Characters ... 249
Heehyeon Park

Navigation for People with Low Vision Using Machine Learning ... 257
Juha Park, Hyebin Lee, Bokwang Shim, and Yangkyu Lim

Infrastructure Optimization for Predictive Maintenance: Enhanced Backend and Artificial Intelligence Integration ... 263
Michael Stern, Michelle Hallmann, Francesco Vona, Ute Franke, Thomas Ostertag, Benjamin Schlüter, and Jan-Niklas Voigt-Antons

Recognizing Table Logical Structure from Re-flowable Documents 273
Runxin Wang, Lin Zhang, and Ning Li

AdvisorAI: Transforming Graphic Advertising with Generative AI-Enhanced Design Strategies 295
Pengfei Wu, Xiaomei Li, Ziming He, and Ling Fan

The Impact of Artificial Intelligence in the World of Finance: A Bibliometric Study 305
Isabel Yepes, Osvaldo Arevalo, Josnel Martínez Garcés, Emilia María Polo Carrillo, Mary Yaneth Rodríguez-Villamizar, and Jorge Roa

Author Index 315

Contents – Part III

Design for Health and Well-Being

A Conceptual Design Framework of GorbhoShongi App for Mental Well-Being Among Bangladeshi Pregnant and Postpartum Women 3
Istiaq Ahmed, Syed Niaz Mohtasim, Faiza Omar Arpita, Ashraful Islam, and M. Ashraful Amin

OxPal: Empowering Children with Stress Regulation Through Biofeedback 14
Arda Özkurt, Arda Edil, Zeynep İrem Gökgöz, Melisa Aşcı, Ahmet Burhan Baş, Sedef Şeker, and Sedat Yalçın

Digital Exclusion in Older Adults: Strengthening Patient Safety and Healthcare Through a Digital Application Designed for the Elderly 25
Mariel Garcia-Hernandez

Modular Platform for Health and Safety Data Monitoring 30
Joao Marques, Mauro Teofilo, Everton Aleixo, Francisco Filho, Agustín Alejandro Ortiz Díaz, and Sergio Cleger Tamayo

Case Study in Interdisciplinary Interface Design to Improve Maternal Health for Marginalized Community in the United States 40
David Oh, Alison Stuebe, and Brooke Jones

Is Technology a Double-Edged Sword: Exploring the Influence of Parental Technoference on Child Psychological Well-Being 47
Abhishek Sharma, Lakshmi Sharma, Kunnumpurath Bijo, and Amandeep Sidhu

Analysis of Emergency Duty Medical Institution Websites in Four Hokkaido Cities 62
Yuki Uenoya and Kang Namgyu

Assessing the Psychological Benefits of 'mood Plants': A Custom Flower System for Caregivers 72
Peize Wu, Yihang Dai, Tianze Wang, Jing Li, Jingbo Ge, and Jiang Wu

Research on the Art Design of Group Psychological Healing Installation Based on User Needs 80
Qi Xiao

A Bionic Robot Dog and UI Design Practice for the Emotional Healing of Self-harming Adolescents ... 96
Jingyi Yuan

Advanced Interactive Technologies for Learning

Let's Talk Digital: Education, Digital Transformation and Digital Humanities ... 111
Alejandra Alvarez, Carlos Varela, Oscar Salavarrieta, Christian Lozano, Harold Castañeda, and Victor Hugo Villamizar

Assistive Toolkit for Teaching Programming to Visually Impaired Children ... 119
Ângelo Amaral, Camila Aparecida Paris Baston, and Marcos Augusto Francisco Borges

Online Safety Videos in Youtube: Typology and Persuasive Techniques ... 128
Liuyu Huang, Dion Hoe-Lian Goh, and Stella Xin Yin

Enhancing Spatial Design Education Through Virtual Reality: An Empirical Study in China ... 138
Jie Ling, Yunyi Zhuang, Dan Li, and Li Ou Yang

Free Software: an Opportunity to Improve University Higher Education ... 151
Jose Ricardo Mondragon Regalado, Grimaldo Heredia Pérez, Jaime Mundaca Araujo, Willam Suárez Peña, Nancy Saldaña Mendoza, Alexander Huaman Monteza, Julio César Montenegro Juárez, Jannier Alberto Montenegro Juarez, Orestes Daniel Adrianzén Guerrero, John Smith Rodríguez Estacio, and Alex Alfredo Huaman Llanos

Enhancing Programming Education Through Algorithm Visualization: A Focus on Teaching Data Structures ... 157
Oswaldo Vélez-Langs and Jose Gaspar-López

The Potential of Large Language Models in Education: Applications and Challenges in the Learning of Language, Social Science, Health Care, and Science ... 165
Yalun Zhou, Mei Si, and Jacky Doll

Interaction Design of Virtual Reality for Scenario-Based Science Popularisation of Chinese Traditional Carpentry Craft Under the Perspective of Ancient Painting Restoration ... 173
Fangzhou Zhu and Dehua Yu

Connectivism Theory and Social Narrative: Innovative Exploration of Platformized Teaching Mode for Creative Practice Design Courses 182
Li Zhuang and Cailin Chang

Gaming, Gamification, and Immersive Design

MASTERM1ND: A Virtual Reality Web-Based Cybersecurity Awareness Game 193
Hussain Assaf Alassaf, Abdulaziz Mohammed Tayeb, Muhammad Sufiyan Shoukat Ali, Eyad Raed Elsadouni, Hassan Harun ur Rashid, Hoda Elsayed, and Muhammed Umair Khan

Unraveling Cybersickness in VR Gaming: Exploring Causes and Strategies for Mitigation 204
Nuha Bahatheq and Hoda Elsayed

Eat Me Up 215
Siqi Hu and Xinyang Yu

Game Interaction Design for Alzheimer's Disease 229
Yinshan Luo

Immersive Experience Design of (e)sports Events 239
George Margetis, Eirini Sykianaki, Ioannis Chatzakis, Artemis Sfakaki, Konstantinos C. Apostolakis, George Paparoulis, Stavroula Ntoa, Ioannis Markopoulos, and Constantine Stephanidis

Gamification in E-Wallets: Impact on User Satisfaction and Experience 249
Kwan Panyawanich, Martin Maguire, and Patrick Pradel

Sentiment Analysis for Drawing Parallels Between Cinema and Video Game Texts 265
Charalampos Rizopoulos, Anna Poupou, and Natalia Arsenopoulou

Technology-Enhanced Experiences in Cultural Heritage

Research on Situational Interactive Intelligent Guiding System for Children in Oceanographic Museums 279
Xijie Gao

From Look to Insight: Unveiling Visitor Engagement in Exhibits via Gaze Interface Technology 285
Tsuei-Ju Hsieh and Yun-Ju Chen

Research on Serious Game Design of Intangible Cultural Heritage for Children—Taking the Guangdong Provincial Museum as an Example 291
Chenxin Huang and Yan Wang

The Impact of Korean Traditional Audience Culture on Digital Performance ... 301
Jiyoung Kim, Kayoung Na, and Yangkyu Lim

Tangible Sumeru: Enhancing AR Interactive Narrative Experience with 3D-Printed Assemblies for Dunhuang Grotto Murals 308
Zixiao Liu

AnoGAN for Tabular Data: A Novel Approach to Anomaly Detection 319
Pavan Reddy and Aditya Singh

Research and Practice of Human-Computer Interaction Design in Museums from the Perspective of Atmospheric Aesthetics 331
Weirui Wang

Design Strategies for Optimizing the Display of Northern Guangdong Yao Ethnic Headgear in Museums 339
Jiawen Zhang, Xiaoping Hu, and Shih-Mou Kuo

Author Index 349

User Interface and Interaction Design

Human Perceptions of Novel Visual and Non-Visual Explanations in High-Stakes Decision-Making Domains

Edwina Borteley Abam[1,2(✉)], Helena Webb[1,3], Liz Dowthwaite[2,3], and Isaac Triguero[1,4]

[1] School of Computer Science, University of Nottingham, Nottingham, UK
{psxea2,pszhmw,pszit}@nottingham.ac.uk

[2] Horizon CDT, University of Nottingham, Nottingham, UK
ezzed@nottingham.ac.uk

[3] Horizon Digital Economy Research, University of Nottingham, Nottingham, UK

[4] Department of Computer Science and Artificial Intelligence, University of Granada, Granada, Spain

Abstract. Technological advancements have led to the widespread adoption of algorithms to automate decision-making tasks in critical domains like credit risk assessment. While algorithms can easily automate decision-making, erroneous outcomes can have severe consequences. Hence, enhancing algorithmic transparency via explanations is crucial. However, effectively designing and communicating algorithmic explanations has remained a challenging task till today. Incorporating end-users perspectives is essential for developing practical, human-friendly explanations in practice. While technical implementations of explainability techniques abound in academic literature, understanding end-users' perceptions of these techniques in the form of visual and non-visual explanations and their value in communicating explanations has remained underexplored. This paper reports on a study exploring individuals' perceptions of visual and non-visual explanations in the context of loan approval. Focus group discussions were conducted to examine lay peoples' perceptions of different types of visual and non-visual explanations. Findings from the thematic analysis showed that visual explanations were appealing and more quickly comprehended than non-visual explanations. The importance of employing all possible avenues and modes of communicating explanations to ensure inclusivity was emphasized. For visual and non-visual explanations, interactive features were preferred for deeper engagement and understanding of the decision-making process. These findings convey significant implications for policy, research, and practice regarding the design of explanations, particularly in contexts of loan approval.

Keywords: algorithmic decision-making · transparency · explanations

C. Stephanidis et al. (Eds.): HCII 2024, CCIS 2319, pp. 3–13, 2025.
https://doi.org/10.1007/978-3-031-78516-0_1

1 Introduction

As black box models are increasingly employed to make important decisions in critical contexts, the demand for transparency from various AI stakeholders is increasing. Transparency in algorithmic decision-making systems is critical for various technical, legal, and social reasons [8]. A way of ensuring transparency in algorithmic decision-making is by providing explanations. An extensive body of academic literature on explainable AI within the machine learning community has proposed various technical approaches to investigate the inner workings of machine learning algorithms[1]. Most machine learning models are black boxes, meaning they are not easily interpretable by design. Post-hoc explainability involves explaining machine learning models that are not transparent by design. The techniques proposed to render machine learning algorithm interpretable range from model-specific to model-agnostic methods. Explainability is linked to post-hoc explainability since it covers the techniques used to convert a non-interpretable model into an explainable one. While several efforts are made to propose technical solutions to the black box problem in XAI literature [2], there are limited studies which provide insights about end user's perceptions of the various technical solutions proposed to enhance interpretability and transparency of algorithmic systems. Very little is known about how end users might perceive different explanations proposed in explainable AI literature. The study conducted in this paper addresses the gap by investigating the effect of varying explanation styles proposed in the literature on end user's overall perceptions of algorithmic decision-making systems.

1.1 Key Questions

As research into practically achievable explanations for machine learning systems accelerates, researchers are considering which explanation styles are more desirable [5]. Understanding how explanation styles might influence users' perceptions of algorithmic decision-making systems in the context of credit scoring is critical for designing user-friendly explanations and increasing the acceptance of algorithmic decision-making systems in society [7]. This paper addressed the research question:

How do different explanation styles affect end users' perceptions of transparency in algorithmic decision-making systems?

What are end-users' preferences about the design of explanations in algorithmic decision-making systems?

2 Study Design and Methods

A series of online focus group sessions were conducted to investigate end user's perceptions of transparency and the effect of different explanation presentation styles. Ethics approval was obtained from the University of Nottingham School of Computer Science to conduct the study. The study methods included a design that allowed participants to assume the position of a fictional character in different hypothetical lending scenarios. Each scenario represents a different lending organisation, creating a unique borrowing experience. In each hypothetical lending scenario, a fictional character has a credit decision made about them automatically by a credit scoring algorithm. As individuals are more likely to request explanations in response to a negative decision, all scenarios end in a negative outcome [4].

In each scenario, participants were to provide feedback on the lending experience about the presence or absence of explanations and feedback on the style of explanation. Each scenario showed the same decision outcome, with the explanations presented either in text or visual format. The first scenario depicted a situation where no answers were provided in the face of a negative outcome to explore participants' reactions compared to scenarios where explanations were provided. Four(4) different types of explanations (anchor explanations, counterfactual explanations, feature importance bar charts, and a LIME plot showing influential features) were investigated.

2.1 Participants

Using the CallforParticipants(CfP) website, a total of N=34 participants were selected to participate in the study. The criteria for selection were that participants must be 18 years or older, reside within the UK and must have had experience with credit or borrowing. About Twenty-one (21) participants were between the ages of 18–25. Seven(7) were between 26–30, and Five (5) were above age 30. The majority Twenty-one (21) of the participants had experience with student loans, 15 had experience with personal loans, 17 had experience with credit cards, and 2 had experience with car loans. Four separate focus group sessions were conducted with an attendance of about 6-11 participants per focus group session. Participants were recruited from different parts of the UK. There were about 62per cent male and 38 per cent female participants. Each participant was paid

The data was analysed using an iterative inductive thematic analysis approach proposed by Braun and Clark [3].

2.2 Scenarios and Application Context

The explanations presented in the different scenarios were only model-agnostic techniques, as they could be applied to any machine-learning algorithm.

Scenario 1: No explanations This scenario presented a scenario where a lending organisation uses a machine learning algorithm to make a decision about a loan applicant. The outcome of the decision was negative. In this case, no explanations were provided for the decline.

Scenario 2: Anchor Explanations This scenario presented another algorithmic lending scenario with the same decision outcome, a rejection. On this occasion, explanations are provided in the form of anchors. Anchors are model-agnostic rule-based methods of giving explanations in the field of Explainable AI [9]. An anchor explanation is a specific rule or condition which, when met, would cause a machine-learning model to (almost) always make the same prediction. For example, ["the model predicted that the borrower is high-risk because they have a history of missed payments on their previous loans."] The conditions in the scenario are presented in human-understandable form to make it easy for end users to understand how the algorithm arrived at its prediction.

Scenario 3: Counterfactual Explanations This scenario presented a negative decision outcome for the same fictional character and provided reasons in the form of counterfactual explanations. Counterfactual explanations are example-based model agnostic techniques used to generate explanations from a machine learning model. They suggest what should be different in the input instance to change the outcome of an AI system [10]. For example, [You were denied a loan because your annual income was Âc30,000. If your income had been Âc15,000 higher than the current one, and if you had fully paid current debts with other banks, you would have been offered a loan.].

Scenario 4: Feature importance bar plot In this scenario, the same decision outcome is given, and explanations are presented in the form of a bar chart showing the relevant features considered in the decision. Feature importance in the field of explainable AI, concerns the evaluation of relevant features affecting a machine learning algorithm's performance and outputs. [6].

Scenario 5: Lime plot This scenario depicted a lending scenario with the same negative outcome but with explanations presented visually as a LIME plot. The LIME plot is a model agnostic technique proposed in explainable AI literature [1]. The explanations presented here in this scenario were inspired by the work of Ribeiro et al. [9].

3 Findings

3.1 Perceptions of Visual and Non-Visual Explanation Styles

This section reports on the perceptions of participants in relation to the different explanation scenarios, highlighting the perceived benefits or drawbacks.

No Explanation Scenario. This scenario, in which explanations are absent in the face of rejection, elicited negative reactions from participants. When asked how participants would feel being in the fictional character's shoes, responses expressed negative feelings. The most dominant feelings participants expressed were frustration (mentioned 9 times in 4/4 focus groups) and disappointment (mentioned 4 times in 3/4 focus groups). Other feelings were expressed using words such as 'demoralising' (p21, 31-35, fg2), devastated (p24, 18-25, fg3), 'disgusted' (p32, 26-30, fg4), 'awful' (p20, 18-25, fg2), unsatisfied(p6,26-30, fg1), 'rejected'(p31, 18-25, fg3), 'weird'(p27, 18-25, fg4). The lack of explanation was seen as improper treatment of individuals. "So ... this is a very bad way to treat a customer,... there should be some .. details.."(P32, 26-30, fg4)." The emotional and psychological reactions to the no-explanation scenario were a topic that occurred in 4/4 focus groups and was mentioned 23 times during the discussions (Fig. 1).

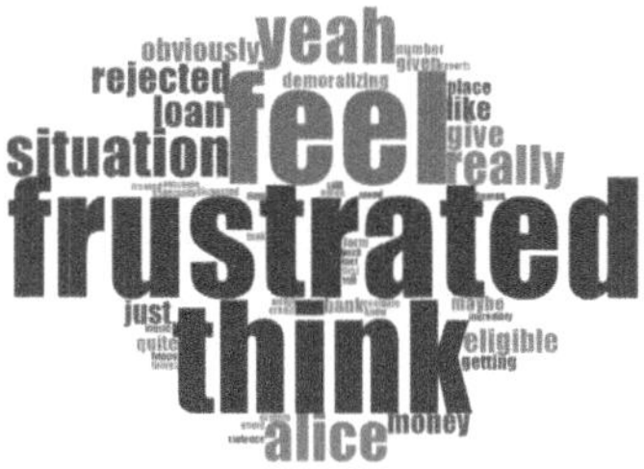

Fig. 1. Word Cloud for emotional reactions to the "no explanations scenario"

Non-Visual Explanation Styles

Anchor Explanation Scenario. Anchor style explanations were perceived as generic and less informative, e.g. "...it's too generic, you know, because it says working towards having a higher credit score..... it's like it gives you like very generic points, which I suppose you can. You can use it as a foundation if you are planning to do your own research." (P13, 18-25, FG2). Other comments revealed that anchor explanations are dismissive and off-putting. "the rather off-putting... saying, for example, try to pay on time that sounds almost vulgar to me...I'm sure there are legitimate reasons why" (P13, 18-25, FG2)

Counterfactual Explanation Scenario. As expected, participants reacted positively to this scenario. Two main subthemes stand out from participants' reactions. Counterfactual explanations were found to be more thorough, with better clarity and actionability. A participant quoted: "...apart from maybe not getting the credit, she benefited from getting the information on how to improve..., now this is the way things should be done, and I really advocate for this" (P32, 26-30, FG4). Due to a greater level of detail, there was a perception that counterfactual explanations provide a higher level of transparency. The drawbacks mentioned were that counterfactual explanations were found to be a bit confusing and lacked guidance on how to take practical steps towards attaining a favourable outcome in the future. A further drawback was that counterfactual explanations lacked practical guidance and a feature for human interaction.

Visual Explanation Styles.

Feature Importance Bar Chart. Views in relation to bar chart explanations were nuanced (Fig. 2).

Participants felt that summarising explanations with visual aids like the bar plot provided quicker comprehension of the presented information. A young participant said, "You don't have to read that much..this is the best way to maybe display all the given explanations. You will understand very quickly, and it contains a lot of information in a very brief manner." (P32, 26-30, fg4)."

Participants found the weightings attached to the relevant factors crucial for understanding the most important factors influencing the decision outcome. One participant said, 'I personally prefer this just because it gives you weightings to the different reasons why you were not, you know, accepted'(p15, 18-25, fg2)

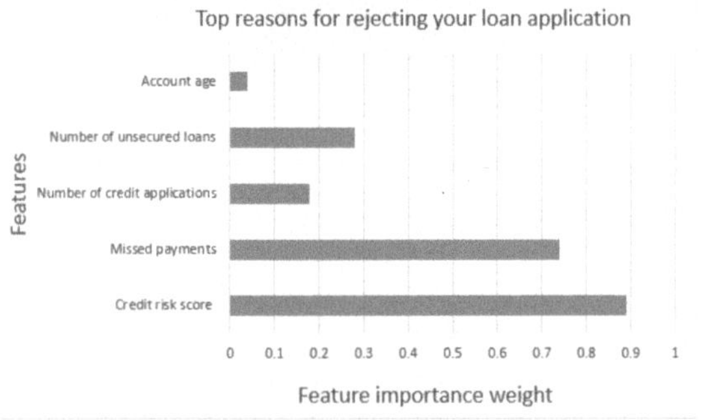

Fig. 2. Explanations showing most influential features presented visually as a bar chart

The order of the bars and orientation of the axis affected participants' ability to effectively interpret the chart. Some comments criticised bar charts and described them as "not useful" and 'totally pedantic' due to the unsorted order of the bars. "I just don't think it's very useful at all. From like being a totally pedantic. To even like the ordering. It would be better to have it so you could clearly see them decreasing... I don't think it's useful." (P2, 18-25, fg1). Some found bar charts to be lacking in detail and guidelines that could be acted on. One participant said, " I suppose you almost have to sort of work it out yourself then what you need to do to improve your credit score because that bit of information is not there on this chart.... that's the only flip side I would say about this chart itself gives you the weightage for the reasons you don't get accepted, but it's probably easier to, you know, work out what you need to do to improve your credit score" (P15, 18-25, fg2). "

Further results showed that the interpretation of bar charts depends on people's level of literacy. One participant said, "Not everyone can read graphs. It doesn't make any sense ... the majority of people can't read graphs." (P14, 26-30, fg2). Similarly, other comments revealed that there is a tendency for bar charts to be misinterpreted. Some found reading the graphs quite confusing due to the rotated axis. The orientation of the axis on the chart affects participants' ability to read and understand the graph correctly. "graph will be easier to interpret ..than words, and it will be faster to interpret the charts if the features were on the on the X axis and the features important switches on the Y axis." (P25, 18-25, fg3)." Another drawback mentioned in relation to bar charts was that they lack the feature for further dialogue and interaction to discuss the explanations provided (Fig. 3).

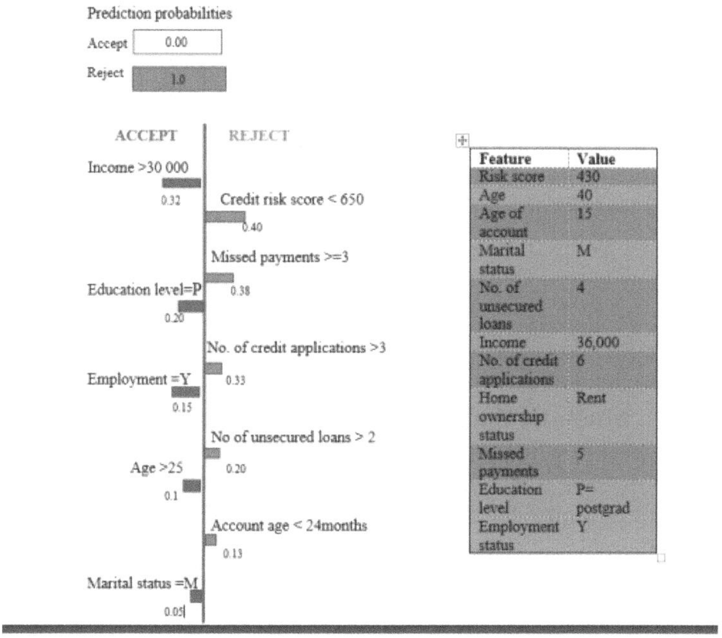

Fig. 3. A LIME plot presented as explanations revealing features influencing the decision outcome in the last scenario

LIME Explanations Scenario. There were very few positive comments about lime explanations. Those comments showed that lime explanations were considered more detailed, especially as they indicated values for the different factors contributing to the decision outcome. These few comments about this may imply that very few people could perhaps make sense of the graph, "it seems very useful in terms of ...it gives you specific values for everything. So I think this graph is probably a bit more complex I think, than the one before, but it's obviously got more sort of useful information" (P13, 18-25, FG2). "

On the other hand, Lime plots were seen as visually overwhelming and cluttered with information with some participants describing it as being 'too busy'

(P1, 18-25, FG1) with 'too much noise, too much going on"(P2, above 40, FG1) and having "too much of data " (P7, 18-25, FG1). Other reactions to this scenario showed that lime plots were seen as complicated, "this is also an overly complicated way of displaying it... (P22, 18-25, FG3) and complex, "this graph is probably a bit more complex .., than the one before (P15, 18-25, FG2).

3.2 Desired Practices and Preferences in Relation to Explanations

During the focus group discussions, participants expressed preferences regarding explanations in general. The main points raised in relation to preferences for explanations are described below:

A High Level of Detail Is Desirable in Explanations. There was a widespread indication that a high level of detail is desirable for information provided in explanations. This became obvious in the trend of responses as participants progressed through the different explanation scenarios. "you don't want general reasons because it could be ...just something in your mind; it's what you are thinking. But that's probably not what the criteria is asking for.... you really want to ... have longer, ... more detailed nitty-gritty reasons." (P14, 18-25, fg2). Preference for a high level of detail was observed in responses across 4/4 focus groups and mentioned 24 times.

Explanations Must Be Actionable. There was a general indication that explanations must provide information which can be acted on. Underlying much of the discussions was a general view that including both reasons for denying and guidelines for improving credit scores is paramount. There was a general perception that explanations must include both laid out reasons why there is a rejection and, secondly, practical instructions or guides as to how to work towards a favourable outcome in future. This preference is highlighted by the following quote from one participant, "at least they've given me some reasons as to why I did not qualify for the credit. ... but uh, I wouldn't be satisfied, and I wouldn't understand... I think some require a detailed explanation because, like, uh, build more credit history, they should at least tell me how I can do that." (P24, 18-25, fg3).

In relation to the scenarios on visual explanations, participants felt the actionability needed to be included, "I suppose you almost have to sort of work it out yourself then what you need to do to improve your credit score because that bit of information is not there on this chart. (P15, 18-25, fg2)" . Overall, this point of having practical guidelines on how to work on the reasons provided in explanations was mentioned in all 4 focus groups and discussed 20 times.

Provide a Reasonable Number of Actionable Advice Points. Other comments showed a need to balance the amount of information and level of detail in explanations. This was evident in some participants' choice of option 3 when responding to the question on the level of detail and scope of information to be provided in explanations. Comments from this group of participants showed some preferred to have fewer reasons in the explanations, suggesting that as a way of avoiding too much information or information overload. One participant said, "OK, I'll go for fewer... It's OK. It's a balance because you have at least an idea of what you're supposed to do., And there's no overload of information at the same time." (P7, 18-25, fg1).

There were a few exceptions in two of the focus groups, stating that the level of detail in explanations should depend on the level of risk associated with the credit product, as pointed out by P2 (above 40, fg1), who explained that "It depends on the level of risk involved.... if I wanted to get a mortgage, I would want [option 4]" .... it's the higher the level of risk, the higher the level of detail for me, whereas if I just wanted to get, credit ..something really small... then maybe [option 1] or [option 3], so depends on what it is that I want to get credit for...if I'm getting something really small, I don't need to bother with [option 4]. .. but if I'm getting something big, then yes, [option 4]. " (P2, above 40, fg1).

Complimenting Explanations with Humans to Explain Explanations. Results showed that human assistance, i.e. experts or other bank staff, is generally desired for both textual and visual explanations (mentioned in all 4/4 focus groups and discussed 31 times). There was a general agreement that participants would like to consult and reason with humans, such as experts, when presented with either counterfactual or anchor explanations. "I would prepare option four, obviously, because that's the most detailed, but I would want a consultation on top of that as well." (P13, 18-25, fg2). Option 4, in this quote, refers to more than 3 actionable, detailed reasons (counterfactual explanations) presented as text. The participant clearly indicates while this seems like the best option to go for, it is desirable to have the opportunity to consult with an expert about the explanations.

The majority of participants preferred to be presented with visual explanations and also have the option of dialoguing with an expert to understand the explanations, "I would prefer to have a graph and have somebody explain or interpret the graph to me, even though I understand it's probably he or she's going to interpret it in a better way than I would interpret it. Probably an expert ..." (P16, 18-25, fg). Another person said, " visual explanations are great if they are user-friendly. If they are not user-friendly, they're pointless, and if they can then be backed up by human beings, fantastic." (P2, above 40, fg1). This topic of complimenting humans with visual aids in explaining credit decisions was reported in all 4 focus groups and mentioned 22 times.

Attach Weights to Factors in Visual Explanations. In relation to both visual explanations, an observation was that participants particularly appreciated weights/magnitudes attached to the features that play a role in determining whether individuals were eligible for credit. In the case of bar charts, the importance of features was associated with the length of the bars, indicating the most significant factors affecting the final decision outcome in the presented scenario. "I personally prefer this just because it sort of gives you weighting to the different reasons why you were not, you know, accepted. " (P15, 18-25, fg2). Participants felt that the weights were useful in determining the most important features. In the case of lime explanations, there were expected values associated with the list of features to show which features contributed most to the decision. There was the impression that weights offered useful information, as participants thought that the weights should be included in visual explanations to offer more information about the factors that play a role. Overall, this was mentioned in 2/2 focus groups and mentioned 3 times.

Visual Explanations Must Be Simple, Easy to Read and User-Friendly. An expected suggestion in relation to visual explanations was that participants felt that graphs and charts must be easy to read and user-friendly. Others showed that graphs and charts would be pointless if they were made overly complicated and hence need simplifying as much as possible, as illustrated in the following quote. "I think the main aim of a visual representation of any information is to make it easy and ready to interpret, so if the credit companies want to use a graph to represent why I was not viable for credit, It should not be difficult for me to understand. It should be spot on, (...), but if it requires much more mental capacity for me to be able to understand and interpret whatever the displayed for me, I think it might not work " (P24, 18-25, fg). This point was agreed upon by most participants in 4/4 focus groups and was mentioned 6 times.

Inclusivity in Designing Explanations. Other comments revealed that participants wanted to have a mixture of modes used to communicate explanations. It was clear that participants were aware that preferences might differ in relation to learning experiences for different audiences; hence, there were some suggestions to provide multiple avenues for explanations as much as possible, implying a combination of both text, visual and human explanations in some form. "And I think it's better to have all avenues of explanations; just as I say, people learn things and process information differently. And so, from an inclusivity perspective, I think it's better to have an option for all people to kind of choose what suits them best." (P1, 18-25, fg1) This implies that in the design of explanations, there is a need to consider carefully how to meet the needs of a diverse set of audiences. This point on inclusivity was mentioned in one of the focus groups and discussed two times.

4 Discussion and Conclusions

The study has demonstrated the significance of explaining algorithmic decisions in high-stakes decision-making domains, specifically in the context of loan approval. Findings from the study highlight a number of implications for policy, research and practice. Individuals place a high value on having explanations about decisions made by algorithms. Having explanations is associated with being treated well. End users require that interactive features must be added to both visual and non-visual explanations to enable dialogue and further discussion about explanations with another entity preferably a human. Overall visual explanations of algorithmic decisions in high-stakes domains are perceived as useful to summarise information and enable quicker comprehension of explanations. Designing both visual and non-visual explanations requires that the information must be presented in an inclusive manner to meet the information needs of different audiences. The quest for inclusive design and presentation of algorithmic explanations calls for greater collaborative efforts on the part of industry practitioners and academic researchers to investigate novel methods towards meeting the information needs and different literacy levels of various categories of end users in society. Insights from the study can inform policy formulation to govern industry practitioners in the design of explanations for end users.

Acknowledgments. This study was funded by UKRI/EPSRC, Horizon Centre for Doctoral Training, University of Nottingham.

Disclosure of Interests. The authors have no competing interests to declare that are relevant to the content of this article.

References

1. Adadi, A., Berrada, M.: Peeking inside the black-box: a survey on explainable artificial intelligence (XAI). IEEE Access **6**, 52138–52160 (2018)
2. Arrieta, A.B., et al.: Explainable artificial intelligence (XAI): concepts, taxonomies, opportunities and challenges toward responsible AI. Inf. Fusion **58**, 82–115 (2020)
3. Braun, V., Clarke, V.: Reflecting on reflexive thematic analysis. Qual. Res. Sport Exerc. Health **11**(4), 589–597 (2019)
4. Brockner, J., Wiesenfeld, B.M.: An integrative framework for explaining reactions to decisions: interactive effects of outcomes and procedures. Psychol. Bull. **120**(2), 189 (1996)
5. Doshi-Velez, F., Kim, B.: Towards a rigorous science of interpretable machine learning. arXiv preprint arXiv:1702.08608 (2017)
6. König, G., Molnar, C., Bischl, B., Grosse-Wentrup, M.: Relative feature importance. In: 2020 25th International Conference on Pattern Recognition (ICPR), pp. 9318–9325. IEEE (2021)
7. Lipton, Z.C.: The mythos of model interpretability: in machine learning, the concept of interpretability is both important and slippery. Queue **16**(3), 31–57 (2018)
8. Miller, T.: Explanation in artificial intelligence: insights from the social sciences. Artif. Intell. **267**, 1–38 (2019)
9. Ribeiro, M.T., Singh, S., Guestrin, C.: why should i trust you? Explaining the predictions of any classifier. In: Proceedings of the 22nd ACM SIGKDD International Conference on Knowledge Discovery and Data Mining, pp. 1135–1144 (2016)
10. Wachter, S., Mittelstadt, B., Russell, C.: Counterfactual explanations without opening the black box: automated decisions and the GDPR. Harv. JL & Tech. **31**, 841 (2017)

Optimizing E-Commerce Warehouse Item Placement: A Three-Pronged Approach

Aakash Bhatt[1(✉)], Matthew Jurado[2], and Amith Tarigonda[3]

[1] Reno NV, USA
aakash.bhatt29@gmail.com
[2] Munich, Germany
[3] Bentonville, AR, USA

Abstract. Placing items optimally to keep up with the fast-paced operations in e-commerce warehouses where humans and automation need to work in a symphony requires complex analysis and a well-defined strategy. This paper introduces a method that combines the strengths of the Slotting Location Assignment Problem (SLAP), Discrete Event Simulation (DES), and Mixed Integer Linear Programming (MILP) to address this issue. SLAP efficiently organizes products within the warehouse, DES models operational flows, including human and automated interactions, and MILP optimizes cost and efficiency, together providing a comprehensive solution to improve warehouse operations. Our results demonstrate notable improvements in operational efficiency and cost savings, indicating the potential of this integrated approach to enhance warehouse management practices in the e-commerce sector.

Keywords: Warehouse Optimization · Slotting Problem · Discrete Event Simulation · Mixed Integer Linear Programming

1 Introduction

1.1 E-Commerce Growth and Warehousing Evolution

Morgan Stanley [1] forecasts substantial growth in the e-commerce market, with global sales projected to increase from $3.3 trillion to $5.4 trillion between 2022 and 2026. This surge underscores the escalating demand for advanced warehousing solutions to accommodate increasing order volumes. Driven by e-commerce's exponential growth, warehousing operations have undergone significant transformations, moving beyond traditional storage strategies to embrace complex automation systems for better productivity [2]. This transition from basic storage facilities to technologically advanced fulfillment centers (FCs) calls for reevaluating warehousing strategies. Modern warehouses are increasingly adopting Automated Storage and Retrieval Systems (ASRS), autonomous mobile robots (AMRs), conveyor systems, and robotics to streamline operational flows and

A. Bhatt, M. Jurado and A. Tarigonda—Independant Researchers

C. Stephanidis et al. (Eds.): HCII 2024, CCIS 2319, pp. 14–24, 2025.
https://doi.org/10.1007/978-3-031-78516-0_2

reduce the reliance on manual labor for tasks such as picking and packing. Based on the business requirements, FCs need a strategic plan to integrate automation with different storage configurations such as pallet flow systems, carton flow racks, vertical lift modules, and bin shelving.

1.2 The Importance of Slotting

At the core of achieving operational efficiency in FCs is the strategic placement of items across the different areas and storage configurations, a practice known as slotting. Slotting involves analyzing product characteristics, order patterns, and storage constraints to determine the most effective locations for items within the warehouse, aiming to minimize picking and storage efforts, reduce travel time, and, consequently, labor costs. Implementing an effective slotting strategy can be a complex task, as it requires finding the right balance between maximizing storage capacity and maintaining efficient flow through warehouse automation to manage bottlenecks. Achieving this balance demands extensive data analysis, a thorough understanding of the facility's infrastructure, and the ability to adapt to constantly changing operational goals.

1.3 Innovative Slotting Strategy for Enhanced Efficiency

Our proposed method addresses a critical gap in the logistics and warehousing industry by offering a comprehensive strategy that tackles the complexities of integrating automation and storage configurations. This approach aims to enhance operational efficiency in FCs by optimizing slotting strategies, minimizing costs, and accelerating order fulfillment. In contrast to traditional slotting methods, which struggle with the dynamic nature of material flow in automated FCs due to their reliance on static, manual analysis, our approach optimizes both cost and flow, adapting to changes in inputs with each iteration.

2 Literature Review

2.1 Slotting Location Assignment Problem (SLAP)

Addressing the Slotting Location Assignment Problem (SLAP) is crucial for warehouse optimization research, aiming to improve operational efficiency by identifying optimal item placements-a challenge intensified by the growing demands of e-commerce. SLAP has been a focal point of warehouse optimization research, aiming to enhance operational efficiency by determining the optimal placement of items within a warehouse. Research by Park and Seo [3], Chen et al. [4], and Ballestín et al. [5] have delved into SLAP's complexities, from innovative heuristics in random storage to outbound container placement in maritime terminals, each study progressively uncovering the nuanced challenges of optimizing item placement. These works underline the complexity of SLAP and its impact on minimizing order-picking costs and improving overall warehouse performance. Leon et al. [6] highlight a pivotal shift in SLAP research towards a holistic and integrated perspective, underscoring a growing recognition of the need to consider broader operational dynamics beyond isolated slotting decisions.

2.2 Discrete Event Simulation (DES)

Given the intricacies of automated warehouse systems introduced by rapid e-commerce growth, Discrete Event Simulation (DES) has emerged as an indispensable tool for dissecting and optimizing the interconnected operational flows within FCs. Gagliardi et al. [7] showed how strategic decisions can be tested and optimized for high-throughput warehouses using discrete event simulation. By simulating real-world systems and their temporal behaviors, DES allows for a detailed examination of operational dynamics, enabling stakeholders to assess the effects of various conditions and decisions on system performance. This modeling precision is instrumental in optimizing process flows, equipment layouts, and workforce allocation, providing a risk-free environment for scenario testing and strategy development.

2.3 Mixed Integer Linear Programming (MILP)

Mixed Integer Linear Programming (MILP) complements the decision framework offered by SLAP and the flow insights provided by DES, presenting a mathematical rigor essential for fine-tuning warehouse optimization strategies. MILP's mathematical framework facilitates the formulation of optimization problems, balancing resource allocation within operational constraints such as capacity limits and fulfillment timelines. Ansari and Smith [8] leveraged simulation with an optimization approach, grouping items based on a gravity affinity model, and also proposed leveraging MILP to optimize picker travel. However, their approach treats MILP for item placement separate from the pick path planning engine directing humans to work.

2.4 Integrating SLAP, DES, and MILP

While advancements in warehouse optimization have been significant, existing research often treats SLAP, DES, and MILP in isolation. Research thus far has overlooked the synergistic potential of their integrated application-a gap our work aims to fill by demonstrating how such integration can provide more adaptable, efficient solutions to modern warehouse challenges. Leon et al. [6] demonstrate that integrating Storage Location Assignment Problem (SLAP) solutions with discrete event simulation (DES) allows for robust warehouse optimization, balancing deterministic planning with stochastic real-world conditions. However, the study does not incorporate MILP, missing an opportunity to explore its potential for further optimization. An integrated approach, leveraging the strengths of each methodology, could significantly advance the state of warehouse optimization, providing solutions that are more efficient and adaptable to the evolving demands of the e-commerce landscape.

While each methodology offers valuable insights into enhancing warehouse operations, there is a clear need for research that explores their integrated application. Such an approach could fill the existing gaps in the literature, offering an innovative solution that leverages the combined strengths of SLAP, DES, and MILP to address the complex challenges of modern warehouse slotting management.

3 Methodology

Our research problem statement highlights the need to improve the operational efficiency of warehouses in order to meet the dynamic demands of the expanding e-commerce market. To address these challenges, we have developed a methodology that integrates three different approaches: The Slotting Location Assignment Problem (SLAP), Discrete Event Simulation (DES), and Mixed Integer Linear Programming (MILP). This three-pronged approach is designed to optimize the placement of items in the warehouse, leading to significant improvements in operational efficiency, cost reduction, and faster order fulfillment process.

3.1 Comprehensive Data Analysis

To effectively address the research problem, our first step involves an extensive collection and in-depth analysis of warehouse operation data. This extensive dataset is categorized as follows, each category playing a pivotal role by serving as input in the subsequent phases of our methodology:

- **SKU Characteristics:** This category encompasses descriptive SKU data, such as physical dimensions (length, width, height), weight, volume, movement frequency, and item classification. Understanding the characteristics of each SKU is pivotal for effective slotting and determining how each item interacts with the warehouse's physical and operational constraints.
- **Order Patterns:** Aggregating SKU characteristics to the order level enables identifying trends within customer order patterns. Order pattern data includes seasonality, recurring orders, item sets, affinities, promotions, and discounts.
- **Storage Location Attributes:** This includes detailed information on the physical storage locations available within the warehouse, such as the type of storage (e.g., shelving, put walls), dimensions (length, width, height), and any physical limitations on SKU storage.
- **Infrastructure and Design:** The physical infrastructure and design of the warehouse, captured through detailed engineering computer-aided design (CAD) drawings, are used to replicate the warehouse environment within the simulation model accurately. This category includes the layout of storage areas, conveyance paths, and the placement of automated systems, providing a visual and structural basis for the simulation modeling.
- **Automation Parameters:** Warehouse automation technology data, such as critical performance metrics on material flow and downtime, are necessary for accurate abstraction in a simulation environment.

3.2 SLAP Application

The Slotting Location Assignment Problem (SLAP) can address one or more warehouse objectives, such as minimizing total retrieval time, minimizing travel distance, balancing workloads, or maximizing space utilization. Mathematically, the SLAP can be formulated as follows:

$$\min \sum_{i=1}^{N} \sum_{j=1}^{M} x_{ij} d_{ij} \tag{1}$$

where N represents the number of items, M the number of slots in the warehouse, x_{ij} is a binary decision variable that equals 1 if item i is assigned to slot j, and 0 otherwise, and d_{ij} denotes the measure of the objective function (such as time to retrieve or distance traveled) when item i is placed in slot j. Further constraints can be added to reflect practical considerations, such as the weight or volume limits of slots, and the need to group related items.

To address the complexity of SLAP efficiently, a two-phase approach is adopted, breaking the problem into manageable segments. The first phase, macro-slotting, involves dividing the warehouse into distinct zones based on item characteristics like demand or size. This phase simplifies the problem by categorizing items into broader groups, making the slotting process more manageable. Macro-slotting can be effectively solved using meta-heuristic algorithms such as Genetic Algorithms [9], Simulated Annealing [10], or Particle Swarm Optimization [11], which are adept at finding near-optimal solutions for complex problems.

Following macro-slotting, the second phase addresses the micro-level SLAP within each zone, assigning specific slots to items. This detailed assignment is executed using exact solvers like Gurobi©, known for its efficiency in solving linear and mixed-integer linear programming problems. This staged approach leverages the strengths of different optimization methods, and the final output is slot assignment for all items within the warehouse.

3.3 DES Flow Modeling

Using the slot assignments from the SLAP phase, combined with the initial flow inputs from automation parameters, a detailed DES model of the warehouse is constructed. A 3D simulation environment is created to accurately replicate the warehouse's infrastructure using high-fidelity engineering CAD drawings and data collected during the input stage. The DES model incorporates specific controls and warehouse management system (WMS) environments with abstracted logic to accurately capture the behaviors of various automation technologies and their interaction with human operations. By varying critical input parameters such as order volume and the activity in the different areas of the warehouse, tiered simulation experiments are run to identify maximum capacity thresholds and operational bottlenecks, facilitating strategic decision-making for operational success. By leveraging tools such as FlexSim© or AnyLogic©, complex interconnected warehouse systems can be modeled to understand flow constraints with a given item-placement strategy.

3.4 MILP for Cost-Effective Optimization

The final stage utilizes MILP formulation to evaluate and conduct experiments with different target shipped volumes out of the warehouse to determine the optimal flow from each zone of the warehouse. This phase is fundamentally aimed at the minimization of operational costs, all the while adhering to flow constraints defined by the DES. MILP helps refine the strategies derived from SLAP and validated through DES, ensuring that the warehouse operations are not only efficient but also cost-effective. he MILP formulation is detailed as follows:

Objective Functions.

Minimize Fulfillment Cost. The objective is to minimize the total fulfillment costs associated with warehouse operations and maxim

$$Z_{\text{min cost}} = \sum (\text{fulfillment costs}) \tag{2}$$

Maximize Shipping Volume. Conversely, the objective is to maximize the total volume of units shipped from the warehouse.

$$Z_{\text{max volume}} = \sum (\text{shipped unit volume}) \tag{3}$$

Constraints. The operational constraints are formulated to ensure the feasibility of warehouse operations while optimizing the objectives.

Area Capacity Constraint

$$\sum_{\text{all items}} \text{Area(item)} \leq \text{Total Area Available} \tag{4}$$

Location Capacity Constraint

$$\sum_{\text{all items in location}} \text{Volume(item)} \leq \text{Volume Capacity(location)}, \quad \forall \text{locations} \tag{5}$$

SKU Type Constraint

$$\text{Type(item)} \in \text{Allowed Types(location)}, \quad \forall \text{items, locations} \tag{6}$$

Picking Cost Constraint

$$\sum_{\text{all items}} \text{Picking Cost(item)} \leq \text{Budget} \tag{7}$$

Lagrangian Relaxation. To effectively balance the dual objectives of minimizing costs and maximizing volume, a Lagrangian relaxation approach is adopted. This involves incorporating Lagrangian multipliers to soften one or more constraints, thereby allowing for a more flexible and focused optimization process.

4 Experimentation and Results

Consider a fulfillment center with four distinct zones, each equipped with different automation technologies and storage configurations:

- **Zone A: High-Volume Automated Shelving** - Utilizes robotic arms for picking items from high-density shelving units, designed primarily for small to medium-sized, high-turnover SKUs.
- **Zone B: Palletized Bulk Storage** - Equipped with automated forklifts and pallet racking systems, optimized for large, bulky items that move at a moderate pace.
- **Zone C: Cold Storage Pick Zone** - A temperature-controlled environment with conveyance systems tailored for perishable goods, ensuring product integrity during handling.
- **Zone D: Manual Pick Zone** - A flexible area with adjustable shelving, designated for items requiring manual picking due to irregular sizes or special handling needs.

Applying an integrated methodology of SLAP, DES, and MILP to optimize the placement of 100 SKUs within the automated FC divided into 4 zones, the experimentation proceeds through the following steps:

4.1 Step 1 Comprehensive Data Analysis

Data on 100 SKUs are analyzed, incorporating dimensions, weight, volume, movement frequency, classification, order trends (seasonality, affinities), storage capabilities, CAD-modeled infrastructure, and automation performance metrics to inform the slotting strategy.

4.2 Step 2 SLAP Application

SLAP is utilized in two phases, macro-slotting and micro-slotting, to allocate SKUs to optimal locations based on their characteristics and order patterns.

In Table 1, the Macro-Slotting Results display the initial broad allocation of 100 SKUs into four distinct areas within the warehouse, categorized based on their physical characteristics and turnover rates. This phase groups SKUs to optimize warehouse organization by ensuring that items are stored in locations best suited to their handling and sales dynamics.

Table 1. Macro-Slotting Results

Area	SKU Range	Characteristics
A	SKU#1-25	Small to medium, high-turnover
B	SKU#26-50	Large, bulky, moderate-turnover
C	SKU#51-75	Perishables, requiring cold storage
D	SKU#76-100	Irregular sizes, manual picking

Table 2, the Micro-Slotting Example for Area A, illustrates the next level of detail in the slotting process, where individual SKUs within Area A are assigned specific shelf heights and arranged to ensure proximity to related SKUs with which they have high affinity. This step fine-tunes the macro-slotting outcomes by addressing the ergonomics of picking processes (by adjusting shelf heights for optimal access) and further reducing picking times (by placing items frequently ordered together in close proximity).

Table 2. Micro-Slotting Example for Area A

SKU	Optimal Shelf Height	Proximity to Related SKUs
SKU#1	Mid-height	Near SKU#5 (high affinity)
SKU#2	Top shelf	Near SKU#6 (high affinity)

Output Metrics: Output Metrics: Allocation efficiency score measures how well are all the constraints of the SLAP satisfied. An initial match of 90% between SKUs and their designated areas is observed, suggesting a high degree of fit.

4.3 Step 3 DES Experimentation

The DES model is built and executed to simulate the flow of items through the warehouse and the picking process, identify bottlenecks, and test capacity thresholds under varying order volumes. From this simulation experimentation, we derive that:

- **Throughput Efficiency:** The system can attain 100% of the throughput required at the average order volume.
- **Bottleneck Identification:** The packing station becomes a bottleneck at 10% above average order volume. Upon resolving this bottleneck by adding additional staffing, the manual ship sortation area becomes the choke point at 30% above the average order volume.

4.4 Step 4 MILP Optimization

MILP focuses on minimizing operational costs by maximizing flow through the most cost-effective zones, taking into consideration the constraints identified in the DES phase. The optimization criteria are to minimize total operational costs while maintaining or improving throughput efficiency. Various flow distributions across the four warehouse zones are evaluated to identify cost-saving measures, tailored to exploit the unique efficiencies and capabilities of the respective areas:

- **Area A (High-Volume Automated Shelving)** is optimized for quicker turnover SKUs to reduce picking times.
- **Area B (Palletized Bulk Storage)** could focus on storing bulk items in a manner that minimizes forklift travel distances.
- **Area C (Cold Storage Pick Zone)** is analyzed for optimal usage to maintain perishable goods' integrity with minimal energy consumption.
- **Area D (Manual Pick Zone)** is scrutinized for ergonomic efficiency to enhance manual picking operations without increasing labor costs.

The outcomes of applying MILP to optimize warehouse operations are demonstrated in Table 3, which includes a baseline scenario (Base) and an optimized scenario (Optimized), along with three additional hypothetical configurations (Scenario 1, Scenario 2, Scenario 3). Each scenario is evaluated based on its ability to reduce operational costs and improve throughput efficiency. The Optimized scenario demonstrates the most substantial gains, achieving a 15% cost reduction and a 5% increase in throughput efficiency, indicating the effectiveness of MILP in enhancing warehouse operational strategies through cost-effective zone utilization and improved item flow.

Table 3. MILP Optimization Output

Scenario	Description	Cost Reduction	Throughput Improvement
Base	Initial setup without optimization	–	–
Optimized	After MILP application, focusing on cost-effective zone utilization	15%	5%
Scenario 1	Increased automation in high-volume areas	10%	3%
Scenario 2	Strategic reallocation of manual picking tasks	12%	4%
Scenario 3	Enhanced ergonomic layout in manual pick zones	8%	6%

5 Discussion and Future Research

The integration of discrete event simulation (DES) with mixed integer linear programming (MILP) to address the slotting location assignment problem (SLAP) represents a warehouse optimization approach that is hard to replicate through manual management. Traditional methods lack the flexibility and scalability of our DES and MILP integration, often resulting in suboptimal item placement and inefficiencies.

The cost implications of our methodology are equally compelling. By optimizing throughput and simultaneously reducing operational costs, mainly labor-we offer a solution that directly addresses one of the central challenges in warehouse management. Furthermore, our approach contributes to the broader goal of supply chain optimization. Businesses can enhance their supply resilience and responsiveness in logistics and e-commerce by iteratively executing this method in a warehouse setting over defined time periods.

The complexity of implementing an integrated DES and MILP approach cannot be understated. It requires a diverse set of skills and, typically, dedicated resources from multiple specialties-a factor that could limit accessibility for some organizations. However, if the infrastructure for both the DES model and optimization engine are laid correctly, a composite model approach like the one discussed in the paper would create a high fidelity model with a great deal of extensibility.

For future research, several avenues are particularly promising. Investigating ways to simplify the implementation process could make our approach more accessible to various organizations. Additionally, exploring the integration of emerging technologies, such as artificial intelligence (AI) and the Internet of Things (IoT), could further enhance the model's predictive capabilities and operational insights. Lastly, a deeper examination of the human factors involved in model interpretation and decision-making could yield valuable strategies for bridging the gap between model abstractions and practical application.

6 Conclusion

This work highlights an innovative approach to refining warehouse operations, uniquely integrating the Slotting Location Assignment Problem (SLAP), Discrete Event Simulation (DES), and Mixed Integer Linear Programming (MILP) to develop a holistic item placement strategy. For warehouses looking to implement this strategy, a systematic analysis of SKU data, storage capabilities, and automation technology is essential. The process begins with SLAP, which guides initial slotting decisions. This is followed by DES to uncover operational insights and identify bottlenecks. The strategy is fine-tuned with MILP, optimizing costs and meeting throughput goals.

This integrated approach offers a pathway to increased warehouse efficiency and aligns with the evolving demands of the e-commerce sector and heightened customer delivery expectations. Implementing such a strategy requires a commitment to data integrity, an openness to technological integration, and a willingness to adapt operational practices based on analytical findings. The methodology outlined in this research offers a practical and effective solution for addressing warehouse slotting challenges through a blend of advanced optimization techniques.

Disclosure of Interests. The authors have no competing interests to declare that are relevant to the content of this article.

References

1. Stanley, M.: The surprising case for stronger e-commerce growth (2022). https://www.morganstanley.com/ideas/global-ecommerce-growth-forecast-2022
2. Dhaliwal, A.: The rise of automation and robotics in warehouse management. In: CRC Press eBooks, pp. 63–72 (2020). https://doi.org/10.1201/9781003032410-5
3. Park, C., Seo, J.: Mathematical modeling and solving procedure of the planar storage location assignment problem. Comput. Ind. Eng. **57**, 1062–1071 (2009)
4. Chen, L., Lu, Z.: The storage location assignment problem for outbound containers in a maritime terminal. Int. J. Prod. Econ. **135**, 73–80 (2012)
5. Ballestín, F., Pérez, Á., Quintanilla, S.: A multistage heuristic for storage and retrieval problems in a warehouse with random storage. Int. Trans. Oper. Res. **27**, 1699–1728 (2017)
6. Leon, J.F., Li, Y., Peyman, M., Calvet, L., Juan, Á.A.: A discrete-event simheuristic for solving a realistic storage location assignment problem. Mathematics **11**(7), 1577 (2023). https://doi.org/10.3390/math11071577
7. Gagliardi, J., Renaud, J., Ruiz, A.: A simulation model to improve warehouse operations. In: Proceedings - Winter Simulation Conference, pp. 2012–2018 (2007). https://doi.org/10.1145/1351542.1351899
8. Ansari, M., Smith, J.: Gravity clustering: a correlated storage location assignment problem approach (2020). https://doi.org/10.1109/WSC48552.2020.9384029
9. Holland, J.H.: Genetic algorithms. Sci. Am. **267**(1), 66–73 (1992)
10. Kirkpatrick, S., Gelatt, C.D., Vecchi, M.P.: Optimization by simulated annealing. Science **220**(4598), 671–680 (1983)
11. Kennedy, J., Eberhart, R.: Particle swarm optimization. In: Proceedings of ICNN 1995 - International Conference on Neural Networks, vol. 4, pp. 1942–1948. IEEE (1995)

Towards the Control of Smart Devices Using a GUI-Free EOG-Based HMI System

Tracey Camilleri[1(✉)], Nathaniel Barbara[2], Matthew Mifsud[1], Salah Ad-Din Al Youbi[1], and Kenneth Camilleri[1,2]

[1] Department of Systems and Control Engineering, University of Malta, Msida, Malta
tracey.camilleri@um.edu.mt
[2] Centre for Biomedical Cybernetics, University of Malta, Msida, Malta
https://www.um.edu.mt/eng/sce/

Abstract. Eye-gaze tracking is a common modality used by individuals with limited fine motor skills to control devices within their environment. This work proposes the use of an electrooculography-based human machine interface system that allows users to control smart devices without requiring a graphical user interface. Instead, the system leverages a person's innate gaze interaction with devices in the environment and by recording the individual's position and head orientation, determines the device the user wants to control. Seven different, simple eye gestures are then used for controlling the device to which the user is connected. This preliminary offline study assesses the feasibility of such a system by quantifying the device selection accuracy as well as the eye movement classification accuracy obtained across six subjects. Specifically, the users could select between seven different smart devices with an accuracy of 97.57% ± 0.03% while their eye gestures could be detected reliably with an accuracy of 97.22% ± 0.03%.

Keywords: Electrooculography · Smart device control · Eye movement classification

1 Introduction

Individuals with severe neuromuscular disorders often find it challenging to control devices within their environment using conventional control interfaces, such as remote controls and touch screens. It is thus necessary to develop alternative human machine interfaces that empower these individuals to control devices independently, without requiring continuous assistance from their caregivers.

Eye-gaze tracking is a common modality used for such purposes, given that individuals with mobility impairments typically retain control over their eye movements [1]. Control of smart devices, such as televisions, lights and air conditioners, have been attempted using both videooculography (VOG) [2] and electrooculography (EOG) [1,3,4]. This work focuses on employing an EOG-based human-machine interface (HMI) system for smart device control.

C. Stephanidis et al. (Eds.): HCII 2024, CCIS 2319, pp. 25–34, 2025.
https://doi.org/10.1007/978-3-031-78516-0_3

EOG involves the placement of electrodes around the user's eyes to record the electrical potential around the eyes. The EOG signal characteristics vary depending on the user's eye movements and hence, processing the recorded signals permits the detection and classification of eye movements, such as left, right, up and down eye movements. These can be carried out intentionally and used in EOG-based smart device control applications to activate the desired device functions. In this work, such intentional eye movements are referred to as eye gestures. To increase the list of possible commands or make the system more robust, patterns comprising sequential eye gestures are also often used [3,4]. For example, a sequence of left, right, left, right eye gestures can be executed to toggle specific devices. Alternatively, Zhang *et al.* [1] developed a system which required users to execute blinks that are in sync with the flashes of the desired device options presented on a computer screen, hence increasing the number of available control commands. While both conventional eye movement patterns and synchronised blink patterns are typically detected with high accuracy rates exceeding 90%, they may not offer an intuitive way of controlling smart devices. This limitation stems from the cognitive burden of recalling eye movement patterns, particularly when managing numerous devices and control functions. Additionally, generating repetitive voluntary eye blinks may prove cumbersome.

Many of the EOG-based applications for smart device control documented in the literature require an intermediary graphical user interface (GUI) [1,3]. This GUI displays various control options and may include multiple menus for user navigation [1]. While this setup provides a clear view of available options, it necessitates continuous visual engagement with a computer screen to activate the desired functions. This approach lacks the naturalness inherent in controlling external devices and confines users to remain in front of a computer screen.

This work proposes an alternative approach that capitalises on an individual's inherent gaze interaction with devices in their surrounding, thereby eliminating the necessity for a GUI. In the proposed system users are free to navigate through their environment, select a device by directing their gaze towards it, and execute specific eye gestures to activate desired control functions. Achieving this objective necessitates three key components: i) accurate localisation of the individual, facilitated by a real-time ultra-wideband localisation system, ii) fusion of this localisation data with recorded head orientation data to determine the device the user intends to control, and iii) processing of EOG data to detect and classify the executed eye gestures.

This paper presents preliminary results from an offline study conducted with six subjects, documenting the performance obtained for device selection and eye movement classification. In what follows, Sect. 2 discusses the system setup, Sect. 3 outlines the data collection process, Sect. 4 details the approach for device selection and eye movement classification, and Sect. 5 presents the results. Finally, Sect. 6 offers a discussion and conclusion of the study.

2 System Setup

The proposed EOG-based system for device selection and control required the real-time monitoring of the user's positional data, head orientation and eye gestures. The setup was implemented within a 9 m × 9.6 m laboratory environment and included seven smart devices: a television, an air conditioner, a smart lock attached to a designated door, motorised blinds, a fan, a lamp and a hi-fi system. The spatial arrangement of these devices within the lab is shown in Fig. 1.

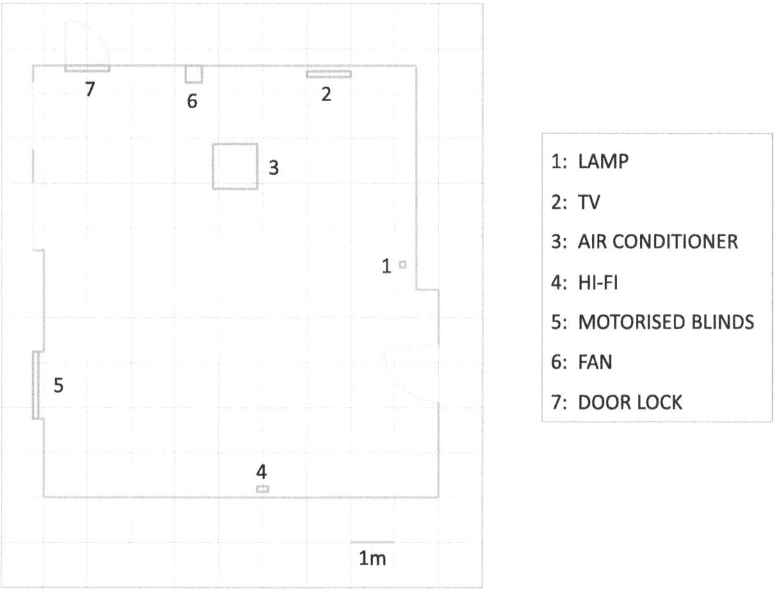

Fig. 1. Lab space showing the location of the seven smart devices

User localisation within the lab was achieved by an ultra-wideband (UWB) real-time localisation system. Specifically, the system developed by Eliko [5] was used to provide the 2D coordinates of the user every 100ms. This functionality was enabled through a set of four anchors strategically affixed to the walls to surround the tracking area, and a wearable tag attached to the user's shoulder.

The user's head orientation was captured using the BNO055 smart sensor [6]. This sensor integrates an accelerometer, a gyroscope, a magnetometer and orientation software, enabling continuous measurement of head orientation in a three-dimensional space through Euler angles.

Subsequently, eye gestures were recorded through an electrooculogram. The JINS MEME EOG glasses [7], which offers a wireless recording of EOG data, was used for this purpose. The glasses are equipped with three electrodes, strategically positioned at the nose pads and nose bridge, and transmit data to a computer via Bluetooth with a sampling frequency of 50 Hz. The real-time vertical and horizontal EOG channels provided by the wearable device were then processed to discern the user's eye movement control signals.

3 Data Collection

A total of six subjects (3 males and 3 females; mean age 28.5 ± 6.1 years), with normal or corrected-to-normal vision, participated in this study. The data acquisition protocol was approved by the University Research Ethics Committee (UREC) at the University of Malta and before each recording session, subjects were asked to provide their consent.

3.1 Dataset for Device Selection

Each subject was positioned at four random locations within the available lab space, making sure that each location was in a different quadrant of the laboratory. From each location, subjects were provided with audio cues instructing them to look at one of seven possible smart devices, positioned in the lab as shown in Fig. 1, for a duration of 10 s. The order of device selection from each location was randomised. A total of 28 trials (1 trial for each device per location) were collected for each subject. During this data collection session, the position of the user was captured through the real-time localisation system while the head orientation data was captured through the orientation sensor.

3.2 Dataset for Eye Movement Classification

Electrooculographic data was recorded from each subject while carrying out seven different eye gestures, specifically up, down, left, right, blink, double blink and eyes closed, according to audio cues. For the first four eye gestures, subjects started from a principal gaze position (PGP), carried out the eye gesture and returned to their PGP. Thus to carry a left gesture, for example, the user gazed from the PGP to the left and back to the PGP. Each trial was 4 s long except those related to the eyes closed gesture which were 6 s long. In each trial an audio cue was provided at 0.5 s stating the eye gesture to be performed. For the eyes closed trials another audio cue at 3.5 s instructed the subjects to open their eyes. A total of 210 trials were recorded for each subject (30 trials for each eye gesture) and the order of eye movements carried out was randomised.

4 Methodology

4.1 Device Selection

The proposed system leverages the user's natural gaze to determine which smart device they intend to control by processing the gaze vector relative to the user's head orientation. Specifically, it uses the real-time localization data to ascertain the user's position and the positions of all available smart devices, then generates a set of expected gaze vectors for each device based on its spatial configuration.

Specifically, in the developed system, each smart device is enclosed within a 2D or 3D bounding box, and the expected gaze vectors are determined by calculating the vectors connecting the estimated head position with the corners of the bounding box as well as its centroid. Thus, the air conditioner, the television, the door lock and the blinds, all of which are very flat, are assigned a 2D bounding box and hence, a set of 5 expected gaze vectors. In contrast, devices like the fan, the hi-fi system and the lamp were assigned a 3D bounding box and hence, 9 expected gaze vectors.

The system then uses the head orientation data to determine the user's actual gaze vector. This actual gaze vector is then compared to the sets of expected gaze vectors for each device. The device whose expected gaze vector is closest to the actual gaze vector in terms of angular proximity is identified as the device the user intends to control.

To prevent accidental device selections, the system incorporates a dwell period requirement. Specifically, the user must maintain their gaze on the selected device for a continuous period of 2 s before the device is considered to be actively selected for control. The dwell period ensures intentionality in the user's selection process, thereby minimizing unintentional selections of smart devices.

4.2 Eye Gesture Detection and Classification

This work considered seven distinct eye gestures: up, down, left, right, blink, double blink and eyes closed. Figure 2 illustrates the expected characteristics of the EOG signals for each eye gesture, as recorded on both the vertical and horizontal EOG channels, EOG_V and EOG_H, respectively. Their specific characteristics are detailed below. Recall that for the up, down, left and right eye gestures, the subject started from the PGP, carried out the eye gesture and then returned to their PGP.

Up Eye Gesture: EOG_V displays a peak due to the initial saccade and a trough due to the return saccade. EOG_H exhibits no prominent peaks or troughs.

Down Eye Gesture: EOG_V is characterised by a trough due to the initial saccade and a peak due to the return saccade. EOG_H exhibits no prominent peaks or troughs.

Left Eye Gesture: EOG_H displays a trough due to the initial saccade followed by a peak due to the return saccade. EOG_V shows no prominent peaks or troughs.

Right Eye Gesture: EOG_H has a peak due to the initial saccade followed by a trough due to the return saccade. EOG_V has no prominent peaks or troughs.

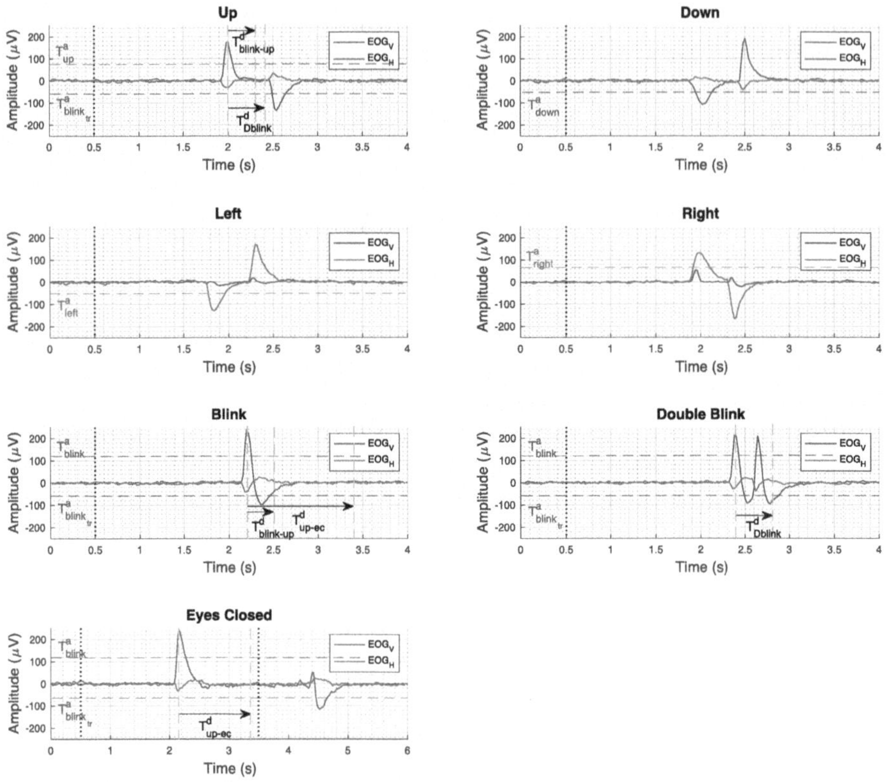

Fig. 2. EOG characteristics on the vertical EOG channel EOG_V and horizontal EOG channel EOG_H for each of the seven eye gestures considered.

Blink: EOG_V is characterised by a large peak which is immediately followed by a trough. EOG_H lacks significant peaks or troughs.

Double Blink: EOG_V exhibits characteristics similar to those of a blink but with two peak-trough events occurring in quick succession.

Eyes Closed: EOG_V shows a pattern similar to a blink. However, due to the eyes remaining closed until instructed, there is a longer duration between the peak and trough.

Given these characteristic peaks and troughs, and aligning with established practices in the literature [8–11], event detection and classification were carried out based on signal amplitude thresholds T_x^a, for $x \in \{up, down, left, right, blink, blink_{tr}\}$ and duration thresholds, T_y^d for $y \in \{blink\text{-}up, up\text{-}ec, Dblink\}$, all of which are illustrated in coloured dotted lines in Fig. 2. The amplitude thresholds for the up, down, left and right gestures were determined considering the EOG amplitude of the initial peak or trough of the respective eye gesture. For blinks, T^a_{blink} and $T^a_{blink_{tr}}$ were determined using the EOG amplitude of the peak and trough in EOG_V, respectively. For the duration thresholds, $T^d_{blink-up}$ was determined such that it lies between the typical duration between the peak and trough of the blink and up gestures. Similarly, T^d_{up-ec} was determined considering the typical duration between the peak and trough of the up and eyes-closed gestures. Finally, T^d_{DBlink} was found by considering the typical duration between the two peaks of the double blink eye gesture. These thresholds were determined using a 5-fold cross validation method, where four folds were used for training the thresholds, while the remaining fold was used to evaluate the eye gesture classification performance.

In this study, detection of left and right eye gestures occurred when the initial peak or trough detected on the horizontal EOG channel surpassed the corresponding amplitude threshold, T^a_{left} or T^a_{right}, respectively. Similarly, for down gestures, if a trough surpassed T^a_{down}, the event was classified as a downward eye gesture. Conversely, if a peak exceeded T^a_{up} but not T^a_{blink}, it was identified as an upward eye gesture. However, even if the peak amplitude exceeded T^a_{blink}, the event could still be considered as a potential upward eye gesture event, as discussed below.

Due to their EOG signal characteristics, distinguishing between blinks, double blinks, upward eye gestures and eyes closed necessitated an analysis not only of the amplitudes of the peaks or troughs but also of the duration between them. A blink is identified when the initial peak surpasses the blink amplitude threshold T^a_{blink}, followed by a trough exceeding the blink trough amplitude threshold $T^a_{blink_{tr}}$. Additionally, the duration between the peak and trough must fall within the duration threshold $T^d_{blink-up}$ for the event to be categorized as a blink. In the event that, within the double blink duration threshold T^d_{DBlink}, another peak and trough are detected by exceeding T^a_{blink} and $T^a_{blink_{tr}}$, the eye gesture is classified as a double blink. Conversely, if the time after the first peak exceeds T^d_{DBlink} and a trough is observed with an amplitude exceeding $T^a_{blink_{tr}}$, the event is identified as an upward eye gesture. Finally, if the duration between the initial peak and the subsequent trough surpasses T^d_{up-ec}, the event is designated as eyes closed.

5 Results

These preliminary results show the performance of both device selection and eye gesture classification across six subjects. Figure 3 illustrates the classification accuracy for each subject and the overall average. Specifically, the average classification accuracy for device selection was of $97.57\% \pm 0.03\%$, while the accuracy for eye gesture classification accuracy was $97.22\% \pm 0.03\%$.

The device selection accuracy exceeded 90% for all subjects, with Subject 4 showing the lowest performance. As documented in Table 1, which details the performance for each smart device by subject, this reduced accuracy is primarily due to the low classification performance obtained for the door lock, which only reached 50%.

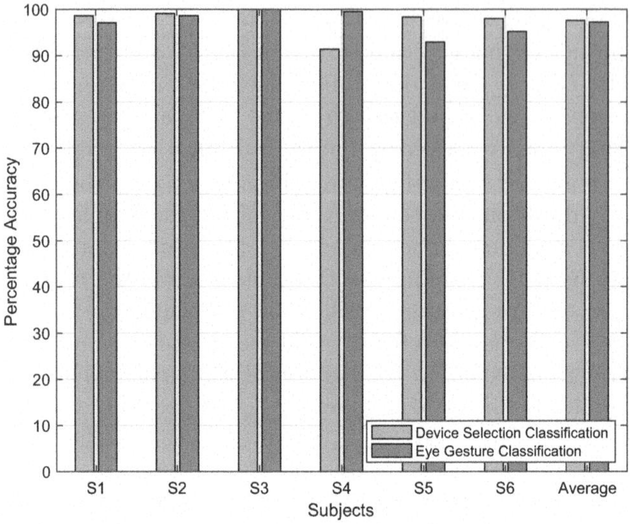

Fig. 3. Classification accuracy for device selection and eye gesture classification.

Table 1. Smart device percentage classification accuracy across subjects.

Subject	Lamp	TV	AC	Hi-Fi	Blinds	Fan	Door Lock	Average
S1	100	100	100	100	100	90.3	100	98.6
S2	100	100	100	100	100	99.5	94	99.1
S3	100	100	100	100	100	100	100	100
S4	90.1	100	100	100	100	100	50	91.4
S5	100	94.2	94.7	100	100	100	99.32	98.3
S6	100	100	90.1	99.5	100	100	96.3	98
Average	98.3	99	97.5	99.9	100	98.3	89.8	97.6

Table 2 presents the classification accuracy of the developed system for each subject across the seven different eye gestures. The detection accuracy reached 100% in most cases, indicating distinct and identifiable EOG signal characteristics for each eye gesture. The lowest performance was observed in Subject 5 for eyes closed and in Subject 6 for double blinks. Overall, the system achieved an average accuracy of 97.2%.

6 Discussion and Conclusion

In real life, when individuals interact with smart devices using standard control interfaces, such as remote controls, they typically look at the device and point the remote control towards it to operate it. This intuitive interaction is often lost when GUI-based human-machine interfaces [1,3] are developed as alternative

Table 2. Eye gesture percentage classification accuracy across subjects.

Subject	Up	Down	Left	Right	Blink	Double Blink	Eyes Closed	Average
S1	96.7	100	100	100	93.3	100	90	97.1
S2	93.3	100	100	96.7	100	100	100	98.6
S3	100	100	100	100	100	100	100	100
S4	96.7	100	100	100	100	100	100	99.5
S5	96.7	100	100	100	93.3	90	70	92.9
S6	93.3	100	100	100	93.3	83.3	96.7	95.2
Average	96.1	100	100	99.5	96.7	95.6	92.8	97.2

control methods for individuals with limited fine motor skills. These users are usually required to use their gaze to select devices presented on a computer screen, and then execute control functions either by selecting options on the screen or performing a sequence of eye gestures [3, 4]. This approach is not very natural and in the latter case, users have to memorize specific sequences of eye gestures for each control function. This can become increasingly complex as the number of available smart devices grows.

This work proposes an alternative human-machine interface system devoid of a GUI, enabling users to interact seamlessly with seven smart devices. Through tracking the user's position and head orientation, the system accurately identifies the device the user intends to control. The limitation of this approach is that devices within the same line of sight may be indistinguishable. Nevertheless, the system can allow the user to select between them or the user can simply change position to avoid this. Offline results obtained from six subjects positioned at various locations in the available lab space demonstrated an average device selection performance of 97.57% ± 0.03%. Notably, the seven smart devices considered varied in dimensions and placement within the room, with differences in height. For instance, the air conditioner was mounted to the ceiling, the lamp on a desk, and the fan as an upright floor-standing unit. This setup facilitated the evaluation of performance across varying user head orientations corresponding to the attended device.

The different control options of the selected device could then be actuated through simple eye gestures. This preliminary study assessed the classification performance achieved in distinguishing between seven different eye gestures using a threshold-based approach on recorded EOG signals. An overall classification accuracy of 97.22% ± 0.03% was achieved. Subsets of these eye gestures could then be used to activate the desired device functions. For instance, upward and downward eye gestures could control the volume of a television set, while left or right eye gestures could navigate through different channels. Additionally, the system is designed to provide audio feedback, indicating the connected device and the forthcoming control function.

This proposed system offers a novel, natural approach of smart device control without the requirement of a GUI. Such a system empowers individuals with mobility impairments, fostering increased independence and an enhanced quality of life.

Acknowledgments. Project financed by the Malta Council for Science & Technology, for and on behalf of the Foundation for Science and Technology, through the FUSION: Smart Cities Programme.

Disclosure of Interests. The authors have no competing interests to declare that are relevant to the content of this article.

References

1. Zhang, R., et al.: An EOG-based human-machine interface to control a smart home environment for patients with severe spinal cord injuries. IEEE Trans. Biomed. Eng. **66**(1), 89–100 (2019)
2. Bissoli, A., Lavino-Junior, D., Sime, M., EncarnaÇão, L., Bastos-Filho, T.: A human-machine interface based on eye tracking for controlling and monitoring a smart home using the internet of things. Sensors **19**(4), 859 (2019)
3. Molleapaza-Huanaco, J., Charca-Morocco, H., Juarez-Chavez, B., Equiño-Quisp, R., Talavera-Suarez, J., Mayhua-López, E.: IoT platform based on EOG to monitor and control a smart home environment for patients with motor disabilities. In: 13th International Congress on Image and Signal Processing, BioMedical Engineering and Informatics (CISP-BMEI), pp. 784–789, Chengdu, China (2020)
4. Samann, F.E., Subhi Hadi, M.: Human to television interface for disable people based on EOG. J. Duhak Univ. **21**(1), 54–64 (2018)
5. ELIKO. https://eliko.tech/. Accessed 08 May 2024
6. BOSCH Smart Sensor: BNO055. https://www.bosch-sensortec.com/products/smart-sensor-systems/bno055/. Accessed 08 May 2024
7. JINS MEME. https://jinsmeme.com/en/. Accessed 08 May 2024
8. Lopez, A., Villar, J.R., Fernandez, M., Ferrero, F.J.: Comparison of classification techniques for the control of EOG-based HCIs. Biomed. Sig. Process. Control **80**, 104263 (2023)
9. Aungsakun, S., Phinyomark, A., Phukpattaranont, P., Limsakul, C.: Development of robust electrooculography (EOG)-based human-computer interface controlled by eight directional eye movements. Int. J. Phys. Sci. **7**, 2196–2208 (2012)
10. Wu, S.L., Liao, L.D., Lu, S.W., Jian, W.L., Chen, S.A., Lin, C.T.: Controlling a human-computer interface system with a novel classification method that uses electrooculography signals. IEEE Trans. Biomed. Eng. **60**(8), 2133–2141 (2013)
11. Champaty, B., Jose, J., Pal, K., Thirugnanam, A.: Development of EOG based human machine interface control system for motorised wheelchair. In: 2014 Annual International Conference on Emerging Research Areas: Magnetics, Machines and Drives (AICERA/iCMMD), (2014). https://doi.org/10.1109/aicera.2014.6908256

Cognitive Dynamics of Theory of Mind in Collaborative Problem-Solving: A Framework for Understanding Teamwork in Complex Environments

Fiona Duruaku[1,2(✉)], Stephen M. Fiore[1,2], and Florian G. Jentsch[1,2]

[1] University of Central Florida, Orlando, FL 32826, USA
{Fiona.duruaku,sfiore,Florian.jentsch}@ucf.edu
[2] University of Central Florida, Institute for Simulation and Training, Orlando, FL, USA

Abstract. The intricate interplay between Theory of Mind (ToM) and Collaborative Problem-Solving (CPS) is a critical but underexplored area of research for understanding and enhancing teamwork across diverse and complex contexts. We argue that ToM, the ability to understand the thoughts and intentions of others, is fundamental to effective collaboration and problem-solving. This paper discusses a framework for studying ToM in collaborative problem-solving, focusing on its role in complex environments characterized by information overload, uncertainty, time pressure, and adaptability demands. We explore how teams manage these challenges while utilizing ToM to stay coordinated and achieve shared goals. We emphasize the significance of social perceptiveness and accurate mental model formation in enhancing communication and decision-making processes in teams. Furthermore, the paper examines the potential role of Artificial Intelligence (AI) in supporting and augmenting human ToM processes within teams through scaffolding social cognitive processes to improve collaborative outcomes. We discuss the potential benefits of AI in facilitating communication, information analysis, and mental model reconstruction, and providing recommendations for the study of AI integration during CPS. By investigating the interplay between ToM, CPS, and AI in complex environments, this paper aims to contribute to our understanding of effective teamwork dynamics and provide insights for future research and practical applications.

Keywords: Theory of Mind (ToM) · Collaborative Problem Solving (CPS) · Teamwork · Artificial Intelligence (AI)

1 Introduction

1.1 Theory of Mind (ToM) and Collaborative Problem-Solving (CPS) Dynamics

Teamwork and collaborative problem-solving (CPS) are fundamental to the success of organizations, societies, and communities. Collaboration is becoming a cornerstone of modern organizations, driven by the complexity of challenges, the need for innovation,

C. Stephanidis et al. (Eds.): HCII 2024, CCIS 2319, pp. 35–50, 2025.
https://doi.org/10.1007/978-3-031-78516-0_4

and the demand for diverse knowledge and skills [10]. From scientific breakthroughs and technological advancements to successful business ventures and meaningful social interactions, the ability to work effectively with others is crucial for individual and collective success. Understanding the nuances of human cognition and social interactions has remained a focal point in psychological and cognitive research. Theory of Mind (ToM), an essential cognitive ability, assumes a pivotal role in comprehending the thoughts, intentions, and beliefs of others. This helps individuals navigate complex social landscapes, anticipate behaviors, and engage meaningfully in interpersonal interactions [40]. It forms the foundation of human capacity for intricate social engagement and could stem from an evolved, inherently predisposed, and domain-specific cognitive mechanism [32]. It is crucial for establishing and maintaining common ground during collaboration and communication. ToM development begins early in life and continues to evolve throughout childhood and adolescence, shaping individuals' social and emotional intelligence [51]. As Theory of Mind matures, individuals become more adept at navigating social interactions, including collaboration and problem-solving within teams [3]. While the developmental trajectory of Theory of Mind is a crucial area of study, this paper focuses on its functioning within established teams. Beyond individual cognition, we suggest that the significance of ToM extends to collaborative efforts, where the capacity to interpret and anticipate the mental states of team members becomes indispensable for fostering successful teamwork and problem-solving.

Collaborative Problem-Solving (CPS) is an important subset of teamwork across diverse settings. In today's interconnected world, where teams tackle multifaceted challenges requiring collective intelligence and diverse perspectives, CPS requires a critical skill set. It involves individuals jointly working together to analyze issues, generate solutions, and reach consensus on action plans by sharing information, resources, and expertise [5]. It necessitates both cognitive and social aptitudes. Cognitively, team members must define problems, assess team knowledge, bridge gaps, formulate solutions, and monitor progress. Socially, successful teams establish shared understanding, engage in joint actions, and coordinate behavior to generate and evaluate solutions [1, 10, 20]. In team settings, CPS often involves complex tasks that require creative problem-solving, critical thinking, and decision-making under uncertainty [38]. Further, teams must navigate various challenges, such as information overload, time pressure, and conflicting priorities, while maintaining cohesion and productivity [3]. The collaborative nature of problem-solving not only enhances creativity and innovation, but also fosters a sense of shared responsibility and accountability within teams.

Artificial Intelligence (AI) has undergone a paradigm shift in various facets of the workplace, profoundly impacting teamwork and social dynamics. The incorporation of AI technologies, encompassing sophisticated machine learning algorithms, natural language processing, and advanced computer vision, holds promise in elevating human cognition and refining collaboration [4]. While extensive research exists on utilizing AI to bolster cognitive functions in complex problem-solving tasks like decision-making, there remains a dearth of research connecting AI with other realms of complex problem-solving, particularly those involving social and emotional cognition. Within team contexts, AI-driven tools focusing on social cognition, can serve as a scaffold for Theory of Mind (ToM) processes by discerning intricate communication patterns, decoding nuanced social cues, and facilitating information exchange and cooperation among team members [53]. Furthermore, AI can serve as a catalyst for amplifying human decision-making capabilities by furnishing tailored recommendations, predicting outcomes, and automating mundane tasks [19]. By harnessing the potential of AI, teams can bolster their problem-solving capabilities, heighten operational efficiency, and navigate through dynamic and uncertain landscapes [55]. This paper explores the intersection of Theory of Mind, Collaborative Problem-Solving, and Artificial Intelligence in understanding effective teamwork. We discuss how individual cognitive abilities impact team performance, the diverse strategies in collaborative problem-solving across teams, and the role of AI in enhancing social cognitive processes. Through this review, our aim is to provide valuable insights for researchers aiming to enhance teamwork effectiveness in complex environments by better understanding the collaboration between humans and technology.

1.2 ToM in Shaping Team-Based Problem-Solving in Complex Environments

Effective problem-solving hinges not only on technical expertise but also on the ability to leverage the collective cognitive abilities of the team [10, 21]. Theory of Mind (ToM) and Collaborative Problem-Solving (CPS) encompass the interplay between understanding others' perspectives and working together to solve complex problems. In problem-solving, people build mental models of a problem (problem space) including initial state, goal, and possible actions (operators). These rely on existing knowledge structures (schemata) and mental models. New information is assimilated into schemata, or if not a fit, accommodation occurs to adjust schemata or build a new mental model for the specific problem. [42, 44]. When engaged in collaborative problem-solving, participants converge diverse perspectives, specialized knowledge, and varied experiences, amalgamating their collective wisdom to address challenges that transcend individual aptitudes [38]. This convergence of knowledge and perspectives in complex environments has been termed 'macrocognition in teams' [10]. We expand on this concept to argue that, not only does it rely on the interplay between individual cognitive processes, but also ToM and social cognition, to optimize team problem solving. To better understand how theory of mind impacts CPS, we distinguish between two facets of ToM, cognitive and affective. On the one hand, "cognitive" (or "cold") ToM pertains to understanding the cognitive states, beliefs, thoughts, or intentions of others [33]. It can be evaluated through various assessments, such as false belief tests (examining comprehension of others' false beliefs about a situation), attribution of intention tasks (deducing the intention behind an individual's action), and social faux pas' scenarios (detecting social blunders or lack of tact). On the other hand, "affective" (or "hot") ToM involves grasping the affective states, emotions, or feelings of others in some kind of first-person interaction scenario [33]. This can be assessed through verbal narratives specifically detailing an individual's emotions, tests of recognizing expressive facial expressions depicting basic emotions (e.g., happiness, sadness, fear), or tools like the Reading the Mind in the Eyes test, which presents complex emotions (e.g., scheming, guilt, threat).

Theory of mind is relevant to team processes more generally. Within teams, individuals must work together to navigate intricate challenges that exceed the capabilities of any single team member; it involves not just the cognitive abilities of individual members, but also a collective cognitive process that emerges uniquely when team members collaborate as a unified group [25]. Given the role of ToM in social cognition [40], we suggest that it enables team members to understand and anticipate the thoughts, intentions, and beliefs of their colleagues, fostering effective communication, empathy, and cooperation. In their review of team cognition theory, [7] note that teamwork involves cognitive processing that unfolds at both individual (intraindividual) and team (interindividual) levels. This interindividual processing heavily relies on Theory of Mind (ToM), as team members need to understand each other's thoughts, intentions, and perspectives to effectively collaborate. By accurately perceiving and interpreting others' mental states, team members can coordinate their efforts more efficiently, leading to enhanced problem-solving outcomes.

Although ToM has not traditionally been discussed in the literature on team cognition, the significance of ToM in shaping team processes and performance is apparent when considering what is required in complex environments. For example, reviews of group cognition show that team effectiveness relies on coordination, information sharing, and decision-making abilities, leading to superior problem-solving outcomes [49]. ToM would be necessary to help team members understand and respond to the needs and perspectives of their peers. Further, ToM would influence the development of shared mental models within teams, which are essential for effective collaboration and problem-solving. Shared mental models represent the team's collective understanding of the task, goals, and strategies, enabling team members to align their actions and make coordinated decisions [36, 37]. Teams with well-developed shared mental models, facilitated by ToM, would exhibit higher levels of cohesion, performance, and innovation, even in complex and dynamic environments.

Understanding the nuanced dynamics of ToM within team-based problem-solving requires familiarity with the diverse terms associated with the more general idea of collective cognition. In the more general study of groups and teams, several terms are commonly used to describe different aspects of social cognition that likely draw from ToM processes (see Table 1). We provide these definitions as a foundation for their discussion in the remainder of this paper.

In sum, we suggest that ToM equips teams with the cognitive tools necessary to navigate the complexities of social interaction and information processing within CPS. They are not isolated processes, but rather interconnected elements of good teamwork. Understanding others' mental states is essential for effective collaboration and problem-solving, enabling teams to utilize varied viewpoints and generate successful results. We turn now to an elaboration of ToM processes and how these relate to CPS.

1.3 Explicit and Implicit ToM for CPS

Research in social cognition and social neuroscience suggest that ToM manifests in explicit and implicit forms [2, 17]. In this section we show how these may play a role in fostering successful teamwork in distinct ways. Effective CPS requires a synergistic interplay between explicit and implicit ToM processes. While explicit ToM facilitates clear communication and mutual understanding among team members, implicit ToM enhances interpersonal sensitivity and adaptability, enabling individuals to navigate

Table 1. Keywords Associated with ToM in Human Teams

Keywords	Definition	Relevant Citations
Social Intelligence	The ability to understand and navigate social situations, appropriately making use of facial expressions, body language, and social cues	[29, 50]
Social Cognition	The cognitive abilities involved in understanding and responding to others' mental states, such as their thoughts, emotions, and intentions	[12, 15]
Social Perception	The ability to perceive and interpret social cues, including facial expressions, body language, and verbal communication	[13, 22]
Metacognition	Awareness and understanding of one's own thought processes including emotions, learning strategies, and limitations	[14, 31]
Collective Intelligence	The ability of a group to perform tasks and solve problems effectively, often exceeding the capabilities of any individual member	[55, 56]

social dynamics and adjust their behavior in real-time. Explicit ToM involves conscious mental state reasoning, allowing team members to strategically consider the perspectives and motivations of others during collaboration [17]. Implicit ToM operates more automatically, influencing team interactions through processes like emotional contagion and nonverbal communication [17]. Note that, in the literature on ToM and social cognition, this is sometimes distinguished as dual-process theories of cognition [e.g., System 1 versus System 2; see 54]. We use the concept of implicit and explicit to more clearly characterize the nature of the processes engaged as these fits more closely with thinking about teamwork. This distinction highlights the multifaceted nature of ToM in shaping team dynamics and problem-solving outcomes.

Explicit ToM, characterized by conscious mental state reasoning [17], would play a vital role in fostering successful teamwork during complex problem-solving. It is crucial for complex problem-solving tasks, as it allows individuals to consciously consider the mental states of others when making decisions or solving problems. It empowers team members to deliberately consider and communicate their understanding of each other's perspectives [40]. Although team research rarely invokes the idea of explicit ToM, its roots can be found in studies of team communication. For example, in the study of shared mental models, explicit acknowledgment of mental states facilitates smooth information exchange and reduces misunderstandings, ultimately enhancing team performance. Specifically, explicit ToM forms the foundation for core parts of shared mental models, for example, actively anticipating colleagues' likely actions and contributions, which helps team members seamlessly adjust their approaches, leading to more efficient role coordination and overall effectiveness. Further, this strengthens the team's shared mental model, ensuring everyone operates with a common understanding of the problem and potential solutions. However, team research shows how too much communication is often problematic. We can, again, view this as an overreliance on explicit ToM. Extensive discussions and detailed explanations, while fostering clarity, can hinder agility in dynamic situations. Additionally, too much information can lead to cognitive overload, hindering creativity and problem-solving. Finally, too much communication, again, as a type of overemphasis on explicit ToM, can inadvertently promote groupthink, where a strong desire for consensus stifles the exploration of diverse viewpoints. Therefore, striking a balance between utilizing explicit ToM for clear communication and maintaining open-mindedness for creative solutions, is crucial for effective teamwork in complex environments.

Much less studied and understood are implicit expressions of ToM in teams. This form of ToM operates at a subconscious level but can also be seen as fundamental for seamless team communication and coordination. It would play a role in complex problem-solving tasks by shaping individuals' perceptions, judgments, and decisions based on their implicit understanding of others' mental states. For example, individuals may unconsciously adjust their behavior to align with the perceived mental states of their teammates, even if they are not consciously aware of doing so. Subtle cues such as non-verbal expressions convey tacit information about team members' mental states, enhancing coordination during intricate tasks [23]. Nonetheless, reliance on implicit ToM presents challenges. We can contextualize implicit ToM in the study of teams by re-interpreting prior findings on team coordination. For example, ambiguities may arise due to opaque expectations, impeding coordination. Newcomers integrating into well-established teams may encounter difficulty aligning with implicit shared mental models, constraining their contribution. Furthermore, implicit alignment can foster groupthink in that it might lead the team to overlook divergent viewpoints. Addressing these challenges is crucial to leverage the benefits of implicit ToM while avoiding potential pitfalls, as it fosters dynamic communication and adaptability within teams.

2 Contextual Factors Affecting CPS

Woolley et al. [56] argue that collaborative problem-solving in small groups is shaped by a multifaceted interplay of bottom-up factors, such as interpersonal skills, and top-down processes including group structures, norms, and routines. [34] underscores three pivotal elements that influence team collective intelligence for CPS: individual intelligence, effective collaboration, and cognitive diversity. In this section, we review a set of factors that can affect success at collaborative problem solving. This includes individual differences in ToM and how diversity in teams alters collaboration dynamics. We additionally consider task factors and the role of ToM in complex environments characterized by information overload, ambiguity, and time pressure. Following, this, in our concluding section, we introduce a framework that integrates artificial intelligence (AI) as a tool to support team cognitive processes, enhancing ToM capabilities within teams operating in complex environments.

2.1 Individual Differences in ToM and Team Performance in Diverse Teams

Variations in ToM ability can markedly affect team performance by shaping perceptions, interpretations, and reactions to teammates' thoughts, intentions, and emotions.

Recognizing and navigating these differences is essential for enhancing team synergy and achieving optimal performance, especially in complex environments. Diverse teams bring together individuals with varying cultural backgrounds, expertise levels, and personality traits, which can influence how team members perceive, interpret, and respond to the thoughts, intentions, and emotions of their teammates. Individuals with strong ToM demonstrate enhanced social perceptiveness, empathy, and perspective-taking skills [24]. These abilities are essential for building trust, fostering collaboration, and maintaining positive team dynamics. Conversely, individuals with lower ToM abilities may struggle with effective communication, coordination, and decision-making within teams. This can lead to suboptimal problem-solving outcomes, where teams fail to leverage the collective intelligence of their members [55]. Further, studies suggest females are better able to manage teamwork because of superiority in ToM [43]. Finally, research suggests that, although certain facets of ToM remain intact over time, others appear to be more susceptible to the impact of aging [48].

Research on heterogeneous teams has demonstrated their propensity to outperform homogeneous counterparts, particularly in the realm of complex problem-solving tasks. This superiority arises from the different perspectives and methods for problem-solving heterogeneous teams possess. Nonetheless, navigating the dynamics of ToM within diverse teams presents its own set of challenges. This is because culture influences ToM [16], meaning that individuals from diverse cultural backgrounds often hold differing views on collaboration, communication, and decision-making, adding complexity to team interactions. Thus, cultural backgrounds may play a pivotal role in shaping ToM dynamics [16]; individuals from distinct cultures may possess differing perspectives on mental states and their implications for behavior. Additionally, expertise levels within teams significantly impact performance, as diverse expertise fosters the introduction of varied problem-solving approaches and perspectives, particularly advantageous for tackling complex tasks [35]. Moreover, individual differences in personality traits, communication styles, and cognitive abilities further contribute to the intricacies of team dynamics and overall effectiveness [45]. By recognizing, managing, and leveraging these differences through targeted interventions such as training programs, promoting diversity, fostering feedback, and mindful team composition, teams can improve their overall performance in complex environments, fostering a culture of trust, cooperation, and innovation within diverse team settings.

2.2 ToM and Problem Task Environment

Gaining insight into the influence of ToM on both well-structured and ill-structured problems illuminates the intricacies of teamwork dynamics. Collaborative problems can be broadly categorized into well-defined and ill-defined [18]. Well-defined problems have clear objectives, constraints, and established solution pathways, while ill-defined problems are characterized by ambiguity, uncertainty, and multiple possible interpretations. Well-defined problems also typically feature a correct solution on which a team can converge whereas ill-structured problems can have multiple possible solutions. [8]. We suggest that the type of problem a team faces – well-defined or ill-defined – may significantly influence the interplay between individual ToM and team success. Because well-structured problems have clearly defined objectives, constraints, and solution pathways, technical expertise, and adherence to established protocols are crucial for success. For instance, imagine astronauts need to engage in a routine equipment repair on their spacecraft. This could represent a well-structured problem because the objective (repairing the equipment) is clear, and there may be established protocols or procedures for conducting such repairs. In this situation, ToM may play a role in understanding each team member's specific expertise and assigning tasks accordingly. Moreover, from the interpersonal standpoint, ToM will influence team interactions by fostering empathy, promoting effective communication, and facilitating conflict resolution [6]. Team members with high ToM skills can interpret subtle social cues, build rapport with colleagues, and collaborate seamlessly to achieve shared objectives; these are all competencies crucial during times of high stress or time pressure.

In contrast, ill-structured problems are characterized by ambiguity, uncertainty, and multiple possible interpretations [41, 47]. These problems necessitate creativity, flexibility, and the ability to navigate complex social dynamics. In ill-defined problems, the absence of specifications may demand more creative problem-solving approaches, which could benefit from the diverse perspectives and problem-solving strategies. This requires effective ToM to leverage a team's capability at divergent thinking, as this can help them explore a variety of ideas [8]. Consider a scenario where astronauts encounter an unexpected technical malfunction upon landing on Mars, jeopardizing their ability to establish a stable habitat. This situation exemplifies an ill-structured problem due to its ambiguity, uncertainty, and absence of a clear solution pathway. To tackle this challenge, the astronauts must leverage their collective knowledge, creativity, and adaptability. ToM becomes indispensable in this scenario as the astronauts must grasp each other's perspectives, concerns, and potential solutions. Again, from the interpersonal and affective standpoint, ToM promotes resilience and flexibility within teams by fostering empathy, perspective-taking, and effective communication. This psychological awareness enables team members to address cognitive biases, overcome groupthink, and capitalize on diverse viewpoints when collaborating.

2.3 ToM in Complex Settings

The majority of real-world problems are complex and multifaceted. Unlike simple, linear, well-defined problems with clear-cut solutions, addressing complex problems requires more advanced cognitive processing to navigate the intricacies and uncertainties they entail effectively [25]. Complex environments, characterized by information overload, uncertainty, and time pressure, can significantly impact teams' ability to utilize ToM effectively. In environments characterized by information overload, teams may struggle to process vast amounts of data, leading to cognitive overload and reduced attentional resources for ToM processing. Problem complexity can overwhelm team members, reducing their cognitive capacity for core aspects of ToM like perspective-taking and mental state attribution. This then hinders the ability to accurately perceive and interpret mental states, impairing communication, coordination, and decision-making. This can also lead to confirmation bias and a reliance on personal heuristics, hindering the ability to leverage the full range of perspectives offered by its members. Uncertainty exacerbates these challenges by leading to reliance on assumptions and errors in mental state attribution, while also increasing cognitive load. In complex problem-solving processes where uncertainty plays a significant role, it is crucial for CPS success that team members are cognizant of the situation and possess the ability to collectively adapt strategically to changes [25]. Additionally, time pressure further complicates matters, as teams prioritize task completion over social cognition, resulting in rushed judgments and suboptimal problem-solving outcomes. Time pressure in complex situations can lead to cognitive biases such as anchoring and groupthink. Anchoring refers to relying too heavily on initial information, while, as already discussed, groupthink describes a tendency to favor consensus over critical evaluation of diverse perspectives [28]. Uncertainty can also breed distrust within teams, leading to a reluctance to share information and openly discuss concerns. We suggest that this lack of open communication hampers the ability to understand each other's perspectives and effectively utilize ToM. Under time pressure, team members might prioritize quick decisions over understanding the nuances of each other's thoughts and concerns. Rushing through problem-solving limits opportunities for brainstorming and creative exploration of diverse perspectives. This stifles innovation, hindering ToM's role in fostering creativity and exploring alternative solutions. These factors collectively hinder teams' utilization of ToM for collaborative problem-solving, highlighting the need for strategies to mitigate their impact in dynamic environments.

In complex environments, communication challenges arise due to information overload and time pressure, impeding the accurate sharing of mental states and perspectives among team members [20]. This can lead to misunderstandings, misinterpretations, and reduced empathy within the team. Additionally, uncertainty disrupts task allocation and coordination, hindering teams' ability to adapt efficiently to changing circumstances and impacting problem-solving outcomes [30]. We suggest that these may foster a "defensive" use of ToM. Here, team members focus more on reading others' intentions for potential threats than on understanding their viewpoints for collaborative problem-solving. Moreover, time pressure and uncertainty force teams to prioritize task completion. This may limit the team's capacity for empathy and perspective-taking, as members do not take time to understand each other's viewpoints, potentially undermining collaboration, and creativity.

3 Role of Artificial Intelligence (AI) in ToM and CPS

Complex problem-solving has evolved with advances in computer science, artificial intelligence (AI), and cognitive psychology. Increased data availability, advanced algorithms, and improved computational infrastructure, including managed data lakes, now enable collaboration among diverse teams [26]. These advances set the stage for teams and the identification of patterns and cues relevant to ToM understanding. AI is evolving in ways that could help humans and AI work seamlessly together, boosting team collaboration. The application of AI in groups, teams, and everyday life has evolved from primarily targeting labor cost savings through automation to enhancing human abilities. This shift is highlighted by the emergence of generative AI tools like ChatGPT, which raises the possibility that AI can actively contribute to tackling complex problems. AI technologies are not only proficient in analyzing large datasets, including unstructured data, in real-time and identifying underlying patterns, but they are developing in such a way that they could play a crucial role in scaffolding team cognitive processes. This could involve, for example, enhancing the collective reasoning, decision-making, and problem-solving abilities of team members, thereby elevating the overall effectiveness of group collaborations [46]. The integration of AI support introduces additional complexities to collaborative problem-solving in teams. AI technologies can augment team capabilities by providing data-driven insights, automating routine tasks, and facilitating information sharing. Moreover, AI tools and technologies possess the capacity to analyze social cues, optimize communication strategies, and monitor team dynamics, potentially enhancing team performance in complex problem-solving tasks. For well-structured problems, AI may streamline processes, reducing the reliance on social cognition. However, in the context of ill-structured problems, AI interfaces may necessitate interpretation and integration into collaborative efforts. In such scenarios, individuals with high ToM skills can effectively navigate and leverage AI-generated recommendation. Nonetheless, the effectiveness of AI support is contingent upon the type of collaborative problem and the team's proficiency in integrating AI tools into their problem-solving processes.

In complex settings, the strain on human ToM capabilities can be significant. This is where AI could be an invaluable asset, providing support for team cognitive functions and thus improving collaborative efforts. But the integration of AI support introduces new dynamics to team interactions, where AI may alter ToM to shape collaborative efforts and outcomes. As such, to leverage AI support, we must account for interactions between ToM and collaborative problem-solving, to better inform strategies for optimizing team collaboration, and achieving collective goals in diverse problem-solving contexts. For example, employing AI as a mechanism to scaffold cognitive operations could involve externalizing cognition to directly support team processes. In this way, AI serves as a collaborative partner. As a complementary example, AI can support taskwork for problem solving by aiding in data analytics, or it can support teamwork by helping to manage role interdependencies [11]. Additionally, research underscores the importance of developing artificial Theory of Mind to foster collaboration between human and AI team members, emphasizing the need to cultivate social intelligence through AI technologies to improve team dynamics and problem-solving outcomes across interdisciplinary domains [53]. Furthermore, adopting a Bayesian Theory of Mind approach highlights the significance of collective intelligence in human-AI teams, where AI shows the potential to augment human cognition by overcoming biases and human limitations in memory and attention [51]. When AI is employed for tackling complex problems, the interaction patterns become more refined. AI counterparts enhance human input and can shape subsequent human actions. In the study of human-human collaboration, the findings highlight the significance of social, emotional, cognitive, and metacognitive elements in the problem-solving process [1]. Therefore, for AI to be an effective collaborator, it needs capabilities that encompass social-cognitive processes like ToM.

To guide the exploration of how artificial intelligence intersects with the theory of mind for successful collaborative problem-solving in teams in complex environments, we provide a notional research framework for both the study of ToM in the context of CPS and how the introduction of AI into these contexts will affect success in CPS. We first ask a general set of research questions foundational for the evaluation of AI as a tool for scaffolding human cognitive processes.

Research Questions as Foundation for the Study of ToM and CPS

1. To what extent does individual ToM ability (mental model formation and communication) predict successful team performance on collaborative problem-solving tasks in human teams?
2. Does the type of collaborative problem (e.g., well-defined vs. ill-defined) alter ToM processing and team success in collaborative problem solving?
3. Does the type of collaborative problem (e.g., well-defined vs. ill-defined) influence the relationship between individual ToM ability and team success in collaborative problem solving?
4. How do complex environments, characterized by information overload, uncertainty, and time pressure, impact teams' ability to utilize ToM for collaborative problem-solving?
5. How do complex environments, characterized by information overload, uncertainty, and time pressure, influence the relationship between individual ToM ability and team problem solving effectiveness?

Research Questions on AI Scaffolds for ToM and CPS

1. How can AI be leveraged to scaffold social cognitive processes by identifying potential breakdowns in ToM to improve team dynamics?

- How does the integration of AI tools change human team members ability to engage in ToM attributions?

2. How can AI be leveraged to scaffold social cognitive processes by analyzing communication to determine potential group dynamics problems (e.g., conflict).

- How does the integration of AI tools change communication patterns for human teammates and alter group dynamics?

3. How can AI be leveraged to scaffold social cognitive processes and provide feedback to improve team dynamics?

- How does the use of AI delivered feedback alter its receptivity when compared to human given feedback?

Next, in Table 2, we provide recommendations for AI integration into CPS. We pay particular attention to complex problem solving. Specifically, because the characteristics of complex problems are, in and of themselves, an impediment to solution finding, we identify areas where AI may be useful to help humans address these challenges. With each of these, we then provide a set of research questions meant to guide the field in understanding how AI may or may not improve CPS.

Table 2. Framework for Research on AI Integration for ToM Enhancement in Team Based CPS

Challenge in Complex Environments	Notional AI Integration Point	Research Questions to Assess Impact on ToM and CPS
Information Overload	**Data Summarization and Filtering:** AI analyzes vast data sets, presenting key insights in clear formats	a. Does AI reduce cognitive load, allowing focus on understanding team member perspectives? b. Does AI enable deeper analysis of information relevant to the problem?
Uncertainty	**Scenario Modeling and Prediction:** AI simulates potential outcomes based on different approaches	a. Can AI provide teams with a broader understanding of potential consequences, facilitating discussions and shared decision-making? b. Can AI assist teams anticipate challenges and adapt strategies?
Time Pressure	**Automated Task Management and Prioritization:** AI manages routine tasks and prioritizes critical decisions	a. Can AI minimize cognitive load associated with task management, freeing up mental resources for understanding teammates' perspectives (ToM)? b. Can AI ensure focus on the most pressing issues during problem-solving?
Communication Gaps (Diverse Teams)	**Language Translation and Processing**: AI facilitates communication by translating languages and processing text for clarity	a. Can AI enable clear communication and understanding of perspectives across different cultural backgrounds (important for ToM in diverse teams)? b. Can AI promote team cohesion and collaboration during problem-solving?
Bias in Decision-Making	**Bias Detection and Mitigation**: AI analyzes decision-making processes and highlights potential biases based on historical data or individual preferences	a. Can AI prompt open discussions about assumptions and potential biases, fostering objective approaches and better use of ToM? b. Can AI encourage consideration of diverse viewpoints during team problem-solving?

4 Conclusion

Our understanding of complex problem-solving has been significantly influenced by advancements in computer science, artificial intelligence (AI), and cognitive psychology. The integration of AI tools to improve ToM in human – human teams for collaboration is still in its infancy. But it has the potential to revolutionize teamwork by providing support for team cognitive processes, enhancing collective problem-solving, and decision-making capabilities. AI's role in scaffolding human cognition and collaboration will become increasingly vital in improving team dynamics and the success of problem-solving in complex environments. As such, it is critical to ground these applications in empirical work. To ensure that theory and practice are aligned, we provided research questions as a framework for integrating AI into CPS. Specifically, how AI can effectively scaffold collaborative cognitive processes, with a focus on social cognitive support like Theory of Mind.

Understanding the intricate relationship among individual Theory of Mind (ToM), collaborative problem-solving (CPS), and the evolving role of artificial intelligence (AI) in complex environments is crucial for supporting effective teamwork. Researchers need to illuminate these dynamics by probing the correlation between individual ToM and team success, examining how problem type influences ToM's impact on team performance, and scrutinizing the effects of complex environments on teams' utilization of ToM for problem-solving. AI offers promising avenues for enhancing teamwork by supporting social cognition, identifying communication breakdowns, and providing feedback to enhance team dynamics and problem-solving capabilities. The framework provided in this paper lays the foundation for advancing our comprehension of ToM, CPS, and the transformative potential of AI in constructing effective and adaptable teams in today's collaborative environment.

Acknowledgements. Writing of this paper was partially supported by US Air Force Office of Scientific Research (AFOSR) grant FA9550–22-1–0151 and by the Defense Advanced Research Projects Agency (DARPA) under Contract No. W911NF-20–1-0008. Any opinions, findings and conclusions or recommendations expressed in this material are those of the authors and do not necessarily reflect the views of the AFOSR, DARPA or the University of Central Florida. The corresponding author is Stephen M. Fiore (sfiore@ucf.edu).

References

1. Andrews-Todd, J., Forsyth, C.M.: Exploring social and cognitive dimensions of collaborative problem solving in an open online simulation-based task. Comput. Hum. Behav. **104**, 105759 (2020). https://doi.org/10.1016/j.chb.2018.10.025
2. Apperly, I.A., Butterfill, S.A.: Do humans have two systems to track beliefs and belief-like states? Psychol. Rev. **116**(4), 953–970 (2009). https://doi.org/10.1037/a0016923
3. Beaudoin, C., Leblanc, É., Gagner, C., Beauchamp, M.H.: Systematic review and inventory of theory of mind measures for young children. Front. Psychol. **10**, 2905 (2020). https://doi.org/10.3389/fpsyg.2019.02905
4. Carter-Browne, B.M., Paletz, S.B., Campbell, S.G., Carraway, M.J., Vahlkamp, S.H., Schwartz, J., O'Rourke, P.: There is no "AI" in teams: a multidisciplinary framework for AIs to work in human teams. Appl. Res. Lab. Intell. Secur. (ARLIS) Report June (2021)

5. Davenport, T.H., Ronanki, R.: Artificial intelligence for the real world. Harv. Bus. Rev. **96**(1), 108–116 (2018)
6. Dillenbourg, P.: What do you mean by collaborative learning? In: Dillenbourg, P. (ed.) Collaborative-learning: Cognitive and Computational Approaches, pp. 1–19. Elsevier, Oxford (1999)
7. Epley, N., Keysar, B., Van Boven, L., Gilovich, T.: Perspective taking as egocentric anchoring and adjustment. J. Pers. Soc. Psychol. **87**(3), 327–339 (2004). https://doi.org/10.1037/0022-3514.87.3.327
8. Fiore, S.M., Salas, E.: Why we need team cognition. In: Salas, E., Fiore, S.M., (eds.), Team Cognition: Understanding the Factors that Drive Process and Performance, pp. 235–248. American Psychological Association (2004). https://doi.org/10.1037/10690-011
9. Fiore, S.M., Schooler, J.W.: Convergent or divergent problem space search: The effect of problem structure on group versus individual problem solving. In: Proceedings of the Human Factors and Ergonomics Society Annual Meeting, vol. 45, no. 4, pp. 483–487. SAGE Publications, Sage CA: Los Angeles, CA: (2001). https://doi.org/10.1177/154193120104500446
10. Fiore, S.M., et al.: Collaborative Problem Solving: Considerations for the National Assessment of Educational Progress (2017)
11. Fiore, S.M., Rosen, M.A., Smith-Jentsch, K.A., Salas, E., Letsky, M., Warner, N.: Toward an understanding of macrocognition in teams: predicting processes in complex collaborative contexts. Hum. Factors **52**(2), 203–224 (2010). https://doi.org/10.1177/0018720810369807
12. Fiore, S.M., Wiltshire, T.J.: Technology as teammate: examining the role of external cognition in support of team cognitive processes. Front. Psychol. **7**, 1531 (2016). https://doi.org/10.3389/fpsyg.2016.01531
13. Fiske, S.T., Taylor, S.E.: Social Cognition. McGraw-Hill Book Company (1991)
14. Fiske, S.T.: Social cognition and social perception. Ann. Rev. Psychol. **44**(1), 155–194 (1993). https://doi.org/10.1146/annurev.ps.44.020193.001103
15. Flavell, J.H.: Metacognition and cognitive monitoring: a new area of cognitive–developmental inquiry. Am. Psychol. **34**(10), 906 (1979). https://doi.org/10.1037/0003-066X.34.10.906
16. Flavell, J.H., Miller, P.H.: Social cognition. In: Damon, W., (ed.), Handbook of Child Psychology: Vol. 2. Cognition, Perception, and Language, pp. 851–898. John Wiley & Sons, Inc. (1998)
17. Frank, C.K., Temple, E.: Cultural effects on the neural basis of theory of mind. Prog. Brain Res. **178**, 213–223 (2009). https://doi.org/10.1016/S0079-6123(09)17815-9
18. Frith, C.D., Frith, U.: Implicit and explicit processes in social cognition. Neuron **60**(3), 503–510 (2008). https://doi.org/10.1016/j.neuron.2008.10.032
19. Ge, X., Law, V., Huang, K.: Detangling the interrelationships between self-regulation and ill-structured problem solving in problem-based learning. Interdisc. J. Prob.-Based Learn. **10**(2), 11 (2016). https://doi.org/10.7771/1541-5015.1622
20. Getchell, K.M., et al.: Artificial intelligence in business communication: the changing landscape of research and teaching. Bus. Prof. Commun. Q. **85**(1), 7–33 (2022). https://doi.org/10.1177/23294906221074311
21. Graesser, A.C., Fiore, S.M., Greiff, S., Andrews-Todd, J., Foltz, P.W., Hesse, F.W.: Advancing the science of collaborative problem solving. Psychol. Sci. Public Interest **19**(2), 59–92 (2018). https://doi.org/10.1177/1529100618808244
22. Hagemann, V., Kluge, A.: Complex problem solving in teams: the impact of collective orientation on team process demands. Front. Psychol. **8**, 1730 (2017). https://doi.org/10.3389/fpsyg.2017.01730
23. Higgins, E.T., Bargh, J.A.: Social cognition and social perception. Annu. Rev. Psychol. **38**(1), 369–425 (1987). https://doi.org/10.1146/annurev.ps.38.020187.002101

24. Holland, C., Phillips, J.: A theoretically driven meta-analysis of implicit theory of mind studies: the role of factivity. In: CogSci. (2020). https://cognitivesciencesociety.org/cogsci20/papers/0387/index.html
25. Hughes, C., Jaffee, S.R., Happé, F., Taylor, A., Caspi, A., Moffitt, T.E.: Origins of individual differences in theory of mind: from nature to nurture? Child Dev. **76**(2), 356–370 (2005). https://doi.org/10.1111/j.1467-8624.2005.00850.x
26. Hung, W.: Team-based complex problem solving: a collective cognition perspective. Educ. Tech. Res. Dev. **61**, 365–384 (2013). https://doi.org/10.1007/s11423-013-9296-3
27. Joksimovic, S., Ifenthaler, D., Marrone, R., De Laat, M., Siemens, G.: Opportunities of artificial intelligence for supporting complex problem-solving: findings from a scoping review. Comput. Educ. Artif. Intell. **100138**,(2023). https://doi.org/10.1016/j.caeai.2023.100138
28. Jonassen, D.H., Hung, W.: All problems are not equal: implications for problem-based learning. Interdisc. J. Prob. Based Learn. **2**(2) (2008). https://doi.org/10.7771/1541-5015.1080
29. Jones, P.E., Roelofsma, P.H.: The potential for social contextual and group biases in team decision-making: biases, conditions, and psychological mechanisms. Ergonomics **43**(8), 1129–1152 (2000). https://doi.org/10.1080/00140130050084914
30. Kihlstrom, J.F., Cantor, N.: Social intelligence. In: Sternberg, R.J., (ed.), The Cambridge Handbook of Intelligence (2nd ed., pp. 756–779). Cambridge University Press (2020). https://doi.org/10.1017/9781108770422.032
31. Kirschner, P.A., Sweller, J., Kirschner, F., Zambrano, R., J.: From cognitive load theory to collaborative cognitive load theory. Int. J. Comput.-Support. Collab. Learn. **13**, 213–233 (2018). https://doi.org/10.1007/s11412-018-9277-y
32. Kuhn, D.: Metacognitive development. Curr. Dir. Psychol. Sci. **9**(5), 178–181 (2000). https://doi.org/10.1111/1467-8721.00088
33. Leslie, A.M., Friedman, O., German, T.P.: Core mechanisms in "theory of mind." Trends Cogn. Sci. **8**(12), 528–533 (2004). https://doi.org/10.1016/j.tics.2004.10.001
34. Li, D., et al.: Comparing the ability of cognitive and affective theory of mind in adolescent onset schizophrenia. Neuropsychiatr. Dis. Treat. **13**, 937–945 (2017). https://doi.org/10.2147/NDT.S128116
35. Malone, T.W.: Superminds: The surprising power of people and computers thinking together. Little, Brown Spark (2018)
36. Mannix, E., Neale, M.A.: What differences make a difference? the promise and reality of diverse teams in organizations. Psychol. Sci. Public Interest **6**(2), 31–55 (2005). https://doi.org/10.1111/j.1529-1006.2005.00022.x
37. Mathieu, J.E., Heffner, T.S., Goodwin, G.F., Salas, E., Cannon-Bowers, J.A.: The influence of shared mental models on team process and performance. J. Appl. Psychol. **85**(2), 273–283 (2000). https://doi.org/10.1037/0021-9010.85.2.273
38. Mohammed, S., Ferzandi, L., Hamilton, K.: Metaphor no more: a 15-year review of the team mental model construct. J. Manag. **36**(4), 876–910 (2010). https://doi.org/10.1177/0149206309356804
39. OECD. PISA 2015 collaborative problem solving framework. PISA 2015 Assessment and Analytical Framework: Science, Reading, Mathematic, Financial Literacy and Collaborative Problem Solving (2017). https://doi.org/10.1787/19963777
40. Perner, J., Roessler, J.: From infants' to children's appreciation of belief. Trends Cogn. Sci. **16**(10), 519–525 (2012). https://doi.org/10.1016/j.tics.2012.08.004
41. Premack, D., Woodruff, G.: Does the chimpanzee have a theory of mind? Behav. Brain Sci. **1**(4), 515–526 (1978). https://doi.org/10.1017/S0140525X00076512
42. Reed, S.K.: The structure of ill-structured (and well-structured) problems revisited. Educ. Psychol. Rev. **28**, 691–716 (2016). https://doi.org/10.1007/s10648-015-9343-1

43. Rumelhart, D.E., Smolensky, P., McClelland, J.L., Hinton, G.: Sequential thought processes in PDP models. Parallel Distrib. Process. Explor. Microstruct. Cogn. **2**, 3–57 (1986). https://doi.org/10.7551/mitpress/5237.003.0004
44. Russell, T.A., Tchanturia, K., Rahman, Q., Schmidt, U.: Sex differences in theory of mind: a male advantage on Happé's "cartoon" task. Cogn. Emotion **21**(7), 1554–1564 (2007). https://doi.org/10.1080/02699930601117096
45. Salas, E., Cooke, N.J., Rosen, M.A.: On teams, teamwork, and team performance: discoveries and developments. Hum. Factors **50**(3), 540–547 (2008). https://doi.org/10.1518/001872008X288457
46. Seel, N.M., Ifenthaler, D.I.R.K., Pirnay-Dummer, P.A.B.L.O.: Mental models and problem solving: technological solutions for measurement and assessment of the development of expertise. In: Model-based Approaches to Learning, pp. 17–40. Brill (2009). https://doi.org/10.1163/9789087907112_004
47. Siemens, G., et al.: Human and artificial cognition. Comput. Educ. Artif. Intell. **3**, 100107 (2022). https://doi.org/10.1016/j.caeai.2022.100107
48. Simon, H.A.: The structure of ill structured problems. Artif. Intell. **4**(3–4), 181–201 (1973). https://doi.org/10.1016/0004-3702(73)90011-8
49. Slessor, G., Phillips, L.H., Bull, R.: Exploring the specificity of age-related differences in theory of mind tasks. Psychol. Aging **22**(3), 639 (2007). https://doi.org/10.1037/0882-7974.22.3.639
50. Theiner, G., Allen, C., Goldstone, R.L.: Recognizing group cognition. Cogn. Syst. Res. **11**(4), 378–395 (2010). https://doi.org/10.1016/j.cogsys.2010.07.002
51. Walker, R.E., Foley, J.M.: Social intelligence: Its history and measurement. Psychol. Rep. **33**(3), 839–864 (1973). https://doi.org/10.2466/pr0.1973.33.3.839
52. Wellman, H.M., Cross, D., Watson, J.: Meta-analysis of theory-of-mind development: the truth about false belief. Child Dev. **72**(3), 655–684 (2001). https://doi.org/10.1111/1467-8624.00304
53. Westby, S., Riedl, C.: Collective intelligence in human-AI teams: a Bayesian theory of mind approach. In: Proceedings of the AAAI Conference on Artificial Intelligence, vol. 37, no. 5, pp. 6119–6127 (2023). https://doi.org/10.1609/aaai.v37i5.25755
54. Williams, J., Fiore, S.M., Jentsch, F.: Supporting artificial social intelligence with theory of mind. Front. Artif. Intell. **5**, 750763 (2022). https://doi.org/10.3389/frai.2022.750763
55. Wiltshire, T.J., Lobato, E.J., Garcia, D.R., Fiore, S.M., Jentsch, F.G., Huang, W.H., Axelrod, B.: Effects of robotic social cues on interpersonal attributions and assessments of robot interaction behaviors. In: Proceedings of the Human Factors and Ergonomics Society Annual Meeting, vol. 59, no. 1, pp. 801–805. SAGE Publications, Sage CA: Los Angeles, CA (2015). https://doi.org/10.1177/1541931215591245
56. Woolley, A.W., Chabris, C.F., Pentland, A., Hashmi, N., Malone, T.W.: Evidence for a collective intelligence factor in the performance of human groups. Science **330**(6004), 686–688 (2010). https://doi.org/10.1126/science.1193147
57. Woolley, A.W., Aggarwal, I., Malone, T.W.: Collective intelligence and group performance. Curr. Dir. Psychol. Sci. **24**(6), 420–424 (2015). https://doi.org/10.1177/0963721415599543

Color Design for Pet App Based on Emotional Human-Computer Interaction

Xuan Gao and Qian Ji(✉)

Department of Industrial Design, School of Mechanical Science and Engineering, Huazhong University of Science and Technology (HUST), Wuhan, China
{m202270434,jiqian}@hust.edu.cn

Abstract. In the burgeoning pet economy of China, pet Apps have emerged as pivotal platforms, catering to the emotional bonds between pets and their owners. However, the prevalent homogeneity in pet app designs often falls short of meeting the personalized and emotional needs of predominantly young users. This deficiency hampers user trust and engagement with these Apps. Addressing this gap, our research introduces an innovative approach of color emotion design in pet applications, aimed at enhancing the visual experience and creating an emotional synergy between users, their pets, and the app interface. Utilizing the K-means clustering algorithm, we extract and refines key color palettes from user-uploaded pet images. This process not only objectively represents pet color but also optimizes the hues, saturation, and lightness to enhance color interface usability, balancing design aesthetics with legibility. This approach emphasizes the profound impact of color on human-computer interaction and its potential to evoke emotional responses. In evaluating our design, we engage users in an interactive process where they upload their pet photos, leading to the generation of multiple personalized color schemes. User satisfaction with the interaction process of these schemes is quantitatively assessed by a five-point Likert scale. Our findings indicate that tailored interface color matching significantly elevates the users' visual experience. This research contributes to the domain of design within human-computer interaction, emphasizing the critical role of color in crafting emotionally resonant Apps. By bridging the emotional gap between users and technology, our work paves the way for more personalized and emotionally engaging App designs in the pet industry.

Keywords: Interface Design · Color Emotion · Personalized Design · K-means clustering

1 Introduction

In recent years, the pet economy has witnessed significant growth, fueled by a shift in consumer lifestyles and increasing emotional investment in pets. Pet applications (apps) have emerged as integral components of this burgeoning market, serving not only as platforms for pet care management but also as bridges fostering the bond between pets and their owners. Despite their potential, many pet apps are characterized by a lack of

C. Stephanidis et al. (Eds.): HCII 2024, CCIS 2319, pp. 51–59, 2025.
https://doi.org/10.1007/978-3-031-78516-0_5

personalization and emotional engagement, particularly in their visual and interactive design elements. This shortfall is particularly noticeable among the younger demographics, who not only dominate the user base but also seek deeper emotional connections with digital content that reflects their individual preferences and lifestyles.

Personalized design in digital applications can profoundly influence user satisfaction and retention by aligning the app's features and aesthetics with the individual preferences of the users. Effective personalization encompasses several dimensions including functionality, aesthetics, and usability, tailored to meet the unique needs and desires of each user [1]. Furthermore, research indicates that emotional design plays a pivotal role in enhancing user interaction and satisfaction by incorporating elements that resonate on an emotional level with users [2–4].

Moreover, color, as a powerful communicative tool, impacts emotional responses and can significantly enhance user experience if utilized thoughtfully within app interfaces [5]. The application of K-means clustering algorithms to analyze and refine color palettes based on user-generated content, such as pet photos, presents a novel approach to achieving such personalization. By systematically analyzing these images to derive color schemes that reflect the pets' characteristics, designers can create more appealing and emotionally resonant interfaces.

This introduction sets the stage for discussing the integration of personalized and emotional design elements in pet apps, specifically through innovative use of color, to enhance the user experience. This study explores how these design strategies can be implemented effectively to meet the evolving demands of users in the pet economy, thus contributing to the fields of human-computer interaction (HCI) and design.

2 Related Work

Color psychology is essential in HCI, particularly in emotionally engaging applications like pet apps, where strategic color use significantly influences user perception. Ouyang [6] demonstrates the effective application of visual emotional color theory in specialized systems, highlighting its relevance in enhancing user engagement through thoughtful color choices. When it comes to design practice, the Color Wheel tool by Bianchi and Neris [7] allows designers to select color that evoke targeted emotions, optimizing user interaction by aligning interface aesthetics with users' emotional expectations.

Other representative research, including studies by Abegaz et al. [8] and Venni et. al [9], establish that color not only provoke emotional responses but also affect memory and user evaluations, suggesting a nuanced approach to color harmony is beneficial in app design. Meqdad et al. [10] and Murphy et al. [11] reinforce this by showing that personalized color adjustments in interfaces can directly influence emotional regulation and cognitive functions like decision-making, which are crucial for the usability and satisfaction of pet apps.

In terms of technical implementation, k-means clustering serves as a robust unsupervised learning algorithm for color extraction and quantization in digital images, which optimizes data compression without significantly degrading image quality. Enhancements such as adaptive cluster initialization and quasi-random [12], alongside the incorporation of K-Means++ and coreset [13, 14], have markedly improved the efficiency and quality of this process.

The reviewed studies affirm the intricate interaction between color, emotion, and cognitive responses within HCI. As pet apps strive to bridge the emotional gap between digital interfaces and users, implementing effective color strategies based on robust psychological principles is essential. This approach not only enhances the user experience but also leverages color's potential to foster deeper emotional connections in personalized digital environments.

3 Methods

This section describes the software prototyping and user test methods used to assess whether personalized themes enhance user satisfaction and emotional engagement. We developed a prototype of a color extraction app using the k-means clustering algorithm, crafted a high-fidelity prototype user interface (UI), and conducted product tests with 60 participants across three different app theme interfaces.

3.1 Software Prototyping

The core of our technical implementation involves the use of the K-means clustering algorithm to extract dominant color from pet images uploaded by the users. This algorithm partitions the set of pixels into clusters where each pixel belongs to the cluster with the nearest mean color value.

In the K-means clustering algorithm applied to color extraction from images, the process commences with the initialization of K centroids, representing the desired number of color to extract. Each pixel in the image is then assigned to the nearest centroid based on the Euclidean distance between the pixel's RGB values and the centroids' RGB values. The distance d is calculated as Eq. (1).

$$d = \sqrt{(R_2 - R_1)^2 + (G_2 - G_1)^2 + (B_2 - B_1)^2} \quad (1)$$

where R_1, G_1, B_1 are the RGB values of the pixel, and R_2, G_2, B_2 are those of the centroid. Following assignment, centroids are updated to the mean of the RGB values of the pixels within each cluster. These steps iterate until the centroids stabilize, indicating a convergence to a solution where each cluster represents a significant color presence within the image. This method is particularly effective for color quantization and theme extraction, providing a robust approach to identifying representative color in complex images [15, 16].

The algorithm's implementation in Python uses functions from the OpenCV library to process image pixels and display the RGB value distribution. We set k to 7, extracting seven main color after 20 iterations, closely matching the primary color of pet images. This process is shown in Fig. 1. The extracted color are displayed as color cards with the number of pixels corresponding to each cluster center shown in percentages.

3.2 UI Design

The UI design of the pet app incorporates personalization features allowing users to customize their themes. This approach underpins the interaction design, aimed at understanding and predicting user behavior to meet psychological needs and enhance user

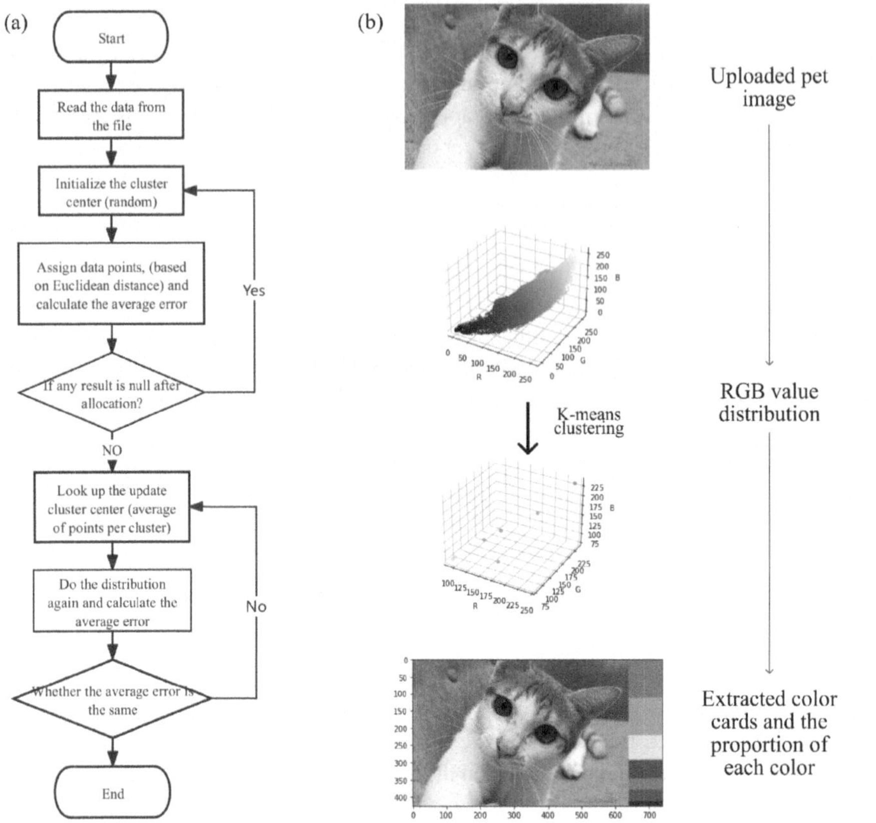

Fig. 1. (a) A flow chart of K means clustering algorithm to extract color; (b) K-means clustering used for color quantization from a pet image.

experience. The "Custom Themes" feature is prominently displayed on the "Me" page, leading users through a three-step process detailed in Fig. 2: uploading pet images, color picker, and theme generation. Users can interact with the color scheme using an "eye-dropper" tool to make adjustments before applying or resetting the generated theme. The main pages are shown in Fig. 3.

3.3 User Test

The user test involved 60 participants recruited from online forums for pet owners, representing diverse demographics. The procedure began with an online briefing session explaining the study objectives. We asked participants to assess the two interface themes we provided, the default theme and the theme generated from color extracted from images uploaded by the participants themselves. After interacting with the app, they completed a questionnaire assessing aesthetic appeal, usability, emotional connection, and provided open-ended feedback. The questionnaire used a 5-point Likert scale for structured questions and free text for general feedback. The study aimed to determine

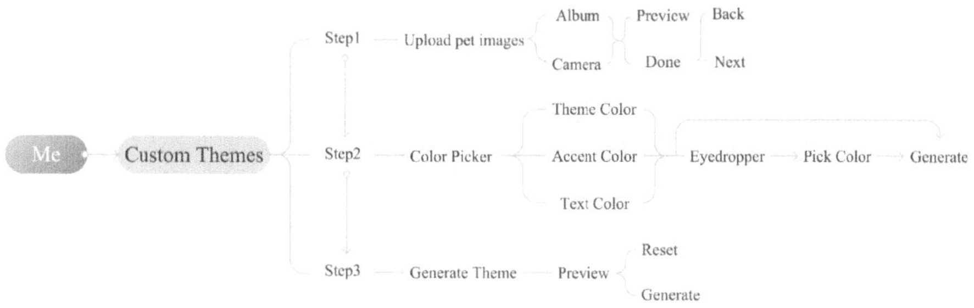

Fig. 2. Interaction steps of the feature "Custom Themes".

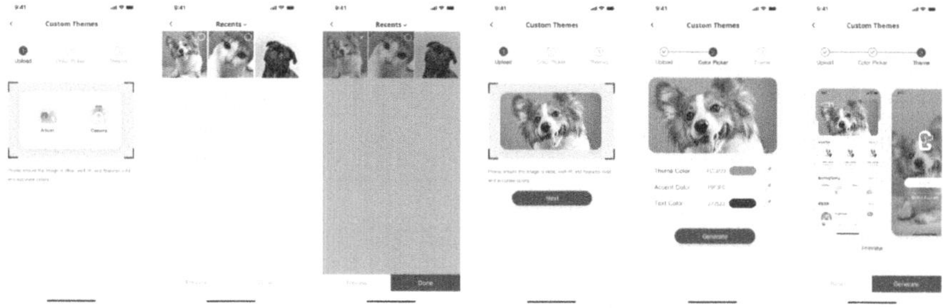

Fig. 3. UI design of main pages.

if personalized themes enhance user satisfaction and emotional engagement, informing further app refinements to meet user expectations effectively.

4 Results and Iteration

4.1 Results of User Test

User test with 60 participants demonstrated that personalized themes significantly enhance user satisfaction and emotional engagement. The structured questionnaire revealed that personalized themes were rated higher for aesthetic appeal with an average score of 4.233 out of 5, compared to default themes. Participants described these themes as "welcoming and vibrant," emphasizing their preference for customization reflecting their pets. Emotional connection scored highest with an average of 4.483, underscoring the value of personalization in enhancing user engagement. These results align with findings from previous research [17–19], suggesting that effective personalization can enhance user satisfaction. However, usability scores averaged at 3.817 out of 5, indicating some challenges with navigation and interface layout which could benefit from further optimization. The results are shown in Table 1.

Participants reported dissatisfaction primarily due to the final interface effects being heavily influenced by the uploaded images, which sometimes led to poor contrast and legibility issues. These challenges arose from inaccuracies in the k-means color extraction process that occasionally produced non-distinct or overly similar color schemes, thereby diminishing the aesthetic and functional quality of the interface. Furthermore, the lack of dynamic adjustments for text and background color often resulted in reduced visibility of interface elements, complicating navigation and overall user interaction. Providing users with the ability to adjust color and choose from alternative themes, as well as ensuring adherence to design standards like Web Content Accessibility Guidelines (WCAG) [20] to maintain accessibility, were identified as potential solutions to enhance usability. These adjustments are crucial to align the app more closely with user expectations and improve retention by optimizing both functionality and user satisfaction.

Table 1. Average scores of user satisfaction.

Items	Default theme	Personalized themes
Aesthetic	4.167	4.233
Usability	4.083	3.817
Emotional connection	4.267	4.483

4.2 Iteration

In response to feedback on the initial user interface, we iterated on our design to enhance readability and user comfort. The revised algorithm now incorporates adjustments based on the Hue, Saturation, and Lightness (HSL) values of the uploaded pictures, with the adjusting method shown in Fig. 4. This adaptation ensures that the text-background contrast is optimized for readability across all user-generated themes. By dynamically adjusting the HSL parameters, the interface maintains visual harmony and enhances the overall user experience, ensuring that both aesthetic appeal and functionality are preserved in the personalized themes. This iteration aligns with best practices in interface design, aiming to address previous usability challenges and improve satisfaction with the app's presentation. Figure 5. Shows the adjusted preview of two themes with different color.

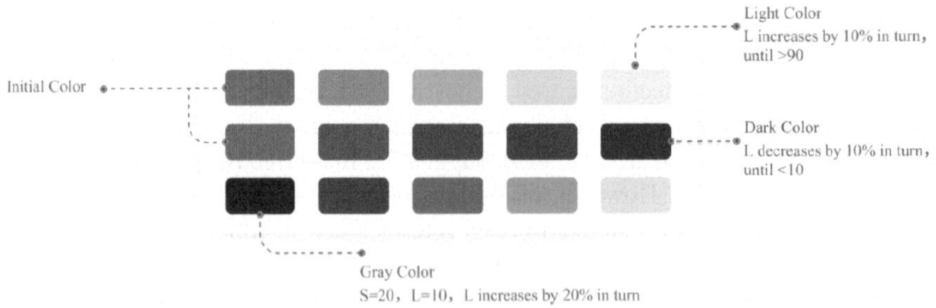

Fig. 4. A method to adjust the extracted color (taking Light as an example).

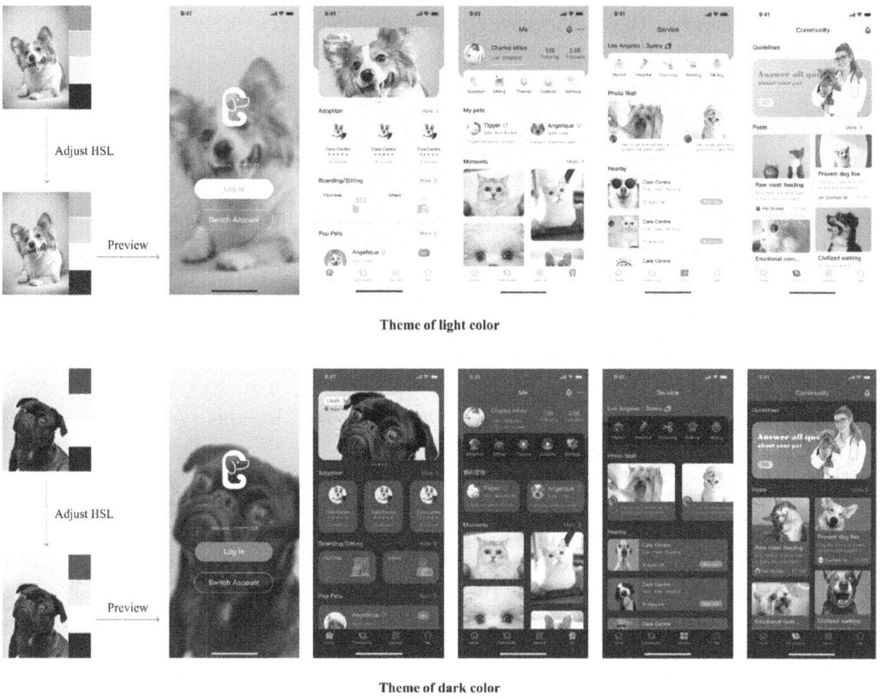

Fig. 5. Adjusted preview of two different themes.

5 Conclusion

This study investigated the impact of personalized themes derived from user-uploaded pet images on user satisfaction and emotional engagement in a pet app. User testing revealed a strong preference for these personalized themes, highlighting their effectiveness in enhancing aesthetic appeal and emotional connection. However, challenges with UI usability indicated the need for further usability improvements.

Subsequent iterations refined the color extraction algorithm to dynamically adjust the interface based on the HSL values of uploaded images, optimizing readability and user comfort. These enhancements addressed the usability issues and demonstrated the potential of personalized design to deepen user engagement and satisfaction.

Overall, this research underscores the value of integrating user-generated content into app design, suggesting that such personalization can significantly improve user experience. Future developments will focus on expanding customization capabilities and further refining interface adjustments to better meet user needs. This approach has broad implications for enhancing human-computer interaction through tailored design elements.

Acknowledgments. This study was funded by Teaching and Research Project of Huazhong University of Science and Technology (grant number 2023042).

Disclosure of Interests. The authors have no competing interests to declare that are relevant to the content of this article.

References

1. Reinecke, K., Bernstein, A.: Improving performance, perceived usability, and aesthetics with culturally adaptive user interfaces. ACM Trans. Comput.-Hum. Interact. (TOCHI). **18**, 1–29 (2011)
2. Kumar, V., Kumar, V., Singh, S., Singh, N., Banoth, M.S.: The impact of user experience design on customer satisfaction in e-commerce websites. Int. J. Res. Appl. Sci. Eng. Technol. (2023). https://doi.org/10.22214/ijraset.2023.52580
3. Norman, D.: Emotional Design: Why We Love (or hate) Everyday Things. Basic Books (2007)
4. Chiang, C.-Y., Boakye, K., Tang, X.: The investigation of E-learning system design quality on usage intention. J. Comput. Inf. Syst. (2017)
5. Tufte, E.R.: Envisioning information. Optom. Vis. Sci. **68**, 322–324 (1991)
6. Ouyang, M.-Y.: Psychology of colour in user experience/interaction: 'emotional colour in visualisation' theory in interaction design for user experience: the design of the Italian medical linkage system as an example. In: 2021 2nd International Conference on Intelligent Computing and Human-Computer Interaction (ICHCI), pp. 339–343. IEEE (2021)
7. Bianchi, R.G., de Almeida Neris, V.P.: Which color should i pick? a study on colors and emotions in human-computer interaction. In: Proceedings of the 14th Brazilian Symposium on Human Factors in Computing Systems, pp. 1–10 (2015)
8. Abegaz, T., Dillon, E., Gilbert, J.E.: Exploring affective reaction during user interaction with colors and shapes. Procedia Manuf. **3**, 5253–5260 (2015)
9. Venni, J., Bétrancourt, M.: Aesthetics in hypermedia: impact of colour harmony on implicit memory and user experience. In: Companion Publication of the 2020 International Conference on Multimodal Interaction, pp. 215–219 (2020)
10. Meqdad, M.N., Abdali-Mohammadi, F., Kadry, S.: Recognizing emotional state of user based on learning method and conceptual memories. TELKOMNIKA (Telecommun. Comput. Electron. Control) **18**, 3033–3040 (2020)
11. Murphy, L., Stanney, K., Hancock, P.A.: The effect of affect: the hedonomic evaluation of human-computer interaction. In: Proceedings of the Human Factors and Ergonomics Society Annual Meeting, pp. 764–768. SAGE Publications Sage CA: Los Angeles, CA (2003)
12. Thompson, S., Celebi, M.E., Buck, K.H.: Fast color quantization using MacQueen's k-means algorithm. J. Real-Time Image Proc. **17**, 1609–1624 (2020)
13. Valenzuela, G., Celebi, M.E., Schaefer, G.: Color quantization using coreset sampling. In: 2018 IEEE International Conference on Systems, Man, and Cybernetics (SMC), pp. 2096–2101. IEEE (2018)
14. Ongkadinata, D., Putri, F.P.: Quality and size assessment of quantized images using K-Means++ clustering. Bull. Electr. Eng. Inform. **9**, 1183–1188 (2020)
15. Krishna, T.V.: Finding the most dominant color in an image using K-means algorithm based on machine learning. Int. J. Res. Appl. Sci. Eng. Technol. (2023). https://doi.org/10.22214/ijraset.2023.57507
16. Celebi, M.E.: Improving the performance of k-means for color quantization. Image Vis. Comput. **29**, 260–271 (2011)
17. Oyebode, O., Alqahtani, F., Orji, R.: Using machine learning and thematic analysis methods to evaluate mental health apps based on user reviews. IEEE Access. **8**, 111141–111158 (2020)
18. Bellman, S., Potter, R.F., Treleaven-Hassard, S., Robinson, J.A., Varan, D.: The effectiveness of branded mobile phone apps. J. Interact. Mark. **25**, 191–200 (2011)

19. Linnhoff, S., Smith, K.T.: An examination of mobile app usage and the user's life satisfaction. J. Strateg. Mark. **25**, 581–617 (2017)
20. Caldwell, B., et al.: Web content accessibility guidelines (WCAG) 2.0. WWW Consortium (W3C). **290**, 5–12 (2008)

Integrating User Perspectives: A Framework for Ad-Hoc Privacy Preference Implementation in Information Systems

Mandy Goram(✉)

Independent Researcher, Dainalytix, Germany
mandy.goram@dainalytix.com

Abstract. This paper presents preliminary results for a comprehensive framework for integrating ad-hoc privacy preferences into information systems. The framework is structured into three layers: Preference Identification, Semantic Representation, and Integration and Enforcement. The Preference Identification Layer analyzes user interactions, feedback, and predefined settings to identify privacy preferences and generate detailed user profiles. The Semantic Representation Layer standardizes these preferences into machine-readable formats using ontologies, XML, and JSON schemas, as well as Semantic Web technologies like RDF and OWL, facilitating interoperability across systems. The Integration and Enforcement Layer embeds and enforces these preferences within application settings, ensuring consistent application and compliance with regulatory standards through policy enforcement mechanisms, context-aware systems, and real-time monitoring tools. This framework enhances user control over personal data and aligns with global privacy regulations such as GDPR and CCPA, addressing challenges like dynamic preference management and system integration complexities. Future research should focus on scalability across different domains and the integration of advanced technologies like machine learning to further refine and validate the framework. This paper contributes to the development of privacy-aware information systems that prioritize user autonomy and ethical design, facilitate trust and compliance in the digital landscape.

Keywords: Privacy Preferences · Privacy Management · Context-dependent

1 Introduction

User privacy has become a primary concern in product development and delivery, driven by global regulatory requirements. To meet these requirements, companies are being forced to implement transparent privacy practices. From the user's perspective, transparent privacy practices alone are useless without effective enforcement of their privacy preferences. While existing research and tools aim to explain privacy practices to users (e.g., visualization [1], privacy notices [2], and nutrition labels [3]), a critical gap remains in understanding the individual user perspective on the processing of personal data across applications within information systems.

C. Stephanidis et al. (Eds.): HCII 2024, CCIS 2319, pp. 60–69, 2025.
https://doi.org/10.1007/978-3-031-78516-0_6

In previous research, we have successfully developed prototypes for ad hoc privacy preference identification that can be used to individualize privacy preferences. However, bridging the gap between identifying users' privacy preferences and operationalizing them within and across applications remains an open challenge. Research on the integration of privacy-related information into applications exists but is tightly coupled to specific applications [4, 5]. This paper presents ongoing work that focuses on the integration of ad hoc privacy preferences into applications in general to ensure that functionalities are tailored to individual user preferences.

While the focus of the research is on a technical approach this paper presents a generic framework used for the prototypical instantiation of semantic data structures for mapping identified privacy preferences to technical privacy preference settings. Using privacy preferences as a key use case, the research presents an approach for contextualizing user preferences within applications.

The paper outlines a process for including user preferences into information systems, addressing the challenge of operationalizing detected privacy preferences in real-world applications. By presenting a framework that links user-centered privacy preferences to technical implementations, this research contributes to the development of privacy-aware information systems and provides a foundation for future advances in the field.

2 Background

The rapid spread of digital technologies has significantly transformed how personal data is collected, processed, and utilized, raising critical concerns about privacy, ethics, and user autonomy. The necessity of a comprehensive framework to manage and enforce user-specific privacy preferences is underscored by these developments.

The Importance of Privacy and Ethics in Digital Systems. Privacy is a fundamental human right, preserved in various international declarations and regulations such as the General Data Protection Regulation (GDPR)[1] and the California Consumer Privacy Act (CCPA)[2]. These regulations mandate rigorous measures for protecting personal data and ensuring that individuals retain control over their information. However, the practical implementation of these principles in digital systems remains challenging.

Ethical considerations in Human-Computer Interaction (HCI) go beyond mere compliance with legal standards. They involve designing systems that respect user autonomy and promote informed consent, minimizing the risk of harm and enhancing trust [6]. Ethical design principles such as Value Sensitive Design (VSD) advocate for the inclusion of stakeholder values in the design process, ensuring that systems align with the broader societal values of privacy and autonomy [7].

The Role of User Autonomy and Self-Determination. User autonomy and self-determination are critical in the digital age. Users should have the ability to make informed decisions about their data, including what is collected, how it is used, and who has access to it. This concept is central to the notion of Privacy by Design (PbD), which

[1] https://gdpr.eu/.

[2] https://oag.ca.gov/privacy/ccpa.

emphasizes the integration of privacy considerations into the design and architecture of IT systems from the outset [8].

However, ensuring user autonomy in practice requires sophisticated mechanisms to translate user preferences into enforceable policies. This involves not only capturing user preferences accurately but also ensuring that these preferences are consistently applied across diverse information systems. The lack of such mechanisms often leads to privacy preferences being ignored or overlooked, undermining user trust and compliance with ethical standards [9].

Technical Challenges in Enforcing Privacy Preferences. Enforcing privacy preferences in real-world applications is associated with technical challenges. These include the dynamic nature of user preferences, the complexity of integrating privacy preferences into existing systems, and the need for real-time adaptation to changing contexts and regulations. Advanced technologies such as machine learning, natural language processing, and semantic web technologies offer potential solutions to these challenges.

Machine learning algorithms can analyze user interactions and feedback to infer privacy preferences, reducing the burden on users to manually configure their settings [10]. Natural language processing tools can parse user feedback and detect nuanced privacy concerns, enhancing the accuracy of preference identification [4]. Semantic web technologies, including RDF and OWL, provide standardized formats for representing privacy preferences, facilitating interoperability across different systems [11].

Incorporating AI into Privacy Management. Artificial Intelligence (AI) plays a critical role in enhancing the capabilities of privacy management frameworks. AI systems, which often rely on huge amounts of data, pose significant privacy risks if not properly managed. Integrating user-specific privacy preferences into these systems is crucial to mitigate potential abuses and ensure compliance with privacy regulations [12, 13].

AI can automate the detection of privacy preferences and anomalies, ensuring that systems remain responsive to evolving user needs and regulatory landscapes. Moreover, AI technologies such as generative models can create synthetic data that mimics real user data without compromising privacy, allowing for robust machine learning applications while protecting personal information [14].

The integration of AI into the framework not only enhances the accuracy and efficiency of privacy preference identification but also ensures that privacy management is dynamic and adaptive. This adaptability is crucial in environments where user interactions and contextual factors are constantly evolving, thereby maintaining user trust and compliance with privacy regulations [9].

3 Method

This study employs a mixed-methods approach, combining qualitative data from user interviews and surveys with quantitative analysis of privacy settings. The goal is to develop and validate a process and semantic data structures for mapping identified privacy preferences to technical settings within applications.

Data collection involved two phases: qualitative user studies to gather detailed information on privacy preferences and concerns, and quantitative analysis of privacy settings across different applications. The qualitative phase focused on understanding differentiated privacy needs, while the quantitative phase aimed to identify patterns and commonalities in preferences. The prototype implementation of the framework is ongoing research and not part of this paper.

Framework Development. The qualitative phase focused on understanding differentiated privacy needs, while the quantitative phase aimed to identify patterns and commonalities in preferences. The prototype implementation of the framework is ongoing research and not part of this paper. The framework was derived from previous interactive research prototypes. Preference detection and semantic mapping were successfully evaluated. Upcoming work includes the enforcement component to enable an end-to-end system for ad-hoc processing of privacy preferences.

4 Framework for Ad-Hoc Privacy Preference Implementation in Information Systems

Given the complexity of privacy management, a layered framework is essential for systematically addressing the identification, representation, and enforcement of user-specific privacy preferences. The proposed framework consists of three layers:

Preference Identification Layer. This layer detects and identifies user-specific privacy preferences based on interactions, feedback, and predefined settings. It uses machine learning and Natural Language Processing (NLP) techniques to analyze user data and extract privacy preferences accurately [15].

Semantic Representation Layer. This layer develops standardized, machine-readable formats for representing identified privacy preferences. By utilizing ontologies and schemas, it ensures interoperability and consistent representation across systems [11].

Integration and Enforcement Layer. This layer embeds and enforces privacy preferences within application settings. It includes policy enforcement mechanisms such as role-based (RBAC) and attribute-based access control (ABAC) [16], context-aware systems for dynamic adjustment, and real-time monitoring tools to ensure compliance.

The proposed framework for ad-hoc privacy preference implementation in information systems is designed with a layered architecture to systematically address the identification, representation, and enforcement of user-specific privacy preferences. This layered approach ensures that privacy preferences are effectively integrated into various applications, enhancing user control and compliance with privacy regulations.

Incorporating AI into the framework enhances its capabilities to dynamically adjust privacy settings based on real-time user interactions and contextual changes. AI can automate the detection of privacy preferences and anomalies, ensuring that systems remain responsive to evolving user needs and regulatory landscapes. The use of AI also facilitates scalability, allowing the framework to handle large volumes of data and complex privacy requirements efficiently.

4.1 Preference Identification Layer

The primary objective of the preference identification layer is to detect and identify user-specific privacy preferences based on interactions, feedback, and/or predefined privacy settings. This layer takes user interactions and behavior data, feedback from surveys and interviews, and predefined privacy settings as inputs.

The processes in this layer include analyzing user interactions through surveys and interviews to gather detailed insights into privacy concerns and preferences, using behavioral analysis and machine learning algorithms to infer privacy preferences from user interactions, employing advanced detection techniques like NLP tools to parse and interpret user feedback, and utilizing pattern recognition to detect trends indicative of specific privacy preferences.

Furthermore, demographic and contextual data can be collected and analyzed to tailor privacy settings to individual users, while personalization engines recommend privacy settings based on identified user profiles and preferences. The use of sparse-data approaches can prevent privacy violations during preference detection [17]. The outputs of this layer are identified user privacy preferences and profiles detailing user-specific privacy needs.

4.2 Semantic Representation Layer

The semantic representation layer focuses on developing a standardized, machine-readable format for representing identified privacy preferences to facilitate interoperability across systems. This layer uses the privacy preferences and user profiles as inputs.

The processes include data modeling through the creation of ontologies that define the relationships between different privacy concepts and the design of XML or JSON schemas to standardize the representation of privacy preferences. Additionally, Semantic Web technologies like RDF (Resource Description Framework) and OWL (Web Ontology Language) are used to represent privacy preferences as triples and enhance the expressiveness of the privacy preference ontology [18].

Metadata annotation techniques are also used to tag data with relevant privacy preferences to facilitate automated processing and enforcement, while provenance tracking ensures compliance with user-specified privacy preferences by tracking the origin and transformation of data. The outputs of this layer are standardized semantic representations of privacy preferences and annotated data with privacy tags.

By employing well-defined schemas and semantic web technologies [11], the framework ensures that privacy preferences are expressed consistently and comprehensively [19].

Semantic Data Structure: Privacy Preference Ontology. The semantic data structure must represent classes and properties which are related to the target domain which is in this case the GDPR. Example ontology classes and properties are listed below:

- *Classes:*
  - `User`: Represents the individual user.

  - `Consent`: Represents the consent given by the user.
  - `DataProcessing`: Represents the data processing activity.
  - `DataItem`: Represents the specific data being processed.
  - `PrivacyPreference`: Represents the user's privacy preferences.

- *Properties:*

  - `hasConsent`: Links a `User` to their `Consent`.
  - `hasPurpose`: Links `DataProcessing` to its purpose.
  - `hasRetentionPeriod`: Specifies the retention period for `DataItem`.
  - `hasProcessingActivity`: Links `User` to `DataProcessing`.
  - `hasDataItem`: Links `DataProcessing` to `DataItem`.
  - `hasPrivacyPreference`: Links `User` to their `PrivacyPreference`.

Operationalized Rules Derived from Privacy Regulations. From the GDPR the following rules can be derived to be integrated in the semantic layer:

- **Explicit Consent**: A `User` must have a `Consent` instance linked via `hasConsent` for any `DataProcessing` activity.
- **Purpose Limitation**: Each `DataProcessing` activity must have a clearly defined `hasPurpose`.
- **Data Minimization**: Only the data necessary for the `hasPurpose` should be processed.
- **Data Retention**: Data should be retained only as long as necessary for the `hasPurpose`.

4.3 Integration and Enforcement Layer

The integration and enforcement layer aims to embed and enforce the standardized privacy preferences into application settings and ensure their consistent enforcement across different systems. This layer uses the standardized semantic representations of privacy preferences and annotated data with privacy tags as inputs. The processes include implementing policy enforcement mechanisms, such as RBAC and ABAC to enforce privacy policies and developing consent management systems to manage and record user consents, ensuring data processing complies with user preferences.

Context-aware systems dynamically adjust privacy settings based on the current context and user behavior [20], while real-time monitoring tools track compliance with privacy preferences and detect potential violations. Interoperability and integration are achieved by developing APIs that allow applications to query and enforce privacy preferences, and creating middleware solutions that act as intermediaries, translating high-level privacy preferences into specific application settings.

Lastly, feedback and revision mechanisms are established to enable continuous user feedback to refine and update privacy preferences, and automated systems update privacy settings in response to changes in user preferences or regulatory requirements. The outputs of this layer are enforced privacy preferences across applications and updated privacy settings and compliance reports.

4.4 Framework Layer Overview

The framework layer uses different methods and technologies to gather user preferences, enrich these with semantic information and enforce these across information systems. The following Table 1 gives a summary of methods and technologies on the framework layers.

Table 1. Summary table of methods and technologies.

Layer	Methods	Technology
Preference Identification	User Interaction Analysis	Surveys, Interviews, Machine Learning
	Advanced Detection Techniques	NLP, Pattern Recognition
	User Profiling	Demographic Analysis, Personalization Engines
Semantic Representation	Data Modeling	Ontologies, XML, JSON
	Semantic Web Technologies	RDF, OWL
	Metadata Annotation	Tagging Systems, Provenance Tracking
Integration and Enforcement	Policy Enforcement	RBAC, ABAC, Consent Management Systems
	Context-Aware Systems	Dynamic Adaptation, Real-Time Monitoring
	Interoperability and Integration	APIs, Middleware
	Feedback and Revision	User Feedback Loops, Automated Updates

5 Discussion

5.1 Implications for Privacy-Aware Information Systems

The proposed framework significantly enhances current privacy management practices by addressing a critical gap: the operationalization of user-specific privacy preferences across diverse applications. By integrating advanced detection techniques, semantic data structures, and robust enforcement mechanisms, the framework provides a comprehensive solution that is both user-centric and technically feasible.

The multi-layered approach ensures that privacy preferences are identified accurately and represented in a machine-readable format, facilitating interoperability and seamless integration into various systems. This not only enhances user control over personal data but also aligns with regulatory requirements, such as GDPR and CCPA, thereby fostering trust and compliance.

Operationalizing detected privacy preferences in real-world applications presents several challenges, which the framework addresses through its Integration and Enforcement Layer. This layer embeds privacy preferences into application settings and enforces them consistently across systems. Policy enforcement mechanisms ensure that data access and processing comply with user preferences and regulatory requirements.

Context-aware systems dynamically adjust privacy settings based on the current context and user behavior, ensuring that privacy management is not static but adaptive to changing conditions and the user's needs. Real-time monitoring tools must track compliance with privacy preferences, detecting and responding to potential violations promptly. This dynamic approach is crucial for maintaining privacy in environments where user interactions and contextual factors are constantly evolving [9, 21].

The proposed framework describes a multi-layered approach integrating and operationalizing user-specific privacy preferences in information systems. Through the use of AI and advanced data structures, the complexity of real-world applications is taken into account, ensuring that privacy management is both effective and compliant with legal standards.

5.2 Challenges and Limitations

Despite its potential, the framework faces several challenges and limitations. One of the primary challenges is the need for comprehensive user data to accurately identify privacy preferences. Collecting and processing such data raises ethical and practical concerns, including data privacy and user consent. Additionally, integrating these preferences into existing systems can be complex and resource-intensive, requiring significant modifications to current infrastructure.

Another limitation is the dynamic nature of privacy preferences [22]. User preferences may change over time, demanding continuous updates and real-time adjustments to privacy settings [21]. Ensuring that the framework adapts to evolving user preferences and regulatory landscapes is crucial for its long-term viability. This requires robust mechanisms for real-time monitoring, feedback loops, and automated updates, which may add to the system's complexity and maintenance overhead.

5.3 Future Research

Future research should focus on evaluating instances of the integration and enforcement layer of the framework to show how the challenges of enforcing ad hoc preferences in different domains and applications can be overcome. Enhancing detection techniques through advanced machine learning models and artificial intelligence can improve the accuracy and efficiency of privacy preference identification [1, 4].

Investigating the application of the framework in specific industries, such as healthcare and e-commerce, can provide valuable insights into its practical implementation and effectiveness.

5.4 Conclusion

The proposed framework for integrating ad hoc privacy preferences into information systems addresses a critical need for user-centered privacy management. By linking user privacy preferences to technical implementations, the framework ensures that privacy settings are accurately identified, represented, and enforced across various applications. This not only enhances user control and trust but also aligns with regulatory requirements, contributing to the development of privacy-aware information systems. Future advancements will refine the framework, making it more effective and adaptable to information systems.

References

1. Habib, H., et al.: Toggles, dollar signs, and triangles: how to (In)effectively convey privacy choices with icons and link texts. In: Proceedings of the 2021 CHI Conference on Human Factors in Computing Systems, pp. 1–25. ACM, Yokohama Japan (2021)
2. Schaub, F., Balebako, R., Durity, A.L., Cranor, L.F.: A design space for effective privacy notices. In: Eleventh Symposium on Usable Privacy and Security (SOUPS 2015), pp. 1–17. USENIX Association, Ottawa (2015)
3. Kelley, P.G., Bresee, J., Cranor, L.F., Reeder, R.W.: A "nutrition label" for privacy. In: Proceedings of the 5th Symposium on Usable Privacy and Security, pp. 1–12. Association for Computing Machinery, New York, NY, USA (2009)
4. Liu, B., et al.: Follow my recommendations: a personalized privacy assistant for mobile app permissions. In: Proceedings of the Twelfth USENIX Conference on Usable Privacy and Security, pp. 27–41. USENIX Association, USA (2016)
5. Sharma, T., Dyer, H.A., Bashir, M.: Enabling user-centered privacy controls for mobile applications: COVID-19 perspective. ACM Trans. Internet Technol. **21**, 1–24 (2021). https://doi.org/10.1145/3434777
6. Friedman, B., Hendry, D.G.: Value Sensitive Design: Shaping Technology with Moral Imagination. The MIT Press (2019)
7. Friedman, B., Kahn, P.H., Borning, A.: Value Sensitive Design: Theory and Methods
8. Cavoukian, A.: Privacy by Design The 7 Foundational Principles. (2011)
9. Schwartz, P.M., Solove, D.J.: The PII problem: privacy and a new concept of personally identifiable information. N.Y.U. L. Rev. **86**, 1814 (2011)
10. Jawaheer, G., Weller, P., Kostkova, P.: Modeling user preferences in recommender systems: a classification framework for explicit and implicit user feedback. ACM Trans. Interact. Intell. Syst. **4**, 1–26 (2014). https://doi.org/10.1145/2512208
11. Antoniou, G., Harmelen van, F.: A Semantic Web Primer. MIT Press, Cambridge (Mass.) (2008)
12. Dwork, C., Roth, A.: The algorithmic foundations of differential privacy. TCS **9**, 211–407 (2014). https://doi.org/10.1561/0400000042
13. Shokri, R.: Privacy Games: Optimal User-Centric Data Obfuscation. Proceedings on Privacy Enhancing Technologies (2015)
14. Ulusoy, O., Yolum, P.: PANOLA: a personal assistant for supporting users in preserving privacy. ACM Trans. Internet Technol. **22**, 27:1–27:32 (2021). https://doi.org/10.1145/3471187
15. Sousa, S., Kern, R.: How to keep text private? a systematic review of deep learning methods for privacy-preserving natural language processing. Artif. Intell. Rev. **56**, 1427–1492 (2023). https://doi.org/10.1007/s10462-022-10204-6

16. Huang, J., Nicol, D.M., Bobba, R., Huh, J.H.: A framework integrating attribute-based policies into role-based access control. In: Proceedings of the 17th ACM Symposium on Access Control Models and Technologies, pp. 187–196. Association for Computing Machinery, New York, NY, USA (2012)
17. Goram, M., Dehling, T., Morsbach, F., Sunyaev, A.: Human-centered design for data-sparse tailored privacy information provision. In: Gerber, N., Stöver, A., Marky, K. (eds.) Human Factors in Privacy Research, pp. 283–298. Springer International Publishing, Cham (2023)
18. Pandit, H.J., Debruyne, C., O'Sullivan, D., Lewis, D.: GConsent - a consent ontology based on the GDPR. In: Hitzler, P., et al. (eds.) The Semantic Web, pp. 270–282. Springer International Publishing, Cham (2019)
19. Goram, M., Veiel, D.: Linking legal and domain-specific requirements in a context-based adaptive personalized learning environment. Procedia Comput. Sci. **170**, 995–1002 (2020). https://doi.org/10.1016/j.procs.2020.03.095
20. Adomavicius, G., Tuzhilin, A.: Context-aware recommender systems. In: Ricci, F., Rokach, L., Shapira, B. (eds.) Recommender Systems Handbook, pp. 191–226. Springer, US, Boston, MA (2015)
21. Nissenbaum, H.: Privacy in Context: Technology, Policy, and the Integrity of Social Life. Stanford University Press, Stanford, CA, USA (2010)
22. Acquisti, A., Brandimarte, L., Loewenstein, G.: Privacy and human behavior in the age of information. Science **347**, 509–514 (2015). https://doi.org/10.1126/science.aaa1465

Research on Emotional Image of Custom Fonts in Chinese Enterprises Based on Kansei Engineering

Shua-Hua Jin[1,3](✉) and Xiang Liu[2,3]

[1] Beijing Institute of Technology, Zhuhai, China
11024@bitzh.edu.cn
[2] Guangdong Polytechnic Normal University, Guangzhou, China
xiang5863@126.com
[3] Studying School for Doctor's Degree, City University of Macau, Macau, China

Abstract. Custom fonts have emerged as a visual trend for Chinese brands. Enterprises and institutions are increasingly adopting uniquely designed corporate typefaces. These fonts symbolize the deepening of corporate branding, serving as a connection between companies and consumers. This paper examines emotional factors in custom fonts by studying those of prominent Chinese enterprises.

This research methodology employs the brand mind theory and Kansei Engineering's emotional images to extract relevant perceptual words. Cluster analysis is then used to form perceptual word pairs, establishing the relationship between emotional and morphological dimensions in fonts. By utilizing image scale diagrams, the study analyzes the factors influencing emotional aspects of custom fonts and user psychology. In examining the emotional dimensions of Chinese enterprise custom fonts, stroke shape and weight of Chinese characters emerge as key design elements for building font personality.

The emotional image projected by a custom font enhances brand conceptual understanding, enriches the brand's value chain, and contributes to assessing brand worth. With the prevalence of Internet information dissemination, sans-serif fonts have emerged as the preferred option for enterprises due to electronic display technology advantages. Despite this, differentiation among custom fonts within the same industry remains insufficient. When designing custom fonts, it is imperative to deeply understand users' emotional requirements for corporate brands and employ suitable design concepts and methodologies.

Keywords: Custom font · Kansei Engineering · Image Scale Map · Emotional Image

1 Introduction

1.1 Research Background and Motivation

Custom fonts represent an intricate facet of branding within the development trajectory of Chinese enterprises. As brands transition into the "heart era," they signify a psychological contract between enterprises and consumers, etched in the depths of emotions—a

C. Stephanidis et al. (Eds.): HCII 2024, CCIS 2319, pp. 70–85, 2025.
https://doi.org/10.1007/978-3-031-78516-0_7

reflection of consumer perception towards a product or service. Consumer psychology significantly influences consumer behavior, underscoring the imperative of fortifying brand image to secure a prime space in the consumer's psyche for brand success [1]; From a systems theory perspective, as standard product functionalities fall short of meeting Chinese consumer demands, value is shifting towards holistic service experiences rather than mere product utility. Service design stands out as a tool that aids enterprises in expanding the sphere for brand growth [2]. In an era of burgeoning information interfaces, consumers encounter myriad touchpoints, with brand offerings serving as pivotal avenues for establishing mental connections with consumers. Embracing custom fonts, Chinese companies employ these soft products to cater to consumers, enhancing brand touchpoints and bolstering brand messaging.

Custom fonts are distinctive typefaces commissioned by font companies to fortify brand image, characterized by exclusivity and uniqueness. Unlike standard fonts commonly used in brand logos, custom fonts predominantly serve corporate publicity purposes for everyday reading and are freely distributed to consumers. Aligned with the enterprise's brand positioning, design agencies extract visual elements from font designs to ensure functional utility while effectively communicating the enterprise's core concepts to consumers, thereby establishing a lasting impact on consumer perceptions.

Custom fonts seamlessly integrate brand concepts and visual identity into a continuum of brand value interests. In marketing realms, an enterprise's ability to deliver sustained perceived value to customers serves as a tangible indicator of its competitiveness. Perceived value encapsulates three key components: product functionality, service speed, technological innovation, supply adequacy, brand value, emotional resonance, and social significance [3]. The customer acts as the focal point in perceiving value, with the enterprise's services serving as the object upon which customers evaluate their overall service experience. Custom fonts represent a sustainable perceived service offering by enterprises to consumers, serving as a pivotal component that shapes customers' evaluation of a brand's perceived value.

Companies and organizations have started to use their own exclusive fonts. For example, BYD, Huawei, Taobao, Jingdong, Xiaomi, Tencent and so on. Coca-Cola China launched the "Zaihu" font, Alibaba launched the "Puhui" font, and Tencent launched the "Tengxun" font. Some cultural organizations also use custom fonts. For example, the Shenzhen Graphic Design Association and Founder Font Company launched the GDC custom fonts, and the China Academy of Art launched the custom fonts based on FangSong. This shows that market demand is undergoing profound changes, brands must expand the category nature of their products, and the fusion of category fringes has become the consensus of enterprises. The competition of Chinese enterprises is upgrading from the competition of product power to the competition of brand premium, and enterprises must seize all possible information touch points to strengthen a good brand image and win the sustainable trust and support of future consumers [4].

The Internet business platform exemplified by Alibaba has provided a breeding ground for numerous small and medium-sized enterprises (SMEs) to flourish swiftly. However, these SMEs often grapple with intellectual property issues while promoting their merchandise. Firstly, fonts are commonly perceived as free for use by many individuals. Secondly, there's a prevailing belief that the correct usage of fonts holds minimal sway over an enterprise's sales. Lastly, due to limited resources, smaller enterprises are hesitant to allocate excessive funds towards promotional activities. Contrary to popular belief, text fonts are meticulously crafted by professional font design companies and safeguarded through patents for legal protection. These design firms protect their rights via mechanisms like patenting font designs and asserting against unfair competition in font repositories. Under current Chinese law, font usage within commercial practices is subject to these regulations. Consequently, enterprises are not at liberty to freely access font libraries on Internet business platforms or other commercial avenues [5]. Alibaba, in conjunction with Founder Fonts, has launched custom fonts free of charge for SMEs to use, which has helped SMEs reduce their sales costs and build a better corporate image. It is such a good demonstration effect that prompts more and more Chinese enterprises to invest in custom fonts.

1.2 Research Purposes

At present, the research on custom fonts for Chinese enterprises is at a basic stage. It mainly focuses on two aspects: on the one hand, it stresses the importance and significance of custom fonts for enterprises. For example, An Xiaomin [6] advocates that custom fonts are related to the development of China's corporate image and are an inevitable product of corporate image improvement. Chen Xinyue [7], Wang Yuqi [8] believe that custom fonts are an important symbol of city and corporate brand differentiation. Pan Jian [9] listed how to design custom fonts in the process of building cultural and tourism brands. Yue Hong [10] proposed the design elements of Hei typeface in custom fonts for Chinese enterprises in his study. The above scholars only emphasized the role of custom fonts and did not explore in depth the emotional imagery existing in custom fonts, which is precisely the emotional point of the consumer mind link.

On the other hand, there are some other scholars who researched the emotional imagery of fonts. For example, Sheng Haohan [11] proposed several visual dimensions that affect the emotion of fonts. Ouyang Jinyan [12] and others proposed a model of emotional relationship between the structure and strokes of Chinese fonts. Zhang Shuo [13] used a quantitative research method to find the emotional commonality of fonts. Guo Sheqi [14] categorized the fonts directly according to the emotion types. From the above, the above scholars only focus on the design elements of corporate custom fonts, or only study the emotional factors of fonts, and do not combine the two studies. Perception and feeling are precisely people's direct association with things, and they are also the key for brands to occupy consumers' minds. Therefore, studying the facets that affect the emotional factors of fonts can help designers to complete the design practice of corporate custom fonts.

2 Research Methodology of Custom Fonts

2.1 Related Theoretical Research

Kansei engineering is the first theory formed in Japan by introducing emotions into industrial design research [15]. This methodology enables the quantification of consumers' latent emotional needs using structured methods to scrutinize the correlation between perceptual imagery and design elements. Designers leverage this understanding to streamline the design process or enhance models. The interplay between emotional vocabulary and design components within perceptual engineering serves as a crucial reference point for design initiatives. Thus, the perceptual lexicon in this paper predominantly revolves around consumers' perceptual linkages with custom font samples from Chinese companies, pinpointing emotional framing elements intrinsic to custom font design.

The primary technique for investigating perceptual imagery is the semantic differential method, initially introduced by American psychologist Osgood [16]. This methodology explores the shared perceptual attributes of objects by constructing a conceptual scale with adjectives of contrasting semantic significance, assessing subjects to unveil emotional inclinations. Perceptual imagery constitutes a cognitive response synthesized by the brain based on an individual's experiential insight. For accurate assessments of the emotional connotations within a design composition, participants must possess pertinent knowledge and practical experience within a specific field.

Image scale maps serve as a tool for assessing individuals' cognitive preferences. People exhibit diverse evaluations of product aesthetics, and their psychological responses are influenced by their educational background and experiences. Image Scale Mapping involves measuring, calculating, and analyzing psychological levels, transforming mental imagery into an imagery scale distribution. This distribution stems from quantitative data obtained from semantic differentials, enabling the use of scientific statistical techniques to dissect constructs and elucidate the broader mental imagery landscape.

2.2 The Research Process of Emotional Imagery of Custom Fonts

Samples of custom fonts from Founder Fonts Company and HanYi Fonts Company were selected for assessment by Chinese companies. Perceptual vocabulary used to evaluate these custom fonts was gathered through expert interviews with designers. Subsequently, word pairs were established through screening, leading to the creation of a Richter scale to define the semantic space. Subjects—primarily designers with relevant experience—were then selected for the study. Data was calculated, statistical analyses were conducted, and an imagery scale map of enterprise custom fonts was generated. By interpreting the imagery scale diagram, the overall emotional tendencies of Chinese corporate custom fonts were deduced. Lastly, existing samples of corporate custom fonts were scrutinized to challenge preconceived mental imagery assumptions, as illustrated in Fig. 1.

3 The Emotional Imagery of Chinese Corporate Custom Fonts

3.1 Sample Selection of Custom Fonts

After research China custom fonts are mainly concentrated in the following categories. One category for government agencies, such as the China Naval Equipment Research Institute, Fuzhou Tourism Bureau, Zhejiang SongYang County, the National Centre for the Performing Arts, etc.; another category for cultural activities, such as the WNBA, the

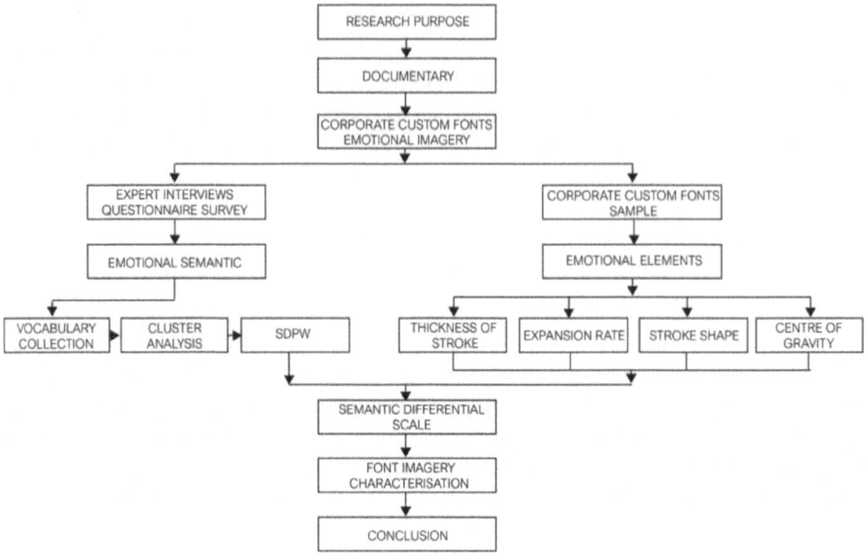

Fig. 1. Research flow chart.

Beijing Winter Olympics, the Chinese Football Premier League, the One Foundation, etc.; and the third category of enterprise custom fonts this category, such as Huawei, XiaoPeng, Alibaba and so on. With the help of experts and Internet surveys, Chinese character font design workload is large, the development cycle is long, the design is difficult, the application scenarios are extensive, and more designers are needed. Therefore, the custom fonts for enterprises in China are mainly done by two large font design institutes, namely, Founder font and HanYi font. At present, a total of 32 Chinese corporate fonts were retrieved from these two font design institutes. Considering the time for the respondents to answer the questions as well as the classification, 10 custom fonts in the famous corporate category were mainly extracted for the questionnaire test (recommended samples from corporate websites). Considering the existence of different font weights, all the fonts were in regular font weights. Meanwhile, considering the existence of different industries of enterprises, multi-industry samples such as Internet industry, cosmetic industry, telecommunication industry, financial industry, etc. were selected. To avoid the potential influence of company names on the testers, all of them use the same Chinese character font, and the testers fill in the questionnaire only according to the font. The font samples are as follows: Vivo, Alida Cosmetics, Dou Shen education, Huawei Font, Coca-Cola China, Lagou, Jingdong, China Union Pay, Alibaba, and Tencent, see Fig. 2.

3.2 Dimension in Chinese Corporate Custom Fonts

- Stroke Width. Stroke width pertains to the variation in stroke thickness within a Chinese character. Fonts featuring embellishments commonly employ diverse stroke widths, ranging from exceptionally fine to exceptionally coarse. Chinese character

Fig. 2. Enterprise custom fonts samples.

strokes are typically categorized into 7 levels of thickness variance. Unlike standardized specifications for stroke weight thickness, the number of variable character weight levels is typically contingent on the intricacy of stroke shapes. This leads to significant visual distinctions in character weights across different font categories.

- Degree of Expansion. The concept of stroke distribution within a square is fundamental to Chinese character design. When strokes are evenly spread within the square, the character appears more proportional, termed "normal." If strokes cluster near the square's perimeter, the character feels fuller, known as "expanding." Conversely, when strokes gravitate towards the square's center, the character exudes introversion and is labeled "contracting." The balance between expansiveness and contraction within a Chinese character is dictated by the shift in the square's center, influencing the character's overall cohesion and structure.
- Center of Gravity. In physics, the concept of the center of gravity defines the point where an object's weight is concentrated due to gravitational force. In typography, the center of gravity signifies the visual focal point within a Chinese character. Each Chinese character also has a standard center located at the intersection of its central horizontal and vertical lines. Research on a character's center of gravity typically involves analyzing the deviation of the center of gravity from this central point. A character with a higher center of gravity than the central point is deemed to have a high center of gravity, while one with a lower center of gravity is considered to have a low center of gravity.
- Stroke Shape. Stroke shape is the shape of a stroke, and the stroke of a Chinese character consists of three parts: the start of the stroke, the movement of the stroke, and the end of the stroke. Because different writing tools can cause different shapes when entering and closing the brush, designers use computer software to simulate different tools to design different shapes of strokes, or different design intentions of writers to form fonts with very different styles.

On the one hand, in Chinese character design, the choice of font style plays a crucial role in conveying specific characteristics. An expanding font typically evokes a sense of reliability and honesty, whereas a contracting font exudes an upright, young, and energetic vibe. Fonts with a low center of gravity tend to appear calmer, suitable for conveying elderly or childlike qualities. On the other hand, fonts with a high center of gravity often project a modern and youthful appearance, while those with a central center of gravity tend to exude a more mature aura. Moreover, the shape of strokes within Chinese characters can significantly influence emotional perception. For instance, straight strokes generally impart a modern and powerful aesthetic, radiating a youthful essence. Variations in starting, running, and finishing strokes contribute to different emotional interpretations. The regular script embodies humanistic traits, showcasing elegance and internal depth due to historical influences. In contrast, the imitation Song font retains stroke movement, providing a sense of handwritten authenticity and profound humanistic implications. As a result, emotional imagery can be effectively conveyed through the diverse elements of font design.

3.3 Emotional Framing in Corporate Custom Fonts

Sentimental vocabulary, integral to font design analysis, stems from diverse sources such as literature, books, online repositories, expert insights, and interviews. A comprehensive compilation of 100 vocabularies related to emotional imagery was gathered through meticulous research efforts. Experts and proficient students meticulously scrutinized and analyzed the assembled vocabularies, employing taxonomy and the KJ method for categorization and synthesis. Through a systematic approach, words with similar or contradictory meanings were identified, leading to the retention of fifty-nine significant terms.

The perceptual vocabularies underwent thorough classification and similarity scoring procedures using card classification techniques and data clustering methods to generate a word distance data matrix. This data matrix was further processed using SPSS software, facilitating cluster analysis that pinpointed eight key sensual words. These words were thoughtfully paired with their antonyms, forming essential word pairs like slim - heavy, gentle - tough, compact - loose, modern - traditional, fancy - rough, sharp - rounded, funny - formal, and gorgeous - pristine. Five additional experts, each boasting over five years of experience in typeface design, were then engaged to delineate the intricate relationship between emotional elements within typefaces and fundamental typeface design components. By systematically categorizing and screening the stroke shape, expansion extent, center of gravity, and stroke width factors, a detailed insight into these relationships was established as illustrated in Table 1.

Following the meticulous selection of semantic words and examination of custom font samples from various Chinese companies, a semantic differential method was employed to construct a seven-level semantic scale spanning from –3 to 3 for eight pairs of perceptual words. This scale was then applied to ten font samples, culminating in the formulation of a questionnaire focused on perceptual imagery analysis. The questionnaire, meticulously crafted, was disseminated with the aid of Internet-based survey platforms, specifically leveraging the capabilities of "Questionnaire Star." A total of 42 participants were involved in the assessment process, comprising 15 male and 27 female subjects, among whom 31 possessed insightful font design experience, while the remaining 11 had no prior exposure to font design. The outcomes of the questionnaire were meticulously tabulated and analyzed to derive the perceptual averages of the representative sample set, as detailed in Table 2.

Table 1. Font sensibility word right.

Typeface Emotional Composition	Sensual Imagery Word Pair
stroke width	slim-heavy
	gentle-tough
degree of expansion	compact-loose
	modern-traditional
stroke shape	fancy-rough
	sharp-rounded
center of gravity	funny-formal
	gorgeous-pristine

Table 2. Average value statistics of perceptual evaluation.

SDPW	Label	sp1	sp2	sp3	sp4	sp5	sp6	sp7	sp8	sp9	sp10
slim-heavy	X1	1.1	−1.5	1.24	−0.07	1.98	−1.1	1.02	0.81	0.5	0.55
gentle-tough	Y1	0.07	−0.36	0.88	0.1	−1.07	−0.48	0.81	−0.91	0.6	0.86
compact-loose	X2	0.81	0.62	−0.12	0.55	0.14	0.74	0.33	0.38	0.12	0.48
modern-traditional	Y2	0.1	−0.05	0.57	−0.29	1.12	−0.55	−0.07	−0.07	−0.12	−0.71
fancy-rough	X3	0.02	−0.76	0.12	−0.38	−0.69	−0.93	0.36	−0.14	0.31	0.38
sharp-rounded	Y3	0.43	−0.38	−0.26	0.02	1.52	0.1	−0.26	0.69	−0.12	−0.67
funny-formal	X4	0.24	0.21	0.64	0.67	−0.34	−0.36	0.43	0.21	1.07	−0.38
gorgeous-pristine	Y4	0.74	0.14	−0.12	0.67	−0.1	−0.12	0.38	0.33	0.5	0.17

4 An Imagery Scale Analysis of Custom Fonts for Chinese Enterprises

Upon integrating font samples with pairs of perceptual words for the questionnaire survey, the resulting perceptual imagery values for each font sample were meticulously analyzed. Subsequently, by calculating the average values, an imagery scale diagram illustrating the perceptual characteristics of the font samples was constructed. As illustrated in Table 1, the imagery scale was meticulously formulated based on four key dimensions: stroke width, degree of expansion, center of gravity, and stroke shape.

For each elemental configuration of font design, two pairs of perceptual intention vocabularies were meticulously assigned, each corresponding to either the X-axis or Y-axis within the imagery scale diagram. These vocabularies were strategically positioned at opposite ends of their respective axes. Taking the degree of expansion as an illustration, "compact - loose" was placed along the X-axis, while "modern - traditional" marked the Y-axis. For instance, the coordinates for sample 1 were (0.81, 0.1), effectively plotting the samples onto the imagery scale diagram.

Through this systematic approach, distinct imagery scale graphs were individually plotted, vividly showcasing user emotional preferences for custom fonts [17]. The resulting imagery scale diagrams, represented in Fig. 3, Fig. 4, Fig. 5, and Fig. 6, offer invaluable insights into the emotional requisites of users regarding custom font designs.

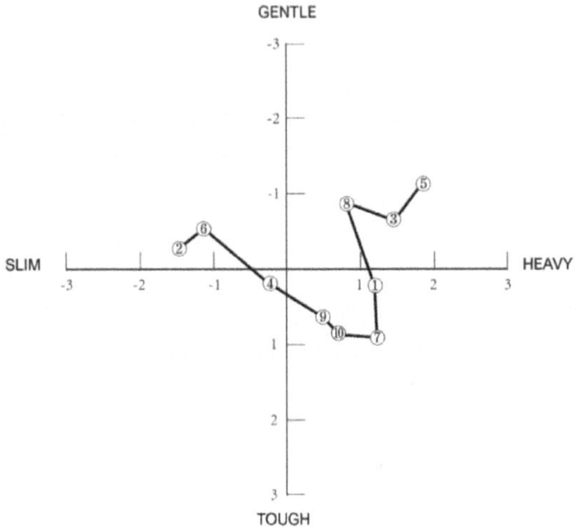

Fig. 3. Stroke width image scale diagram.

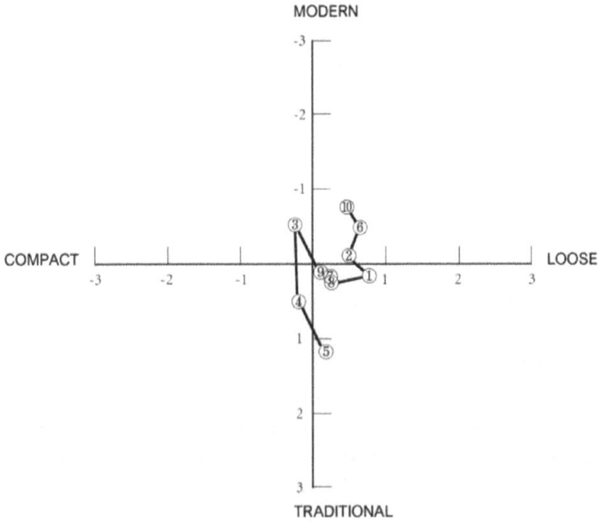

Fig. 4. Degree of expansion image scale diagram.

The analysis of the four imagery scale diagrams for Chinese corporate custom fonts has led to several fundamental conclusions. Firstly, a notable observation from the graphs reveals that stroke width exhibits the most significant variation, resulting in a wide

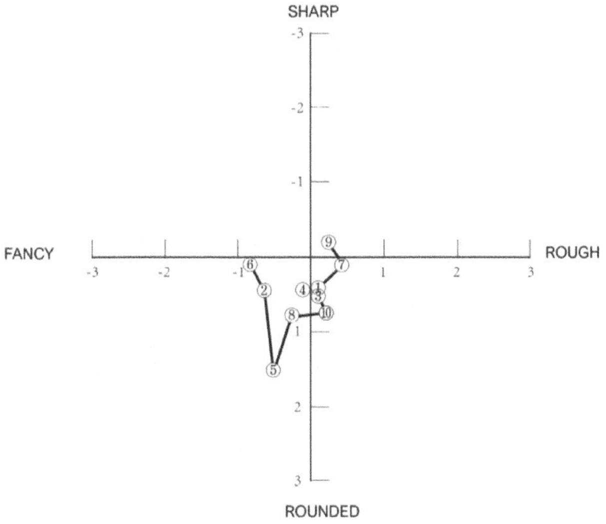

Fig. 5. Stroke shape image scale diagram.

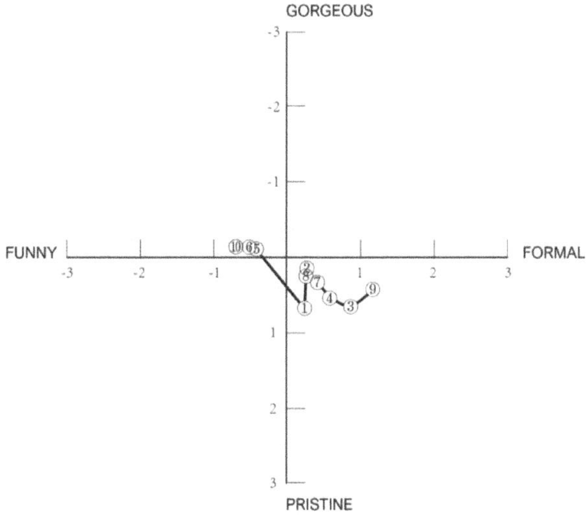

Fig. 6. Center of gravity image scale diagram.

range of emotional fluctuations that effectively delineate the fonts' emotional tendencies. Notably, 7 out of the 10 samples are situated towards the heavy end of the x-axis, indicating that the stroke width prevalent in corporate custom fonts tends to lean towards larger sizes. This characteristic aptly conveys a sense of rigidity and power, resonating with psychological perceptions.

Secondly, the degree of expansion among custom fonts displays minimal variance, as evidenced by the dense clustering of data points on the imagery map. While font designs vary, the perceptual differences in degree of expansion remain negligible, representing merely slight variations within the normal spectrum.

Thirdly, there is a discernible preference for rounded stroke shapes as indicated by the relative emotional inclination towards this form. With 9 out of 10 data samples positioned above the positive axis of the Y-axis, it becomes evident that rounded strokes evoke a friendlier perception, fostering increased affinity and user appeal.

Lastly, concerning the center of gravity within fonts, corporate custom typefaces tend to exude a formal aura. The prevalence of seven sample metrics along the x-axis underscores the fonts' inclination towards a more formal aesthetic. Fonts intended for lengthy textual content prioritize a straightforward, unembellished feel, highlighting users' preference for security and understated sophistication over ostentatious designs.

Based on the insights garnered from the imagery scale diagram, font design elements undergo metamorphosis in accordance with the emotional perceptions delineated. This transformative process leads to the identification of prevalent design traits inherent in Chinese enterprise custom fonts, ultimately culminating in the determination of the collective stylistic orientation characterizing these corporate typefaces. Drawing upon the data presented, it is evident that custom fonts within the corporate category tend towards a modern, eye-catching, simple, rounded, and rustic aesthetic. Notably, the most significant variable influencing the design of corporate fonts is stroke width, a parameter that demands meticulous attention from designers due to its pronounced impact on consumer perception and receptivity. Given consumers' heightened sensitivity to stroke width characteristics, designers must adeptly navigate this aspect to ensure optimal visual appeal and user engagement.

Furthermore, the variation in stroke shape emerges as another pivotal factor shaping consumer acceptance levels towards custom corporate fonts. By strategically manipulating stroke shapes to evoke specific emotional responses, designers can enhance consumer affinity and foster a deeper resonance with their target audience. Conversely, the relative constancy observed in the center of gravity and degree of expansion aspects underscores the importance of adhering to conventional norms and user expectations. By maintaining consistency in these areas, designers can effectively cater to users' preferences while ensuring seamless readability and usability, thereby striking a harmonious balance between innovative design elements and user-centric functionality.

In essence, by aligning design choices with consumer emotional perceptions and focusing on key variables such as stroke width and stroke shape, designers can craft compelling custom corporate fonts that embody a contemporary, visually arresting, and user-friendly aesthetic, catering to the evolving needs and preferences of both enterprises and end-users alike.

5 Enterprise Custom Font Case Study

5.1 Changan Automobile Brand Positioning

Take the gravity typeface launched by Changan Automobile as an example [18], see Fig. 7. To adapt to the arrival of the intelligent era, Changan Automobile has adjusted its brand concept to the fusion of science and technology and nature and provides a brand-new experience of a new way of travelling through new technologies such as "intelligence and science and technology". Under the concept of new technology and intelligent aesthetics, users will re-conceptualize the brand of Changan Automobile.

Fig. 7. Changan automobile custom font.

5.2 Emotional Imagery of Changan Automobile Custom Fonts

Changan custom font uses three stroke width variations, including regular, light, and bold. Sans-serif is used as the base font to represent modernity and technological sensibilities. As a long text font, Sans-serif font is heavier than serif font, and custom font retains the basic visual characteristics of its font weight based on sans-serif font. In addition, the smaller variable interval for the three levels of weight means that each level is heavier than fonts with multiple levels of width.

The new font adopts the treatment of starting straight strokes and folding curved strokes to reflect the feeling of writing. In addition to the commonly used horizontal and folding strokes at the corners, the strokes are also processed with continuous strokes, and the curved at the continuous strokes are also carried out to ensure the overall temperature and affinity. The design treatment of "left straight and right arc" makes the abstract concept of "science and technology" and "care" have a concrete visual embodiment, so that the font has both a sense of science and technology and a humanistic atmosphere, and at the same time, it also has a significant memory point [19].

Gravity typeface adopts a formal design, with horizontal and vertical strokes, vertical and uniform axes, and consistent direction, giving a comfortable sense of order and reflecting the perception of formality. The center of gravity is slightly upward and smooth, appearing upright and energetic, with a smooth and comfortable visual perception, giving people a sense of youth without losing stability, which is in line with the aesthetic pursuit of Changan Automobile's user group. The degree of expansion is enlarged and slightly flattened, reflecting modernity with flattened qualities, and adapting to the visual requirements of screen display.

5.3 An Evaluation of the Emotional Imagery

The emotional imagery of the Changan custom font was redesigned for the questionnaire. It still unfolds the four dimensions of the font's word weight, middle court, stroke shape and center of gravity, and uses the four previous terms to rate them separately. The seven-step rating method of Likert scale was used, which was set as very dissatisfied, dissatisfied, relatively dissatisfied, average, satisfied, and very satisfied. Corresponding scores –3, –2, –1, 0, 1, 2, 3. 71 questionnaires were issued, and the scores of the fonts in each emotional word were counted, see Table 3. Its comprehensive rating score is 2.13. The above data can prove that the main emotional performance of the current enterprise custom font is concentrated in the two aspects of the stroke width and the stroke shape, which confirms the experimental results of the previous section.

Table 3. Font image word score.

Dimension	Stroke Width	Degree of Expansion	Stroke Shape	Center of Gravity
word	heavy	modern	rounded	formal
score	2.1	2.5	2.4	1.5

The Chinese character font is divided into four basic categories, Hei, Song, FangSong, and Kai. They correspond to different emotional vocabularies, Song - historical, Hei - modern, Kai - traditional, and FangSong - humanistic. Enterprises can choose different types of fonts according to their brand attributes, and then integrate them into their brand concepts to form visual emotional imagery. Changan custom font is positioned as a new energy technology, so it chooses Hei(sans-serif) to represent science and technology as the basic typeface, and then integrates the concept of modern fashion, and the stroke shape adopts the characteristics of horizontal thin and vertical thick Song font stroke shape, which highlights the humanistic care appeal. Therefore, modern enterprise custom fonts can be considered from the above aspects.

6 Conclusion

6.1 Custom Fonts Can Determine the Attributes of Chinese Companies

Chinese enterprises' custom fonts can be visually classified into two main categories:

1. Sans-serif Fonts for Internet and Industrial Companies: Entities on the internet and automotive sectors, such as Changan Automobile, BYD, Huawei, Xiaomi, and other technology-focused industries, predominantly opt for sans-serif fonts. These fonts embody a modern, technological aesthetic, aligning with the forward-thinking and innovative nature of these enterprises. Sans-serif fonts are chosen to convey a sense of modernity, sophistication, and emotional engagement with consumers.

2. Serif Fonts for Consumer-Oriented Enterprises: Consumer-centric enterprises like Coca-Cola China and Doushen towards serif fonts for their custom typography. The selection of serif fonts reflects the rich heritage and humanistic values associated with these brands. These fonts evoke a sense of tradition, reliability, and care towards consumers, resonating with the emotional aspects of their brand identities.

The exposure of consumers to enterprise custom fonts is often intertwined with the core products of the company. The immediate psychological impression evoked by the outer appearance of the product plays a pivotal role in determining the design of enterprise custom fonts. It is imperative that the font choices harmonize with consumers' psychology, ensuring a seamless connection between the brand's visual representation and consumer perceptions. In essence, the emotional resonance and overall perception of Chinese character design should be rooted in the general psychological inclinations of consumers. By aligning custom font designs with consumer expectations and emotional responses, enterprises can cultivate stronger brand connections and foster meaningful engagements with their target audience, mirroring the essence of their offerings and the core values they seek to communicate.

In the current landscape of enterprise custom fonts in China, the predominant focus lies on globally recognized companies, notably Fortune 500 corporations or cultural entities affiliated with government backgrounds. This emphasis primarily stems from the fact that many local companies, particularly small and medium-sized enterprises (SMEs), have shown limited interest or investment in this specialized design service. The primary barrier hindering the participation of SMEs in custom font design services is the intricate nature of Chinese character fonts, which necessitate meticulous completion for approximately 7,000 characters. This extensive requirement translates to significant time commitments and elevated labor costs, thereby constraining SMEs' ability to compete effectively in this domain. In contrast, multinational enterprises, aiming to expand across diverse countries, regions, and industries, are compelled to engage in custom font design services as part of their global branding strategies. Consequently, corporate custom fonts have emerged as a discernible indicator for evaluating the scale and stature of a company. By investing in bespoke font designs that encapsulate their brand identity and resonate with international audiences, multinational corporations can reinforce their market presence, foster cross-cultural connections, and establish a distinct visual identity that transcends linguistic boundaries. As the significance of custom font design continues to grow in the corporate sphere, enterprises—both domestic and international—are recognizing the pivotal role that tailored typography plays in enhancing brand recognition, consumer engagement, and overall competitiveness in an increasingly globalized marketplace.

6.2 Custom Fonts Are Visually Identical

In the contemporary era of rapid development in China, the Internet plays a pivotal role in consumer lifestyles, with mobile internet devices serving as the primary medium for enterprises to engage with consumers. When designing custom fonts for Chinese enterprises, it is imperative to consider the screen presentation on mobile terminals, given the prevalence of self-illuminated media displayed in a pixelated format. With small screen sizes and limitations in displaying curves and angles effectively, fonts featuring visually straight lines are favored for optimal visibility and clarity.

Analysis of sample data reveals that despite varying consumer aesthetic preferences across industries, the predominant choice for most Chinese companies aligns with sans-serif fonts. Among the samples examined, 8 out of 10 feature sans-serif fonts, while 1 employs a serif font and another utilizes a handwritten font. Serif fonts are strategically employed to soften stroke variations at the beginning and end of characters, enhancing visual cohesion and readability within non-serif designs.

It is important to acknowledge that technical constraints currently influence the differentiation of custom fonts among Chinese enterprises, resulting in limited visual distinctiveness that may challenge consumers in quickly identifying brands based on typography alone. As electronic display technology advances and monitor resolutions approach paper-like clarity, it is anticipated that more serif fonts will emerge in Chinese custom font designs. Serif fonts, aligning more closely with traditional Chinese character writing styles and promoting enhanced reading experiences over extended periods, are poised to gain prominence as display technologies evolve.

As the convergence of digital and print-like display quality progresses, Chinese enterprises are likely to explore a broader spectrum of font choices, infusing their custom typography with a blend of modern sans-serif designs and classic serif aesthetics to optimize visual appeal, readability, and user engagement across diverse media platforms.

6.3 Custom Fonts Need Emotional

Enterprise custom fonts play a pivotal role as an extension of corporate brand concepts, embodying the principles of value-based co-creation services and serving as a vital conduit for user-perceived value. They facilitate the establishment of enduring visual connections between users and brands, fostering a sustainable brand image that resonates with consumers and embodies distinct personality elements for brand differentiation.

By delving into users' emotional imagery requirements and comprehensively grasping consumers' psychological preferences towards enterprise custom fonts, designers can leverage four core font design elements and employ quantitative research methodologies to derive fundamental style characteristics specific to custom font designs. Utilizing tools such as imagery scale diagrams aids in externalizing tacit knowledge related to perceptual factor cognition, empowering designers to craft bespoke font solutions that align with user expectations and emotional perceptions. Abstract concepts find tangible expression through mediums that permeate daily life, with custom fonts emerging as a potent vehicle for frequent interactions and heightened brand visibility. While the custom font landscape in China is still evolving, it is poised for rapid growth alongside the expanding footprint of Chinese enterprises. Emotional imagery considerations represent just one facet of the multifaceted design process for custom fonts; Chinese brands must continually enhance the depth and quality of their brand services to establish a competitive edge and fortify their brand positioning over time.

As Chinese enterprises navigate the realm of custom font design, they must remain attuned to evolving consumer preferences, elevate the symbolic richness of their brand offerings, and perpetually refine their brand services to solidify their market presence and carve out enduring brand advantages amidst a dynamic and competitive business landscape.

References

1. Yue, J., Zhan, F., Wu, Q.: Brand strength mold based on the consumers mental resources development. J. China Ind. Econ. **3**, 88–95 (2007)
2. Hu, F., Li, W.: Definition of service design. J. Packag. Eng. **3**, 37–50 (2019)
3. Geng, X., Huang, B., Wei, S.: The logic explanation of system philosophy on brand formation. J. J. Syst. Sci. **2**, 86−91(2023)
4. Li, M., An, G.: A brief analysis of the relationship between customer perceived value and perceived quality, brand image and customer experience. J. Prod. Res. **22**,149−150, 165 (2008)
5. Zhao, F.: An analysis of copyright ability and protection mode of fonts in the view of publishing. J. Publishing Res. **3**, 72–80 (2022)
6. An, X., Wang, J.: Application of customized font in enterprise image design. J. Packag. Eng. **12**, 124–128 (2019)
7. Chen, X.: Research on Customized Font in Urban Brand Image. Beijing Institute of Fashion Technology (2020)
8. Wang, Y.: Research on Brand Custom Typeface Design of Inner Mongolia. Inner Mongolia Normal University, Hohhot, Hohhot (2020)
9. Pan, J.: Research on rural custom font design methods under the background of cultural revitalization - taking "Sheng-shi font" as an example. J. Chutzpah. **4**, 24–31 (2021)
10. Yue, H.: The modeling of Chinese Heiti font Research. Chinese National Academy of Arts, Beijing (2020)
11. Sheng, H., Feng, L.: Research on the structure and emotional design of chinese character fonts'. Design. **7**, 122–125 (2019)
12. Ouyang, J., Gao, X., Zhang, S., Wang, X., Zhou, A.: Relationship model between chinese character font stroke shape and emotional image. J. J. Graph. **12**, 348–355 (2021)
13. Ouyang, J., Sheng, H., Zhou, A., Su, J., Zhang, S.: Multi-image prediction model based on cognitive computing of chinese font structure. J. J. Graph. **10**, 945–952 (2019)
14. Zhang, S.: Research and Application of Emotional Imageries of Typefaces Based on Kansei Engineering. Beijing University of Posts and Telecommunication, Beijing (2019)
15. Gao, S.: Research on Emotional Expression of Fonts in Visual Communication Design. Jilin university, Changchun (2021)
16. Zhou, Z., Cheng, J., Zhang, X.: Application of kansei engineering in nursing beds design. J. Packag. Eng. **6**, 102–105 (2016)
17. Huang, L., He, C., Fang, F., Li, M.: Form design of heavy truck based on image scale. J. Packag. Eng. **12**, 11–16 (2016)
18. Founder Type: Changan Automobile new brand custom font - Changan Gravity. https://www.foundertype.com/index.php/FontofMade/caseDetail/id/33.html. Accessed 26 Sept 2020
19. Gao, Y., Ma, D., Qian, H., Zhi, W.: Design of a series of cultural and creative products based on gestalt principle. J. Packag. Eng. **6**, 115–122 (2020)

Designing Warmth: Enhancing School Belonging and Identity Through Student-Generated Photographic Content

Jie Ling[1], Li Li[1], and Li Ou Yang[2](✉)

[1] Zhongkai University of Agriculture and Engineering, Guangdong 510220, China
[2] The Guangzhou Academy of Fine Arts, Guangdong 510261, China
oylee@163.com

Abstract. This study explores the role of user-generated content in enhancing emotional connections and feelings of belonging within educational settings, focusing on participatory photography at a 2024 province-wide school-themed photography event in Guangdong. Students and teachers from various educational levels participated, and the analysis involved both descriptive and quantitative methods to assess how elements like human figures, environments, and color temperatures influence emotional expression and ambiance in photographs. An experiment with thirty students, split into two groups, evaluated the impact of training in photographic techniques on capturing emotionally resonant scenes. The findings highlight that participatory photography not only boosts students' expressive skills but also enriches their social media engagement and community integration within schools. By effectively using user-generated content, this approach promotes social learning and a supportive community atmosphere, suggesting that it can significantly enhance educational practices and students' mental health. Future research is encouraged to adapt these strategies across diverse educational and cultural contexts.

Keywords: User-Generated Content · Educational Design · Emotional Expression · Community Engagement · Photography Techniques

1 Introduction

The university phase is a critical period for student socialization, where learning shifts from passive reception to active exploration. Students often face a variety of psychological challenges as they adapt to new environments and social relationships, with coping mechanisms varying by grade and gender [1]. To alleviate stress, universities encourage students to participate in clubs and sports activities [2], fostering better integration into campus culture. With the widespread adoption of 5G networks, mobile photography and video recording have become integral to students' daily lives, often sharing their lives on social media, which aids in a more direct understanding of their psychological states [3].

C. Stephanidis et al. (Eds.): HCII 2024, CCIS 2319, pp. 86–96, 2025.
https://doi.org/10.1007/978-3-031-78516-0_8

This study leverages the provincial campus-themed photography event organized by universities in Guangdong in 2024 to explore how participatory photography can enhance students' sense of belonging and identity on campus. Through descriptive and quantitative analysis of the visual elements (such as characters, environment, lighting, and color) of the award-winning works, this study assesses their role in expressing emotions and atmosphere. Participatory photography activities not only transform students from passive observers to active creators of content but also promote emotional connection and national pride through artistic expression, which is crucial for enhancing students' psychological health and academic performance.

The study designed experiments to assess the impact of professional photography guidance on students' ability to express emotions, further understanding how this type of training can deepen students' sense of campus belonging and identity. The students' works were not only displayed on campus social media and public areas, accompanied by personal narratives, significantly enhancing community engagement and expressive power. These activities have been observed to greatly enhance empathy and community dialogue among students, fostering an inclusive and emotionally supportive campus atmosphere.

With the popularity of social media, student-generated photographic content has become a part of campus culture. This study explores how this content can effectively enhance students' sense of belonging and identity. By systematically employing participatory photography, this research aims to provide insights for educational practices, potentially shaping educational policies and being adopted by other educational institutions to enhance student experiences. These findings are expected to have a profound impact on the formulation of global educational policies.

2 Literature Review

2.1 Related Research on Participatory Photography

Participatory photography initially involved providing cameras to the public to capture images of their interests or concerns. This method has been particularly beneficial for giving a voice to socially disadvantaged groups [4] or immigrants [5], later expanding to include tourist engagement with travel destinations [6] and community literacy education [7]. Besides acting as photographers, participants like those in JR's "INSIDE OUT" project have also been subjects [8], significantly enhancing their sense of identity through participation. Although research on participatory photography includes both short-term and long-term assessments, the results are somewhat unpredictable due to uncontrollable factors. As a catalyst and tool, participatory photography plays a crucial but uncertain role in enhancing critical awareness. This uncertainty arises because its effects are influenced by context, conditions, and participant initiative, which can vary. Nevertheless, its importance cannot be overlooked; as a tool for fostering critical consciousness and self-awareness, the impact of participatory photography may persist for decades, profoundly affecting people's perceptions and behaviors [9]. Byrne et al. (2016) highlighted that while participatory photography empowers participants [10], the photographs produced are often undervalued or not further utilized, suggesting that the research and practice of participatory photography still need deeper exploration.

2.2 Factors Affecting Sense of Belonging and Identity

Belonging and identity are key factors affecting an individual's social and psychological functions, involving interactions with their reference groups. Mahar et al. (2013) define belonging as a subjective sense of value and respect stemming from a reciprocal relationship with a reference group, which typically comprises communities or environments that individuals choose and aspire to be part of. This sense of belonging, rooted in shared experiences, beliefs, or personal characteristics, may be facilitated or hindered by the complex interplay between environmental and personal factors [11]. St-Amand et al. (2017) further refine the definition of belonging, identifying four critical elements: positive emotional experiences, maintaining good relationships with peers and teachers, personal enthusiasm for participating in group activities, and the ability to adapt behavior to group needs when necessary [12]. Voelkl (1997) emphasized that classroom participation and academic achievements significantly influence students' sense of school identity, noting these as key to building such identity [13]. Ang et al. (2019) found that the sense of purpose in university education, adaptability, curriculum and teaching cognition, and the availability of online technology are positively correlated with students' identity, indicating that enhancing students' sense of purpose, improving their adaptability to educational environments, enhancing teaching quality, and providing advanced online learning tools are necessary to foster a positive student identity [14]. These studies collectively highlight the critical role of belonging and identity within educational and social contexts, revealing that nurturing these feelings through comprehensive support and environmental optimization is crucial. Organizing theme-centered group activities can significantly enhance students' sense of purpose and teamwork skills. Furthermore, establishing related theme workshops not only strengthens interactions between teachers and students but also helps enhance students' sense of belonging and identity with the school. Such activities not only promote students' social skills but also deepen their overall engagement and satisfaction with the educational environment.

2.3 Research on Student Participation in Campus Photography

Li and others (2020) suggest that university photography competitions are beneficial for cultivating students' holistic qualities including moral, intellectual, physical, aesthetic, and labor skills. These competitions serve as platforms where students can showcase their talents and acquire knowledge that is not typically taught in classrooms [15]. In such events, students are more interested and motivated to learn about photography and traditional culture. Existing research indicates that participating in campus photography enhances students' sense of belonging and identity. Through photography, students can express their perceptions and emotions about the campus environment, sharing their stories and experiences. This form of self-expression and sharing strengthens their connection to the campus community, enhancing their participation and satisfaction.

Furthermore, participating in campus photography acts as an educational tool, helping students develop various skills including aesthetic appreciation, critical thinking, and social responsibility. For example, the Guangdong Education Department's "My Country, My Dream" Most Beautiful Campus Photography Contest invites students from all educational levels across the province to capture campus scenes. This initiative showcases how students express their love for the campus and their personal aspirations through photography, encouraging them to explore and document beautiful moments in campus life while conveying positive values. The competition not only provides a platform for students to display their photography skills but also inspires them to identify with campus culture and reflect on their roles in society.

Students' motivation to participate may include personal interest, a sense of belonging to the campus, and the desire to win awards. By participating in the photography contest, students not only improve their photography skills but also use their cameras to express their affiliation and emotions towards the school. This involvement and method of expression play a crucial role in enhancing students' emotional warmth and sense of belonging. Additionally, the personal narratives displayed alongside the photographs add dynamic stories to the static images, allowing viewers to understand the emotions and experiences behind the photos more deeply. Sharing these narratives helps build empathy among students, deepening their understanding and respect for each other's experiences.

3 Research Methods

3.1 Research Design

This study employs a mixed-methods research design, combining quantitative and qualitative approaches to comprehensively assess how participatory photography activities enhance students' sense of belonging and identity. By integrating experiments and case studies, the research aims to explore how students express their perceptions and emotions about campus life through photography and analyze how this expression influences their social interactions and community involvement.

Case Study. The study further examines the award-winning works from the 2024 Guangdong Province campus-themed photography event. Using content analysis, the research team evaluated the key visual elements (such as characters, environment, lighting, and atmosphere) in these works and how these elements collaboratively contribute to emotional expression and community building. Additionally, tools like Photoshop and Excel were used to perform quantitative color analysis to investigate how variations in color temperature affect the accuracy of emotional expression and the conveyance of ambiance.

Experimental Design. To gain a deeper understanding of the specific impact of photography techniques on students' modes of expression, a controlled experiment was designed. In the experiment, 30 students were randomly assigned to two groups. The first group, consisting of 15 students, undertook shooting tasks without any prior photography training, while the second group of 15 students received systematic training on photographic content and color expression. Both groups were instructed to use digital devices to capture "warm" scenes around the campus, such as interactions between people and nature, sunny atmospheres, animal interactions, and campus landscapes. The photographs taken were then used on school social media, displayed in public areas of the campus, and accompanied by personal narratives from the students, facilitating community dialogue and interaction within the campus.

Qualitative Assessment. Through semi-structured interviews, this study randomly selected 20 teachers and students involved in the photography activities to assess the significance and effects of the photographs in social dissemination. This participatory approach not only enhanced the students' expressive abilities but also strengthened their contributions to the school's social media landscape, thus deepening the sense of involvement and empathy among students. The analysis of interviews and social feedback data demonstrated that participatory photography, as a form of user-generated content, is an effective tool for promoting social learning and strengthening emotional connections.

This comprehensive research methodology allows for the exploration from multiple perspectives of how students use participatory photography activities to express and strengthen their sense of belonging and identity to the school, as well as how these activities help foster an inclusive and emotionally supportive community atmosphere.

3.2 Data Collection

Case Data Collection. Case data collection forms the foundation of this study, involving the acquisition of award-winning pieces from the 2024 Guangdong Province campus-themed photography event. To ensure the relevance and diversity of the data, the following steps were undertaken for case data collection: First, a detailed descriptive analysis was conducted for each awarded work, documenting key visual elements such as characters, environment, lighting, and atmosphere, while noting the emotions and messages conveyed by the works. Subsequently, all collected works and their descriptive information were digitally archived to facilitate further analysis and retrieval.

Collection of Student Photographic Works. The collection of student photographic works was divided into two directions: one group took photographs autonomously without any guidance, and another group did so after receiving training on photographic content and color expression. For the guided group, standards for collecting case data were established, including the theme, creativity, technical quality, and depth of emotional expression of the works. These standards aimed to filter out photographs that broadly and deeply represent students' perceptions of campus life. Selected works were categorized by theme and content, and basic information about each piece, including title, author, location and time of shooting, and the equipment and techniques used, was recorded.

Interview Data Collection. Interview data were collected using a semi-structured format, where 20 students were randomly selected for in-depth discussions. The interview content revolved around the creation process of the photographic works, their personal significance, social impact, and experiences of belonging and identity.

3.3 Data Analysis

Descriptive Analysis. For photographic works, descriptive analysis included categorizing and documenting the visual elements (such as characters, environment, lighting, composition) and thematic content of the works. Additionally, basic information about each piece, including the author, location and time of shooting, and the equipment and techniques used, was recorded.

Color Quantitative Analysis. Color quantitative analysis, a distinctive feature of this study, involved extracting and quantifying the colors in the photographic works using Photoshop and Excel tools. Initially, digital images of each work were opened in Photoshop, and the main colors were extracted using the stained glass filter from the filter library. These color data were then input into Excel for further quantitative analysis. The aim of the color quantitative analysis was to explore how variations in color temperature affect the accuracy of emotional expression and the conveyance of ambiance.

Interview Data Analysis. Firstly, the interview recordings were transcribed into text, followed by data cleansing to remove content irrelevant to the research. Qualitative analysis software was then used to code and analyze the themes in the transcribed texts. The results of the semi-structured interview data analysis were used to gain deeper insights into how students express emotions and build community through photography, and how these processes impact their sense of belonging and identity.

3.4 Ethical Considerations

During the research process, the research team strictly adhered to relevant ethical guidelines. All students participating in interviews and experiments were informed in advance about the purpose, process, and potential risks of the research and voluntarily signed consent forms. The research team also ensured the privacy and confidentiality of all collected data, and all publicly displayed photographic works were done so with the authors' consent.

4 Data Analysis and Discussion

4.1 Case Data Analysis

The collection of case data involved selecting award-winning works from the 2024 Guangdong Province campus-themed photography event. A total of 30 winning photographs were collected, all taken by students, covering various aspects of campus life.

The case analysis revealed the impact of the depiction of characters and settings in photographic works on students' emotional expression. Color analysis indicated that works in warm tones (such as red, orange, and yellow) tend to convey warmth, comfort, and positivity, closely associated with interpersonal interactions and social activities on campus. Conversely, works in cool tones (such as blue and green) are generally linked to tranquility, contemplation, and natural landscapes, reflecting students' appreciation of the campus's natural environment (Table 1).

4.2 Analysis of Student-Photographed Works

Beauty is all around us, omnipresent. A truly aesthetic photographic work, capable of embodying beauty, requires more than just advanced photography skills; it also necessitates an eye for discovering beauty. Therefore, the photographic works were scientifically

Table 1. Award-Winning Works Color Analysis

Award Placement	Photograph	Color Analysis
First Prize	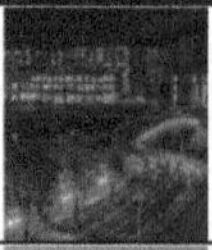	
Second Prize		
Third Prize		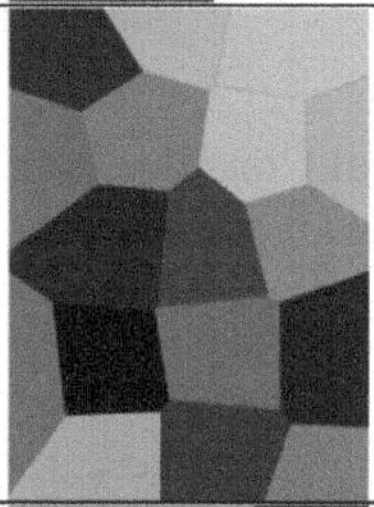
Popular Choice Award		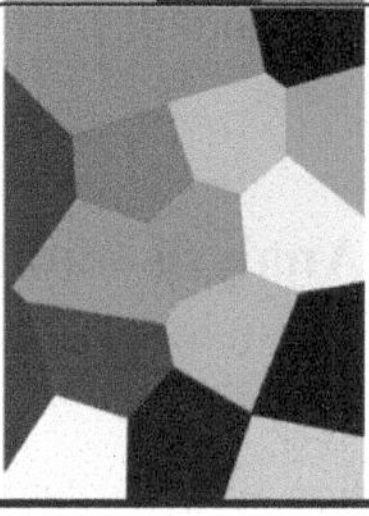

guided in terms of framing, composition, the modeling of picture elements, color, and creativity. The experimental group, which consisted of 15 students who received photography training, submitted a total of 15 photographic works. The control group, comprising 15 students who photographed autonomously, also submitted 15 works. Analysis of the photos taken by the students showed that the control group's subjects included cats, landscapes, or specific scenes within the campus, with generally broad thematic content. In contrast, the works from the experimental group were richer and more precise in theme, composition, color usage, and emotional expression (Fig. 1).

4.3 Interview Analysis

Through semi-structured interviews with 20 students, this study delved into how students experience and express their campus life through participatory photography, and how

Fig. 1. Left: Photographs taken by the experimental group (n = 15), Right: Photographs taken by the control group (n = 15)

these activities affect their sense of belonging and identity. The qualitative data analysis based on student feedback from the interviews revealed the following themes:

Theme 1: Photography as a Tool for Exploration and Connection. Most students expressed that photography allowed them to discover previously unnoticed beautiful scenes on campus with new perspectives (Student 1, Student 11). Additionally, the photography activities provided a platform for them to explore the campus's natural settings (Student 5, Student 17) and culture (Student 12, Student 19), thereby deepening their identification with and respect for the campus environment. Experiences shared by Student 8 and Student 20 specifically highlighted photography as a medium that enhances social interaction and personal storytelling, which in turn strengthened their sense of community belonging.

Theme 2: Enhancement of Technical and Expressive Skills. Many participants mentioned that participating in photography training helped improve their technical skills, especially in lighting and composition (Student 3, Student 14), enabling them to more effectively express their thoughts and emotions. Student 10 and Student 16 emphasized the role of color and light in conveying emotions and aesthetics, illustrating how technical advancements aid in better visual storytelling.

Theme 3: Photography and Personal and Community Identity. Photography served not only as a means of personal expression but also as a vital tool for establishing and deepening a sense of community identity. For example, Student 4 and Student 18 captured interpersonal relationships and landscape design on campus, showcasing their understanding of aesthetics and their commitment to creating a positive campus environment. Feedback from Student 7 and Student 9 highlighted their experiences of feeling more integrated into the community through sharing their photographs on social media.

Theme 4: Photography as a Means of Philosophical and Cultural Exploration. Some students used photography to explore deeper philosophical and cultural themes (Student 15, Student 13). They utilized photography to delve into existential and perception issues or to reflect on their personal roles and positions within society by capturing details of everyday life.

Summary. The interview data demonstrated that participatory photography significantly enriched students' campus life experiences. Through technical training and creative expression, not only were students' personal skills enhanced, but their sense of belonging and identity within the campus community was also deepened. This educational practice, facilitated through visual arts, proved effective in promoting students' emotional, social, and cultural identities.

5 Conclusion

5.1 Summary of Key Findings and Their Significance

This study, through the 2024 Guangdong Provincial Campus Photography Event, delved deeply into the role of user-generated content in educational settings, particularly its potential to enhance students' sense of belonging and identity at school. Students in the experimental group, who received training on photographic content and color expression, showed significantly better outcomes in social communication and impact compared to the unguided control group. Through experiments and semi-structured interviews, the study found that participatory photography not only enhanced students' expressive capabilities but also significantly increased their contributions to the school's social media landscape, thereby deepening their engagement and empathy with each other. This indicates that strategic use of student-generated content can effectively enhance students' psychological well-being and advance the educational environment.

5.2 Summary and Outlook on Methods and Strategies for Designing Warmth

Our findings underscore the importance of color and atmosphere in design and the potential of photography in establishing identity. Here is a summary and outlook on methods and strategies for designing warmth:

Use of Color. Quantitative analysis revealed that variations in color temperature are crucial for accurately conveying emotions and ambiance. Future designs should consider color psychology to enhance emotional connections.

Creating Environments. Elements such as human interaction with nature and sunny atmospheres shown in photographic works play a key role in creating a warm campus environment. Schools should encourage students to explore and document these elements to enhance a sense of campus belonging.

Integration of Narratives. The combination of students' personal narratives with photographic works provides rich content for community dialogue. Future educational designs should value the power of storytelling to enhance student engagement and empathy through narrative.

Cultural Adaptability. Future research should explore how to adapt these strategies to different cultural and educational backgrounds to maximize their benefits.

5.3 Limitations and Future Outlook

Despite the positive outcomes, this study has limitations, such as a relatively small sample size focused on educational institutions in Guangdong Province. Future research should expand the sample to include students from different regions and cultural backgrounds to verify the universality of the findings.

Additionally, while this study focused on the role of photographic techniques in enhancing belonging and identity, the impact of other forms of user-generated content, such as videos, audio, or text, has not been fully explored. Future studies could explore the potential of these different content forms and how they collectively contribute to emotional and community building in educational settings. This research provides new perspectives and tools for the fields of social computing and educational design to promote students' emotional development and community building. We hope these findings inspire more educational practices and contribute to creating more inclusive and supportive learning environments.

Acknowledgments. This study was supported by several projects:the Provincial-Level Top-Tier Offline Course (KA24YY044,6040324137), the 2024 Guangdong Provincial Graduate Education Innovation Plan (2024SFKC_054), the New Agricultural Science Teaching Research and Reform Practice Project at Zhongkai University of Agriculture and Engineering (PX-44231059), and the Design Fundamentals Virtual Teaching and Research Office (ZG20230011).Their generous support greatly facilitated the research.

Disclosure of Interests. The authors have no competing interests to declare that are relevant to the content of this article.

References

1. Zhang, L., Che, W., Li, B.: Research on the characteristics of college students' psychological stress coping styles. J. Psychol. Sci. 36–41 (2005). https://doi.org/10.16719/j.cnki.1671-6981.2005.01.009
2. Du, X., Zhang, L.: Experimental study on the impact of yoga fitness techniques on physical functional quality and mental health level of college students. J. Capital Univ. Phys. Educ. Sports. 100–101 (2005)
3. Li, G., Zhu, H.: Why did Moments arise: a study on college students' WeChat self-presentation strategies and influencing factors from a social psychological perspective. Shanghai Journalism Rev. 25–35 (2019). https://doi.org/10.16057/j.cnki.31-1171/g2.2019.05.003
4. Clover, D.E.: Out of the dark room: participatory photography as a critical, imaginative, and public aesthetic practice of transformative education. J. Transform. Educ. **4**, 275–290 (2006). https://doi.org/10.1177/1541344606287782
5. Gomez, R., Vannini, S.: Notions of home and sense of belonging in the context of migration in a journey through participatory photography. E J. Info. Sys. Dev Countries. **78**, 1–46 (2017). https://doi.org/10.1002/j.1681-4835.2017.tb00569.x
6. Barry, K.: Unsettling the aesthetics of air travel through participatory tourist photography. Tourist Studies

7. Prins, E.: Participatory photography: a tool for empowerment or surveillance? Action Res. **8**, 426–443 (2010). https://doi.org/10.1177/1476750310374502
8. Inside Out Project. https://www.insideoutproject.net/en/. Accessed 07 June 2024
9. Fairey, T.: These photos were my life : understanding the impact of participatory photography projects. Community Dev. J. **53**, 618–636 (2018). https://doi.org/10.1093/cdj/bsx010
10. Byrne, E., Daykin, N., Coad, J.: Participatory photography in qualitative research: a methodological review **4** (2016)
11. Mahar, A.L., Cobigo, V., Stuart, H.: Conceptualizing belonging. Disabil. Rehabil. **35**, 1026–1032 (2013). https://doi.org/10.3109/09638288.2012.717584
12. St-Amand, J., Girard, S., Smith, J.: Sense of belonging at school: defining attributes, determinants, and sustaining strategies. IAFOR J. Educ. **5** (2017). https://doi.org/10.22492/ije.5.2.05
13. Voelkl, K.E.: Identification with school. Am. J. Educ. **105**, 294–318 (1997). https://doi.org/10.1086/444158
14. Ang, C.-S., Lee, K.-F., Dipolog-Ubanan, G.F.: Determinants of first-year student identity and satisfaction in higher education: a quantitative case study. SAGE Open **9**, 215824401984668 (2019). https://doi.org/10.1177/2158244019846689
15. Li, J., Su, J., Sun, Z., Li, X.: Research on the educational function of college photography competition from the perspective of comprehensive education. Guide Sci. Educ. 65–67 (2020). https://doi.org/10.16400/j.cnki.kjdkz.2020.04.031

A Help System for Optimizing Complex Ordering Configurations Based on Cognitive Decision Model

Yuanyuan Liu(✉) and Ying Xia

China Mobile (Suzhou) Software Technology Co., Ltd, Jiangsu, China
liuyuanyuan2@cmss.chinamobile.com

Abstract. The order page configuration items of the cloud computing platform are numerous and complex, and a perfect help system can reduce the difficulty of user to understand and operate the configuration, otherwise, the cloud purchase processes would be blocked, or even abandoned. Therefore, the effectiveness of the help system is crucial to user experience and the commercial value of cloud products. The purpose of this study is to guide the optimization of the order page help system through the investigation based on cognitive decision model. This paper is divided into three parts. First, the functional characteristics and corresponding design components of different help systems are analyzed. Next, based on the definition and composition of the cognitive decision model, a mapping relationship is formed with the help process of users. Finally, by comparing availability data indicators before and after optimization, it is verified that the optimized help system improves the self-help rate, task completion rate and satisfaction.

Keywords: Cloud computing platform · Help system · Cognitive decision system · Self-help rate

1 Introduction

The cloud computing platform has rich functions, including instances, images, system disks, networks, and other functions. Its ordering page has more than 15 major configuration items, which means the page is filled with many professional terms. Therefore, the effectiveness of the help system determines the success rate of ordering.

At present, the product ordering page, the help system is incomplete, the number of help tips is small, and the help form is single. In the recent experience evaluation process, more than half of the evaluation officers reported that the product ordering experience was poor, they could not complete the order independently, and they needed to spend a lot of extra time researching and analyzing the use of a certain function or configuration; At the same time, in the product use stage, do not understand the function, repeated mistakes make their experience of product use decline.

Therefore, product designers optimize the help system of product ordering page based on the user's cognitive decision-making psychology, and at the same time, usability testing verifies the optimization effect.

C. Stephanidis et al. (Eds.): HCII 2024, CCIS 2319, pp. 97–101, 2025.
https://doi.org/10.1007/978-3-031-78516-0_9

2 Help System Component Analysis

The methods of help system for complex pages are diversified. Common help methods include help document, manual customer service and embedded help, etc. The help document usually provides detailed information and is suitable for in-depth learning by users. Human customer service provides users with immediate interaction; Embedded tips usually offer help proactively. According to the function of components, the common design components in interface design are counted.

Overview Function. Assist users to roughly understand new pages or new functions, and actively provide information to give users an overall understanding of the system. Design components include modal popup, tour guide, announcement popup, help document, etc.

Query Function. Users can search information independently and help solve problems. The design components include help documents, artificial customer service and intelligent customer service.

Operation Aid Function. The page actively provides prompts or instructions in the nearby area of the operation to avoid user mistakes or reduce user decision-making pressure and provides corresponding feedback according to user operations to correct user operations. The design components include step bar, embedded help prompt, exclusive boot, intelligent customer service, etc.

3 Application of Cognitive Decision Model

User help-seeking behavior includes fact finding, process finding, decision support, system discovery [1]. The cognitive processing is driven by a cycle of five phases - inputting, proposing, deciding, applying and outputting [2] The cognitive decision model is based on the psychological process of user information processing, including problem identification, information search, information evaluation and choice. The cognitive decision-making stage of the user and the function of the help system component form a corresponding relationship (see Fig. 1).

In the problem identification phase, users need to explain the configuration items quickly and intuitively, and the overview function components can guide users to deepen their understanding of the page and improve their global cognition. When the user faces a new page, it is necessary to inform the user's role and main tasks and guide the core tasks. For users who have already used it, inform them of new features and new optimizations.

In the stage of information search, users are already confused and eager to solve the confusion with instant and effective information. Query function help components such as intelligent customer service, users can get answers to questions through text dialogue; The bubble window can give hints on important functions and professional terms in a reasonable position.

In the stage of information evaluation and selection, the user is guided to the appropriate and correct action by the information on the page. The operation aid component provides real-time feedback on the user's actions, provides feedback on exceptions when errors occur, and provides feedback on the results when the completion is complete.

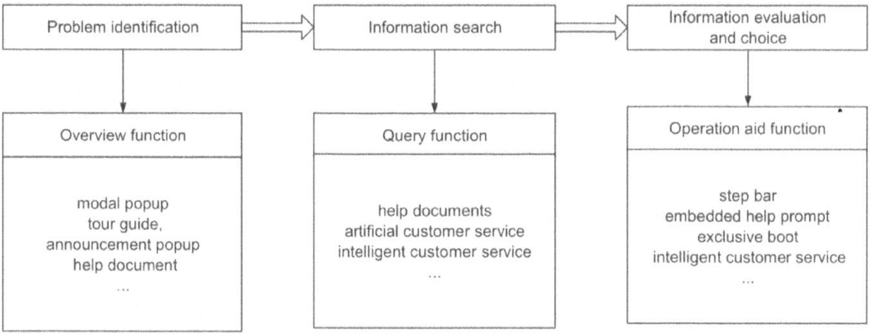

Fig. 1. Mapping relationship between cognitive decision model and help component

Based on the cognitive decision model and the functional characteristics of the components of the help system, the help components are integrated throughout the use process of the complex ordering configuration, as shown in the Fig. 2.

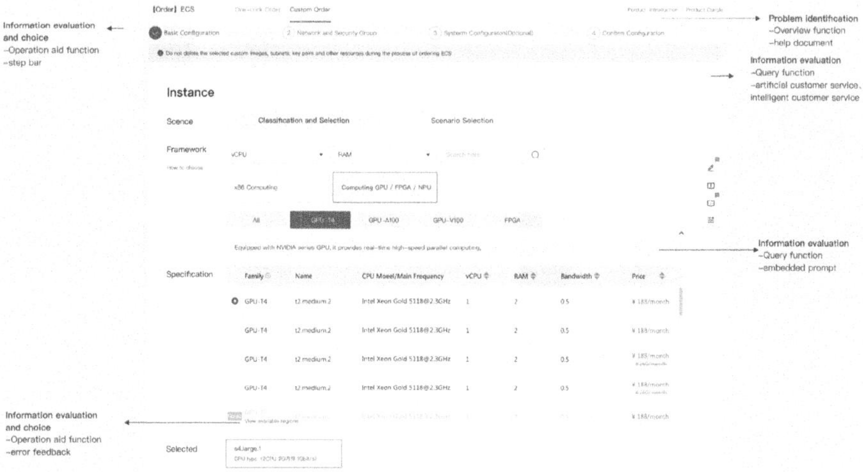

Fig. 2. Optimization of aided system design based on cognitive model analysis

4 Usability Testing

4.1 Evaluation Method

Usability and user experience (UX) are important concepts in the design and evaluation of products or systems intended for human use [3]. User Experience assessment is an evaluation of user's experience with the product, system or service during 'use' (i.e., actual interaction experience) as well as 'anticipated or before use' (i.e., pre-interaction experience) [4].

A total of 15 internal employees were selected for the user experience evaluation. The evaluation task was to order a cloud host on the cloud host ordering page, with a total of 20 task nodes. The test device was a laptop, and the browser was chrome.

The assessment is composed of objective behavioral data and subjective scores, namely self-help rate, task completion rate and satisfaction rate. Self-help rate refers to the proportion of people who are helped by self-inquiry rather than by testers, and task completion rate refers to the proportion of people who complete all task nodes.

4.2 Evaluation Result

After the optimization of the help system, the self-service rate is 70.27%, which is 18.21% higher than before the optimization; The task completion rate reached 95.61%, 8.02% higher than before optimization (see Fig. 3); Satisfaction is optimized to 7.92, which is 0.5 higher than before optimization.

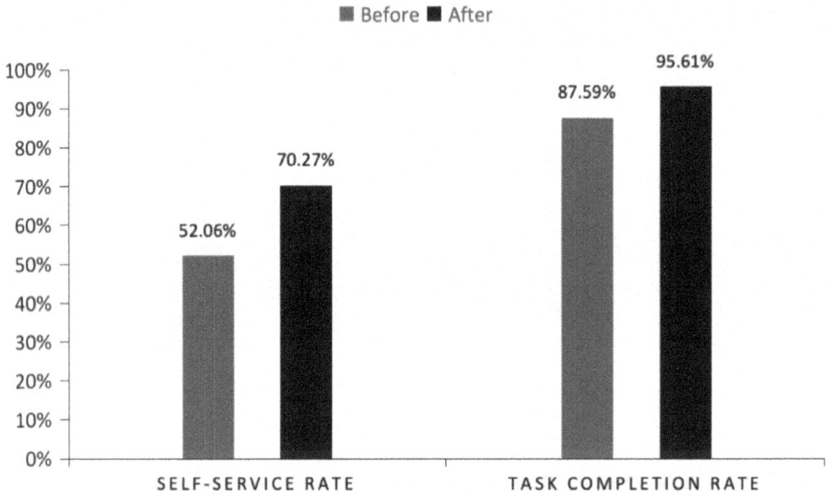

Fig. 3. Bar chart of self-help rate and task completion rate before and after optimization

Through the comparison of self-service rate before and after optimization, the optimized help system obviously improves the ability of users to complete the ordering process independently. Before optimization, users relied on manual support or even gave up purchasing, but after optimization, the self-service rate was significantly improved, which not only reduced the burden of customer service, improved order completion rate, but also improved user ordering satisfaction.

5 Conclusion

This research is based on the cognitive decision model and different help methods to effectively guide the optimization of the help system of the order page of the cloud computing platform. Through subjective and objective data analysis, the results show that the new help system provides users with a more efficient autonomous ordering experience. By analyzing the cognitive decision-making process of users ordering help, and combining the characteristics of different help components, we can select effective help components for users to improve user experience. At the same time, it can increase the profits of enterprises. The above research methods can provide useful guidance for the design of help system of other cloud computing products.

References

1. Dworman, G., Rosenbaum, S.: Helping users to use help: improving interaction with help systems. In: CHI 2004 Extended Abstracts on Human Factors in Computing Systems, pp.1717–1718. ACM, Vienna Austria (2004)
2. Pang, J., Wang, J., Tao, H., et al.: Design and implementation of a cognitive decision architecture. In: 2012 International Conference on Systems and Informatics (ICSAI2012), pp. 705–710. IEEE (2012)
3. Lewis, J.R., Sauro, J.: Usability and user experience: design and evaluation. Handbook Hum. Factors Ergon. 972–1015 (2021)
4. Eilu Phd, E.: Using Cognitive Psychology to Understand Anticipated User Experience in Computing Products (2017)

Human-Centered Organizational Renewal: Transformative Design Science in Action

Jessica Lowry(✉)

Penn State University, 201 Old Main, University Park, PA 16802, USA
jessica.lowry@gmail.com

Abstract. Purpose: Organizational transformation is one of the biggest challenges businesses face in today's global economy. Businesses need to adopt radically different operational requirements to satisfy the expectations of consumers and shareholders. This study proposes methods to shift organizations from survival mode to effective transition through human-centered design methodologies.

Design/methodology/approach. A systematic review of academic and professional literature framed the problem statement working hypothesis for this investigation. A qualitative research design was employed within an organization that was actively transforming its major systems. The researcher recruited experienced Human Resource (HR), operations, technology, marketing, customer service, and sales experts to serve as participants in interviews, creative workshops, diary studies, surveys, and concept validation.

Findings. The research conceptualized how human-centered systems thinking and service design influence innovation, agility, and human-centricity while organizations adjust to Industry 4.0. The findings suggest that organizations can leverage systems thinking and apply service design principles to institute effective continuous quality improvement processes. The outcomes specifically support the use of collaborative approaches to organizational transformation in order to foster an adaptive culture. When research participants allowed themselves to adopt a curious mindset, they were able to generate ideas for reducing pain points and gaps within organizational transformation initiatives. Employees could connect seemingly unrelated information, leading to fresh insights and solving change adoption challenges within a digital network. Once research participants saw that their input was being directly applied to continuous improvements, they embraced belonging to a culture that acknowledges areas for improvement and perceives gaps as valuable opportunities rather than failures.

Originality/value. There is a significant need for business strategy to incorporate human-centered design because only 10% of new strategies are fully executed [10]. The aim of this study was to create a path forward for companies amid organizational transformation to thrive in complexity and uncertainty by promoting human-centered design methods to encourage employees to share the responsibility for solving problems. Ultimately, the goal is to avoid organizational change failure, referred to as planned organizational changes that do not achieve their intended objectives or outcomes [23].

C. Stephanidis et al. (Eds.): HCII 2024, CCIS 2319, pp. 102–112, 2025.
https://doi.org/10.1007/978-3-031-78516-0_10

Keywords: Service Design · Organizational Renewal · Human-centered Methodologies · Innovation · Design Science · Systems Thinking · Change Adoption · Digital Employee Experience (DEX) · Service Design · Trauma Informed Design

1 Introduction

The strategic challenges of transforming entire systems are daunting and most approaches are fundamentally flawed [24]. Traditional transformation efforts often focus on large-scale, one-time changes, while continuous organizational renewal involves a sustained approach to innovation, improvement, and agility. Everything connects within an organization, meaning change must be understood as an ecosystem [8]. Service design enables the systematization of organizational change by measuring cause and effect [19]. The current study aims to propose an approach to continuous organizational transformation and methods to improve internal service ecosystems, including value-in-cultural context and co-construction of context [4]. This study further proposes the use of a digital employee experience (DEX) to achieve those goals [9]. There is tremendous potential to improve how organizations operate as long as employees are involved in co-creating an ideal future state.

Technology has outpaced our ability to manage it, accelerating change at an unsustainable rate for our wellbeing and the environment [26]. The result is future shock, a physical and psychological reaction to experiences that do not fit into existing ways of making sense of external events [22]. This phenomenon is familiar to designers who work on user experiences that introduce new ways of interacting and performing actions. Human-centered design has always focused on the people who need to use a solution, the problems users need to solve, and how to best deliver the most appropriate solutions. Designers consider technology after accurately understanding human needs. When technological capabilities lead solutions, the outcomes can create new problems that are much harder to solve. Often, bureaucracy is perceived as a significant point of friction that limits progress and stalls innovation; however, when it comes to industrialization, it is essential to establish principles that consider the ethical implications of future shock. There are limits to how much change people can tolerate within a given time. People respond to change differently, highlighting the need for trauma-informed design which is a technique to address the impact of future shock. Future shock affects the mind (emotional, psychological) and body (physical, physiological), which is why it is not merely stressful. The effects of massive, collective trauma linger and can lead to depression and other health issues if it is not addressed [17]. Change adoption can only happen when future shock and its traumatic impact are treated as an essential problem to address on a systems level. Since the first waves of the Industrial Revolution, design has considered the relationships between people and technology in ways that influence culture and society. This research is a continuation of a legacy of design that balances the needs of the business and the use of technology as a tool for elevating the human experience.

1.1 Problem Statement

Resistance to change arises during organizational transformation because of a cognitive bias [2]. People inevitably see a loss in almost any change. When change is imposed upon people, it can create a culture of dependency, where individuals wait for instructions and avoid taking any initiative. The lack of agency among employees gets organizations stuck in survival mode and potentially leads to change failure. Organizations must effectively implement continuous change adoption while overcoming resistance, particularly by fostering an open mindset among employees and aligning their needs with those of the business.

2 Literature Review

The strategic challenges of transforming entire systems are daunting and most approaches are fundamentally flawed [24]. Traditional change management practices emphasize the reliance on a single positive leader who actively guides the organization through change and participates visibly throughout the change lifecycle [4]. By contrast, adaptive leadership strongly emphasizes the ethical dimension of transformation and positions followers at the heart of the change process [21]. Adaptive leadership promotes inclusivity, ownership, resilience, cultural transformation, and alignment with organizational values, ultimately increasing the likelihood of successful change adoption. Adaptive leadership addresses basic human needs, such as safety, belonging, and trust, at an individual level by empowering employees to solve problems for themselves and others.

When people work together to solve problems, what happens is defined as the "network effect," which is understood in this research as any situation where the value depends on the number of people who share an experience [18]. Typically, the greater the number of people, the greater the network effect, which can work towards productive or destructive outcomes. An example of a network may be a forum for advice or technical support. An organization can measure the value of a network by examining each unit of content as a cost (or effort) and effectiveness as units of benefit (value). If only a few people produce content, the value of the support forum is more likely to be low because there is a limit to how much information a small group of producers can create. Social media provides many examples of how value is co-designed by network members. A workplace example is GitLab, created by Github [6]. This Microsoft-owned company is a type of organizational support network that enables employees to nominate themselves for an unambiguous task outside their job description. The Directly Responsible Individual (DRI) is ultimately accountable for completing that task. They can request and receive suggestions, but they are free to accept or reject suggestions. The network has much value for the company, but especially for employees who are supported to step outside their comfort zone and take calculated risks.

Digital experiences need to be a support system tailored to an employee's unique requirements based on their personality, maturity, role, and skill sets. It is only possible to accomplish continuous transformation at scale with software solutions such as intelligent digital workers [26]. Artificial intelligence (AI) solutions solve several issues introduced by future shock because intelligent software can handle most administrative, data-entry-type tasks, allowing employees to access their higher-level thinking. Reducing the number of tasks an employee needs to complete significantly reduces the change an employee might struggle to adopt within a short timeframe. Machines are excellent at repetitive tasks, and digital employees should be able to assign mundane tasks to tools that do not have an opinion on whether something is tedious or stressful. Equipping employees with a digital assistant can free managers to spend time on higher-level thinking instead of trying to coach employees to take on tasks that reduce their job performance and well-being. DEX inherently involves flexible and adaptable digital solutions to help employees overcome the natural tendency to perceive new technology as additional stress that outweighs the potential benefits [9]. AI is a technology that radically reduces manual tasks, copious process training, knowledge management, and wasted time requesting support.

3 Methodology

This study aimed to co-create collaboration tools with research participants to help employees conceptualize what they might gain by adopting change. The research used design science methodologies, which question existing beliefs and assumptions to uncover new insights and possibilities [1]. As a practice, design scientists persistently pursue answers to questions, even when difficult or time-consuming, and differ from other disciplines because the emphasis is creating tangible solutions rather than collecting discoveries. It involves iterative cycles of design, testing, and refinement to improve the effectiveness and usability of the artifacts being developed. To this end, the following research questions were framed to gather design criteria that met the needs of the target employee groups.

RQ1: How might we integrate human-centered design at an organization undergoing transformational change, given the likelihood of facing considerable skepticism about the effectiveness of a design-led approach?

RQ2: How might human-centered methodologies facilitate continuous change adoption across the entire organization?

A small team comprised of cross-disciplinary skills determined the constraints of a research-based approach to identifying ways to improve support. The group aligned on having the research deliver validated solution(s) to improve how employees are supported with change adoption. There was consensus that the company was stuck in survival mode based on their sense of loss, apathy, and mistrust, and the recognition of how those feelings were negatively impacting morale and productivity. Although the negative effects were company-wide, they felt it was important to prioritize issues among members of the client services department. As a professional services company, any disruption or delay in delivering services on time, within budget, and meeting customer expectations could result in lost opportunities for future business (Fig. 1).

Surveys and sentiment analysis confirmed that the greatest need for solutions exists among employees who directly deliver value to customers. The surveys also revealed a need for micro-learning, peer-based asynchronous support, reoccurring office hours, and more effective interpersonal communication. Using this criterion, the research was designed to focus on those key aspects of change adoption support.

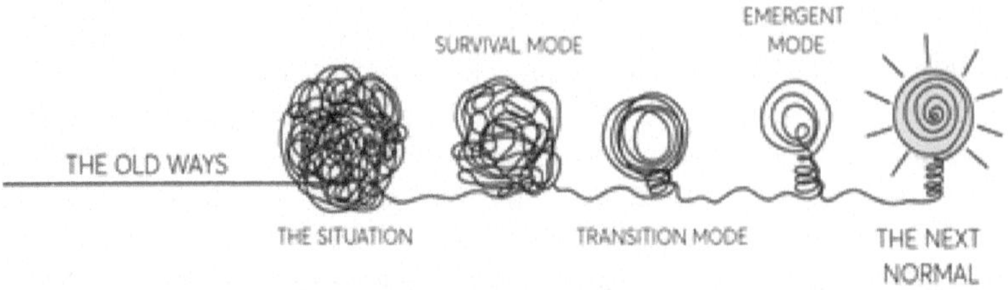

Fig. 1. Visualization of the organizations path towards change adoption.

The total number of employees within the client services department is roughly – 400 and they work remotely throughout North and South America. The objective was to gather enough data from a sample of participants who represent critical roles within the customer services department. Understanding the differences and similarities of primary tasks, which designers often refer to as "jobs to be done," participants provided an ability to identify priorities concerning the gaps in change adoption support. The sample size needed to accurately reflect the percentage of employees with a specific job function. For these reasons, a stratified sampling technique was applied to divide the population into subgroups (e.g., seniority, role, responsibilities), this helped to ensure the sample was representative of the entire client services department (Table 1).

Table 1. Summary of participant recruitment criteria.

Sample Size	Role	Seniority	Responsibilities
3	Designer	Director	Manager
5	Designer	Lead	Supervisor
6	Designer	Senior	Individual Contributor
2	Project Manager	Director	Manager
1	Project Manager	Lead	Supervisor
1	Project Manager	Senior	Individual Contributor
2	Strategy	Lead	Supervisor
3	Strategy	Senior	Individual Contributor
1	Technology	Director	Manager
4	Technology	Lead	Supervisor
10	Technology	Senior	Individual Contributor

In order to co-design with participants, it was necessary to use systems thinking and service design methods to create human-centered guiding principles focused on the desired outcomes. This required incorporating trauma-informed design to consider the need for emotional safety, which ensured participants could align with broader goals in an authentic way. Trauma-informed design greatly informed the types of activities that fostered psychological safety resulting in a safe environment to "fail" [24] (Table 2).

Table 2. Research activities and outcomes.

Co-Design Activities	Purpose	Insights
Iceberg Systems Model	A tool to look beneath the surface of a situation to understand why the organization is stuck in survival mode.	Survival mode is the result of reactive decision-making, short-term fixes, siloed departments, stagnation in innovation, and a focus on immediate results over long-term sustainability.
DEX Service Blueprint	Visualize what support looks like today and identify the most significant opportunities for improvement.	Employees have to work hard to access support because there are too many support touchpoints spread across 10+ standalone platforms.
360 Empathy	Holistic overview of the human experience fosters empathy, leading to better decision-making and employee-centric solutions.	Employees are not receiving the appropriate communication to address their future shock and it is resulting in a prolonged trauma-induced state.
Rapid Prototyping	Co-design tool that facilitates shifting mindsets towards creative thinking, experimentation, collaboration, and a willingness to try new things.	Employees want to streamline support services and establish guidelines to ensure services are simple and accessible.
SME Interviews	Engaging experts is important for generating informed findings, building relationships, managing resistance, and driving alignment during organizational transformation.	The expert view is that the organization is overcoming debt for work that should have been done years ago and they believe that the entire operating system needs to be redesigned.
Diary Study	Context around the circumstances and events helps identify patterns, triggers, and contributing factors to both positive and negative outcomes, informing opportunities to improve change adoption.	Employees benefit the most from their peer network regarding support. As a community, they reduce each other's stress through encouragement and sharing their experiences.

4 Findings

A design science approach resulted in the creation of tools that effectively addressed the reasons why employees resist change during organizational transformation. These tools, guided by design criteria, not only provided a clear understanding of the change process but also empowered employees to take an active role. By involving employees in co-design activities, the key stakeholders were able to further develop the solutions produced during the co-design research activities. This allowed the operations team to swiftly resolve issues and begin to transition out of survival mode. The approach was successful in fostering a dynamic and innovative work environment, where engaged employees are more likely to be satisfied and committed, thereby reducing resistance to change adoption.

4.1 Transparency Builds Trust

It is okay to only know some of the answers. Employees want to have a way of asking questions and receiving information within a reasonable timeframe.

4.2 The Network Effect

Peer knowledge sharing is a powerful tool. By sharing information through dedicated channels, the organization created a sense of community and expedited the dissemination of knowledge. These channels are the perfect place to address questions and provide training through peer support. Unlike general channels, they offer a more focused and supportive environment.

4.3 Snack-Size Instruction

Micro-learning is a game-changer in the change adoption strategy because no one wants to deal with the burden of sitting through training sessions and searching through copious documentation. It provides short, interactive, and engaging pieces of content that reduce cognitive load. The aim is to reduce learner fatigue and give you control over what and when you learn. Each micro-learning module should be designed to be less than 2 min long, focusing on a single learning objective or topic.

4.4 Voice of the Employee (VoE)

Employee feedback is invaluable because it provides real-time insights into how the changes are perceived and experienced across the organization. By understanding these perspectives, the organization can make informed decisions that are more likely to align with employee needs and expectations.

Change method cards were created using the research findings and distributed among stakeholders responsible for delivering successful outcomes. Insights from the study were weaved into the deck of cards that positioned decision-makers to begin shifting from survival into transition mode. The cards provide a structured and interactive way to explore different design methods, evaluate their suitability for specific contexts, and make informed decisions about which concepts to use for continuous change adoption. The deck can be used across the organization to facilitate discussions, brainstorming, and conduct decision-making related to change initiatives. The categories include the drivers that initiate change, human-centered design principles, and methods accessible to everyone impacted by organizational transformation (see Appendix A).

5 Limitations/Implications

Designers need to understand the language of the business world to collaborate with leaders in the organization effectively [20]. The challenge when introducing design to a business environment is that the methodology tends to be deconstructed, reduced, and moved back toward inductive/deductive reasoning, losing its holistic, systems-oriented, and abductive reasoning orientation [12]. Leaders commonly understand the logic of being human-centered; however, when the concept moves from theoretical into an organizational process, several challenges and gaps come to the surface. These gaps are partially because the organization needs time to adjust to a human-centered culture. Incorporating service design is a fundamental change from assigning an implementation manager who considers the business, corporate, and operational needs [14].

Leaders know that the failure rate for organizational transformation initiatives is relatively high, often cited between 60%-88% [23]. For those accountable to deliver impactful change there is a fear of failure that can cause reactive decision-making and overly focusing on short-term goals. The criteria used for defining "failure" are typically attributed to factors such as insufficient leadership, inadequate communication, resistance to change, poor planning, and failure to sustain momentum over the long term. The research highlights the need to be open to feedback [5], willing to make necessary adjustments, and supportive of initiatives that drive renewal.

6 Conclusion

Transparency, peer knowledge sharing, micro-learning, and employee feedback are essential elements in building trust, fostering collaboration, and ensuring effective change adoption. However, designers must bridge the gap between design methodology and business language to effectively collaborate with organizational leaders. Despite the high failure rate of organizational transformation initiatives, leaders must embrace feedback, remain flexible, and focus on long-term goals to drive meaningful change and improve business operations, DEX, and customer loyalty. By addressing these challenges and embracing a human-centered culture, organizations can navigate the complexities of change and emerge stronger and more resilient in an ever-evolving business landscape.

Appendix A.Change Method Cards

Image 3: Change Method Cards

Source: Jessica Lowry

References

1. Antunes, P., Thuan, N.H., Johnstone, D.: Nature and purpose of visual artifacts in design science research. IseB **20** (2022). https://doi.org/10.1007/s10257-022-00559-2
2. Bazerman, M., Moore, D.: Judgment in Managerial Decision Making. 8th ed. Wiley (2012). https://www.perlego.com/book/3866105/judgment-in-managerial-decision-making-pdf
3. Brown, T.: Change by design, revised and updated: How Design Thinking Transforms Organizations and Inspires Innovation. HarperBusiness (2019)
4. Creasey, T.J., Taylor, T.: Best practices in change management: 822 participants share lessons and best practices (2014)
5. Dahlander, L., Frederiksen, L., Rullani, F.: Online Communities and Open Innovation. 1st edn. Routledge (2014). https://www.perlego.com/book/1665344
6. GitLab Mission. The GitLab Handbook (14 May 2024). https://handbook.gitlab.com/handbook/company/mission/#mission
7. Gomes, J.: Leading in a Non-Linear World: Building Wellbeing, Strategic, and Innovation Mindsets for the Future, p. 11. Wiley (2022). ISBN 1119672724, 9781119672722
8. Hoque, F., Baer, D.: Everything connects: Cultivating Mindfulness, Creativity, and Innovation for Long-Term Value (Second Edition) (2022)
9. Gheidar, Y., ShamiZanjani, M.: Conceptualizing the digital employee experience. Strateg. HR Rev. **19**(3), 131–135 (2020). https://doi.org/10.1108/SHR-01-2020-0004
10. Goodwin, K.: Designing for the Digital Age (1st ed.). Wiley (2011)
11. Gomes, J.: Leading in a non-linear world: building wellbeing. Wiley, Strategic and Innovation Mindsets for the Future (2022)
12. Kotter, J.P., Akhtar, V., Gupta, G.: Change: How Organizations Achieve Hard-to-Imagine Results in Uncertain and Volatile Times. John Wiley & Sons (2021)
13. Koskela-Huotari, K., et al.: Service system transformation through service design: linking analytical dimensions and service design approaches. J. Bus. Res. (2021). https://doi.org/10.1016/j.jbusres.2021.07.034
14. Kuratko, D., Hoskinson, S., Kuratko, D., & Hoskinson, S.: The Challenges of Corporate Entrepreneurship in the Disruptive Age. Emerald Publishing Limited (2018)
15. Mouazen, A., Hernández-Lara, A., Abdallah, F., Ramadan, M., Chahine, J., Baydoun, H.: Transformational and transactional leaders and their role in implementing the kotter change management model ensuring sustainable change: an empirical study. Sustainability **16**(1), 16 (2024)
16. Rathninde, A.: Tackling complexity: Tough-Love interactions to navigate uncertainty, promote positivity, and deliver performance excellence. S-Iila Business (2022)
17. Repa, V., Repa, V.: Why business leaders need a trauma-informed approach. Fast Company (31 May 2024). https://www.fastcompany.com/91132890/why-business-leaders-need-a-trauma-informed-approach
18. Romanovich, M.: Expand Employee Learning with Communities of Practice. [edition unavailable]. Association for Talent Development (2014)
19. Salgado, M., De Castro Martínez, M.V., Marcos Martínez, E., López-Sanz, M., Martín-Peña, M.L.: Driving organizational change in SMEs using service design. J. Serv. Theory Pract. (2022)
20. Stickdorn, M., Schneider, J.: This is Service Design Thinking: Basics. John Wiley & Sons, Tools, Cases (2012)
21. Tetenbaum, T., Laurence, H.: Leading in the chaos of the 21st century. J. Leadersh. Stud. **4**(4), 41–49 (2011). https://doi.org/10.1002/jls.20191
22. Toffler, A.: Future Shock. Random House Publishing Group, United Kingdom (2022)

23. Tucker, D., Cirella, S., Kelly, P.: Organizational Change Management. 1st ed. SAGE Publications (2024)
24. Weber, K.M., Rohracher, H.: Legitimizing research, technology and innovation policies for transformative change: combining insights from innovation systems and multi-level perspective in a comprehensive 'failures' framework. Res. Policy **41**(6), 1037–1047 (2012). https://doi.org/10.1016/j.respol.2011.10.015
25. Yen-Chun, W., Chen, W.H.: Service innovation and quality assessment of industry 4.0 microservice through data modeling and system simulation evaluation approaches. Appl. Sci. **12**(9), 4718 (2022)
26. Wilson, R.: Age of Invisible Machines: A Practical Guide to Creating a Hyperautomated Ecosystem of Intelligent Digital Workers. John Wiley & Sons (2022)

How Might We Improve HCI on a Platform Designed to Improve Interagency Collaboration?

Beth A. Martin[1](✉), Basil White[2], and Jason Traquair[2]

[1] Maryland Institute College of Art, Baltimore, MD, USA
bmartin01@mica.edu
[2] U.S. Department of Agriculture, Washington, DC, USA
{basil.white,jason.traquair}@usda.gov

Abstract. The ability of an organization, particularly a government agency, to deliver value to its target audience and mission partners depends on its ability to deliver programs and projects. Delivering value requires integration and alignment of a complex array of policies, objectives, and key results. The Growing Good in Government Initiative (G3I), sponsored by the USDA's Marketing and Regulatory Programs, aims to promote stakeholder value through the Integrated Value Network (IVN), data analytics, and the USDA P/PM Community of Practice to address gaps in program management. We aim to create an integrated, responsive framework to serve citizens effectively, deliver solutions to break down silos, and explore the intersection of competing domains, through building a data and analytics infrastructure that provides answers to critical portfolio, program, and project-level business questions. By leveraging a collaborative platform that supports the needs of decision-makers, we seek feedback from conference attendees to enhance the user experience of a data analysis tool in the creation of useful, usable, and desirable decision-making products for stakeholders and participants using this collaborative platform to translate strategy into tangible improvements in program outcomes.

Keywords: communication · collaboration · change management · innovation · user experience · customer experience · product management · business analytics · policy informatics · integrated value

1 The Integrated Value Network (IVN)

1.1 The Integrated Value Network (IVN) Project

Laws and regulations often include requirements that organizations create policies, plans, priorities, programs and performance measures. When we view them as a logical diagram, these requirements function as a network of governance documents as an emergent property of these requirements. Analysis of these networks yields insights about how to revise governance documents, increase the business value transacted, and furnish evidence to support changes to the laws and regulations that mandate them, increase

C. Stephanidis et al. (Eds.): HCII 2024, CCIS 2319, pp. 113–117, 2025.
https://doi.org/10.1007/978-3-031-78516-0_11

functionality both as individual governance documents, and increase the net functionality of the organization. We present a case study of a multi-year joint effort among USDA and several partner agencies to drive intra-agency and cross-agency collaboration; we include lessons learned, current progress, and future vision.

The Integrated Value Network (IVN) is a project sponsored under the Growing Good in Government Initiative (G3I) [2] by the US Department of Agriculture's (USDA) Marketing and Regulatory Programs (MRP) Business Services. G3I is a holistic approach to coordinate program and project management efforts and maximize value to stakeholders through the synergy of two initiatives: the IVN–a neural network of policy, laws, and regulations, including data and analytics architecture–and the USDA P/PM Community of Practice (CoP), a collaborative initiative across USDA mission areas to solve capability gaps in program and program management (P/PM).

As a data tool, the IVN provides a schematic of programs, plans, metrics, regulations, and laws based on how they inherit authority from the U.S. Constitution. In other words, this data schema comprised of Federal policy has the U.S. Constitution as its root node, flowing down the U.S. Legislative Branch to laws and regulations and policy on one branch and down the U.S. Executive Branch to Executive Orders and policy that support those orders.

When we know how this data schema connects back to the source of authority, it becomes easier to hold our organizations accountable and we can trace decisions and actions to their roots. Policymakers, legislators, and administrators can make decisions informed by the flow of authority, the context, and the implications of their choices. New policies or regulations based on alignment with their context of authority ensures the legitimacy of those authorities.

By integrating the components of these governance documents into a network of value, G3I aims to provide the tools, knowledge, and framework necessary to optimize impact while remaining hyper-responsive to the needs of the citizens we serve. G3I functions as an "ecosystem" of requirements managed and implemented as a coordinated effort to apply lessons learned from policy and program analysis to better tools and decision support and increase the breadth and depth of policy and program integration in the organization.

1.2 Policy as a Neural Network for Change

The IVN represents a knowledge architecture approach to data architecture and policy analysis, as it uses a neural network to depict how Federal laws, regulations, policies, strategies, and performance metrics deliver business value to each other. The visual representation (Fig. 1) looks like a node for each governance document with arrows that show the movement of business value. Network visualization software, such as the "Network Navigator" visualization in Microsoft Power BI, can render alignments from a data table as a network of nodes.

Business architecture and policy informatics provide frameworks to depict the relationships of business processes, systems, and strategies as a network of requirements. These frameworks help us understand how rules, offices and roles interact to deliver the work of the organization. An IVN is one visual model of how parts of the business

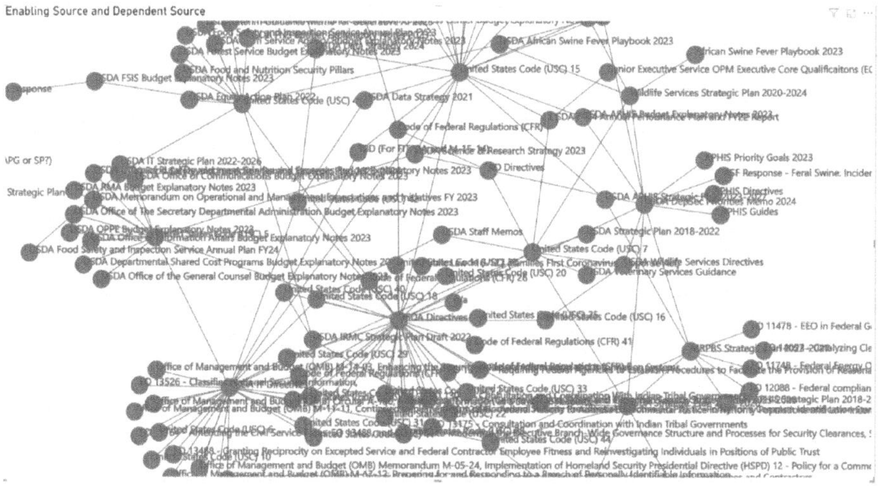

Fig. 1. Microsoft Power BI Network Navigator visualization of an Integrated Value Network.

enable and depend on each other to achieve organizational goals. Within these frameworks, delivering a requirement often progresses another requirement closer to delivery, because requirements in a system enable and depend on each other to succeed. An IVN represents those requirements as nodes. When the IVN connects requirements with arrows that show how requirements supply and receive delivery value, the IVN reveals insights about how to communicate, coordinate, and change that organization systemically. As a result, decision-makers gain insight on how to effectively communicate, collaborate, and change organizations with an IVN.

We want to measure the effect of requirements interactions effectively, so we often separate requirements or aggregate them together, so that delivering each requirement has enough effect to be measurable, but not so much effect that it can be split into multiple, measurable requirements. This helps us measure the effect of interactions more accurately.

2 Feedback Loops

2.1 The Need to Coordinate

Delivering resilient service to citizens requires interdependence of policies, goals, objectives, programs and projects [1] in a way that generates value and resource support. However, in its current state, viewing these integrations and alignments as a neural network show provides an opportunity to improve coordination of roles and responsibilities across the Federal Performance Framework. Crucial legislation intended to have systemic effects on Federal operations, like the Foundations for Evidence-Based Policymaking Act of 2018, Federal Information Technology Acquisition Reform Act, and Program Management Improvement Accountability Act, often seems to have been applied to the hierarchy directed to enforce them. Moreover, the absence of a unified approach that integrates program and project management with program and project creation weakens the capabilities of all of these activities.

Over time, this lack of coordination affects internal capabilities, erodes institutional knowledge, and deprives policymakers and leaders of a holistic understanding of the benefits the organization provides and the necessary capabilities to deliver them. The absence of a holistic understanding of the inventory of benefits we deliver, as well as the requirements (capabilities) needed to deliver them, leads to linear rather than systemic solutions. Without clear metrics and accountability for measuring the actual benefits delivered through various initiatives, these initiatives risk becoming self-serving and difficult to measure for performance [3] to citizens.

The combination of these factors can lead to an environment where an organization will struggle to keep pace with evolving demands, management technologies, and expectations. This disjointed approach has far-reaching consequences, including reduced trust, failure to effectively address emerging challenges, and missed opportunities for innovation and improvement.

2.2 How Might We Effect Change?

We seek to address these complex problems by using G3I to unify and optimize operations and operational change to ensure that they deliver sustainable benefits to the American public. Through G3I, we aim to reinvigorate our organization's ability to communicate, collaborate and change the business of government.

Through this effort, we ask: How can we provide an interactive database and visualization of the interactions of laws, regulations, programs, measures, strategies and requirements in a way that provides an effective, rewarding user experience to decision-makers, stakeholders, employees and researchers? How might we measure and deliver the value of these heightened business optics to citizens and mission partners? How might we create useful products that provide incentives and reduce barriers to breaking down silos, and answer critical portfolio, program, and project-level business questions? How do we leverage current information technology and skill sets to evolve governance data management towards knowledge management that support organizational decisions and capabilities?

Disclosure of Interests. The authors have no competing interests to declare that are relevant to the content of this article.

References

1. White, B., Martin, B., Wold, R.: The integrated value model (IVM): a relational data model of business value. In: Kautish, S.K., (ed.) Using Strategy Analytics to Measure Corporate Performance and Business Value Creation, pp. 198–220. IGI Global (2021)
2. Growing Good in Government: Cultivating the Feedback Loops of the Future - ATARC Federal IT Newscast. https://open.spotify.com/episode/0MXBUFmLe0rQH6XDTUi3Lb. Accessed 15 May 2024

3. Growing Good in Government Initiative Uses Data-and-Evidence-Based Approach to Program Design and Performance - https://federalnewsnetwork.com/management/2024/02/growing-good-in-government-initiative-uses-data-and-evidence-based-approach-to-program-design-and-performance/. Accessed 16 May 2024

From Designer to Imagineer: Personal Fabrication Embedded in Designer's 3D Printing Practice

Jue Ren[1(✉)] and Leirah Wang[2]

[1] Future Institute of Industrial Design for Additive Manufacturing, Shanghai, China
[2] Xubrance, Shanghai, China
leirah.wang@xuberance.com

Abstract. According to 3D printing technology is increasingly adopted in fields of fashion, jewelry, and exhibitions, the work of 3D printing is no longer limited to toys, figures, and other desktop-level products. With steadily expanding of application areas of additive manufacturing of large-scale applications, such as more than 6 m' high outdoor sculptures with steel structures, are winning attention from the industry. Industry need more 3D printing designers who could design and conduct large-scale 3D printing projects, but the research on designer's personal fabrication in large-scale 3D printing is limited. Taking Xuberance's designers experience in large-scale additive manufacturing as a case study, this paper presents a changing pattern of interactive computing in the digital fabrication of large-scale addictive manufacturing. We find that personal fabrication pattern of 3D printing designer changes when the product size shifts from small to large. The research explore that digital fabrication is not the whole map of designers' 3D printing practice. And the whole manufacturing process includes not only onsite design but also re-mote manufacturing. It help the researcher to image more re-mote additive manufacturing scenario, imaging that 3D printing machines work on Mars directed by the 3D printing imagineers work on Earth together to build a Mars Migration Project in one day. Also, It could leading to explore embodied intelligence in the field of additive manufacturing in future.

Keywords: Personal Fabrication · Large-Scale 3D printing · Embodied Intelligence

1 Introduction

Large-scale 3D printing technology has become an important tool in fields such as architecture, art, and furniture design (see Fig. 1.and Fig. 2.). Compared to traditional manufacturing methods, 3D printing excels in creating complex structures and significantly shortens the production cycle. At the core of this emerging technology, 3D printing designers play a key role in every stage of a project, from initial concept design to final delivery. Their expertise and skills determine the success of the project.

C. Stephanidis et al. (Eds.): HCII 2024, CCIS 2319, pp. 118–127, 2025.
https://doi.org/10.1007/978-3-031-78516-0_12

Fig. 1. 3D printed banqueting hall in a Hennessy event in front an ancient city wall,6 m tall [1] (data designed by Xubrance)

This study was initiated in 2014, from the beginning of Xubrance, which is the first professional 3d printing design company in China. We trace the development of 3D printing in China from desktop projects to large-scale projects in the past 10 years.

This study hopes to provide a preliminary exploration to 1. How 3D printing design workflow changed following the changing needs from industry? 2. What is designer's role in the changing design workflow? 3. In order to fulfill the developed need for qualified 3D printing designers from industry, what are the new talents for 3D printing designers need to handle in the new protocol of 3D printing?

Taking Xuberance's designers experience in large-scale additive manufacturing as a case study, this paper presents a changed pattern of interactive computing in the digital fabrication of large-scale addictive manufacturing.

2 Research Approach

This research uses mix-method, such as in-depth interview, online questionnaire, participate observation, multi-site ethnography in Shanghai, Luoyang and Huangshan [3, 4].

24 informants, half of them are in 31–40 years old (see Fig. 3.), and more than 58% of them are new coming into 3D printing industry (see Fig. 4.), are interviewed with a structure online questionnaire. And 8 informants are in-depth interviewed. These 3D printing designers most are major in architecture, environment design, art design, etc.. One informants who are major in English to be a 3D printing imagineer with 3years experience in this industry.

Fig. 2. Large-scale 3D printed sculpture with steel components in VIVO mobile phone launch event, 6.5 m tall (data designed by Xubrance)

Fig. 3. China's 1st 3D-printed retractile bridge in Shanghai (designed by Bin Lu) [2]

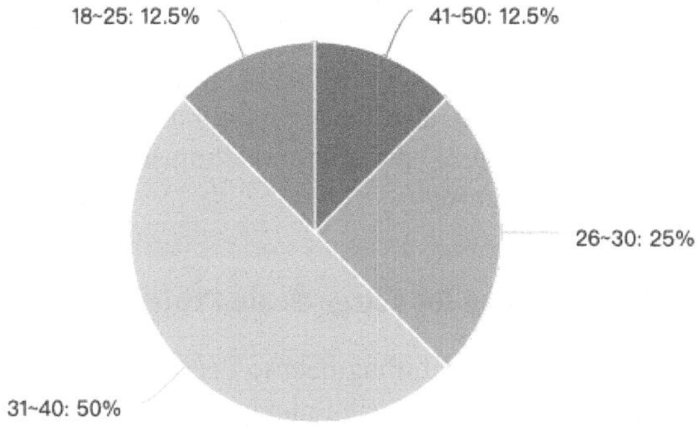

Fig. 4. Age of informants (n = 24)

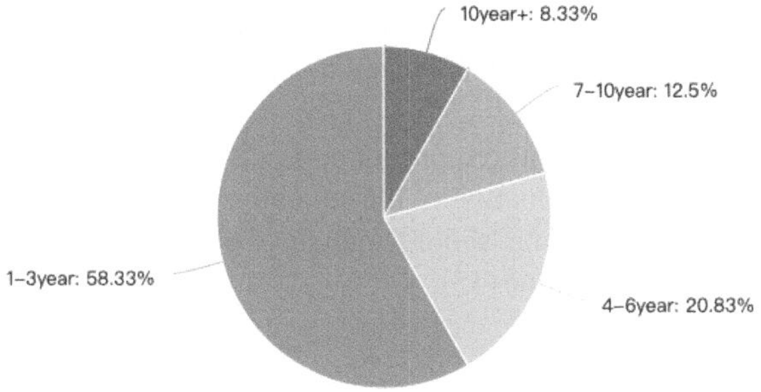

Fig. 5. Working years in 3D printing of informants (n = 24)

3 The Findings

We find that personal fabrication pattern of 3d printing designer changes when the product size shifts from small to large. In large-scale additive manufacturing projects, 3D printing designers need to play multiple roles as both 3D designers, digital sculptors, and structure engineer which changing them from a designer to a digital imagineer, in charging of creating and manufacturing simultaneously. Practitioners from different professional backgrounds have enriched the skills of the 3D printing industry, not only meeting the work requirements of different processes in large-scale 3D printing, but also promoting the diverse development of talents among designers through the collaborative creation of multiple. These experiences transform them from designers to versatile talents, which we call them digital imagineer.

Digital imagineer takes a non-linear workflow to design and manufacturing the large-scale 3d printing project, which needs them to master the final physical manufacturing processes and be familiar with contextual information of various manufacturing materials for final products. That means a digital imagineer also needs to consider the scenario of large-scale 3D printed steel structure components how to being installed on-site during the 3D modeling process (see Fig. 6.).

The new pattern of digital fabrication significantly reduces working time, shorten the supply chain of traditional addictive manufacturing, which make the whole workflow more economical and more portable, and also give digital imagineer new challenges.

With the skills more than using 3D printing modeling software, digital imagineer. can in charge the whole workflow.

3.1 Project Origin and Planning for Large-Scale Projects

The large-scale projects require digital imagineer to deeply understand and analyze the client's requirements to ensure that the design plans meet the client's expectations.

In the project planning stage, digital imagineer need to formulate detailed plans, including timelines, budgets, and possible technical challenges. One in-depth interviewed informant mentioned that digital imagineer typically first understand the client's needs, then identify creative points, and collaborate with project managers to develop a feasible plan. This stage of planning is crucial as it lays the foundation for subsequent design and production.

The needs from industry clients requires large-scale 3D printing designer to consider design feasibility, as well as evaluation of the suitability of technology and materials.

Additionally, project planning should include risk assessment and management strategies to address potential issues [5].

3.2 Design Process

Dimension and Structure Handling. When designing large-scale 3D works, digital imagineer need to accurately handle dimensions and structural issues. Interviews mentioned that designers consider how to support large structures, ensuring material strength and stability. This requires digital imagineer to have extensive engineering knowledge and experience to solve potential structural weaknesses. For instance, to avoid collapses due to insufficient support structures, designers add necessary supports and reinforcements to the model.

Material Selection. The choice of materials is critical for the success of large-scale 3D printed works. Different materials have different physical and chemical properties, suitable for various application scenarios. Interviews mentioned that designers commonly use ABS and ASA materials due to their excellent strength and durability. Research indicates that material selection is one of the key factors affecting the quality of 3D printed works [6]. Different materials perform differently in the printing process, and designers need to select appropriate materials based on project requirements to ensure the performance and stability of the final work [7]. For works requiring higher strength, digital imagineer might choose metals or composite materials.

3.3 Modeling and Preparation

Modeling Software and Techniques. The modeling and preparation stage is critical to the success of 3D printing projects [8]. 3D printing digital imagineer typically use professional modeling software such as Maya, Rhino, and Magics for detailed model creation and optimization. Interviews mentioned that designers use these software tools for multiple simulations and tests to ensure print-ability. The modeling skills and techniques of digital imagineer are particularly important at this stage as they determine the quality and detail presentation of the final work.

Model Optimization and Preparation. Before printing, digital imagineer need to optimize and repair the model. Interviews mentioned that designers use Magics software for model repair and inspection, ensuring all details meet the printer's requirements. Additionally, designers make necessary optimizations, such as adding support structures or adjusting model details, to improve the success rate of printing.

3.4 Printing Process

Printing Technology Selection. Different 3D printing technologies such as FDM, SLA, and SLS each have their advantages and disadvantages. Each of them has significant differences in accuracy, speed, and material utilization [9]. Digital imagineer need to choose the most suitable technology and equipment based on the needs of the work. Interviews mentioned that designers typically use FDM technology to print large-scale works because this technology performs well in printing large structures.

Quality Control During Printing. During the printing process, digital imagineer need to continuously monitor quality and speed, adjusting parameters to ensure smooth printing and high-quality output. Interviews mentioned that designers adjust the printer settings in real-time based on printing progress and actual conditions to optimize printing results.

3.5 Printing Site and Post-processing

Challenges at the Printing Site. During the actual printing process, designers need to deal with various challenges such as print interruptions and material waste. Interviews mentioned that designers must have the ability to quickly solve problems to ensure the continuity of the printing process. For example, when material blockages or print interruptions occur during the printing process, designers need to quickly identify the cause and solve the problem to avoid wasting time and materials.

Post-processing and Assembly. Post-processing work after printing has an important impact on the final quality of 3D printed works [10]. High-quality post-processing can significantly improve the appearance and function of the work, increasing its market value [8]. Additionally, the skills and experience of designers in the post-processing process are also key factors in ensuring the success of the work [7].

After printing is completed, digital imagineer need to perform detailed post-processing and assembly work. Interviews mentioned that these tasks include sanding, painting, and assembling to ensure the final quality and stability of the work. The post-processing process usually requires a lot of time and effort, and designers need to have good manual skills and patience.

Fig. 6. Xubrance digital imagineer team works for a large-scale 3D printed with steel components installed on-site.

3.6 Reflection and Improvement

After project is completed, digital imagineer reflect and summarize to identify areas for improvement. Interviews mentioned that digital imagineer draw lessons from each project to continuously improve their techniques and processes. This continuous improvement not only enhances the professional level of digital imagineer but also promotes the development of the entire large-scale 3D printing industry. This workflow is not only suit for large-scarle project but also suit for desktop project. One informant said she use one year to research a material changed of 3D printed vase (see Fig. 7.)

Fig. 7. 3D printed vases(designed by Himmel Wang)

4 Conclusion

In this exploratory case study, we found that:

1. Personal fabrication is not the whole map of designers' 3D printing practice. By observing and tracing the full workflow of digital imagineer manufacturing process in large-scale 3D printing projects, we find that the whole manufacturing process includes not only onsite design but also re-mote manufacturing.
2. 3D printing designers, called digital imagineer, play a key role in the design process of large-scale 3D printing works,which make them change their role from a designer to a imagineer.
3. The expertise, technical skills, and problem-solving abilities of digital imagineer ensure the smooth progress and high-quality completion of each project. Changed role of digital imagineer require them expand their domain skills to the skills needed in each stage of the whole workflow in large-scale 3D printing projects. This the key change from a 3D printing designer for desktop project [11] to large-scale 3D printing imagineer.
4. From project origin and planning, design process, modeling and preparation, printing process, printing site and post-processing, to project acceptance and delivery, digital imagineer play an irreplaceable role at each stage. With the continuous advancement of technology, 3D printing imagineer will continue to drive the development of this field, bringing more innovation and breakthroughs.
5. The result in this research can be used to study other digital imagineers of architects, fashion engineers, fabric engineers, jewelry designer, etc., who use 3D printing tools for their fabricating practice in various scenarios, in order to construct a large language model database about designers' personal fabrication behavior.
6. For digital imagineer, they need to lead ending stage of large-scale 3d printing project, such as post-processing and assembly into their design at beginning, then their personal fabrication can be embedded in the whole workflow of large-scale 3D printing project, which make it possible to change personal fabrication to be an Embodied Cognitive Fabrication.
7. With digital imagineer's working data, this research also provides possibilities for future studies on transferring learning from small data modeling to a large language model of imagineers' design behavior patterns. It could potentially lead us to the research in embodied intelligence within the field of additive manufacturing.
8. Following the protocol for digital imaginer can apply 3D printing for new approach, such as large-scale 3D printed reproduction of historical and culture heritage for heritage protection and education(see Fig. 8.). Also, it could be used for innovation for studying traditional national ethnic intangible cultural heritage handicrafts to create new color material for 3D printing project (see Fig. 9).
9. This technology also enables researchers to envision advanced remote additive manufacturing within an embodied cognitive fabrication framework. Specifically, it imagines embodied cognitive 3D printing machines, equipped with AI-generated content (AIGC) designs based on the digital expertise of human engineers, operating on Mars under the guidance of digital imagineer on Earth. This human-computer collaborative could effort aims to complete the Mars Migration Project in future. Furthermore, this approach has the potential to advance the exploration of embodied intelligence in the field of additive manufacturing in the coming days.

Fig. 8. First 3d printed replica of Yungang Grottoes [12]

Fig. 9. 3D printed Jewelry with grass and wood dyeing (designed by Himmel Wang)

Acknowledgments. We would like to thank all the informants who are interviewed.

References

1. Hennessy, Hennessy.X.O. https://weibo.com/1801462015/N7w9wektP,last Accessed May 20 2024
2. Global Times, China's 1st 3D-printed retractile bridge unveiled in Shanghai;it can hold 20 ppl at a time.https://enapp.globaltimes.cn/article/1227887. Accessed May 20 2024
3. Marcus, G.E.: Ethnography in/of the world wystem: the emergence of multi-sited ethnography. Annu. Rev. Anthropol. **1**, 95–117 (1995)
4. Xambó, A., Jewitt, C. and Price, S.: Towards an integrated methodological framework for understanding embodiment in HCI. In: CHI'14 Extended Abstracts on Human Factors in Com- puting Systems, pp. 1411–1416 (2014)
5. Smith, R.C., Anderson, E.C.: 3D Printing for Artists. Designers and Makers. Bloomsbury Publishing, London (2018)
6. Wang, X., Jiang, M., Zhou, Z., Gou, J., Hui, D.: 3D printing of polymer matrix composites: a review and prospective. Compos. B Eng. **110**, 442–458 (2019)
7. Gibson, I., Rosen, D.W., Stucker, B.: Additive Manufacturing Technologies: 3D Printing, Rapid Prototyping, and Direct Digital Manufacturing, 2nd edn. Springer, New York (2015)
8. Pham, D.T., Gault, R.S.: A comparison of rapid prototyping technologies. Int. J. Mach. Tools Manuf **38**(10–11), 1257–1287 (2016)
9. Turner, B.N., Strong, R., Gold, S.A.: A review of melt extrusion additive manufacturing processes: II. Materials, dimensional accuracy, and surface roughness. Rapid Prototyp. J. **20**(3), 241–255 (2014)
10. Thomas, D., Gilmore, D.: The roles of 3D printing in design: A practical guide for designers. John Wiley & Sons, Hoboken (2014)
11. Baudisch, P.: Personal fabrication in HCI: trends and challenges. In: Proceedings of the International Working Conference on Advanced Visual Interfaces, pp. 1–2, ACM (2016)
12. Global Times, Shanghai unveils First 3d printed replica of Yungang Grottoes https://enapp.globaltimes.cn/articleImages/3758. Accessed May 20 2024

Investigating the Relationship between Anthropomorphic Expressions and Preferences Based on Kansei Design

Haruki Tanaka(✉) and Kang Namgyu

Future University Hakodate of Japan, Hakodate, Japan
tanaharu04328@gmail.com

Abstract. A good example of anthropomorphism is an animated movie and a toy for children, and it is spread into a product design and a robot field. That means the value of anthropomorphism is needed for not only children but also adults. Anthropomorphism has positive effects, but adverse effects have also been reported in various research. However, only a few studies still discuss the conditions of them. Therefore, this study aims to clarify the relationship between expression and preference for product designs that incorporate anthropomorphic expressions based on the viewpoint of Kansei Design. The participants were shown 45 stimulus images of anthropomorphic product designs evaluated their preference for each stimulus image and answered the reasons freely. After that, the selected participants' answers were analyzed using the Text Mining Method. We could identify and separate these stimuli rated as preferences, likes, and dislikes. In addition, we clarified the preferred impressions of anthropomorphic expression in design were linked with words such as "Cute," "Funny," "Human-like," and "Friendly." Whereas the impression of dislike was linked with words such as "Creepy," "Grotesque," and "Realistic," and the parts of our body such as "Face" and "Teeth." The results suggested that the participants preferred the anthropomorphic designs, which incorporated the whole body of a human being as an anthropomorphic feature with cute, and charming, whereas they disliked the realistic and anthropomorphic designs incorporating only human body parts due to uncomfortable feelings. Through this study, we clarified the tendency and characteristics of preference product designs with incorporated anthropomorphism.

Keywords: Anthropomorphism · Preference · Kansei Design

1 Introduction

1.1 Definition of Anthropomorphism

Anthropomorphism refers to "treating a god, animal, or object as if it had human qualities" [1]. Another related term is 'Animism,' which is "the belief that natural phenomena such as plants, objects, and weather have living souls" [2]. Piaget [3] emphasizes that animistic thinking, in which objects have a human soul, is specific to children. In addition, he explained that this animistic thinking is an immature form that stems from the

C. Stephanidis et al. (Eds.): HCII 2024, CCIS 2319, pp. 128–137, 2025.
https://doi.org/10.1007/978-3-031-78516-0_13

self-centeredness seen in children's early developmental process, and it is lost as they grow older and develop an objective perspective, becoming more decentered. However, Sueda [4] refutes Piaget's argument based on the prevalence of Japanese anime culture. He emphasized that animistic thinking, like anime culture, is not an immature and infantile thought or feeling but a part of the adaptation style universally possessed by adults. Anime culture has become a popular form of entertainment worldwide and for all ages today. He explains that the human cognitive structure, perception, and sensation that responds to manga and anime is not a psychological trait unique to Japan but a transgenerational psychological trait that exists at the base of all cultures. If we support Sueda's argument above, animistic thinking is a way of thinking that humans generally have. In other words, anthropomorphism is one of the values common to all human beings and is a typical behavior and expression that anyone can engage in.

Based on the background, in this research, we define anthropomorphism as 'actions and expressions that reflect animistic thinking which means objects have a human soul.'

1.2 Influence of Design that Incorporates Anthropomorphism

Nishii [5] argues from previous research on anthropomorphism in products that anthropomorphism positively impacts product evaluation and sales. Regarding products and brands that incorporate anthropomorphism, consumers perceive an interpersonal connection to the object; as a result, they feel warmth and familiarity toward the target product or brand, which improves their evaluation and purchase intention. On the other hand, she also considered that the perception of anthropomorphism has a negative impact on consumers depending on the context. Based on the above, it can be concluded that anthropomorphism is generally perceived and can positively or negatively impact people who perceive it. However, there are still few research cases on the conditions under which anthropomorphism has a particularly negative impact on design in general, including products and brands.

2 Purpose of This Research and Hypothesis

This study aims to clarify the relationship between expression and preference for anthropomorphic designs from the viewpoint of Kansei Design. Specifically, we will explore the relationship between the expression of anthropomorphic design and users' evaluation; that is, we will clarify anthropomorphic design's positive and negative effects and the reason for effects through its factors.

Like the precious researcher Nishii [5], she considered that the perception of anthropomorphism can have both positive and negative effects on consumers. However, she argued that most previous studies focused on positive influences and that it is necessary to clarify the conditions under which negative influences of anthropomorphism can occur. If there are factors that positively influence consumers, it is conceivable that there are also factors that have a negative influence simultaneously. Therefore, the following hypotheses are formulated in this study.

'Anthropomorphism in design has positive and negative effects, and there are factors as a reason.'

3 Experiment Methods

3.1 Stimulus

We collected a total of 52 images related to product design, including anthropomorphism, that appeared at the top of a search for "anthropomorphism_products_design" on the online photo-sharing service "Pinterest" (as of April 19, 2023). From these 52 images, we selected 45 images after discussing with nine co-researchers and removing seven images considered inappropriate for this experiment. The collected images were edited to a uniform image size of W143.5 mm H100 mm (W100 mm H143.5 mm for vertical images) using Adobe Illustrator. The image cards were then printed using A4 size photo paper and used as stimuli in this experiment (from now on referred to as "stimulus images").

3.2 Period and Subjects

This experiment was conducted from May 12 to June 6, 2023, with 52 male and female subjects (37 males and 15 females, mean age $M = 22$, standard deviation $SD = 1.3$). Nine subjects could not participate in the experiment in person, so a similar evaluation experiment was conducted online.

3.3 Procedure

Before starting the experiment, each subject completed a consent form indicating whether they would participate. After checking the experiment's flow, they evaluated all 45 stimulus images and answered whether they "liked" or "disliked" the presented images. They were instructed to use their intuition as much as possible to answer the questions. After completing the responses, the subjects were classified into the stimulus image group, where the subjects answered "like" or "dislike." After the classification, they selected three favorite stimulus images among their "liked" ones. After that, they selected their three disliked stimulus images. Finally, they answered why the first to third "liked" and "disliked" stimulus images were selected. The subjects used "Google Forms," an online questionnaire service provided by Google, as the response format for answering the reason for their selection.

3.4 Analysis Method

The following procedure was used to process and analyze the response data to the stimulus images obtained in this experiment.

1. The first, second, and third most "liked" stimulus images were given a score of 3, 2, and 1, respectively. The sum of the scores for each stimulus image was calculated, and this was used as the total "liked" score for them. Then, based on the total score of "liked" in the stimulus images, we ranked them.
2. The first, second, and third most "disliked" stimulus images were given a score of 3, 2, and 1, respectively. The sum of the scores for each stimulus image was calculated, and this was used as the total score of "disliked" for them. Then, based on the total score of "disliked" in the stimulus images, we ranked them.

3. We did text-mining for the reasons for the 1–3 most "liked" stimulus images. Similarly, we did text-mining the reasons for the 1–3 most "disliked" stimulus images.

4 Results

4.1 Preference Scores for "Liked" and "Disliked"

Preference Scores for "Liked". Figure 1 shows the results of the scores for each "liked" of the stimulus images, and the top five "liked" images are displayed. The stimulus image the respondents liked the most was No. 17 [6], with 35 points. In addition, the second place was No. 16 [7] with 30 points, the third place was No. 13 [8] with 29 points, the fourth place was No. 25 [9] with 18 points, and the fifth place was No. 36 [10] with 16 points ($M = 6.93$, $SD = 8.11$).

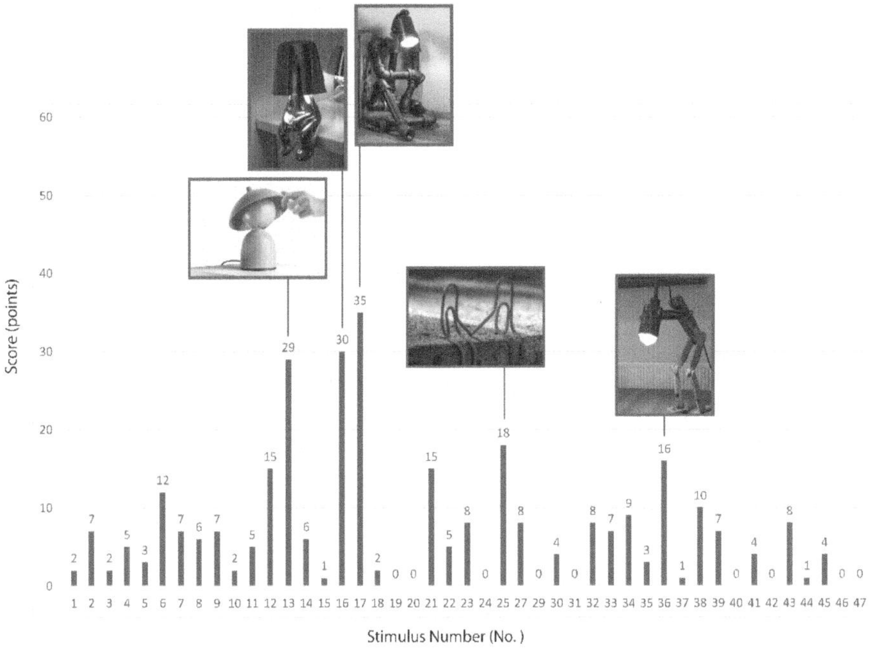

Fig. 1. Score totals and top 5 "liked" [6–10]

Preference Scores for "Disliked". Figure 2 shows the results of the "disliked" scores for each stimulus image, and the top five "disliked" images are displayed. The most disliked stimulus image the respondents "disliked" was No. 29 [11], scoring 49 points. In addition, the second place was No. 31 [12] with 47 points, the third place was No. 19 [13] with 41 points, the fourth place was No. 45 [14] with 33 points, and the fifth place was No. 5 [15] with 29 points ($M = 6.93$, $SD = 12.5$).

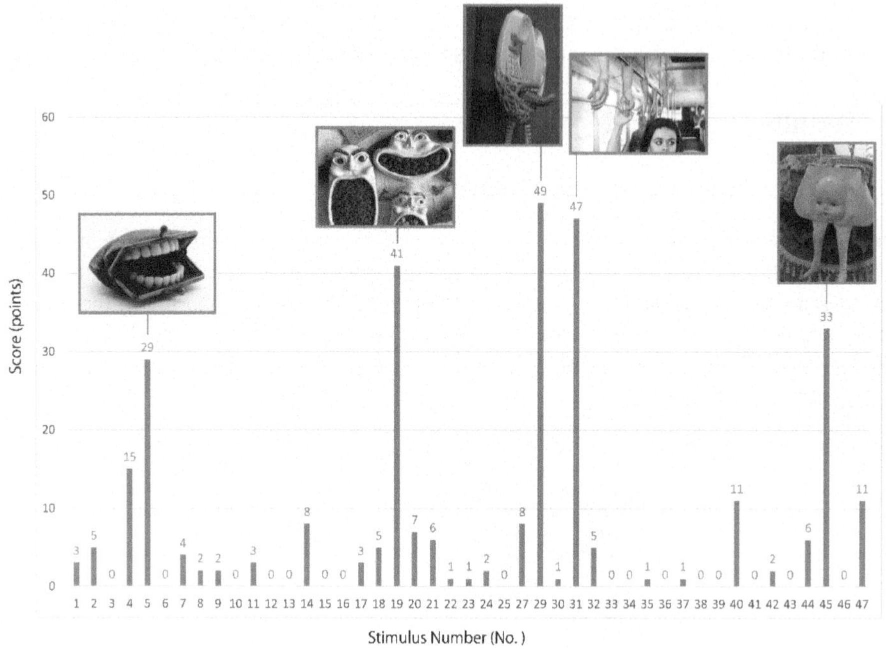

Fig. 2. Score totals and top 5 "disliked" [11–15]

4.2 Text-Mining

Word-Cloud (Sort by Frequency). Text mining using "AI text mining" [16] was performed for each of the "liked" and "disliked" reasons, and the words were arranged in a word cloud in order of frequency of appearance. Thus, the more frequently a word appeared in the preference reasons, the larger it was displayed.

Figure 3 shows the words included in the "liked" reason, ordered by frequency of occurrence. especially, the nouns "好き(like)" (39 times) and "デザイン(Design)" (24 Times), the verbs "感じる(Feel)" (53 times), "思う(Think)" (45 times), and "見える(Look)" (21 times), the adjectives "かわいい/可愛い(Cute)" (51 times) and "面白い(Funny)" (24 times) were identified. Other words that were identified were "ライト(Light)" (18 times), which indicates the characteristics of the product, "キャラクター(Character)" (9 times), and "人間らしい(human-like)" (8 times), which refers to anthropomorphism.

Figure 4 shows the words included in the reasons for "disliked" in order of frequency of occurrence. The nouns were "気持ち(Feeling)" (54 times), "顔(Face)" (43 times), "リアル(Real)" (32 times), "デザイン(Design)" (21 times), and "不気味(Creepy)" (20 times); the verbs were "感じる(Feel)" (63 times) and "思う(Think)" (36 times); and the adjective was "怖い(Scary)" (39 times). Other words related to the human anatomy, such as "歯(Teeth)" (19 times) and "骨(Bones)" (10 times), and words referring to expressions such as "生々しい(Vivid)" (8 times) and "強い(Strong)" (6 times) were also identified.

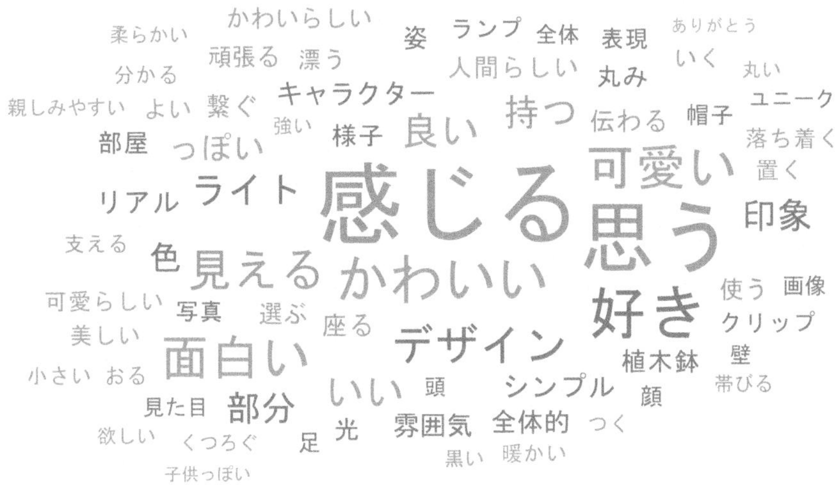

Fig. 3. Reason for Japanese word cloud for "liked" (ordered by frequency of occurrence)

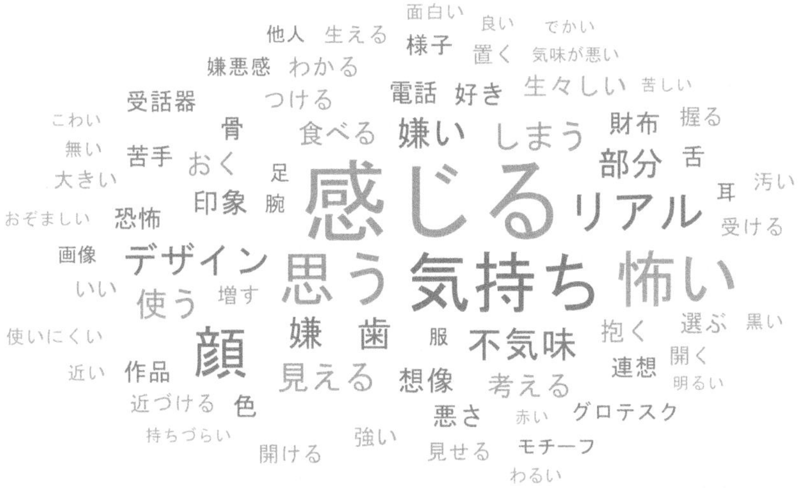

Fig. 4. Reason for Japanese word cloud for "disliked" (ordered by frequency of occurrence)

Co-occurrence Network. Pre-processing was performed using "KH Coder" [17] to exclude pronouns and particles, and morphological analysis was performed on the reasons for "liked" and "disliked". A co-occurrence network was displayed to visualize the relationship between the words. The lines in the figure indicate the relationship between words, the size of the circle indicates the frequency of occurrence of the word, and the circle's color indicates the word's categorization.

Figure 5 shows the co-occurrence network for the reason "liked". A total of nine categories were created based on word associations. First, with the "部分(Part)" in the center, "ポーズ(Pose)"-"光(Light)"-"ランプ(Lamp)" -"丸み(Roundness)"-"全

体(whole)” -”可愛らしい(Cute),” “シンプル(Simple)”-”形(Form)”-”人間(Human),” and “感じる(Feel)”-”持つ(Have)”-”ライト(Light)” -”体(Body)”-”漂う(Waft)” words connection was confirmed. Second, “好き(Like)”-”思う(Think)”-”感じ(Feel like)” -”可愛い(Cute”-”リアル(Real)” -”頑張る(Work hard)”-”キャラクター(Character)”-”似る(Be similar)” -”出る(Appears)” words connection was confirmed. Third, “手(Hand)” - “繋ぐ(Connect)” - “姿(Figure)”- “クリップ(Clip)”- “見える(Look)”- “色合い(Hue)”- “直感(Intuition)”- “雰囲気(Atmosphere)”- “落ち着く(Calm)”words connection was confirmed. In addition, “座る(Sit)”- “様子(Appearance)”words, such as represents human behavior connection was confirmed.

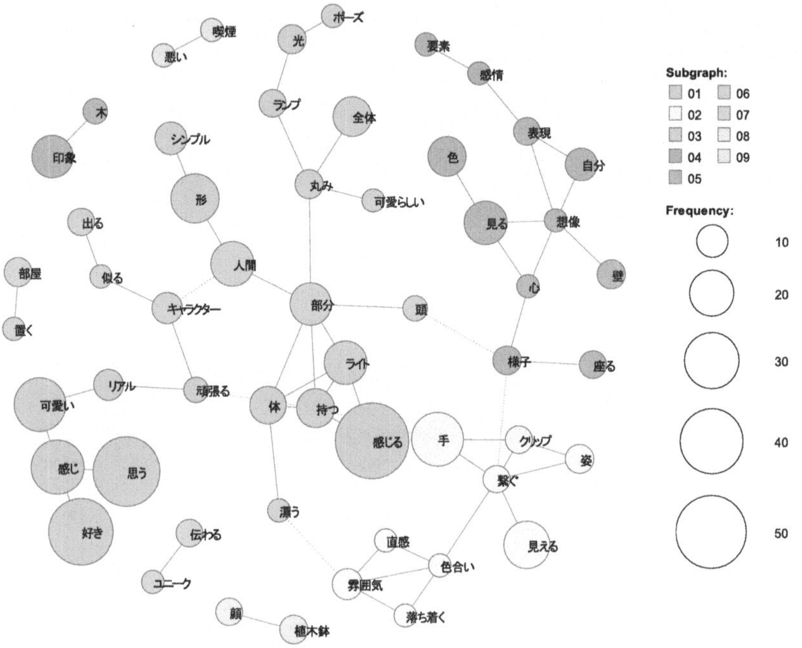

Fig. 5. Co-occurrence network in reasons for “liked”

Figure 6 shows the co-occurrence network for the “disliked” reason. A total of eleven categories were identified based on word associations. First, “リアル(Real)”-”気持ち(Feeling)”-”悪い(Bad)” -”手(Hand)”-”握る(Seize)” -”腕(arm)”-”人(Human)” words connection was confirmed. Second, “口(Mouth)”-”目(Eyes)”-”怖い(Scary)” -”顔(Face)” words connection was confirmed. Third, “受話器(Real)”-”近づける(Feeling)”-”普段(Bad)” -”電話(Phone)”-”使う(Use)” -”舌(Tongue)”-”歯(Tooth)”-”汚い(Dirty)”-”不快(Displeasure)” words connection was confirmed. In addition, “不気味(Creepy)”-”生える(Grow)”-”足(Legs)” words and “出る(Appears)”-”ホラー(Horror)”-”映画(Movie),” “グロテスク(Grotesque)”-”様子(Appearance)”-”作品(Works)” -”強い(Strong)”-”連想(Association)” words, such as recall from the work words connection was confirmed.

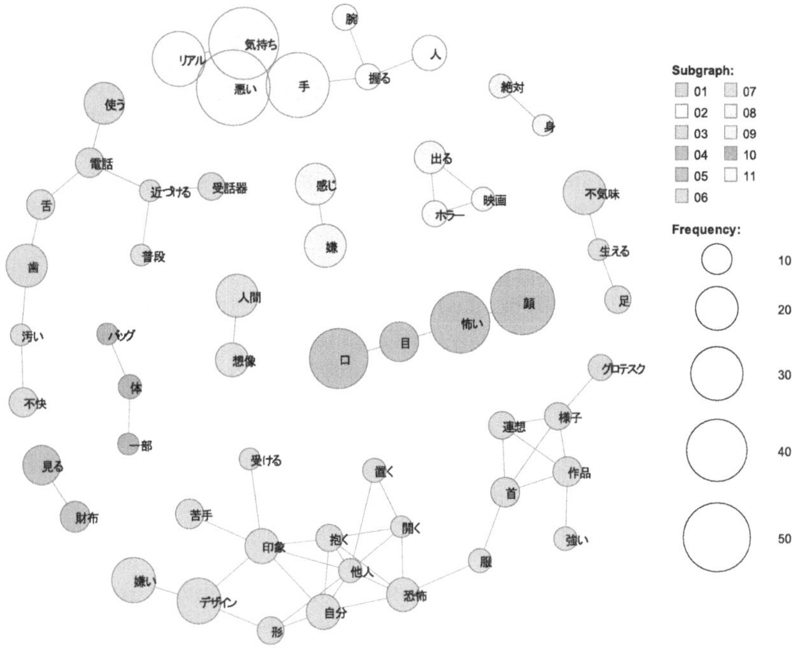

Fig. 6. Co-occurrence network in reasons for "disliked"

5 Discussion

First, Fig. 3 shows that positive words such as "かわいい/可愛い(Cute)," "面白い(Funny)," and "親しみやすい(Friendly)" were selected as the reasons for "liked." In addition, words that indicate humanity were also mentioned, such as "キャラクター(Character)" and "人間らしい(Human-like)," were also cited. On the other hand, Fig. 4 shows that negative words such as "怖い(Scary)" and "不気味(Creepy)" were cited as reasons for "disliked." In addition, it was confirmed that the word "気持ち(Feeling)" was connected to the word "悪い(Bad)" by analyzing the words before and after the word in the sentence. In addition, "リアル(Real)" and "生々しい(Vivid)" were mentioned as expressions close to the natural body. These results suggest that "humanness" and "realism" in anthropomorphic designs can sometimes be positively or negatively evaluated.

Second, Fig. 1 suggests that the top-ranked stimulus images that the respondents "liked" had in common were designs that incorporated the whole body of the human body. Figure 2 indicates that the commonality of the top stimulus images that the respondents "disliked" was a design that incorporated each part of the human body. This can be explained using a word cloud that indicates the reason for each difference and a co-occurrence network that indicates the relationship between words. Figure 3 shows that the word cloud representing the reason for "liked" did not include any human body parts but included words that describe the whole body, such as "全体的(Overall)." Fig. 5 shows that the co-occurrence network for a reason of "liked" is "全体(Whole)" - "丸

み(Roundness)" - "可愛らしい(Cute)," confirming the connection of words that positively evaluate the whole body of an object. On the other hand, Fig. 4 shows that the word cloud representing the reason for "disliked" included words describing human body parts such as "歯(Teeth)," "舌(Tongue)," "耳(Ears)," "顔(Face)," and "足(Legs). Figure 6 shows the co-occurrence network for the reason for "disliked" and the connection between words that negatively evaluate parts of objects such as "リアル(Real)," - "気持ち(Feeling)," - "悪い(Bad)," - "手(Hand)," "口(Mouth)," - "目(Eye)," - "怖い(Scary)" - "顔(Face)," and "不気味(Creepy)" - "生える(Grow)" - "足(Legs)" was confirmed. This suggests that expressions of "humanness" and "realism" in anthropomorphic designs are likelier to be liked if they incorporate the whole human body. In contrast, expressions that include body parts are more likely to be disliked.

Third, another common feature of the stimulus images is the type of object that incorporates anthropomorphism. Figure 1 shows that a table lamp was four out of the top five types of objects that could be anthropomorphic. In addition, Fig. 2 shows that objects such as telephone handsets, hanging straps, bags, and purses were the most common objects that incorporate anthropomorphic qualities. Desktop lamps dominate a part of private spaces such as one's room, but there are few opportunities for the human body to touch them directly. On the other hand, objects such as telephone handsets, hanging straps, bags, and wallets, although they rarely dominate the private space, are often in direct contact with the human body, such as directly on the face, held in hand, or always carried around. This suggests that the type of object that incorporates anthropomorphism influences the preference. In particular, the results of this experiment indicate that the subjects prefer objects that are neither too close nor too far away from the design that incorporates anthropomorphism.

Lastly, in the co-occurrence network for the reason of "liked" in Fig. 5, we confirmed the connection between the words "手(Hand)" - "繋ぐ(Connect)" - "姿(Figure)," 座る(Sit)" - "様子(Appearance)," and "キャラクター(Character)" - "頑張る(Work hard)." On the other hand, for the co-occurrence network in the reason for "disliked" in Fig. 6, the following word connections were confirmed: "グロテスク(Grotesque)"-"様子(Appearance)"-"連想(Association)," "ホラー(Horror)"-"映画(Movie)"-"出る(Appears). This suggests that, in addition to the impression of the overall appearance of the design, the context in the story of the design is also a factor in judging "liked" or "disliked" of the design.

The above results suggest that a design incorporating anthropomorphism is preferred if it includes the whole body of a human being and has a charming expression. On the other hand, the results suggest that designs that incorporate human body parts that are realistic and unpleasant are disliked. In addition, the types of objects that incorporate anthropomorphism and the context of the design story were suggested to influence the preference.

Based on the conclusion, the hypothesis was thus verified.

6 Prospects

This study examined the factors determining likes and dislikes when a product design has anthropomorphism expression. By reflecting on the factors that determine the positivity and negativity of real products, it will be possible to create effective anthropomorphic products. For example, when we want to create an anthropomorphic product liked by the target users or when we want to create an anthropomorphic product that warns the target users, we can use this study's findings. However, one of the problems of this study is that the analysis is not limited to one type of product. Therefore, to continue the research in the future, it is necessary to set the products to which anthropomorphism is applied. In the future, we will define one type of product that incorporates anthropomorphic elements and investigate changes in impressions according to anthropomorphic expressions.

References

1. Oxford Learner's Dictionaries anthropomorphism noun. https://www.oxfordlearnersdictionaries.com/definition/english/anthropomorphism. Accessed 13 March 2024
2. Oxford Learner's Dictionaries animism noun. https://www.oxfordlearnersdictionaries.com/definition/english/animism?q=animism. Accessed 13 March 2024
3. Piaget, J.: The Child's Conception of the World. Routledge & Kegan Paul, London (1929)
4. Keiji, S.: Is the sense of animism quite immature personality traits or not? - On the functional role for inner adjustment. J. Koshien Junior Coll. **38**, 1–6 (2020). (in Japanese)
5. Mayuko, N.: The effect of perceived anthropomorphism on consumer behavior. Chiba University of Commerce Review **59**(3), 233–245 (2022) (in Japanese)
6. Yaplakal (in Russian). https://www.yaplakal.com/forum2/topic2072907.html. Accessed 15 Mrach 2024
7. Tiktok-Lushue.Official. https://www.tiktok.com/@lushue.official/video/7107677313176767750. Accessed 15 March 2024
8. Yanko design -this emotive desk lamp embodies the fondest memories of your childhood rainy days! https://www.yankodesign.com/2021/03/21/this-emotive-desk-lamp-embodies-the-fondest-memories-of-your-childhood-rainy-days/. Accessed 15 March 2024
9. X - Ra'afat. https://twitter.com/raafat_saleh/status/1762822760080752977. Accessed 15 March 2024
10. Etsy –VintageBarrelCrafts. https://www.etsy.com/jp/listing/620357318/robot-lamp-barrel-lamp-desk-lamp-vintage?epik=dj0yJnU9UUhELWEtZkNyREMzM2JOWnhVN05HTGpMN3d5WWFjWWMmcD0wJm49S0FUaEdpVkoxallIN3IycnpzWFRPUSZ0PUFBQUFBR1gwWjZj. Accessed 15 March 2024
11. Cool Pictures to Improve Your Mood. https://www.ebaumsworld.com/pictures/37-cool-pictures-to-improve-your-mood/85278291/?image=85278312. Accessed 15 March 2024
12. Boredpanda - Creative Uses of Handles in Transit Advertising. https://www.boredpanda.com/creative-subway-bus-handle-ads/. Accessed 15 March 2024
13. Instagram -ab_khak_jam. https://www.instagram.com/ab_khak_jan/p/CYMiZuioLAB/?img_index=1. Accessed 15 March 2024
14. Tumblr -Claire Corruptible. https://i-cunt-believe-it.tumblr.com/post/28467361969. Accessed 15 March 2024
15. Etsy -PrettyUnique Molds. https://www.etsy.com/listing/758414916/fake-human-teeth-tooth-mould-silicone?epik=dj0yJnU9VVExbTdOdlJZWEpqeS11bk5IUEtRT2I4WGd0S2Q2SGQmcD0wJm49NHBHOXF3RHVDQVM0dmV5QWNuSTJ6QSZ0PUFBQUFBR1gwYWhF, Accessed 15 March 2024AI Text Mining by User Local, https://textmining.userlocal.jp/. Accessed 15 March 2024
16. AI Text Mining by User Local. https://textmining.userlocal.jp/. Accessed 13 March 2024
17. Koichi, H.: Quantitative Text Analysis for Social Researchers: A Contribution to Content Analysis. 2nd edn. Nakanishiya Shuppan, Kyoto (2020) (in Japanese)

Optimization of SSVEP-BCI Interface Design - a Study Based on Visual Comfort

Mu Tong[1](✉) and Yun Lin[2]

[1] School of Design, South China University of Technology, Nanjing 211189, China
230198790@seu.edu.cn

[2] School of Design Arts and Media, Nanjing University of Science and Technology, Nanjing 210094, China

Abstract. Due to the high information transfer rate and accuracy, SSVEP-based BCI interfaces are widely used in the engineering field. However, the SSVEP paradigm can induce various symptoms of visual discomfort in users after long-term work because it relies on the user's continual attention and confirmation towards flickering objects on the interface. To improve this condition, our study organized an simulated typing experiment with 20 subjects to investigate the impact of frequency and size of flickering icons on visual comfort within a BCI interface. Throughout the experimentation process, subjects' subjective comfort levels and ocular characteristics were monitored to assess their overall comfort.

The experimental results showed that both frequency and size significantly affect the visual comfort of subjects when performing BCI tasks. As the frequency range increased, users' visual comfort ratings were higher, while an increase in size led to the opposite effect. Considering the interaction between these two factors, a icon size smaller than 4 ° and a flickering frequency above 40Hz would yield the optimal visual experience. The findings can be directly applied to optimizing design for SSVEP-based BCI interfaces.

Keywords: Human-Machine Interface Design · Visual Comfort Assessment · Brain-computer interface · Dynamic visual cognition

1 Introduction

As an emerging technology, brain-computer interface has been widely used in rehabilitation medicine, cognitive enhancement, fatigue monitoring and other fields [1, 2, 3]. As a kind of brain-computer interface paradigm based on electroencephalogram (EEG), the SSVEP (steady-state visually evoked potential) paradigm is implemented by presenting flickering stimuli with specific phase or frequency combinations on the screen to induce electrical activity of primary visual cortex neurons [4]. By recording EEG and processing signals, it is possible to analyze and obtain the user's interactive intentions. Compared to other brain-computer interface (BCI) paradigms such as P300 and motor rhythm-based approaches, the SSVEP is extensively used in domains like text spelling and cognitive evaluation due to its high interaction speed and accuracy [5, 6]. However,

C. Stephanidis et al. (Eds.): HCII 2024, CCIS 2319, pp. 138–144, 2025.
https://doi.org/10.1007/978-3-031-78516-0_14

SSVEP implementation requires users to continuously focus on flickering stimuli on the BCI screen during tasks. This continuous eye movement and fixation can lead to problems. For instance, prolonged exposure to flashing stimuli during task performance was known to cause a range of visual discomforts including reduced vision, blurriness, dryness, dizziness, and even photosensitive epilepsy [7, 8, 9].

Previous research has attributed the causes of visual discomfort to fundamental properties of flickering images, such as brightness [10], color [11], frequency [12], and patterns of variation [13]. Among these attributes, flicker frequency is considered to be the critical factor affecting visual comfort in BCI. How to choose the appropriate frequency for flickering images in a BCI interface remains unclear, as both high and low frequencies have their respective advantages and disadvantages. For instance, frequencies lower than 65Hz may directly trigger photosensitive epilepsy [14], whereas lower frequencies are more likely to induce migraines compared to higher rates of flicker [15]. Secondly, since larger flickering stimuli generate stronger SSVEP responses [4], icons of bigger size are preferred when designing BCI interfaces. However, a larger flashing area means more light flow entering the visual field, which can lead to increased visual discomfort [16]. Although the phenomenon of visual fatigue in BCIs due to stimulus property settings has received some attention [3], research simultaneously examining the relationship between both key attributes—frequency and size—and induced visual comfort is still lacking.

Therefore, this study focuses on the size and frequency of flickering icons in the SSVEP-BCI interface. By organizing user participation in simulated BCI typing tasks and monitoring users' subjective visual comfort and eye movement characteristics during task execution, it aims to understand changes in users' visual comfort with different flickering frequencies and sizes. The results obtained for flicker frequency and stimulus size can be directly applied to the design of human-computer interfaces for SSVEP-BCIs.

2 Methodology

2.1 Experimental Design

The experimental Brain-Computer Interface (BCI) used for the study is illustrated in Fig. 1. It involved a simulated SSVEP-BCI typing task, where participants were required to locate target words among numerous flashing stimuli according to prompts. The eye movement patterns during this simulation matched those of an actual BCI task execution. Participants' subjective visual discomfort and eye movement characteristics were monitored over a continuous 20-min typing activity, assessing their levels of visual comfort. Subjective assessments of visual comfort employed a 5-point scale that included factors such as dry eyes, eye discomfort, and deterioration of vision. Measuring eye movement characteristics was done by tracking pupil diameter and monitoring signs of ocular discomfort. Previous research has indicated significant correlations between these two features and objective fatigue indicators [17, 18].

The flicker frequency of the interface icons has been categorized into three ranges: low-frequency (1–20 Hz), medium-frequency (20–40 Hz), and high-frequency (40–60 Hz). The selection of frequencies was informed by previous research [11, 12] [19].

In the interfaces corresponding to each frequency group, all icons will flicker at a random frequency within that range. The interface contains a total of 20 words arranged as depicted in Fig. 1; all icons are randomly placed and reshuffled after each participant's selection. Icon sizes were chosen to be four different degrees: 2deg, 3deg, 4deg, and 6deg. To enhance display quality and minimize fatigue, icon color was selected as white against a black background setting for the interface.

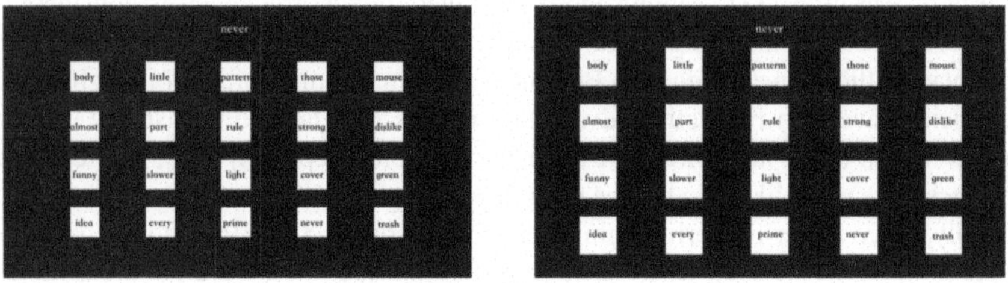

Fig. 1. Schematic representation of the experimental interface materials.

2.2 Participants

A total of 20 graduate students from Southeast University and Nanjing University of Science and Technology were recruited as participants for this experiment. Their ages ranged between 22 and 32. All had normal vision or corrected-to-normal vision. None of the participants had a history of mental illness or photosensitive epilepsy. All participants were required to read and sign an informed consent form before the experiment.

2.3 Equipment and Environment

The experimental program was based on the Unity platform and was written using C#. The experiment was conducted in a quiet laboratory isolated from the external environment. The experimental program ran on an HP workstation with a Windows 10 operating system. Stimuli were presented on a 27-inch Dell monitor with a resolution of 1920*1080. Participants were asked to sit on a chair with their eyes 510mm from the screen, and their line of sight-maintained level with the centerline of the screen. The monitor's brightness was set to 150cd/m^2. Eye movement data were collected using a Tobii Pro Fusion, with a maximum sampling rate of 120Hz. Eye movement data collection and analysis were performed using Tobii Pro Lab.

2.4 Procedure

Before the experiment began, the experimenter provided instructions on precautions, procedures, content, and operation of the experiment to the participants, and adjusted the eye-tracking equipment to ensure effective data collection. Participants were first required to complete a 2-min practice session. Only after finishing the practice could they proceed to the formal experiment. During the formal experiment, participants had to

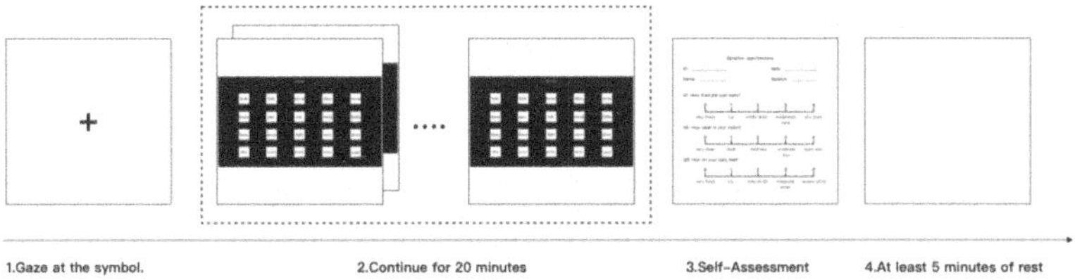

Fig. 2. Schematic Diagram of the Experimental Procedure

complete 12 task segments, frequency [3] x size [4]. The procedure for each task segment is shown in Fig. 2. In each task segment, participants were required to identify and click on target words among all flashing targets on the screen, based on the instructions at the top of the interface. To simulate the latency characteristic of BCI interactions, selected words would continue to flash for 1–2 s before switching to the next stimulus interface. The program continuously generated experimental materials throughout each task segment until the task ended after 20 min.

2.5 Data Processing

In the experiment, a total of 20 sets of data were collected, and the discrete points in the data were removed. Descriptive statistical analysis was conducted on the collected correct answer rate and subjective comfort scores, and A [3] XB [4] repeated measures variance analysis was performed on processed eye movement data and subjective comfort scores. Data processing used IBM SPSS 26.0. All data passed normality testing.

Table 1. Descriptive statistical results of the experimental data

Independent variable	Accuracy Rate		Comfort level		Pupil Diameter		Blink frequency	
	M	SD	M	SD	M	SD	M	SD
Size								
2	92.3	2.92	4.32	0.24	5.73	0.20	12.6	0.34
3	93.7	2.56	4.05	0.30	5.66	0.18	12.4	0.38
4	95.8	3.12	3.57	0.18	5.63	0.16	12.8	0.25
6	94.4	1.98	2.95	0.32	5.54	0.13	11.7	0.17
Frequency								
Low	94.1	2.85	3.39	0.19	5.52	0.11	13.8	0.41
Medium	94.3	2.94	3.73	0.35	5.64	0.23	12.6	0.26
High	93.9	3.07	4.04	0.28	5.77	0.13	10.7	0.29

3 Expected Results

3.1 Accuracy Rates

As shown in Table 1, the descriptive statistics results of task accuracy indicated that the accuracy at all levels was greater than 92.3%, thus confirming that the subjects seriously participated in the tasks during the experiment. Since task accuracy was only used to judge whether the subject seriously participates in the experiment, there was no need for further analysis.

3.2 Subjective Visual Comfort Scores

The results of the ANOVA variance analysis indicated that both flicker frequency ($F = 26.538$, $p < 0.05$) and icon size ($F = 35.609$, $p < 0.05$) significantly affected the visual comfort. Furthermore, there was an interaction between flicker frequency and size ($F = 31.826$, $p < 0.05$). The results of the simple effect analysis showed that when the frequency under low-intervals (1-20Hz) conditions, icon size significantly affected participants' visual comfort scores ($p < 0.05$), and observing larger sizes could lead to lower visual comfort scores. In the mid to high-frequency ranges, vision comfort score was significantly affected only when the size exceeded 4 °, decreasing with further increases in size Table 2.

Table 2. The result of variance analysis of experimental data.

Independent variable	Comfort level		Pupil Diameter		Blink frequency	
	F	P	F	P	F	P
Size	35.609	0.026	19.626	0.026	0.605	0.311
Frequency	26.538	0.041	52.101	0.001	25.133	0.040
Size x Frequency	31.826	0.032	0.782	0.159	0.837	0.158

3.3 Eye Movement Characteristics

The ANOVA analysis results indicated that the pupil diameter was significantly affected by flicker frequency ($F = 52.101$, $p < 0.05$) and icon size ($F = 19.626$, $p < 0.05$). This suggested that a lower flicker frequency lead to pupil constriction, while larger icon sizes were associated with an expansion of the pupil diameter.; no interaction was found between flicker frequency and icon size ($F = 0.782$, $p = 0.159$). Blink frequency was also found to be significantly influenced by the flicker frequency ($F = 25.133$, $p < 0.05$), with low-frequency flickering stimuli causing an increase in blink numbers.

4 Discussion

The overall results of the experiment indicated that in a 20-min visual observation task, both the flicker frequency and size of an icon can affect observers' visual comfort. The higher the flicker frequency, the better was participants' visual experience, possibly because when frequency exceeded 40Hz, it was difficult for human eyes to recognize significant flashing due to exceeding the human's CFF. Flickering less than 20Hz had also been proven in previous studies to cause significant ocular surface and extraocular symptoms. However, size played an opposite role: Among a group of tested sizes, larger ones (4 deg and 6 deg) led to worse viewing experiences. The data on eye movement characteristics supported the aforementioned findings. Pupil dilation tended to increase with higher flicker frequencies and smaller sizes of visual stimuli, which typically indicated a reduction in fatigue (20)(18). Conversely, blink frequency significantly increased when the flicker rate of the stimulus image was lowered, which could generally be interpreted as an increase in ocular fatigue for the observer.

In addition, considering that too small icon size could make users waste more time searching for targets and was not conducive to eliciting effective responses under the SSVEP paradigm. Therefore, this study suggested that when presenting flashing icons in the BCI interface, high frequency (greater than 40Hz) and appropriately sized icons should be chosen as stimuli.

5 Conclusion

This study conducted a simulated typing task with 20 subjects to examine the impact of size design and frequency selection of flickering icons on user visual comfort in SSVEP-BCI human-computer interfaces. Results revealed that flickering icons with a frequency greater than 40Hz and size smaller than 4 deg provide better visual experience. The experimental results can be used as references for SSVEP-BCI human-machine interface design to enhance user's visual experience.

It should be noted that due to limitations in experimental conditions, the current study employed simulated BCI tasks. In actual BCI typing tasks, users may experience more significant visual discomfort and fatigue; therefore, future research would be conducted in more ecologically valid settings and take into account the impact of different types of tasks, such as monitoring and search tasks.

References

1. Bockbrader, M.A., Francisco, G., Lee, R., Olson, J., Solinsky, R., Boninger, M.L.: Brain computer interfaces in rehabilitation medicine. PM&R. **10**(9), S233–S243 (2018)
2. de Albuquerque, V.H.C., Damaševičius, R., Garcia, N.M., Pinheiro, P.R., Filho, P.P.R.: Brain computer interface systems for neurorobotics: methods and applications. BioMed Res. Int. **30**(2017), e2505493 (2017)
3. Cao, T., Wan, F., Wong, C.M., da Cruz, J.N., Hu, Y.: Objective evaluation of fatigue by EEG spectral analysis in steady-state visual evoked potential-based brain-computer interfaces. BioMed Eng OnLine. **13**(1), 28 (2014)

4. Ng, K.B., Bradley, A.P., Cunnington, R.: Stimulus specificity of a steady-state visual-evoked potential-based brain–computer interface. J. Neural Eng. **9**(3), 036008 (2012)
5. Data Analytics in Steady-State Visual Evoked Potential-Based Brain–Computer Interface: A Review I IEEE Journals & Magazine I IEEE Xplore [Internet] (2024). https://ieeexplore.ieee.org/abstract/document/9170622
6. Li, M., He, D., Li, C., Qi, S.: Brain-computer interface speller based on steady-state visual evoked potential: a review focusing on the stimulus paradigm and performance. Brain Sci. **11**(4), 450 (2021)
7. Coles-brennan, C., Sulley, A., Young, G.: Management of digital eye strain. Clin. Exp. Optom. **102**(1), 18–29 (2019)
8. Kuze, J., Ukai, K.: Subjective evaluation of visual fatigue caused by motion images. Displays **29**(2), 159–166 (2008)
9. Harding, G.F.A., Harding, P.F.: Photosensitive epilepsy and image safety. Appl. Ergon. **41**(4), 504–508 (2010)
10. Yan, W., Xu, G., Xie, J., Li, M., Zhang, S., Luo, A.: Study on the effects of brightness contrast on steady-state motion visual evoked potential. In: 2017 39th Annual International Conference of the IEEE Engineering in Medicine and Biology Society (EMBC) [Internet] (2024). https://www.infona.pl//resource/bwmeta1.element.ieee-art-000008037306
11. Duart, X., Quiles, E., Suay, F., Chio, N., García, E., Morant, F.: Evaluating the effect of stimuli color and frequency on SSVEP. Sensors. **21**(1), 117 (2021)
12. Ladouce, S., Darmet, L., Torre Tresols, J.J., Velut, S., Ferraro, G., Dehais, F.: Improving user experience of SSVEP BCI through low amplitude depth and high frequency stimuli design. Sci. Rep. **12**(1), 8865 (2022)
13. Baek, H.J., Kim, H.S., Ahn, M., Cho, H., Ahn, S.: Ergonomic issues in brain-computer interface technologies: current status, challenges, and future direction. Comput. Intell. Neurosci. **7**(2020), 4876397 (2020)
14. Leccese, F., Rocca, M., Salvadori, G., Oner, M., Burattini, C., Bisegna, F.: Laptop displays performance: compliance assessment with visual ergonomics requirements. Displays **1**(68), 102019 (2021)
15. Kowacs, P.A., Piovesan, E.J., Werneck, L.C., Fameli, H., Zani, A.C., da Silva, H.P.: Critical flicker frequency in migraine. A controlled study in patients without prophylactic therapy. Cephalalgia **25**(5), 339–343 (2005)
16. Terenzi, L., Zaal, P.: Rotational and translational velocity and acceleration thresholds for the onset of cybersickness in virtual reality. In: AIAA Scitech 2020 Forum [Internet]. Ameri-can Institute of Aeronautics and Astronautics https://arc.aiaa.org/doi/abs/10.2514/6.2020-0171
17. Schleicher, R., Galley, N., Briest, S., Galley, L.: Blinks and saccades as indicators of fatigue in sleepiness warnings: looking tired? Ergonomics **51**(7), 982–1010 (2008)
18. Bafna, T., Hansen, J.P.: Mental fatigue measurement using eye metrics: a systematic literature review. Psychophysiology **58**(6), e13828 (2021)
19. Won, D.O., Hwang, H.J., Dähne, S., Müller, K.R., Lee, S.W.: Effect of higher frequency on the classification of steady-state visual evoked potentials. J. Neural Eng. **13**(1), 016014 (2015)
20. Hopstaken, J.F., van der Linden, D., Bakker, A.B., Kompier, M.A.J.: The window of my eyes: task disengagement and mental fatigue covary with pupil dynamics. Biol. Psychol. **1**(110), 100–106 (2015)

Competency-Driven Strategies for Sustainable Professional Growth

Florence Williams(✉)

University of Central Florida, Orlando, Florida, USA
florence.williams@ucf.edu

Abstract. This paper discusses strategies for identifying competency-driven approaches to sustain professional growth for educators, particularly in the context of online teaching and learning. It outlines a framework employed by an accredited higher education institution to provide mandatory professional development for online facilitators, emphasizing practical skills, ongoing training, competency assessment, and performance evaluation tied to compensation levels. The approaches covered include aligning with learner needs and institutional policies, promoting inclusive design, and supporting facilitators' continuous development to enhance online teaching quality and student outcomes.

Keywords: Sustainable Professional Development · Inclusive Design · Comptency-Driven Strategies · Experiential Development

1 Approaches to Professional Development Practices

Instructional designers employ a variety of strategies to identify competency-driven instructional design approaches (strategies for effective teaching and learning) for sustainable professional growth (ongoing development of educators to ensure they remain effective in their roles). What though are the key approaches for identifying these competency-driven strategies and how do they impart sustainable professional growth? Several authors have contributed to this field and can help to provide an answer to this question. For instance, Gross (1981) laid the groundwork for instructional design approaches, emphasizing the need to align learner and learning environment characteristics to optimize performance on differentiated learning tasks. Hastings and Rasmussen (2021) expanded on this by advocating for a diverse set of strategies at both macro- and micro-levels. They believe that System-focused decisions should prioritize participant needs and address academic policy and infrastructure barriers.

Williams et al (2015) emphasized the importance of aligning faculty readiness with professional development, particularly in the context of quality education. They found that higher education institutions usually employ adjunct faculty who are usually experts in their disciplines and have industry experience, but generally lack teacher training or preparation to deliver digital–blended, hybrid, online–courses. Therefore, professional development that helps faculty understand how course design aligns with delivery strategies assumes critical importance. More recently, Costanza-Chock (2020) and Williams

C. Stephanidis et al. (Eds.): HCII 2024, CCIS 2319, pp. 145–153, 2025.
https://doi.org/10.1007/978-3-031-78516-0_15

(2024) have argued for inclusive design as a social justice concern, highlighting the role of both the teacher and the learner in this process. These studies collectively highlight the importance of a learner-centered, contextually relevant, and sustainable approach to competency-driven instructional design. This approach is rooted in consistent professional development and underscores the need for instructional designers to help faculty to continually update their skills and knowledge.

1.1 Navigating Professional Development

Competency in online facilitation skills is the cornerstone of teaching and learning excellence (Williams 2021). To adhere to the student charter that promises qualified and experienced teachers, at the regionally recognized HEI under discussion, the administration espoused a management philosophy with its focus on supporting the development of effective online and distance learning practices for student success. To develop a pertinent competency-based professional development strategy, instructional designers and curriculum specialists prioritize the cultivation of practical skills and the application of knowledge to address the challenges of professional practice. The training department at the institution believes that effective facilitation skills are crucial for the development of self-efficacy among existing facilitators. This, in turn, benefits the students, who are the shared asset of the institution.

To support this belief that students are central to institutional sustainability, the institution has implemented a policy to provide professional development and ongoing training for all facilitators teaching online. This training is mandatory before a contract is offered. In line with this initiative, all new facilitators contracted from 2019 onwards received training in managing and facilitating online instructions before being assigned to deliver courses online. This practice ensures that facilitators are equipped with the necessary skills to provide high-quality online education, thereby fulfilling the commitment to the student charter.

1.2 Competency Training Requirement

In addition to training being a requirement for teaching online, studies have found that meticulously designed courses delivered by well-trained facilitators tend to:

- meet quality standards (Brown, Williams & Dunn, 2024).
- have more productive student interactions (Pacansky-Brock et al., 2022).
- have better instructional materials, (Hastings & Rasmussen, 2021) and
- facilitate student achievement of learning outcomes (Williams & Gaines, 2023).

Moreover, proactive professional development boosts facilitator satisfaction and this improves the quality of online teaching and learning, students' satisfaction, and their achievement of learning outcomes (Nilson & Goodson, 2021; Williams 2021). The professional development process offers opportunities for the development of online teaching practice for all facilitators (Risien & Nilson, 2018). This is done by supporting the development and implementation of effective instructional strategies. Figure 1 outlines the professional development training pathways with multiple entry and exit points based on (1) a self-paced technology evaluation and (2) equivalent training evaluation.

The technology evaluation reviews institutional expectations in line with selected technology skills, knowledge, and competencies. Each training pathway was tied to Credly so participants could connect their training journey, track their progress and share their credentials externally.

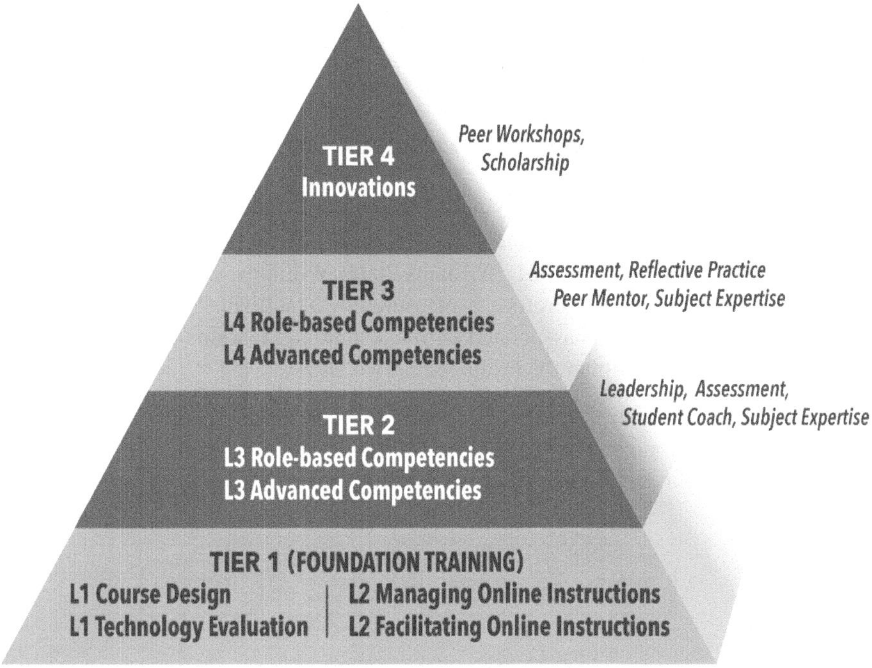

Fig. 1. Training Pathways (Fig. 1. Training Pathways by Donavan Grant and Florence W. Williams is licensed under CC BY 4.0.)

These professional development offerings feature multiple training pathways that consider external training experience and allow training exceptions. Incoming faculty provide their training record, course outlines and hours of training requirement for equivalency evaluation. Based on their prior experience, they are assigned to a training level. The foundation training (beginning at Level 2) operates within a cohort-based, facilitated lockstep approach, ensuring that faculty trainees progress at the same pace. This method requires fewer trainers and is with smaller cohorts is more easily managed than self-paced learning. However, there is flexibility to add new members to the cohort at the point of entry, aligning with their prior training experiences. For instance, new trainers joining the institution would audit the training to familiarize themselves with competencies and required skills. By a similar token, incoming faculty with prior training (or experience) will have an equivalency evaluation completed by members of the training team. After satisfying the audit or the training evaluation, they could skip the foundation training levels one and two and directly join an available cohort at level three.

Upon completing each professional development course, participants receive a competence certificate that is tracked in their faculty development records and acts as prerequisites to the next training level. Faculty can further enhance their knowledge and practical skills by continuing professional development during their first year with the institution, eventually earning a composite certificate that lists the courses they have completed (including those for which they earned an exemption). This tiered model accommodates faculty members at various entry points based on their prior experience, allowing them to progress toward more advanced training levels.

2 Commitment to Professional Development

The ever-changing environment of the virtual classroom requires that facilitators remain abreast of advancements in the field and be efficacious in their own pedagogical practices (Hastings & Rasmussen, 2021; Williams 2021; Williams, 2024). A commitment to professional development, therefore, is measured by a facilitator's continued involvement in educational activities associated with teaching and learning in digital learning environments. This commitment is evaluated in two ways:

- Annual participation in training: The requirement to attend a specified number of professional developments hours each year, and,
- Completion of Mastery Tracks associated with the role they perform

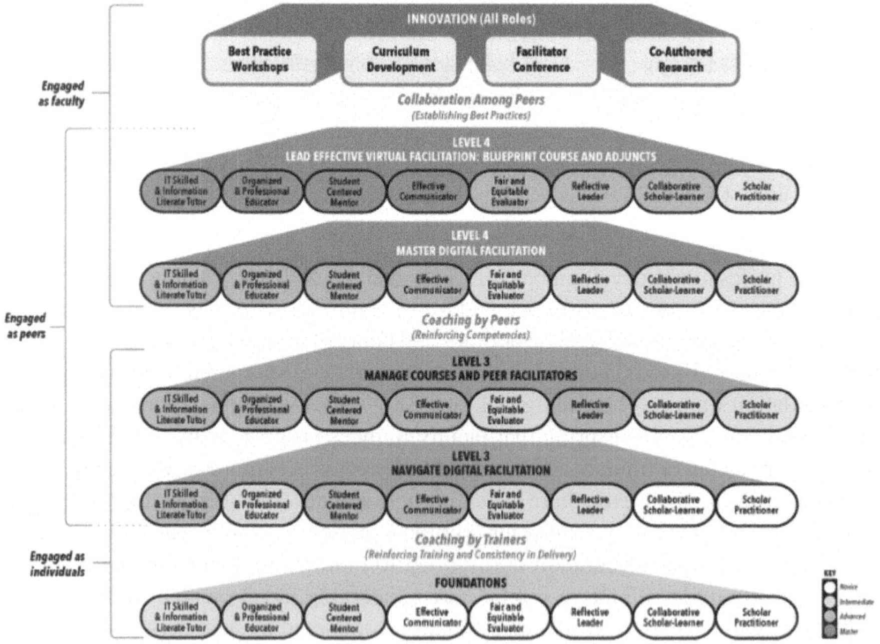

Fig. 2. Development of Attributes and Competencies (Fig. 2. Development of Attributes and Competencies by Donavan Grant and Florence W. Williams is licensed under CC BY 4.0.)

2.1 Demonstration of Attributes and Competencies

The institution's framework for professional development is based on attributes and key performance indicators identified within the University's Strategic Plan. These attributes have been mapped to specific skill competencies of professional performance in Fig. 2, which are addressed through training and other professional development opportunities.

All facilitators, upon completion of the foundation level programs, are contracted, and compensated in their role. In order to be considered for advancement to the next tier of compensation within the role, a facilitator serves, the facilitator must demonstrate the competency level designated for the higher compensation ranking. Levels of performance are classified in four levels: Novice, Intermediate, Advanced, and Expert.

3 Evaluation of Performance in Role

Performance evaluation is designed to ensure that facilitators are meeting the contractual obligations of their positions, as well as providing meaningful learning experiences for students. Loseva (2019) posits that it is not a coincidence that the words "support", and "professional development" can often be seen used next to each other when talking about teaching. The core idea is tying together the interdependency of support and professional development as two sides of developing and empowering a strong teaching workforce. Trainers expanded this connection to reinforce a comprehensive, synergistic professional development approach. The review of performance (based upon the training provided) includes both formative and summative components and involves representatives from all roles within a training department including instructional support (instructional designers), technical support (web administrators and technology specialists), and student perception of instruction (SPIs).

Without adequate support mechanisms like mentoring, resources, time allocation, and follow-up, professional development efforts are likely to fall short. Conversely, well-designed professional development opportunities can provide critical support by building skills, knowledge, and confidence in teachers. The two concepts of support and professional development are co-dependent - one enables and reinforces the other in the pursuit of improving teaching practice. Institutions must recognize this symbiotic relationship and prioritize both support services and structured development programs as complementary investments in developing a highly effective teaching workforce. The assessment of the facilitator's performance and competency achievement serves to document decisions made with respect to advancement. Qamar, (2015) identified six levels of experiential development that might provide a lens through which to view teaching effectiveness: Novice, Advanced Beginner, Competent, Proficient, and Expert. They suggest that teachers who don't meet standards should receive professional development, remediation, and opportunities to observe their peers. Additionally, they should be given adequate time, support, and assistance to meet the standards. In many institutions, student feedback on evaluations of teaching is a primary and frequently convenient tool to measure teaching effectiveness.

3.1 Experiential Development

Table 1 outlines the levels of experiential development used to identify digital course design and facilitation competency. Qamar's framework (2015) was used as a guide for creating the professional development approach described in this paper. An unclassified level was included for all faculty who had not gone through an evaluation of performance. Novice identifies the first level of experience and the support required in that point. Advanced Beginner was replaced with an Intermediate level since the level could include characteristics from the novice and advanced levels of the spectrum. The advanced level in the new framework replaced the competent and proficient levels since those characteristics identified faculty who met the standard expectations for the job. The expert level was retained as part of a peer support framework for those faculty who consistently surpass expectations in the advanced level.

Table 1. Experiential Development Levels

Experiential Development Levels	Characteristics	Types of Support	Rates
Unclassified	This level denotes a new facilitator or observer who has shown some classroom use of technology through small steps, such as posting syllabi online, while this could be viewed as a technology visitor status, the term, unclassified is used to indicate that the facilitator has no records of technology use, through tech quest or other external certification	Participates in virtual tours, reviews exemplars, hears success stories, works on increasing use in traditional courses, considers best practices	0
Novice	Use online technologies for disseminating information (syllabi) and communication (typically email). This level is also used for persons whose certification may be checked for alignment with the self-evaluation process in Technology Evaluation 1	Explores LMS/ CMS functions, reviews exemplars, attends webinars, expands use in classroom courses or shifts to blended	1–49

(*continued*)

Table 1. (*continued*)

Experiential Development Levels	Characteristics	Types of Support	Rates
Intermediate	In this intermediate level, the facilitator is seen to have taught online a few times (1–2-semesters), typically one course. Not 100% clear about what skills are required to teach online, this level can be applied to the lead or tutor roles where the self-evaluation in Evaluation 2 is below the pass grade	Works with mentor, focuses on pedagogy, consider student activity, increases blended mix to online	50–79
Advanced	Taught more than two semesters and at least one course per semester. Comfortable online, probably have designed courses. This facilitator is seen as an insider with technology use and has a score above mastery in the technology assessment	Explores other courses in field, mentors others, publishes	80–89
Expert	This facilitator is an expert user of technology in 80% of the areas required to teach in the institution. This user is noticeably confident and comfortable with the requisite skills, and technology (typically beyond the Learning Management System LMS). Having taught many courses over multiple semesters they mentor others	Mentors others, conducts [action] research, publishes, helps design supports for others	90–100

3.2 Conclusion

Sustainable professional growth for educators requires a comprehensive, competency-driven approach that aligns institutional goals with facilitator development. It is not just about training but includes critical support that builds the capabilities of faculty. By developing skills, knowledge, and confidence, high-quality professional development opportunities empower teachers to enhance learning experiences and drive student success. It is important that those who plan professional development understand that it cannot exist in a vacuum. To truly enable sustainable growth, institutions must take a holistic view that integrates professional development with comprehensive support services and resources. Mentoring, communities of practice, instructional design assistance, and time allocation are just some examples of support structures that allow training to be implemented effectively.

Building teaching excellence requires more than just one-off training sessions. It demands an institutional culture and commitment to continuously developing our most valuable asset - our faculty. Training faculty ensures that institutions prioritize a strategic investment that intertwines strong professional development pathways with robust support mechanisms. The outline demonstrates how one institution's professional development pathways build practical skills for online teaching excellence. By tying facilitator competencies to compensation through performance evaluation, the institution incentivizes a commitment to continuous improvement.

Combining learner-centered instructional design, inclusive facilitation practices, and ongoing upskilling opportunities, this competency-based model supports quality online education. As the demands of virtual learning environments evolve, such holistic professional development strategies are crucial for empowering facilitators and ensuring positive student experiences and outcomes. Investing in facilitator growth through competency-focused training reinforces an institution's dedication to its student charter and the sustainable development of effective online teaching practices.

Acknowledgments. This study was developed from secondary research conducted at a Caribbean institution that is regionally accredited in the United States, Canada, and the United Kingdom.

Disclosure of Interests. The author has no competing interests to declare that are relevant to the content of this article

References

1. Brown, V., Williams, F., Dunn, S.: A responsive, consultative professional development model for online engagement. In: T. Martindale et al. (eds.) Handbook of Research in Online Learning: Insights and Advances, pp. 106–132 (2024)
2. development model for online engagement. Trey Martindale Handbook of Research in Online Learning. Brill
3. Costanza-Chock, S.: Design justice: Community-led practices to build the world's we need. The MIT Press (2020)
4. Gross, G.M.: Instructional design: bridge to competence. J. Educ. Soc. Work. **17**(3), 66–74 (1981)
5. Hastings, N.B., Rasmussen, K.: Designing and developing skills- and competency-based environments. Career Ready Education Through Experiential Learning, pp. 240–260 (2021). https://doi.org/10.4018/978-1-7998-1928-8.ch013
6. Loseva, A.: Self-initiated teacher support: owning your professional development. New Dir. Teach. Learn. English Discuss. **7**, 246–255 (2019)

7. Nilson, L.B., Goodson, L.A.: Online teaching at its best: Merging instructional design with teaching and learning research. John Wiley & Sons (2021)
8. Pacansky-Brock, M., Smedshammer, M., Vincent-Layton, K.: In search of belonging online: Achieving equity through transformative professional development. J. Educ. Res. Pract. **12**(4) (2022)
9. Qamar, K.: Teacher's assessment process. Pak. Armed Forces Med. J. **65**, 721–723 (2015)
10. Risien, J., Nilson, R.: Coordinated reform and local solutions: transforming the university systems of reward and professional advancement (2018)
11. Williams, F.: Applying culturally responsive strategies to promote engagement and student success in online courses. In: Humanizing Online Teaching and Learning in Higher Education, pp. 140–161. IGI Global (2024)
12. Williams, F., Gaines, L.T.: Implementing foundations of quality through online and hybrid course design: a study-away course case study. J. Adult Educ. Tanzania **25**(2) (2023)
13. Williams, F.: Flexible learning design: a turning point for resilient adult education. J. Adult Educ. Tanzania **23**(2) (2021)
14. Williams, F., Fleming-Banks, P., Drakes, C., Gilzene, S.: Rules of Engagement: Improving Teaching Through Online Faculty Development Training. In: Proceedings from the UWI Regional Conference on Higher Education (2015)

Usability and User Experience Evaluation

Study on Motion Sickness Cases in Multiple Driving Simulator Studies

ISol Bae[1](✉), Bogyu Choi[1], and Ji Hyun Yang[2]

[1] Graduate School of Automobile and Mobility, Kookmin University, Seoul 02707, Republic of Korea
rasido130@kookmin.ac.kr

[2] Department of Automotive Engineering, Kookmin University, Seoul 02707, Republic of Korea
yangjh@kookmin.ac.kr

Abstract. This study analyzed cases of motion sickness induced in multiple experiments utilizing a vehicle simulator equipped with a motion platform (KMU-DS) and a simulation program, SCANeR Studio. This is to identify the major factors and mitigation strategies of motion sickness and contribute to the development of technologies preventing motion sickness. Three experiments conducted in a vehicle simulator environment over four years from 2018 to 2021 were analyzed for cases of motion sickness. In the first experiment, 31 participants out of a total of 186 dropped out due to motion sickness. In the second experiment, 7 out of 110 participants experienced motion sickness. The third experiment included a total of 95 participants, and none of them experienced motion sickness. The occurrence of motion sickness varied depending on factors such as manual/autonomous driving, gender, and age group. The results of motion sickness case analysis derived from this study are expected to be utilized for reducing motion sickness in participants during future simulator-based experiments. Furthermore, these findings can be applied to research and development of motion sickness mitigation technologies. For future research, simulator driving experiments incorporating quantitative indicators such as electrocardiography and qualitative indicators such as interviews will be conducted.

Keywords: Motion Sickness · Simulator-based Experiments · Case Analysis

1 Introduction

Motion sickness is a symptom of physical discomfort, such as nausea, dizziness, or vomiting, caused by traveling in a vehicle, such as a car, ship, plane, or spacecraft, or by visual stimuli, such as simulations or computers [1, 2]. The factors that cause motion sickness are complex and include sensory mismatch, individual sensitivity to motion sickness, gender, age, and genetics. It is estimated that approximately 5–10% of the population is highly susceptible to motion sickness, with the young and elderly, children between the ages of 6 and 12, and females being more susceptible [3, 4].

The Society for Automotive Engineers (SAE) taxonomy defines six levels of driving automation. At level 4 and above, the driver no longer needs to monitor the environment

C. Stephanidis et al. (Eds.): HCII 2024, CCIS 2319, pp. 157–164, 2025.
https://doi.org/10.1007/978-3-031-78516-0_16

and, under certain conditions, can perform non-driving related tasks (NDRTs) [5]. We can see that beginning with an active driver, automation gradually transforms the driver into a system supervisor and ultimately into a passenger role at automation level 4 and 5. As these levels of driving automation become more advanced, we can expect to see an increase in the use of the vehicle as a passenger instead of a driver, and an increase in the likelihood and severity of the phenomenon we call motion sickness due to the decrease in vehicle control activities due to NDRTs [6].

Therefore, it is necessary to study the indicators of motion sickness to prevent motion sickness or reduce the severity of motion sickness. This study analyzes the cases of motion sickness induced in experiments using a vehicle simulator (KMU-DS) equipped with a real cabin motion platform and a driving simulation program (SCANeR Studio). By doing so, we aim to identify the main factors and countermeasures of motion sickness to provide a better understanding and contribute to the development of technologies that can prevent motion sickness in future vehicles.

2 Research Methods

2.1 Test Apparatus

We used KMU-DS; a full-scale driving simulator equipped with the 2016 LF Sonata cabin as shown in Fig. 1. Three projector screens, two LCD side mirrors, and one LCD rearview mirror provide simulated driving images to the driver. Driver behavior can be monitored via cameras installed within the cabin. For software, AV Simulation's SCANeR Studio was used to implement the scenarios and acquire driving data. Modalities included audible notifications via 5.1 channel speakers in the cabin, visual notifications via LED lights on the A-pillar and the instrument panel screen, and tactile notifications via vibration of the backrest and seat.

Vehicle simulators are known to be a very useful tool for measuring and evaluating a driver's driving performance or driving competency [7]. The advantages of driving simulations are numerous, with the most significant being their ability to offer realistic driving scenarios that closely mimic real-world conditions. Additionally, they afford a high degree of control over a wide range of variables, which is crucial in the conduct of experimental studies [8]. In addition, driving simulations can be configured to create different scenarios to evaluate essential driving tasks (e.g., hazard avoidance) without exposing the driver to danger [9]. Driving simulations also present certain limitations. Firstly, they may not accurately replicate real-world driving conditions. Despite efforts to closely emulate real-world scenarios, the visual representation, and the physical sensations, especially during deceleration, might not fully match the actual experience. Secondly, participants often require time to acclimate to the simulator environment, potentially impacting the reliability of early experimental data.

2.2 Research Procedures

In this study, an exploratory case study method was chosen to analyze the cases of motion sickness during the use of vehicle simulators in multiple experiments. Data from

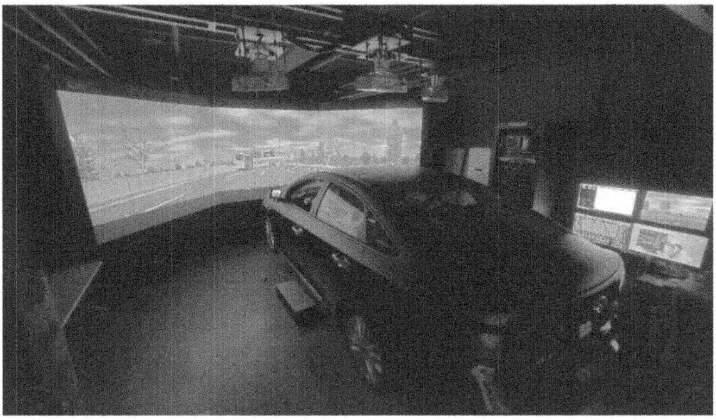

Fig. 1. Test apparatus (Full-scale driving simulator KMU-DS)

a total of 391 participants from three experiments conducted using a vehicle simulator over four years from 2018 to 2021 were analyzed. The three experiments had their own experimental purposes, which are not related to motion sickness. They analyzed the interaction between the driver and the autonomous system from different perspectives, including the characteristics of driver behavior in risk perception situations. Additionally, they examined the methodology of providing information to the autonomous function interface and the transition of control during autonomous driving. This enables the study to cover a wide range of driver reactions and behaviors.

2.3 Overview of the Three Simulator Studies

Study on Driver's Behavioral Characteristics in Hazardous Situation. This study, conducted between 2019 and 2020, was funded by the National Forensic Service. The following hazardous situations were studied: (1) encountering a vehicle crossing the centerline, (2) encountering a vehicle parked in the shoulder lane, (3) encountering a jaywalker, and (4) encountering a vehicle running a red light at an intersection. A total of 186 adults with driving experience participated in the experiment. Among them, 99 were males and 87 were females. The participants were divided into the following age groups: 32 in their 20s, 31 in their 30s, 42 in their 40s, 42 in their 50s, and 39 in their 60s.

Development and Evaluation of Automated Driving Systems for Motorway and City Road. This study, conducted between 2017 and 2022, was funded by the Ministry of Trade, Industry and Energy. A total of 110 adults with driving experience participated in the experiment. Among them, 61 were males and 49 were females. The participants were divided into the following age groups: 47 in their 20s, 22 in their 30s, 20 in their 40s and 21 in their 50s. Two road conditions were created for the experiment. First, the virtual environment of the Osan-Shingal IC section with a driving time of 7–8 min on a dedicated road. Second, the virtual environment of the city center with a driving time of 5 min on a section near the Sangam World Cup Stadium. The participant uses the automated driving system (ADS) normally and reads as NDRTs without looking ahead.

Then, voice guidance is provided to help the participant check the visual information, and one of five service driving situations is selected: maintaining lane & lane distance, changing lanes, driving at low speed due to traffic congestion, entering a branch, and turning right at an intersection.

Safety Evaluation Technology and Social Acceptance of Automated Vehicle Take Over. This study, conducted between 2017 and 2020, was funded by the Ministry of Land, Infrastructure, and Transport. A total of 118 adults with driving experience participated in the experiment. Among them, 51 were males and 44 were females. The participants were divided into the following age groups: 59 in their 20s, 17 in their 30s, and 19 in their 40s. This experiment was conducted with a driving scenario that provided a single/multimodal notification method in an unexpected Operational Design Domain (ODD) departure situation.

3 Results

3.1 Cases of Motion Sickness in Each Experiment

Study on Driver's Behavioral Characteristics in Hazardous Situation. Of the total 186 participants, 31 or 16.67% discontinued the experiment due to motion sickness. Of these, 16 were males and 15 were females. The age breakdown was as follows: 1 in their 20s, 1 in their 30s, 10 in their 40s, 10 in their 50s, and 9 in their 60s (see Fig. 2). Notably, there was a significant increase in the dropout rate due to motion sickness among participants aged 40s, 50s and 60s. We also found that motion sickness symptoms occurred primarily during rapid turns and deceleration.

Following the first round of testing, the team implemented the following measures to mitigate motion sickness. First, they adjusted the traffic signals to prioritize the test vehicle, except for the continuous turning sections, thereby minimizing the braking and stopping time caused by signals. Second, they revised the Visual Map logic. The simulator map for the scenarios is composed of an RND (logic) file, which dictates the movement of vehicles and pedestrians, and an IVE (image) file, which displays the virtual environment to the driver. For optimal performance, the RND and IVE files must be precisely aligned; any misalignment can lead to discrepancies between the visual and actual driving paths, potentially inducing motion sickness. Consequently, the team conducted a thorough review of the entire scenario and optimized the RND and IVE files during the second year to reduce motion sickness among participants.

In the second year of the experiment, only participants in their 50s and 60s were tested. The incidence of motion sickness induced dropouts remained comparably high, similar to the rates observed among participants in their 40s during the first year. This suggests that the measures to reduce motion sickness may not have been significantly effective, or that factors such as age had a more substantial impact on the occurrence of motion sickness than the driving environment.

Development and Evaluation of Automated Driving Systems for Motorway and City. 7 out of 110 participants or 6.36% experienced motion sickness symptoms. Among these, 4 were males and 3 were females. The age distribution was as follows:

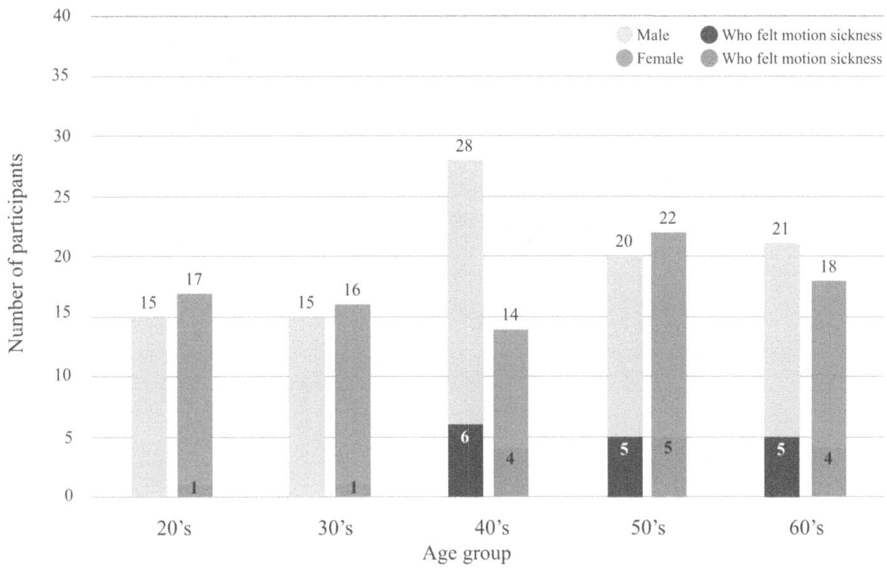

Fig. 2. Results of motion sickness in "Study on Driver's Behavioral Characteristics in Hazardous Situation"

1 in their 30s, 1 in their 40s, and 5 in their 50s, as shown in Fig. 3. This experiment was a user interface study on the use of driving automation levels 3 and 4. While seven participants experienced motion sickness, none of them dropped out of the experiment. There was a slight tendency for participants to experience motion sickness during the NDRTs requested during the experiment when looking forward.

Safety Evaluation Technology and Social Acceptance of Automated Vehicle Take Over. None of the 95 participants reported experiencing motion sickness. The age and gender distribution of the participants are depicted in Fig. 4. This experiment was also conducted on driving automation level 3.

3.2 Comprehensive Results of Case Analysis of Motion

This study, conducted from 2018 to 2021 with 391 participants across three different experiments, explored motion sickness occurrences across various driving conditions. Key findings include:

(1) Manual driving in urban settings, especially during rapid vehicle maneuvers such as cutting in and sharp turns, was the most common scenario for motion sickness. (2) Although fewer participants experienced motion sickness in Level 3 autonomous driving, some experienced more motion sickness when looking straight ahead. (3) Age seems to influence susceptibility to motion sickness: 0.72% in their 20s, 2.86% in their 30s, 13.58% in their 40s, 23.81% in their 50s, and 23.08% in their 60s experienced motion sickness. (4) Gender differences were observed: 9.48% of males and 10.00% of females reported motion sickness, reinforcing previous research on gender susceptibility.

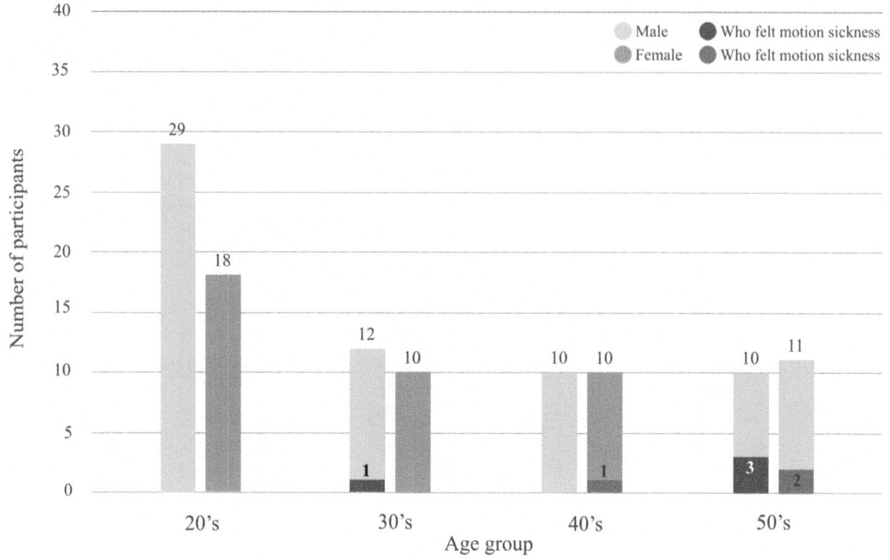

Fig. 3. Results of motion sickness in "Development and Evaluation of Automated Driving Systems for Motorway and City Road"

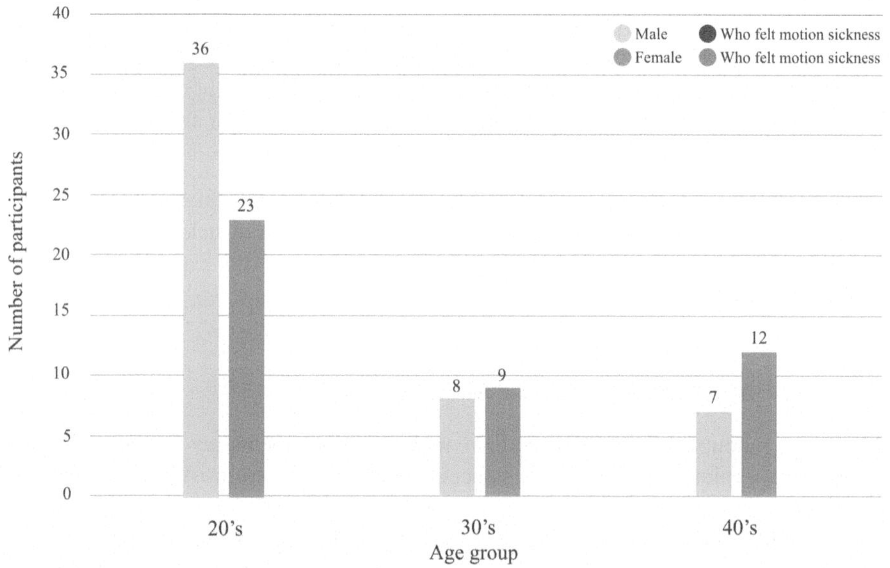

Fig. 4. Results of motion sickness in "Safety Evaluation Technology and Social Acceptance of Automated Vehicle Take Over"

4 Discussions and Conclusion

This study aimed to analyze motion sickness in full-scale vehicle simulators to identify significant correlations. Our methodology summarized the research procedures and motion sickness case analysis, highlighting the potential for comparison and validation with prior studies. The findings are expected to contribute to reducing motion sickness in future simulator experiments and to the development of technology enhancing passenger satisfaction.

However, the study's limitation lies in its reliance on recorded data without using qualitative (e.g., Motion Sickness Questionnaire) and quantitative (e.g., vital signs) indicators. In future research, it will focus on developing a model to minimize motion sickness by comprehensively examining individual physical conditions, health status, and sensitivity to motion sickness for more effective prevention.

5 Disclosure of Interests.

Disclosure of Interests. The authors have no competing interests to declare that are relevant to the content of this article.

Acknowledgments. This work was supported by the Technology Innovation Program (20018101, Development on Automated driving with perceptual prediction based on T-Car/vehicle parts to intelligent control/system integration for assessment) funded By the Ministry of Trade, Industry & Energy(MOTIE, Korea), This paper was supported by Korea Institute for Advancement of Technology(KIAT) grant funded by the Korea Government(MOTIE) (P0017120, The Competency Development Program for Industry Specialist), This paper was supported by Korea Institute for Advancement of Technology(KIAT) grant funded by the Korea Government(MOTIE) (P0020536, HRD Program for Industrial Innovation), This work was supported by the BK21 Four Program (5199990814084) of the National Research Foundation of Korea (NRF) funded by the Ministry of Education, Korea.

References

1. Jung, S.H.: Motion sickness. Aerosp. Med. J. **19**(3), 87–90 (2010)
2. Sivak, M., Schoettle, B.: Motion Sickness in Self-Driving Vehicles. University of Michigan, Ann Arbor, Transportation Research Institute (2015)
3. Schmäl, F.: Neuronal mechanisms and the treatment of motion sickness. Pharmacology **91**(3–4), 229–241 (2013)
4. Paillard, A.C., et al.: Motion sickness susceptibility in healthy subjects and vestibular patients: effects of gender Age and Trait-Anxiety. J. Vestib. Res. **23**(4–5), 203–209 (2013)
5. SAE, T.: Definitions for Terms Related to On-Road Motor Vehicle Automated Driving Systems-J3016. Society of Automotive Engineers: On-Road Automated Vehicle Standards Committee, SAE Pub. Inc., Warrendale, PA, USA (2013)
6. Hainich, R., Drewitz, U., Ihme, K., Lauermann, J., Niedling, M., Oehl, M.: Evaluation of a human-machine interface for motion sickness mitigation utilizing anticipatory ambient light cues in a realistic automated driving setting. Information **12**(4), 176 (2021). https://doi.org/10.3390/info12040176

7. Brooks, J.O., et al.: Simulator sickness during driving simulation studies. In: Accident Analysis & Prevention (Vol. 42, No. 3, pp. 788–796) (2010)
8. Lee, J.: Comparisons of middle-and old-aged drivers' recognition for driving scene elements using sensitivity, response bias, and response time. J. Korean Data Anal. Soc. **20**(6), 3185–3199 (2018)
9. Marmeleira, J., Ferreira, I., Melo, F., Godinho, M.: Associations of physical activity with driving-related cognitive abilities in older drivers: an exploratory study. Percept. Mot. Skills **115**(2), 521–533 (2012)

Conducting Usability Testing with Tweens on Mobile AR Platforms

Hanah I. S. Correa(✉), Marcos Silbermann, and Mariana Lopes

Sidia Instituto de Ciência e Tecnologia, Manaus, AM 69055-035, Brazil
Hanah.santos@sidia.com

Abstract. In October 2022, the Sidia (Sidia Institute of Science and Technology is a research and development institute. This article is the result of the Digikin Adventure Pockets PD&I project carried out in partnership with Sam-sung Eletrônica da Amazônia Ltda., using resources from Federal Law No. 8,387/1991, and its dissemination and advertising following the provisions of article 39 of the Decree No. 10,521/2020.), research and development institute launched a game for mobile platforms. The game aimed at children aged between 8 and 12 years old, called Digikin Pocket Adventures, involves the projection of a 3D scenario into the real environment, in which the child needs to find a character hidden in the virtual scenario in a certain amount of time, accumulating points and gifts. The development of this game included a final phase of validation and iteration of the experience, in which the application was tested with a sample of children from Amazonas to evaluate elements of the user's experiences and their gameplay. This article discusses the development of this testing tool with children and the construction of a rigorous protocol and test script targeting the particularities of this context, where we will discuss the construction of this methodology and share some test results.

Keywords: Validation · Mixed Reality · Usability · Augmented Reality · Game

1 Introduction

This article aims to briefly discuss the preparation and conduct of playtests with children through the experience gained during the validation of the Digikin Pocket Adventures application. He carries out this discussion through the presentation of the preparation processes for the playtest and brings important insights for the construction of a set of good practices for applying research with children. Digikin Pocket Adventures is an augmented reality (AR) experience exclusively for Samsung Kids mode, a controlled environment (Fig. 1) that parents can activate and monitor so that the child can interact with the digital world safely on Samsung mobile devices. Samsung (Samsung, 2024). The game was developed by the Sidia Research and Development Institute, focusing on children in the age group between Generations Z and Alpha, the so-called Tweens (KOSTMAN, 2003). The term that was coined is based on the English word "between", something in the middle of two or more things. It is a term generally used to refer to

C. Stephanidis et al. (Eds.): HCII 2024, CCIS 2319, pp. 165–176, 2025.
https://doi.org/10.1007/978-3-031-78516-0_17

so-called pre-adolescents, boys, and girls who are between 8 and 12 years old (CASTELLON, 2007). They share the characteristics of the Alpha generation and are created by individuals from Generation Z and/or Millennials. In Digikin, the player-user joins four friends: Lolly Bunny, Jack Fox, Ted Bear, and Alice Bee, as they embark on a journey in a digital environment to play a game of hide and seek (Fig. 2).

Fig. 1. Kids mode on the Samsung system (Samsung Website, 2024). Figure 2 Characters from the AR game Digikin Pocket Adventures (Author's compilation, 2024).

When starting the game, the player-user defines the chosen character and then needs to anchor the virtual scene on some flat surface of their choice, such as the floor, a table, or a chair. Then the player selects a character to play hide and seek, and then he will observe the digital world anchored in the real world. In the game, the child uses the smartphone to see the virtual elements projected in the environment and make angle changes in the scene, moving around the real environment to look for characters hidden in the virtual scene among plants, animals, and other objects (Fig. 2). The user has a set amount of time and three chances to find the character and 'take a photo' of him to earn points.

Before its launch, still, in the first half of 2023, Digikin was undergoing a stage of validating concepts and mechanics presented by the game, which needed to be validated with its target audience. In this context, the project leadership called on the institute's research team to evaluate and validate with participants from the target audience, the usability aspects, interface, and flows of the application by carrying out a playtest. In addition to observing the levels of understanding of its mechanics, it was essential to assess the degree of fun children had when playing. Analyzing the degree of the fun of an application implies building an experimental process that makes it possible to observe and understand the significant appreciations, thoughts, and mixed feelings experienced by player-users during the game, rather than just the positive effects expressed by them (Oliver et al. al 2016). Observing whether the game is fun or not could tell us whether the child minimally understood the game experience, whether they were interested in continuing to play, or whether they enjoyed the narrative and its characters.

The validation phase of the Digikin user experience had a very central value in conducting the project, as, in addition to bringing important findings about usability and game mechanics, the playtest was a way of validating the concepts proposed by the game among users with the target age of the product. Still, from a UX research point of

Fig. 2. Digikin gameplay dynamics. (Author compilation, 2022)

view, carrying out a playtest bringing together augmented reality interfaces and children from generations Alpha and Z was a new process for our team and required a level of preparation unknown to our team of researchers. From the beginning of the planning process for this playtest, we established some questions about the technical and ethical conditions for carrying it out, possible biases, and limitations. Questions such as: How to carry out the playtest offering greater freedom of opinion for children? Or even, how to conduct the test without the adult's authority becoming an inhibitor of the child's opinion or excessively restricting how they interact with the application?

In the next sections of this article, we will present the process of planning, preparing, and executing the test, reporting the care taken during its conduct, and sharing the lessons learned. We will talk about the methods we exercise, and the tools used during the Playtest sessions and finally, we will end with the presentation of the results achieved through behavioral observation of children and application of the test protocol that we developed to deal with children during the sessions.

2 Method

To organize the Digikin validation process, we first defined the research questions we wanted to answer, as a way of establishing the validation tools and starting to build your roadmap. It is important to highlight that the validation tools used by user experience research mostly have a qualitative focus and, therefore, are tools for observing users' understanding of the mechanics and values proposed by an experience. As well as identify learning curves and obtain insights into how users appropriate and make sense of the technological products offered to them.

Understanding the needs of the project, we chose to use a Playtest methodology with children of a pre-determined age group. The playtest differentiates itself from other validation tools by bringing important aspects of the gaming experience into an experimental context. In other words, like other validation tools, this methodology inserts the participant in an experimental situation, in which he/she goes through the flow of experience of a game. Regarding the reasons that justify the choice of this tool, the bibliographic references define the playtest: "The ultimate objective is to provide game designers with practical feedback from consumers on how they perceive critical aspects of their games." (Davis et al, 2005). Likewise, authors such as Fullerton et al. (2004) and Schell (2008), emphasize that playtesting is an important Design methodology, as it helps game designers to obtain insights about the game and respond to whether the concepts proposed by the application meet the player/user experience objectives.

2.1 Definition of the Target Audience

In the case of Digikin, the questions about validating the game mechanics, which structured the construction of the semi-structured playtest script, had as their starting point care and questions related to the age group of the players/users. Based on our previous research that explored the construction of generational profiles relevant to the project, we defined the target audience. According to Parry & Urwin (2011), to configure a generation it is necessary "a set of historical events and related phenomena that creates a distinct generational gap." or "some form of social 'proximity' to shared cultural events or phenomena". To talk about generations, we need to understand that social, geographic, and economic aspects can generate considerable differences in the behavior and characteristics of a given generational group. Even today there is no consensus among authors and other scientific references on the exact delimitation of time between generations. Thinking about the needs of the Digikin project, we studied two specific generations, Generation Z and Generation Alpha.

According to the literature, Generation Z individuals are those born between 1995 and 2010 (Priporas et al., 2019; Djafarova et al., 2021). They are currently between 14 and 29 years old, and are considered 'digital natives' (Smith, 2017; Djafarova et al., 2021), as they are the first generation that was born in a context of diffusion of technologies such as smartphones and computers, unlike, from previous generations in which the pervasive use of the internet is an important temporal milestone. The Alpha generation refers to children born from 2010 to 2024 (McCrindle, 2024), who are currently between 0 and 14 years old. According to McCrindle (2024), in 2025 when all alpha generation individuals are born, they will be the largest generation ever, numbering almost 2 billion. According to GWI (2021), "researchers call them "upagers" – they are more socially aware from a young age and become consumers more quickly".

Children of these generations were born with access to screens directly and indirectly. Every day they are bombarded by a series of content that makes them access knowledge and information quickly. One of the most consumed contents by Gen Alpha is games, according to the study conducted in several countries by GWI (2021), where around 51% of participants between 12 and 15 years old consume Gaming videos on social networks first. Much more than previous generations, these children spend more time in front of screens consuming content or playing games than spending time outdoors (GWI, 2021). Due to these characteristics highlighted by the bibliography as typical of the Alpha and Z generations, we chose to establish a sample size that circumscribes individuals in transition from childhood to adolescence and who are between these two generations, the Tweens (CASTELLON, 2007). To observe whether there are decisive differences in the use and understanding of the experience due to the age difference in this age group, we divided the participants into 2 groups as follows:

- Group 1: children from 8 to 10 years old
- Group 2: children from 11 to 12 years old

According to the literature, the differentiation of groups within the Tweens category is quite relevant and is based on the children's own physical development (Fei Fei Liu, 2018). For this author: "As children's physical development changes throughout childhood, so do their physical abilities, restrictions, and device preferences." In this sense, this difference can be found in the touch gestures performed by children. Swiping and tapping on large targets is easy for all ages, unlike fine mouse or trackpad gestures like dragging and selecting, which are difficult for younger children. Considering the relevance of this variation in age groups, we chose to segment the sample of participants into two groups, as we considered that the differences between 8-year-old and 12-year-old children would lead to variations in test results and our input inputs to obtain important comparative insights.

In this sense, the Playtest was structured to answer questions such as the level of understanding of the usability of the AR game. We wanted to observe whether the player/participant understood the mechanics and features of the game. For some children, this could be their first contact with this type of technology. Another important aspect to be observed is whether the age difference between the Tweens would cause any type of divergence in the understanding of the narratives, understanding of usability, and use of mechanics using augmented reality (AR) functionalities. Having highlighted that the physical development of children during childhood changes rapidly and knowing that AR technology continues to be relatively new among the public. We wanted to pay attention to how children used the space, the forms of mobility, and which gestures they explored to carry out the missions proposed by the game.

Another factor that we used to recruit playtest participants, but which did not constitute a criterion for excluding children from the study, was to identify whether the children had experience with games or applications that involve Augmented Reality (AR) concepts or similar to Digikin, such as PK XD, Roblox, and Pokémon Go, and they used smartphones frequently. With this type of data, we could understand whether the users who demonstrated a greater understanding of the game's mechanics and narrative would be those with greater expertise in AR games, similar games, or who had greater contact with the type of device. These factors represent the need to consider the particularities of augmented reality games for smartphones. For example, the need to anchor a virtual scenario through the smartphone screen may not be a simple task for those users with little or no experience with this type of game.

3 Construction of the Playtest Script

Defining the target audience brought a variety of challenges and learning to the research team, it was the first time we would carry out research with children. Our first step was to seek references to understand what measures and behaviors we should adopt to carry out playtests that were understandable, respectful, and ethical with the children participating in the validation research. This survey aimed to create a set of initial good practices to be followed by researchers when constructing the test script and, mainly, to function as a conduct manual to be used when carrying out playtests.

3.1 Survey of Good Practices

When we talk about users, we almost unconsciously refer to an adult person, a consumer of technological consumer goods with formed opinions about their tastes and routines. Adding children to the game validation process raises technical and ethical questions for user-centered design. UX design aims to bring the development of technological solutions and products closer to their end consumers, bringing research input into the points of view, behaviors, and consumption habits of their users. For some time now, the inclusion of children in design processes has drawn the attention of authors in the field, as we identified references from the 1990s that explain the difficulty of understanding the practices and procedures necessary to design centered on users, children: as they grow the body of literature on children's use of computer products, a necessary step is to detail exactly how to include children in the design of computer products." (Libby Hanna et al., 1997). The issue at stake is not just about the need to include children in research and define them as users, but whether we should do this and how to do it while respecting the ethical limits of this activity.

Taking this statement into account and the challenges encountered in the process, we began to survey good practices through a reference search. We searched among several references such as Norman Nielsen Group (2024) and Playtest with Kids (2024) and other authors for tips and methods to approach children before and during the application of playtests. So, we try to create a comfortable environment for participants in the Digikin playtest, making the necessary adaptations to collect relevant and in-depth data. We studied the following topics that will be covered in depth in our results:

- Build a relationship of trust with the child and guardians
- Be friendly.
- Avoid questions that favor immediate yes or no.
- Pay attention to non-verbal language
- Show interest
- When something did not go as expected
- Only the essentials
- Short sessions
- Segment the sample

3.2 Itinerary and Selection of Participants

We start with the selection of children for the Playtest sessions. We contacted a non-governmental institution in Manaus, Amazonas, which works with social projects for children's education, Instituto Ágape. In agreement with the institute, we sent a survey form aimed at parents, and from there we selected participants considering the criteria mentioned above. After selecting potential participants, we delivered the Free and

Informed Consent Form (TCLE) only to those responsible for their children who registered an interest in participating in the study. So that those responsible were fully aware of the experience their children would participate in and registered their consent. We recruited 10 children who were divided into two groups based on the pre-defined age range, 5 children for the first group (8 to 10 years old) and 5 for the second group (11 to 12 years old). We started by developing two pilot tests, that is, two sessions that we used to validate our Playtest script and narrative. If the script needed adjustments or improvements, we would do them before other tests. During the construction of the script, we focused on the main thematic axes that designers, developers, and researchers thought of as the current needs of the project:

- Understanding the game's proposal
- Understanding gameplay
- UI/UX aspects
- Degree of fun

We clarified good conduction practices in the document so that the moderator could follow them, ensuring the quality of the material collected and the comfort of the child in the testing room. To define the Playtest phases, we studied the phases of the game itself so that we could establish what directions we would give and what we should observe at each stage. We created a table where we inserted the stages of the game, the questions that would be directed to the child, and what we should observe. To manage data collection during the Playtest we created some tools:

Virtual Board. Where the behaviors, speeches, and general observations about the participant during the test were described.

Success Rate Table. To record whether the participant performed the required task.

Memo Cards. Cards with emojis were used during the test to facilitate the understanding of participants' emotions during the experience. Through them, children classified the sections of the application according to how they felt at that moment: Very good, Good, Fair, not very good, and Horrible. Using the Memo Cards tool to understand the emotions of participating children, we were able to analyze their opinions regarding the application's components, characters, and activities. So, we tried to evaluate, together with qualitative observations, which parts of the experience the children considered fun, uninteresting, or difficult.

3.3 Definition and Assembly of the Setup

Before running the sessions, we determined what would need to be organized for the test environment. Originally, only three professionals would be in the room, the moderator, an observer, and the person responsible for the child represented by a professional from Instituto Ágape. We decided that we would hold the sessions in a reserved room close to the institute and prepared our equipment such as a table, smartphones, tripod, notebook, and other tools necessary for recording, transmitting, and cataloging data to be discreetly around us so that the child would not feel pressured. This way we prepare the environment to be as less intimidating as possible. To validate the effectiveness of this organization, we carried out two pilot tests that helped us verify points of divergence in this organization that could be aligned, before the other sessions.

3.4 Playtest with Assisted Sessions

We held a total of 10 sessions with children aged 8 to 12 years, with two pilots, and divided into two pre-defined age groups. We prepared the room with all the necessary materials to receive the participating child who entered accompanied by a person responsible from Instituto Ágape who remained in the room to monitor the session. The participant was welcomed by the moderator, who contextualized them about the game and the flow of activities carried out during the session. From the beginning, the moderator clarified that what would be tested was only the game and not the participant, so he was instructed to always share his thoughts and doubts about the application.

Free Practice. After the minutes of instruction and icebreakers with the participant, we handed the smartphone into the child's hands and followed the introductory phases of the game alongside the child to gather their perceptions and what level of understanding they had about the different sessions of the game. Application. After the initial character selection phase, anchoring flow, and tutorial, we left her free to experience the game however she wanted, we indicated that she could move around the room or try different positions, whatever was most comfortable for her when playing. First, we allowed the child to get used to the application, before moving on to the other activities in the semi-structured script, so that we could observe the behavior of participants during their first contact with the application. Some children demonstrated greater shyness than the other participants, which is why they avoided performing certain actions such as walking around the space and exploring the angles to view the virtual environment unless requested. Others were already exploring diligently, seeking new positions, and exploring the virtual environment through their cell phone screen. This type of divergence was expected and was important for us to map different profiles. When we were dealing with shyer children, we tried to be very attentive and show that we were very interested in what they could tell us. We understand that when faced with a group of unknown people, some children may feel uncomfortable and may not be able to talk to us. Following recommendations from Joyce (2018), we decided to recruit a slightly larger number of participants so that we could find participants who were more "sociable" than shy (Joyce, 2018), as a way of facilitating communication between participants and moderators.

Practice with a Semi-structured Script. The first game was considered an observation game, we left the participating children free to experiment and get used to the game mechanics. We then observed two more matches, but now focusing on the activities of the semi-structured itinerary. In this Playtest session, we observed the children play while we directed them with tasks and questions that helped us identify the levels of understanding of the game's functions and mechanics.

While the moderator directed the child, the observer wrote down all the comments and behaviors that the child expressed and observer two marked on the success table whether the child was performing the activities with difficulty, without difficulty, or was unable to do so. The moderator himself also asked, at the end of each script session, that the participant choose a memo card that best demonstrated their emotions during that session. Finally, we asked some questions to allow participants to express their opinions about the experience as a whole and, finally, we handed out thank you gifts.

4 Results

Through the Playtest sessions with children, our expectation that there are crucial differences between the application of tests with children and adults was confirmed. The results of this process are presented here in two different axes highlighted above: the formation of good practices for conducting the test and the technical aspects of building data collection tools and organizing the test set-up. The process of researching good practices and tips for conducting tests with children proved to be the main point, in this section we will share good practices related to preparing and conducting playtests. Even so, we reinforce that the main conduct to be established by researchers is continuous attention to dealing with children and the search for establishing an appropriate form of communication. Attention and communication are the instruments that avoid situations of disrespect for the test's ethical and technical limits by focusing the test on listening to the child, distancing itself from the excessive authority on the part of the adult, or situations of embarrassment on the part of the participant.

4.1 Training in Good Practices for Conducting Tests with Children

Build a Relationship of Trust with the Child and Guardians. Before contacting the child, we informed those responsible about the test step by step what type of data would be collected, how they would be treated, as well as the type of findings generated by the playtest. At this stage, it is important to seek the most transparent form of dialogue possible, as a way of demonstrating that the playtest is a safe space and, at this moment, demystifying the objectives and type of information generated by the methodology for those responsible, to also acquire consent of the person responsible, expressed, and documented.

Be Friendly. The way we connect with the participating child is important to observe. She needs to feel as comfortable as possible and, therefore, the test moderator must avoid posturing and using overly formal and technical language. (Rajendran, 2019). Trying to develop a less formal posture that is closer to the child is a way of reducing the risk of them being embarrassed or intimidated by the adult.

Avoid Questions that Favor Immediate Yes or No. We avoid phrases like "Do you like this?" When dealing with someone unknown asking questions, children may give in to trying to please the researchers conducting the test (Sesame Workshop, 2022). Instead, we chose to ask questions that gave them the opportunity to present and discuss their points of view and perceptions of the game. For example, the question "Would you use this app/game?" was replaced with "Who do you think would like this app? Why?". In this sense, the test with children does not differ from those carried out with adults, the moderator must express interest in the participant's speech and respect for their language, without establishing an asymmetrical hierarchical stance.

Pay Attention to Non-verbal Language. When carrying out the playtests, we deal with different personalities and realities, which is why we started the playtest with a neutral tone of voice and adapted it according to the mood the child demonstrated during the session (Rajendran, 2019). It was essential to pay attention to the children's non-verbal language (Henriques, 2020) so that at the sign of discomfort or difficulty we were ready to ask the right questions.

Show Interest. Encourage moments in which the child talks about things that interest him before and during the test (Rajendran, 2019). Our attention was fully on the child and what they were doing (Henriques, 2020). This way we encourage children to feel valued and thus find confidence to continue expressing themselves. When we did not understand a speech, behavior, or action, we asked the participant what they meant, avoiding applying our bias regarding the answer we expected.

When Something Didn't Go as Expected. We always avoided interrupting them, even if the response or action was not what we imagined. When necessary, we would re-ask the questions or ask the child to do a task again, but if the child showed reluctance, we would move on (Rajendran, 2019).

Only the Essentials. Only one moderator, one observer and one person present for the child must be in the testing environment. If more people needed to be in the room, we reinforced that they did not interrupt and just observed. Being in a new environment and with new people can be uncomfortable for the child, so the ideal is for only the moderator to talk to the child and establish this closer connection.

Short Sessions. Young children understand each other easily and may not have the patience to spend more than an hour in front of a computer or smartphone. That's why we hold Playtest sessions lasting a maximum of 45 min, so as not to make the experience boring and so that the participant remains interested in using the game and providing in-depth feedback.

Segment the Sample. To Alita Joyce (2019), "When designing for children there are certain cognitive and physical considerations to remember". During childhood, children change quickly, and the difference of a year between one child and another can generate great contrasts. According to Fei Fei Liu (2018), children between 5 and 8 years old can perform simple gestures to interact with devices because their gross motor skills are partially developed, while their fine motor skills are limited, as is their motor coordination. Children aged between 9 and 12 have well-developed gross and fine motor skills while motor coordination is partially developed. Imagining these differences applied to our study sample is crucial to understanding the variations in our results and observations. There are three concepts that we can observe in both children and adults that help us identify which interactions they may be capable of carrying out:

- Global motor skills: use of large muscle groups that involve the skills of walking, jumping and kicking (Rebelo et al, 2020).
- Fine motor skills: use of a set of smaller muscles that generate fine interactions, such as pinching the hands, closing buttons, and writing (Rebelo et al, 2020).
- Motor coordination: involves the ability to combine global and fine skills in a coordinated way to carry out an activity (Fei Fei Liu, 2018).

5 Structure and Set-up for Testing in AR Mobile

Different Perceptions. We identified very explicit differences related to the difference age of the participants in relation to how they understood the possibility of using the space and the gestures required to carry out the tasks. At the same time, we can observe how participants developed strategies to facilitate their ways of playing.

Use of Space. In the first sessions, we imagined that the children would like to continue playing around a single space where the virtual environment was anchored. However, we noticed that some children preferred to anchor the virtual environment to the floor and play while sitting or crawling, and others preferred to play around a table. Most participants faced difficulties in understanding the concept of anchoring the virtual world on a real-world surface, we realized that the anchoring flow itself was not clear enough to the children. At certain times we had to intervene to help the participant anchor. Some of the children did not understand that they needed to move around the world instead of staying in one place, to be able to see all angles of the virtual environment.

Gestures. We noticed that at various times the player-users tried to 'zoom' the cell phone screen to take a closer look at an object. Or they tried to 'rotate the world' with their fingers so that it was not necessary to cross the environment or get closer. Observing these particularities during the sessions provided important input for our designers and game designers to devise improvements or new forms of interaction. There are still many gestures and inputs that the technical feasibility can be studied for AR applications on mobile devices.

6 Conclusion

This article chronicled our process of implementing Playtest with children for the first time. Accompanied by our development and survey of good practices that would support the Playtest exercise with minors as there are fundamental differences between the research process with children and adults. Our objective is to contribute so that this methodology and good practices can continue to be continuously supported and there are more references in the area. The good practices raised made a big difference during the application of the tests, helping us to conduct and communicate with the participating children, strengthening a comfortable interaction. Children in general demonstrated that they were open to experiencing new virtual worlds and sought new ways to explore them by translating gestures used in 2D apps into the AR context. There is an open window here for exploring inputs and means of interaction that are comfortable for users, especially those who, even at a young age, are already voracious consumers of technology. We can engage children in new contexts in the area of XR development where they will help build user-centered usability for generations to come.

References

Davis, J.P., Steury, K., Pagulayan, R.: A survey method for assessing perceptions of a game: the consumer playtest in game design. In: The International Journal of Computer Game Research, volume 5, issue 1 (2005)

Fullerton, T., Swain, C., Hoffman, S.: Game Design Workshop: Designing, Prototyping, & Playtesting Games. CRC Press (2004)

Schell, J.: The Art of Game Design: A Book of Lenses, 1st edn. Taylor & Francis, CRC Press (2008)

Oliver, M.B., Bowman, N.D., Woolley, J.K., Rogers, R., Sherrick, B.I., Chung, M.-Y.: Video Games as Meaningful Entertainment Experiences (2016)

Libby, H., Kirsten, R., Kirsten, A.: Guidelines for usability testing with children. Interactions **4**(5), 9–14 (1997)

Feifei, L.: Design for Kids Based on Their Stage of Physical Development (2018). https://www.nngroup.com/articles/children-ux-physical-development/

Rebelo, M., Serrano, J., Duarte-Mendes, P., Paulo, R., Marinho, D.A.: Child motor development: relationship between global motor skills, fine motor skills and age. Cuadernos de Psicología del Deporte **20**(1), 75–85 (2020)

Joyce, A.: Usability Testing with Minors: 16 Tips (2019). https://www.nngroup.com/articles/usability-testing-minors/

Koster, R.: Theory of fun. 2nd ed. O'Reilly Media (2013)

Lazzaro, N.: Why we play games: Four Keys to More Emotion without Story. Game Dev Conf. (2004)

Castellón, L.: Ultra young power. Isto É São Paulo, August 1, 2007. In: <http://www.istoe.com.br/reportagens/1081_PODER+ULTRAJOVEM>

Priporas, C.V., Stylos, N., Kamenidou, I.E.: City image, city brand personality and generation Z residents' life satisfaction under economic crisis: Predictors of city-related social media engagement. Journal of Business Research (2019)

Kostman, A.: They have the strength. Veja, São Paulo, n. 1.791, pp. 84–91, 26 fevereiro 2003

Djafarova, E., Bowes,T.: 'Instagram made Me buy it': Generation Z impulse purchases in the fashion industry. J. Retail. Consum. Serv. **59**, 102345 (2021). ISSN 0969–6989

Mccrindlle: Understanding Generation Alpha. https://mccrindle.com.au/article/topic/generation-alpha/generation-alpha-defined/

GWI: Gen Alpha: The Real Picture (2022). https://www.gwi.com/reports/gen-alpha

Rajendran, S.: User Research Tips for Interviewing Kids (2019). https://uxdesign.cc/user-research-tips-for-interviewing-kids-ae686e5324ac

Henriques C., Pilar, D., Ignácio, E.: UX com sotaque brasileiro (2020). ISBN 978–85–5519–319–4

Samsung.: Children's first steps into the world digital with Samsung Kids. https://www.samsung.com/br/apps/samsung-kids/

Playtest with kids.: Get Actionable insights for your product. https://playtestwithkids.org/

Nielsen norman group. Articles.: https://www.nngroup.com/search/?q=kids

Immersive Test Study to Evaluate XR Device Performance and Usability

Anderson V. C. de Oliveira(✉), Pio H. Ordozgoith F. S., Hanah I. S. Correa, and Renato A. O. Andrade

Sidia Instituto de Ciencia e Tecnologia - SW Solutions, Avenue Darcy Vargas 654, Manaus, Chapada 69050-020, Brazil
{anderson.oliveira,pio.sobrinho,hanah.santos,renato.andrade}@sidia.com

Abstract. In this work, we propose a methodology to measure the performance and usability of virtual, augmented, and extended reality (VR/AR and XR) devices, providing a number score instead of traditional questionnaire-based assessments. In order to accomplish this goal, we have designed a target selection test in immersive environment, and we carried out a mathematical study to measure the test quality. We defined three quality metrics that provided a score within a scale from 0 to 10. The idea is that, instead of assessments based on questionnaires which are filled out by the users in the end of an immersive test, the quality experience can be provided by a number with no bias, taking into account the factors relevant for that application. Then we validate our methodology by performing a user test with Meta Quest 2 with ten participants. The proposed methodology can be used to compare VR/AR/XR devices without the subjectivity of questionnaires.

Keywords: Metrics · Immersive test · Comparing devices · VR reality · Fitts' law

1 Introduction

Despite the growth of immersive technology market, it is not a new technology, since the first virtual reality (VR) device is dated from 1968 [10]. Some head-mounted displays (HMD) emerged in the 1980 s and 1990 s but without achieving massive commercial success. Among them, we can mention "EyePhone HRX" by VPL Research [12], one of the first commercial HMDs, "Virtual Boy" by Nitendo [13], which offered a 3D virtual reality experience, and "Forte VFX1" [7], a Forte virtual reality headset manufactured. These devices pioneered and helped lay the foundation for the development of modern VR/AR/XR devices. They differed in functionality, from simple stereoscopic visualizations to more complex virtual reality experiences. Important later releases include "Glass" by Google in 2013 [9], which represented a major advance in immersive technology at the time, but also failed to achieve mass adoption, HoloLens by Microsoft in 2015 [2], which introduced the concept of mixed reality (MR), and Quest by

C. Stephanidis et al. (Eds.): HCII 2024, CCIS 2319, pp. 177–187, 2025.
https://doi.org/10.1007/978-3-031-78516-0_18

Meta in 2019 [11], the most affordable device in price terms. Over the years, continuous development in hardware and software has been enhancing the MR experience, and subsequent versions of some of these devices have been released with significant improvements.

The quality of the immersive experience offered by these devices to users is influenced by ergonomic factors, as well as the accuracy of the device sensor and the precision of the detection of the controller. In addition, this kind of evaluation is extremely difficult to measure. In general, it is done by using predefined questionnaires which are filled by the participants at the end of user tests. Theses questionnairies includes items such as "I felt present in the environment", "I felt like I was really there" and "I felt the environment reacts to my actions", so that the participants rate these items on a scale. Some of these questionnaires include "System Usability Scale" (SUS) [1], "Software Usability Measurement Inventory" (SUMI) [5], "Standardized User Experience Percentile Rank Questionnaire" (SUPR-Q) [8] and "Questionnaire for User Interaction Satisfaction" (QUIS) [4].

In [6], a quick scale for measuring immersion, feeling of control, and simulator sickness was developed and tested with three different immersive devices: a headband (OptiTrack VR trackers with a MiddleVR software platform), 3D glasses (XPAND) and a head-mounted display (Sony HMZ-T2). The scale works by assessing the participants' experiences based on several questionnaire items related to immersion. After completing the questionnaire items, the responses are averaged to create a summated scale for immersion for each device. The goal of that experiment was to measure the levels of immersion people experience in their virtual environments interactions, and the head-mounted display proved to be the most immersive device.

Given the subjectivity in evaluating the quality of user experience with immersive devices, we propose a methodology based on an unbiased calculation of the user performance when carried out an immersive test. Since the main feature of these devices is to integrate the user into immersive experiences among virtual objects, a suitable way to assess the usability of the device is by a "target selection test". We can numerically measure a test quality by modeling equations to provide a final score, since Fitts' Law [3] states that the difficulty of a target selection task can be quantified.

2 Target Selection Test

Target selection is a fundamental application of MR interaction. We designed a test where a ball appears in a random position within a rectangular plane as in Fig. 1, and the user must point and click over it by using the pointer control or other available selection mechanism, depending on the device. In our experiments with Meta Quest 2, the test could also be done with hands, but we chose to use control for all users. When the click is over the object region, the ball disappears and a hit is counted. Immediately, another ball appears at a random position within the plane. Otherwise a error is count. In every test, ten balls appear. As shown in the Fig. 1b, the rectangular region has sides of 113 × 71 cm, and the target is a ball with a diameter of 10cm. The plane area was empirically defined on the basis of the *field of vision* (FOV) of the user at a distance of 1 m. Ball lifespan was set up in 3 s. If it is not hit during this time, it disappears and another one appears at a random position on the plane.

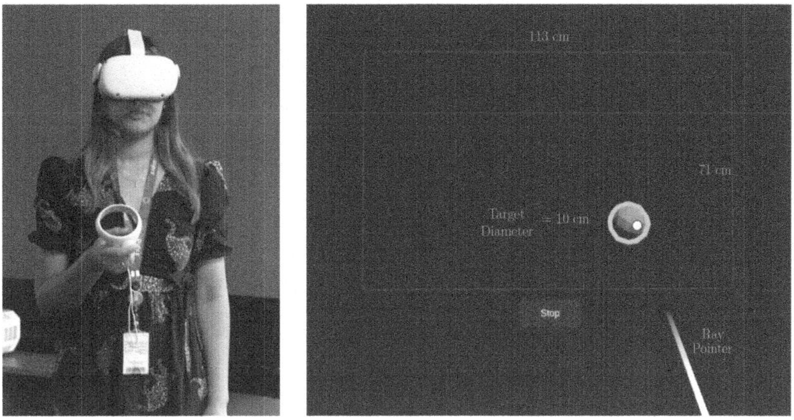

(a) (b)

Fig. 1. Target pointer click test. a) User performing the test with a Meta Quest 2. b) Field of vision during the test (text in green was placed later to illustrate.). (Color figure online)

Although the test may seem like a simple game, target selection is an essential task in immersive environments since it represents how the user will perform tasks of selecting and clicking buttons in menus and general applications during the use of the device. Therefore, our goal is to measure user performance when taking the test. As ten balls appear to be clicked, we can assign 1 individual quality point q to each one, so that at the end the user can get a maximum of 10 test quality points Q, as in Eq. 1, where $N = 10$.

$$Q = q_1 + q_2 + ... + q_N \tag{1}$$

The simplest way to set up a score in this scenario is to assign 1 point if the user hits the ball and 0 otherwise. However, a fairer measurement should take into account that during the test, some of the balls can be hit quickly as soon as they appear on the plane, and others may take and be reached almost at the end of the ball timelife. Of course, they cannot have the same score. Likewise, the user can hit the ball sometimes by clicking near the center and sometimes near the edge. Therefore, we have two variables to consider in a target selection test: click time and distance to the center of the target.

Since the test quality depends on two variables, we can establish some equations to measure the quality of individual interaction q for the ball i such that each equation gives as a result a floating number between 0 and 1. In this way, the final result Q with N balls will give a floating real number ranging from 0 to N. If we define ω_t as the weight relative to the time and ω_d as the weight relative to the distance in the quality score, it is wanted that both ω_t and ω_d are as low as possible (close to 0), since it means a fast click and close to the center of the ball. But when this happens, they must have a high score (close to 1). In this way, we can define the following equations:

$$q_i = \frac{(1 - \omega_t) + (1 - \omega_d)}{2} \tag{2}$$

$$k_i = (1 - \omega_t \omega_d) \tag{3}$$

$$h_i = \left(1 - \frac{T_T}{N \cdot T}\right) \cdot (1 - \omega_d) \tag{4}$$

In Eq. 2, the quality interaction q_i of the ball i is defined as the sum of the two portions, time and distance (so it can achieve a maximum value of 2), divided by 2 to ensure that q_i varies from 0 to 1. In Eq. 3, the quality interaction k_i is defined as follows: time and distance parts are multiplied, so that good performance (fast and close to the target center clicks) will provide a low value of multiplication. Then 1 minus that multiplication will provide a score close to 1 when it is well and close to 0 otherwise. In Eq. 4, different from q_i and k_i, the quality interaction h_i of the ball i does not use the individual portion ω_t of each ball i but the total test time T_T of the N balls. T_T is normalized by the possible total time of the test, i.e. N plus the ball lifespan T. As before, 1 minus this portion ensures a partial score close to 1 if the time is short and close to 0 otherwise. This part of the time is obtained only at the end of all the N balls and it is multiplied by the individual distance performance for each ball i. $\omega_t = 0$ means that the user hit the ball in a theoretical time of 0 s, and $\omega_t = 1$ means that the user clicked on the maximum lifespan limit T of the ball (when it disappears). In the same way, $\omega_d = 0$ means that the user hits the ball exactly in the center, and $\omega_d = 1$ means that the user hits the ball at its maximum edge limit, that is, distance d is equal to the radius R of the ball.

Since we want to vary ω_t and ω_d from 0 to 1, there are many ways to model it. Two intuitive ways are to use a linear variation as shown in Fig. 2a and exponential variations as shown in Fig. 2b, so that exponentials can have positive or negative concavity.

Note that, once we have quality equations that depend on two variables, time and distance, and both can vary from 0 to 1 using a linear or exponential behavior, we can also combine the time and distance portions in Eqs. 2, 3 and 4 as shown in Table 1 and increase the possibility of quality equations.

Another way to create other quality equations depending on the test objectives is to assign different weights to time and distance. For instance, Eq. 5 is a variation of Eq. 2 with weight 2 for time, and Eq. 6 with weight 2 for distance.

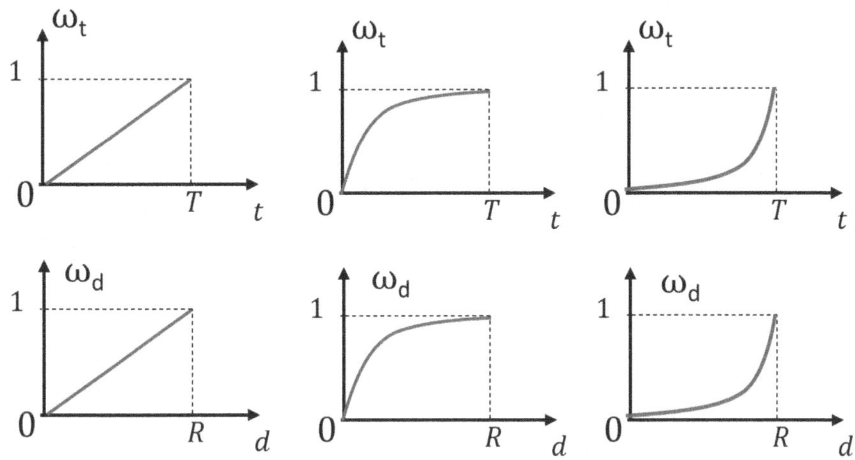

Fig. 2. Time and distance variation from 0 to 1 to score the quality of interaction.

Table 1. Combination of linear and exponential variations for time and distance.

Time	Distance
Linear	Linear
Linear	Exponential
Exponential	Linear
Exponential	Exponential

$$q_i = \frac{2 \cdot (1 - \omega_t) + (1 - \omega_d)}{3} \quad (5) \qquad q_i = \frac{(1 - \omega_t) + 2 \cdot (1 - \omega_d)}{3} \quad (6)$$

We will follow our study using only linear behavior for time and distance. Exponential variations, weights for time and distance, as well as combinations in the Table 1 are mentioned as future work and investigation of the best metrics to be used. Focusing on linear variation for time and distance, we can model ω_t and ω_d to have the line behavior on the graph shown in Fig. 2a. In this way, the individual score for the ball i relative to time portion, ω_t, is defined in Eq. 7, where t_i is the time to click on the ball i and T is the lifespan of the ball i. Similarly, the individual score for the ball i relative to the distance portion, ω_d, is defined in Eq. 8, where d_i is the distance between the click and the center of the ball i, which has radius R.

$$\omega_t = \left(\frac{t_i}{T}\right) \quad (7) \qquad \omega_d = \left(\frac{d_i}{R}\right) \quad (8)$$

By replacing the results of ω_t and ω_d of Eqs. 7 and 8 into Eqs. 2, 3 and 4, we obtain the following results for the quality equations q_i, k_i and h_i:

$$q_i = \frac{(1 - \frac{t_i}{T}) + (1 - \frac{d_i}{R})}{2} \quad (9)$$

$$k_i = \left(1 - \frac{t_i}{T}\frac{d_i}{R}\right) \quad (10)$$

$$h_i = \left(1 - \frac{T_T}{N \cdot T}\right) \cdot \left(1 - \frac{d_i}{R}\right) \quad (11)$$

As q_i, k_i and h_i are individual quality scores for the ball i, the overall test quality score will be the sum of these quantities for all the N balls. Then if we named these sums of q_i, k_i and h_i as the quality test score Q_1, Q_2 and Q_3 respectively, we obtain the final Eqs. 12, 13 and 14:

$$Q_1 = \sum_{i=1}^{N} \left[\frac{(1 - \frac{t_i}{T}) + (1 - \frac{d_i}{R})}{2}\right] \quad (12)$$

$$Q_2 = \sum_{i=1}^{N} \left(1 - \frac{t_i}{T}\frac{d_i}{R}\right) \quad (13)$$

$$Q_3 = \left(1 - \frac{T_T}{N \cdot T}\right) \sum_{i=1}^{N} \left(1 - \frac{d_i}{R}\right) \quad (14)$$

where t_i is the time to click on the ball i, d_i is the distance between the click position and the center of the target ball, R is the diameter of the ball, which is a fixed constant number, T is the lifespan of the ball, N is the numer of ball in the test, and T_T is the final test time for the N balls. Both Q_1, Q_2 and Q_3 will provide a floating number ranging from 0 to 10 at the end of the test, as shown in Fig. 3.

If M people perform the test with two devices D_1 and D_2, we can build a vector of results for each of them. These vectors can be used to plot a normal distribution for each of the devices, as shown in Fig. 4. The device with best performance will be the one with distribution further ahead in the scale.

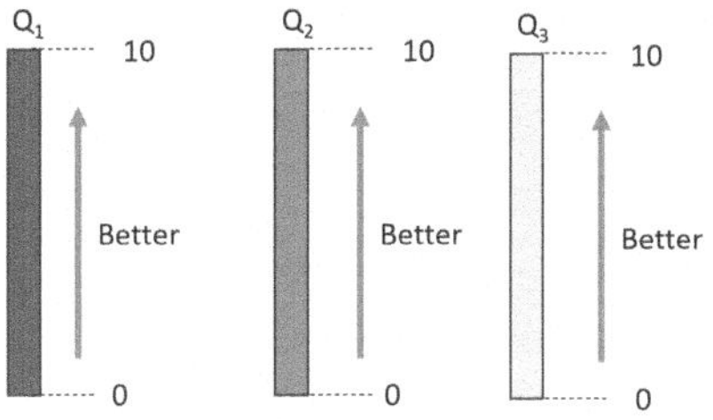

Fig. 3. Scales for metric quantities Q_1, Q_2 and Q_3.

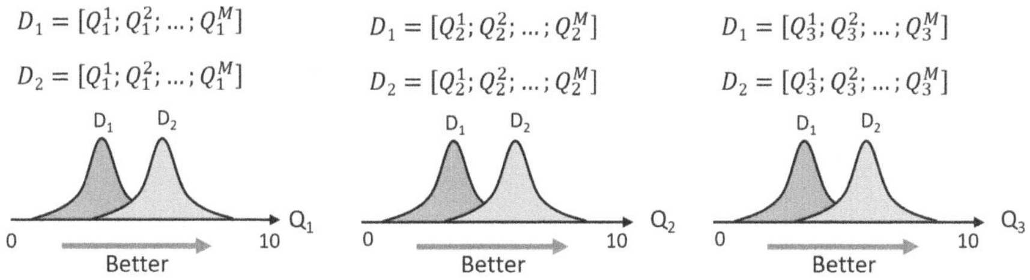

Fig. 4. Normal distribution for a set of M users evaluated with Q_1, Q_2 and Q_3.

3 Experimental Results

As our objective here is not to directly compare some devices but rather to show the proposed methodology, we performed a user test with Meta Quest 2 with 10 participants. Each of them performed the tests five times. Table 2 shows the score results for all users. Figure 5 shows the normal distribution of these values. We can see that, when evaluated with the metric Q_1 in Eq. 12, Meta Quest 2 gets a mean score of ~ 6.8, on a scale from 0 to 10, with a standard deviation of ~ 0.493. Note that, if the same participants carry out the tests with other device, it would be possible to compare them with numerical data without the subjectivity of the questionnaires mentioned in the introduction.

When the same tests are measured with the metric Q_2 of Eq. 13, they present the results shown in the Table 3. When these values are grouped to build a normal distribution, they show the curve shown in Fig. 6, with a mean of ~ 9.08 on a scale from 0 to 10, with a standard deviation of ~ 0.294. Note that despite having a higher mean and lower standard deviation, it represents exactly the same tests measured with the metric Q_1, since the absolute value of quality depends on how the equation is modeled.

Finally, when these tests are measured with the metric Q_3 of Eq. 14, the quality score results for all users presented the values shown on Tab. 4 and the normal distribution of Fig. 7, with mean ~ 6.03 on a scale from 0 to 10, with standard deviation of ~ 0.606.

Table 2. User test results for Meta Quest 2 evaluated with metric Q_1.

User	Test 1	Test 2	Test 3	Test 4	Test 5
User 1	6.03	6.81	6.59	6.73	7.09
User 2	5.87	6.65	6.29	7.15	6.98
User 3	6.13	6.62	6.55	7.38	6.60
User 4	7.01	7.33	7.27	7.64	7.52
User 5	6.64	6.62	7.10	7.08	7.12
User 6	6.94	6.46	6.82	7.05	6.58
User 7	7.05	7.06	6.37	7.30	6.61
User 8	6.07	7.51	7.41	7.10	7.25
User 9	5.99	7.18	6.93	5.94	6.73
User 10	5.33	7.20	6.81	6.45	7.38

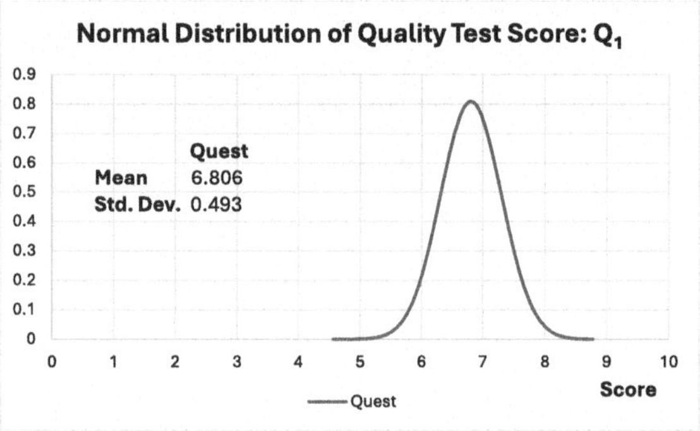

Fig. 5. Normal distribution for results using metric Q_1.

Table 3. User test results for Meta Quest 2 evaluated with metric Q_2.

User	Test 1	Test 2	Test 3	Test 4	Test 5
User 1	8.93	9.01	8.70	9.13	9.45
User 2	7.92	8.65	8.99	9.17	8.94
User 3	9.19	8.84	9.17	9.54	9.14
User 4	9.16	9.31	9.36	9.43	9.47
User 5	8.95	9.00	9.35	9.21	9.33
User 6	9.11	8.72	8.90	9.29	8.78
User 7	9.10	9.36	8.90	9.43	9.12
User 8	8.77	9.33	9.19	9.08	9.16
User 9	8.72	9.35	9.21	8.84	9.11
User 10	8.60	9.10	9.01	9.14	9.56

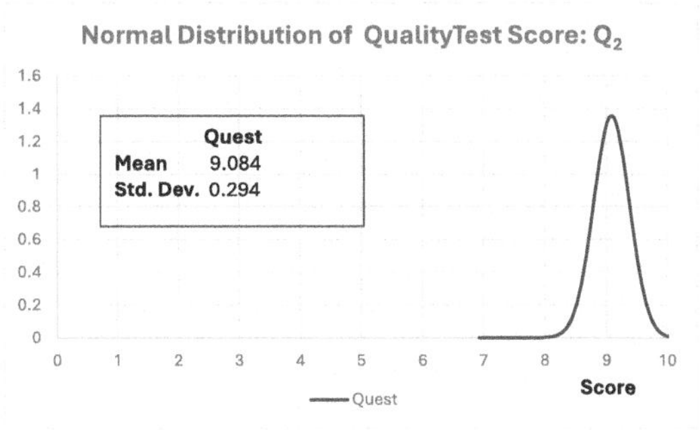

Fig. 6. Normal distribution for results using metric Q_2.

Table 4. User test results for Meta Quest 2 evaluated with metric Q_3.

User	Test 1	Test 2	Test 3	Test 4	Test 5
User 1	5.86	6.17	5.70	6.12	6.73
User 2	5.04	5.67	5.85	6.14	5.73
User 3	6.35	5.80	6.15	7.04	6.04
User 4	6.19	6.46	6.61	6.78	6.88
User 5	5.96	5.58	6.66	6.56	6.52
User 6	6.14	5.51	5.91	6.52	5.74
User 7	5.96	6.73	5.61	6.78	5.95
User 8	3.90	5.92	6.11	6.12	6.08
User 9	5.08	6.00	6.30	5.37	5.71
User 10	4.29	6.17	6.00	6.22	6.99

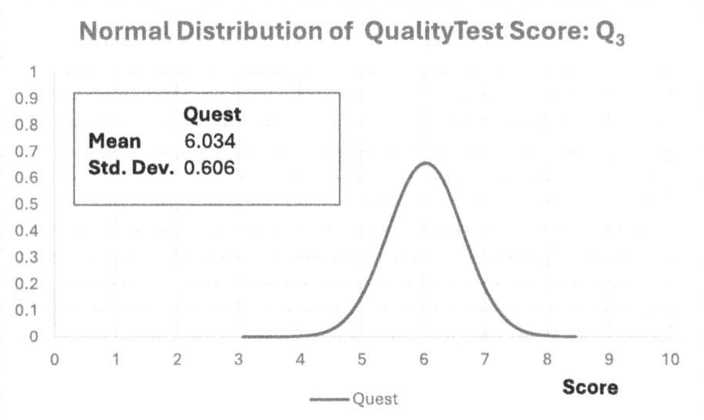

Fig. 7. Normal distribution for results using metric Q_3.

4 Conclusions

In this work, we proposed a methodology to compare virtual environments devices, when the result is provided by a number score instead of a questionnaire to be filled out by the participants at the end of the test. Provides a fair assessment with no bias compared to the subjectivity of choosing a grade for the questions. We have successfully designed a target selection test to be built in XR devices and we did a mathematical development to define three quality equations to provide a score within a range from 0 to 10.

Depending on the equation chosen to measure performance, final results will show different values, but since you use the same metric for more than um device it is possible to compare them in a fair way with warranty of a mathematical background. In future work, as previously mentioned, we mention carrying out tests using metrics derived from those we define here, according to the Tab. 1, and mainly carry out an investigation about, given several metrics available to measure a test, how to find the one that is the best or most appropriate to a target selection test.

Acknowledgment. This work was presented as part of the results from the Harp Platform 2.0 Project, carried out by Sidia Instituto de Ciência e Tecnologia in partnership with Samsung Eletrônica da Amazônia LTDA, according to the IT Law n.8387/91 and article 39 from Decree 10.521/2020.

References

1. Brooke, J.: SUS: a quick and dirty usability scale. Usability Eval. Ind. **189**, 4–7 (1995)
2. Chen, H., Lee, A.S., Swift, M., Tang, J.C.: 3D collaboration method over Hololens and Skype end points. In: Proceedings of the 3rd International Workshop on Immersive Media Experiences, pp. 27–30 (2015)
3. Fitts, P.M.: The information capacity of the human motor system in controlling the amplitude of movement. J. Exp. Psychol. **47**, 381–391 (1954)
4. Harper, B.D., Norman, K.L.: Improving user satisfaction: the questionnaire for user interaction satisfaction version 5.5 **224**, 228 (1993)
5. Kirakowski, J., Corbett, M.: SUMI: the software usability measurement inventory. Br. J. Educ. Technol. **24**, 210–212 (2006). https://doi.org/10.1111/j.1467-8535.1993.tb00076.x
6. Kronqvist, A., Jokinen, J., Rousi, R., et al.: Evaluating the authenticity of virtual environments: comparison of three devices. In: Advances in Human-Computer Interaction (2016)
7. Murray, J.W.: Building Virtual Reality with Unity and SteamVR. CRC Press (2020)
8. Sauro, J.: SUPR-Q: a comprehensive measure of the quality of the website user experience. J. Usability Stud. **10**(2), 68–86 (2015)
9. Starner, T.: Project glass: an extension of the self. IEEE Pervasive Comput. **12**(2), 14–16 (2013)
10. Sutherland, I.E.: A head-mounted three dimensional display. In: Proceedings of the December 9-11, 1968, Fall Joint Computer Conference, part I, pp. 757–764 (1968)
11. Time magazine: review: the oculus quest is virtual reality best bet yet (2021). https://time.com/5584275/oculus-quest-review/. Accessed 17 Apr 2024

12. Veron, H., Hezel, P., Southard, D.A.: Head-mounted displays for virtual reality. Helmet-and head-mounted displays and symbology design requirements **2218**, 41–50 (1994)
13. Willcox, J.K.: Boy toy: nintendo virtual Boy 3-D game system. Video Mag. **19**(7), 100–102 (1995)

Automated Evaluation of Metrics for Immersive Test Using Reinforcement Learning

Roberto G. Estrada L.(✉), Anderson V. C. de Oliveira, Agustin Alejandro Ortiz Diaz, Jeferson B. da Costa, and Emerson S. Domingos

Sidia Instituto de Ciência e Tecnologia - SW Solutions, Avenue Darcy Vargas 654,Manaus, Chapada 69050-020, Brazil
{roberto.leyva,anderson.oliveira,agustin.diaz, jeferson.costa,emerson.domingos}@sidia.com

Abstract. In this work, we designed a target selection test in order to investigate the most appropriate metric to measure the quality of an immersive experience. The test was designed in Unity, and instead of usual subjective tests with a group of volunteers, we incorporate to it a reinforcement learning system which represents an impartial agent to carry out the tests. The idea is that the network will learn to hit the target along the training and grows its precision when evaluated by a quality metric. The precision will increase until it reaches its maximum score. If we define different metrics, we can analyze the behavior from the beginning of the training until it reaches its maximum value, and then we define the best metric. We use three quality equations that provide a performance score ranging from 0 to 1 with the following behavior when they vary from along the range: (1) a linear variation, (2) a positive concavity exponential, and (3) a negative concavity exponential variation. Experimental results show that metric 1 presents the best results, followed by metrics 2 and 3 respectively.

Keywords: metrics evaluation · interaction test · mixed reality · reinforcement learning · Fitts' law

1 Introduction

In the dynamic landscape of virtual, augmented, and mixed reality (VR, AR, MR), where an universal standard is absent, user experiences are influenced by factors such as device sensor accuracy, controller detection precision, pose detection speed and user perception. Even subtle changes in these elements can significantly impact overall user satisfaction [7]. Furthermore, there is currently no defined standard for interaction models in AR and VR glass [10]. While some industry-leading companies like Microsoft and Meta are gradually shaping interaction methods with concepts such as controllers, pointers, and reticles, no clear standard has been established for these platforms [9]. The absence of

C. Stephanidis et al. (Eds.): HCII 2024, CCIS 2319, pp. 188–197, 2025.
https://doi.org/10.1007/978-3-031-78516-0_19

definitions and standards exacerbates the issue of user comfort when using MR systems.

Comparison between devices is often carried out by experiment with a group of participants following some conditions [2,8]. In general, usability results for applications and devices are based on pre-defined forms which are filled by these participants at the end of the test. Some of these methods include "System Usability Scale" (SUS) [1], "Software Usability Measurement Inventory" (SUMI) [6], "Standardized User Experience Percentile Rank Questionnaire" (SUPR-Q) [12] and "Questionnaire for User Interaction Satisfaction" (QUIS) [5].

Given these conditions of high subjectivity, we propose to compare measures of user experience quality using an impartial agent: use a machine learning system to perform the test instead of the traditional human subjective tests. Quality will be measured by pre-defined metrics, so that the score will tend to increase as the network learns. Fitts's law [3] states that the difficulty of a target selection task increases as the distance between the user and the target increases and the difficulty decreases as the target size increases. By using different metrics, we can investigate which one learns faster and therefore is the more appropriate. To accomplish this, we devised a "target pointer click" test in the Unity platform, a fundamental MR interaction application.

Many researchers, for study, divide machine learning methods into three broad areas: supervised learning (prediction using labeled data), unsupervised learning (learning structure from unlabeled data), and reinforcement learning. Currently, most of the state-of-the-art methods in all three areas are based on deep learning techniques [11].

In general, reinforcement learning can be defined as a field of machine learning that aims to train an agent to perform optimally in a given environment, concerning a particular goal" [4].

Some key terms to understand this learning process are as follows:

- **Agent**: the entity that performs actions in the environment.
- **Environment**: set of rules that control the process of updating the game and assigning rewards.
- **Game state**: information that represents a particular situation that the agent may encounter.
- **Action**: a possible move that an agent can take.
- **Reward**: the value with which the agent is rewarded by the environment due to a given action (it can be reward or penalty).
- **Episode**: A completed task of the agent on the environment.

The fundamental objective of reinforcement learning methods is to maximize the long-term reward of an agent in a given environment. To achieve it, the agent must learn optimal strategies through repetition of the game [4].

2 Test Design

We devised an application using Unity platform as shown in Fig. 1. It represents a target selection test, where there is a 2D plane in a square form with side of 2 m.

On it, a target appears in a random position (x_t, y_t) over the plane, so that it is a ball with diameter of 20cm. In front of the plane, there is a pointer representing the user. It is a ray with an origin at a distance of 1 m and is positioned on the plane in a moveable position (x_r, y_r). Main goal is move the ray pointer over the target area and click over it. Then a new ball (target) will appears in a random position. In order to move the ray pointer along the plane to reach the target, there are four possible actions: move the origin along horizontal and vertical direction (Hor and Ver in Fig. 1) and ray inclination at horizontal and vertical angles. Target ball has a lifetime of 3 s. If there is no click while the ball is alive or there is a click outside of the ball area, the actual target disappears and another one appears in a random position. Quality is considered to be better as the click is faster and closer to the ball center.

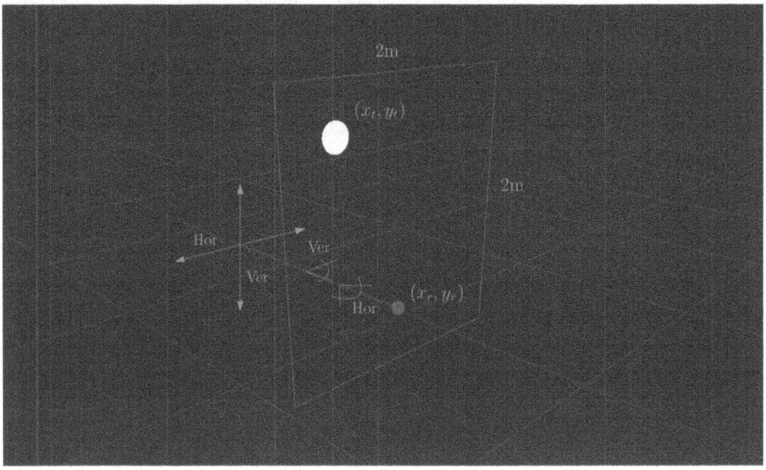

Fig. 1. Unity scene: target selection test.

3 Network

Unity platform provides a machine learning toolkit named ML-Agents [14]. enabling games and simulations to serve as environments for training intelligent agents. Our goal is to incorporate it to our devised target selection application as an impartial agent in such a way that it prevents possible bias from subjective testing with groups of people. First, it is expected that the network will learn to hit the ball. Once it learns that it must leads the pointer ray to the target, the click action will be more and more accurate, i.e. clicks will be faster and closer to the ball center.

Network was designed as in Fig. 2, i.e. it is a 3-layer fully connected network, with 128 neurons at each layer. The inputs are the position coordinate of the target center (x_t, y_t) and the actual ray pointer coordinate on the plane, (x_r, y_r). The output is the following actions: slope of the angle of the ray in vertical or horizontal directions, movement of the origin of the ray in vertical (up and down) or horizontal (right or left) directions, and a "click".

When the network come to decision of move the pointer ray in some of the directions, it receives a reward feedback which will be greater the closer it gets to the target and vice versa. It represents a "step", so that one episode can have up to 50 steps. When the click action happens, the current episode is finished off, doesn't matter if the click was inside or outside the target, and another ball appears in a random place on the plane.

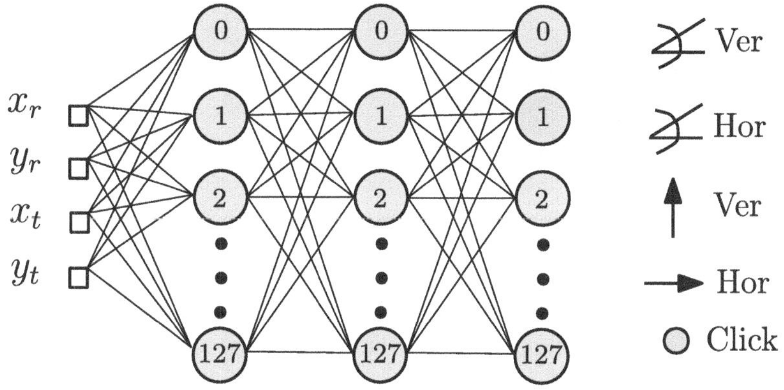

Fig. 2. Fully-connected network: 3-layered with 128 neurons.

4 Metrics

Metrics will define the score for a target hit attempt. We designed the score to be a real float number ranging from 0 to 1. According to the test design shown in Fig. 1, there are two main quantities to define the test quality "*Q*": the distance "*d*" between the click coordinate position and the center of the target, and the time "*t*" from the beginning of the episode (when the target appears on the plane) until the moment of click. For the distance evaluation, it must has the maximum score value 1 when the click is exactly at the center of the ball ($d = 0$). It reduces to 0 as the distance moves away from the center to the edge of the ball ($d = R$). In the same way, for the time corresponding evaluation, the maximum score value 1 occurs when the click has a hypothetical time of 0 s ($t = 0$) from the moment when the target appears on the plane, and it decreases to 0 as the time approaches the lifetime "*T*".

In both quantities, d and t can vary from 0 to 1 in many ways. The simplest way is a linear variation as shown in Fig. 3b. Since we want the final score (considering both d and t) to have a value ranging from 0 to 1, one way to get it is to add the individual scores for distance and time and then divide by 2. Then, we define the first quality metric Q_1 as shown in Eq. 1. All possible values for Q_1 when d vary from 0 to R and t vary from 0 to T are represented in the plane shown in Fig. 3a.

$$Q_1 = \frac{(1 - \frac{d}{R}) + (1 - \frac{t}{T})}{2} \tag{1}$$

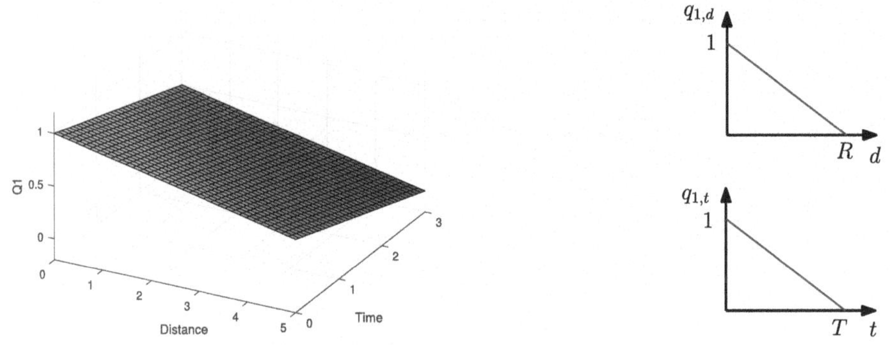

(a) (b)

Fig. 3. Metric 1: (a) all possible Q_1 values; (b) distance and time variation.

In the same way, d and t can vary from 0 to 1 by an exponential variation as shown in Fig. 4b. Adding the two quantities and dividing by 2, we define the second quality metric Q_2 as shown in Eq. 2. All possible values for Q_2 are represented in the plane shown in Fig. 4a.

$$Q_2 = \frac{\left(\frac{e^R - e^d}{e^R - 1}\right) + \left(\frac{e^T - e^t}{e^T - 1}\right)}{2} \tag{2}$$

Finally, the third metric Q_3 is another exponential behavior function for d and t, but with negative concavity as shown in Fig. 5b (note that metric 1 has positive concavity). Adding the two quantities and dividing by 2, Q_3 is defined in Eq. 3 with all the possible values represented in the plane of Fig. 5a.

$$Q_3 = \frac{\left(\frac{e^{R-d} - 1}{e^R - 1}\right) + \left(\frac{e^{T-t} - 1}{e^T - 1}\right)}{2} \tag{3}$$

Equations 1, 2 and 3 are valid when the click occurs inside the target, and the reward will be a positive float number between 0 and 1. When it does not, the reward score will be a negative value (penalty), with the modulus greater the further away the target is from the click. As the 2D plane in Fig. 1 has a side of 2 m, the maximum error distance inside the plane should be the plane hypotenuse H (in this case $\sim$ 2.8284). Since, we are measuring the error, i.e.

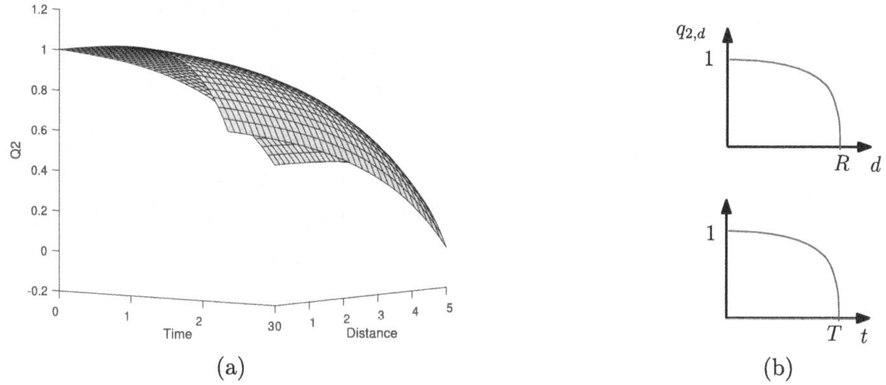

Fig. 4. Metric 2: (a) all possible Q_2 values; (b) distance and time variation.

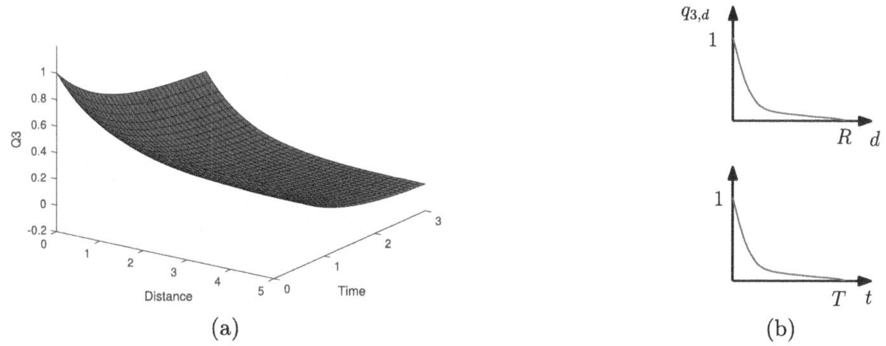

Fig. 5. Metric 3: (a) all possible Q_3 values; (b) distance and time variation.

clicks outside the ball, the distance d must be subtracted by the radius R given that the region of interest goes now from the ball edge to the plane edge. If we normalize the error to range from -1 to 0, with -1 the maximum possible error distance inside the plane and 0 being the closest limit outside the ball, the error reward score E is defined by the Eq. 4. Another possible situation that can occur during the test is that the ray is brought out of the plane and then clicks. In this case, we set a penalty of -1.

$$E = -\frac{d - R}{H} \tag{4}$$

In order to ensure a fair comparison between the equations defined before: (1) linear, (2) positive concavity exponential and (3) negative concavity exponential, we use the same error equation for all of them and the same out of plane click criterion to avoid different events while the system is learning to hit the ball, and the convergence behavior for each of the equations can be analyzed without bias from the moment the hits start to happen.

5 Experimental Results

There are some training configurations available to use in Unity platform together with ML-Agents toolkit. We use the "Proximal Policy Optimization" (PPO) [13]. It is expected that the network click in a random way along the plane at the beginning of training, then a particular configuration to be mentioned is named "curriculum". It allows to change the difficulty setup as the network learns. We use the configuration shown in Table 1. It means the training starts in lesson 0 with the target being a 40cm-diameter ball. When the average reward reaches 0.55 and has at least 100k steps, it will go to lesson 2, with the diameter reducing to 30cm diameter. It continues until the last lesson, when the target becomes a 10cm diameter ball.

Table 1. Curriculum lessons configuration.

Lesson	Min steps	Reward threshold	Ball diameter
0	100,000	0.55	40 cm
1	100,000	0.60	30 cm
2	100,000	0.65	20 cm
3	100,000	0.70	10 cm

The plot shown in Fig. 6a shows the average reward behavior along the training when that reward is provided by each of the three quality equations defined in Sect. 4. Rewards are shown in function of the steps along the training, i.e. it is wanted that it reaches a high quality score with fewer steps. Note that in addition to the oscillations in all three curves, there are also some sudden drops in the quality scores, since it represents the moment when training moved to the next lesson in the "curriculum" configuration. When this happens, the target reduces in size and becomes more difficult to hit. So, the first attempts fail, and the network follows learning until it manages to increase the average score again. This will repeat in every lesson in Table 1.

As it is expected that the network will make mistakes in the first attempts, all the curves in Fig. 6a start with negative values. As the network learns and begins to hit the first clicks, rewards begin to have positive values, which will be greater the better the precision of these clicks according to Eqs. 1, 2, and 3. We can see in Fig. 6a that metric 2 has the biggest peaks for score rewards, with values close to those of metric 1. However, we can see that metric 1 first meets the requirements to go from lesson 0 to lesson 1, which means that metric 2 also present good results for score quality but needs more steps to achieve them. Metric 3 presents slightly lower values compared to metrics 1 and 2, and it takes the longest to complete the first lesson.

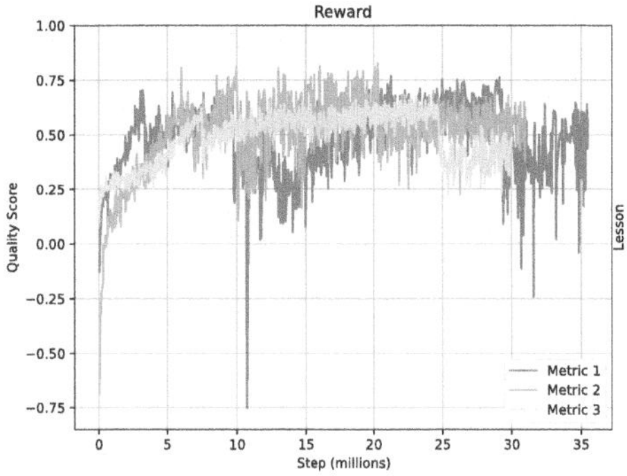

(a) Reward

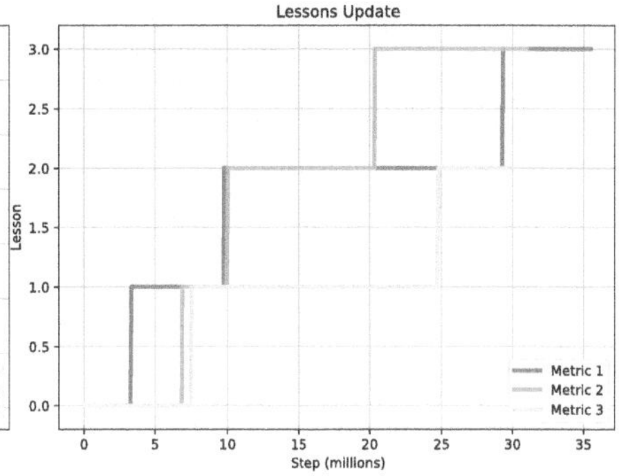

(b) Lessons

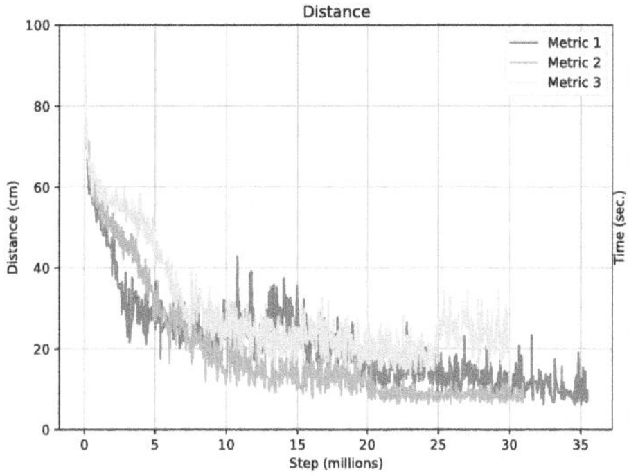

(c) Distance

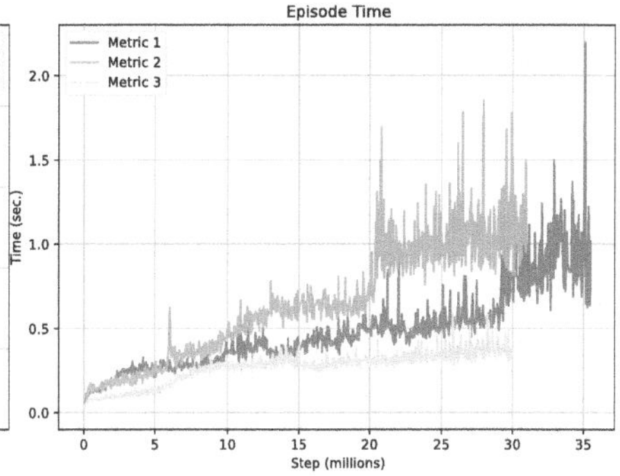

(d) Time

Fig. 6. Training result plots.

The plot shown in Fig. 6b a) shows the exact moment when metrics 1, 2 and 3 reach the next lesson in the Table 1. Note that metric 1 goes from lesson 0 to lesson 1 in about 3.2 million steps. Metric 2 does it in ~6.9 millions steps and metric 3 in ~7.5 millions steps. Then metric 1 goes to lesson 2 in ~9.8 millions steps, very close to metric 2 in ~10.0 millions while metric 3 does it only in ~24.5 millions steps. Finally, note that lesson 3 is achieved first by metric 2 in ~20.3 million steps and then by metric 1 in ~29.3 millions steps. Note also that metric 3 does not reaches the lesson 3 in 30 millions steps.

It is important to note that the absolute value of quality score is not sufficient to define the best metrics, as depending on the equation, the quality value Q may be higher in an equation even with worse distance and time values than in another one. Then in order to analyze it, plots in Figs. 6c and 6d show the distance and time behavior respectively for the three equations. For distance, as expected, all they start with high distances, which means that a lot of clicks are done outside the target. During training, these distances become smaller as the network improves accuracy. Metric 1 crosses 40cm before followed by metrics 2 and 3. Metric 2 reaches the lowest values for distance and presents smaller oscillations than the others. For time evaluation, all metrics start by clicking quickly and, of course, missing the target. During training, the network takes more time to bring the cursor closer to the target and then click. Metric 3 presents the lowest time values, but clicks are more distant to the target center as we see in Fig. 6c and learning is slower as we can see in Fig. 6b. Metric 1 presents shorter times than metric 2 and less fluctuations in values.

6 Conclusions

In this work, we propose to carry out an investigation into the assessment of quality metrics to measure the performance of a target selection test in an immersive environment where the performer should be a neural network instead of traditional human subjective tests. We successfully design an Unity immersive test, and we have defined three equations as metric to provide quality score taking into account the distance and time to click. Equations characterized by the way they go from minimum to maximum possible value, as follows: (1) linear, (2) positive concavity exponential, and (3) negative concavity exponential. In the Unit test, we incorporate a fully-connected network with 3-layered and 128 neurons on each, and we train under the same conditions up to a number of 30 million steps for each equation.

Given the average reward results, number of steps to complete the lessons, distance and time behavior along the training, we note that metric 3 has a lower quality and requires more steps to reach a high quality score. Moreover, it was the only one who did not meet the requirements to reach the last lesson. Metrics 1 and 2 present close quality score behavior, so that metric 1 completed lessons 0 and 1 first, in addition to reducing and stabilizing the distance faster and presents a shorter average click time. Metric 2 also presents good results for quality score, distance, and time behavior, but it needs more steps to reach them. Therefore, metric 1 has the best performance, followed by metric 2 and then metric 3.

In future work, we mentioned the use of different weights for the distance and time portions in the equations. For example, multiply the distance portion by 2, add it with the time portion, and divide by 3. The same is true for the time portion in the equations. This may provide information about which of these two factors is more important for measuring test quality. Another suggestion is to combine distance and time portion with different equation types, for example:

use the distance portion of the equation with a linear variation as in the metric 1 and time portion with an exponential variation as in metric 2, and investigate what combination provides best results.

Acknowledgment. This work was presented as part of the results of the Harp Platform 2.0 Project, carried out by Sidia Instituto de Ciência e Tecnologia in partnership with Samsung Eletrônica da Amazônia LTDA, according to IT Law n.8387/91, article 39, Decree 10.521/2020.

References

1. Brooke, J.: SUS: a quick and dirty usability scale. Usability Eval. Ind. **189**, 4–7 (1995)
2. Craig, P., Willemsen, P., Downs, E., Lover, A., Barber, W.: Learning environments in AR: comparing tablet and head-mounted augmented reality devices at room and table scale. In: IEEE Conference on Virtual Reality and 3D User Interfaces Abstracts and Workshops, pp. 892–893 (2022)
3. Fitts, P.M.: The information capacity of the human motor system in controlling the amplitude of movement. J. Exp. Psychol. **74**, 381–391 (1954)
4. Foster, D., Friston, K.: Generative Deep Learning: Teaching Machines to Paint, Write, Compose, and Play. O'Reilly Media, Incorporated (2023)
5. Harper, B.D., Norman, K.L.: Improving user satisfaction: the questionnaire for user interaction satisfaction version 5.5 **224**, 228 (1993)
6. Kirakowski, J., Corbett, M.: SUMI: the software usability measurement inventory. Br. J. Educ. Technol. **24**, 210–212 (2006). https://doi.org/10.1111/j.1467-8535.1993.tb00076.x
7. Kojic, T., Spang, R., Vergari, M., Meier, L., Moller, S., Voigt-Antons, J.N.: Effects of user factors on user experience in virtual reality: age, gender, and VR experience as influencing factors for VR exergames. Qual. User Exp. **8**, 3 (2023)
8. Lin, G., Panigrahi, T., Womack, J., Ponda, D.J., Kotipalli, P., Starner, T.: Comparing order picking guidance with Microsoft Hololens, Magic Leap, Google Glass XE and Paper. In: Proceedings of the 22nd International Workshop on Mobile Computing Systems and Applications, pp. 133–139. Association for Computing Machinery (2021)
9. Mayer, J., Auer, S., Friedl, J., Anthes, C.: Volumetric data interaction in AR and VR using a handheld touch-sensitive device. transitional interfaces in mixed and cross-reality: a new frontier?, KOPS Universität Konstanz (2021). https://books.google.com.br/books?id=s4nGzgEACAAJ
10. Papadopoulos, T., Evangelidis, K., Kaskalis, T.H., Evangelidis, G., Sylaiou, S.: Interactions in augmented and mixed reality: an overview. Appl. Sci. **11**(18) (2021). https://doi.org/10.3390/app11188752
11. Prince, Simon J.D.: Understanding Deep Learning. MIT Press (2023)
12. Sauro, J.: SUPR-Q: a comprehensive measure of the quality of the website user experience. J. Usability Stud. **10**(2), 68–86 (2015)
13. Unity technologies: training configuration file. https://github.com/Unity-Technologies/ml-agents/blob/develop/docs/Training-Configuration-File.md, github repository
14. Unity technologies: the unity machine learning agents toolkit. https://github.com/Unity-Technologies/ml-agents, github repository

Exploring the Effectiveness of Augmented and Virtual Reality for Visualizing Complex Lighting Simulation Data Structures and Evaluating User Experience

Elham Mohammadrezaei(✉), Fatemeh Sarshartehrani, Majid Behravan, and Denis Gračanin

Virginia Tech, VA, Blacksburg 24061, USA
{elliemh,fatemehst,behravan,gracanin}@vt.edu

Abstract. We investigate the application of augmented reality (AR) and virtual reality (VR) technologies, utilizing Unity's light probes, in visualizing complex lighting simulations to enhance interior design practices. The focus is on the strategic placement and dynamic analysis of light probes within virtual environments to assess and improve the distribution and quality of lighting. By examining light characteristics across different spatial locations, the research aims to address significant challenges in creating well-illuminated and aesthetically pleasing living spaces. A Unity-based framework is proposed, offering a novel approach to understanding light volumes and identifying areas lacking sufficient lighting. The methodology integrates AR/VR technologies with real-time data capture, enabling detailed and adaptive lighting analysis. Preliminary findings suggest that this approach not only facilitates a more nuanced understanding of interior lighting conditions but also enhances the user experience in design visualization. The potential implications of this research extend beyond interior design, offering insights into architectural visualization, healthcare environments, and the general quality of living spaces. Future directions include refining the framework's precision through improved probe placement algorithms and exploring machine learning techniques for predictive lighting optimization. AR and VR technologies are positioned as transformative tools for the visualization and analysis of complex lighting data, paving the way for advancements in design practices and environmental well-being.

Keywords: Augmented and Virtual Reality (AR/VR) · Human-Computer Interaction · Dynamic Lighting Visualizations · Visualization Techniques

1 Introduction

The advent of augmented reality (AR) and virtual reality (VR) technologies has ushered in a new era of visualization capabilities, particularly within the

C. Stephanidis et al. (Eds.): HCII 2024, CCIS 2319, pp. 198–205, 2025.
https://doi.org/10.1007/978-3-031-78516-0_20

realms of architectural design and interior planning [1,2]. Among the various challenges faced by designers and architects, the accurate representation and analysis of lighting within spaces remain paramount due to its profound impact on aesthetics, energy efficiency, and occupant well-being. Traditionally, the simulation of lighting has relied on static models and approximations that often fail to capture the dynamic and complex nature of light interactions within varied environments. This limitation not only hinders the optimization of natural and artificial lighting but also restricts the creative potential of designers [3].

In recent years, the integration of AR and VR technologies with advanced simulation tools has emerged as a promising solution to these challenges. These immersive technologies provide an unprecedented ability to visualize and manipulate lighting simulations in real-time, offering a more intuitive and comprehensive understanding of light distribution and its effects on space [4]. Particularly, Unity's light probes have become a focal point in this technological evolution, offering means to capture and analyze lighting data with remarkable precision and flexibility [5].

The significance of this research lies in its focus on leveraging AR and VR technologies to transcend traditional barriers in lighting simulation [6]. By enabling detailed and dynamic visualizations, these technologies facilitate a deeper understanding of how light behaves and interacts with different materials and surfaces, which is crucial for creating environments that are not only visually appealing but also conducive to occupants' comfort and well-being [7,8].

Furthermore, the exploration of light characteristics as a function of spatial location addresses a crucial aspect of interior design—the creation of balanced and harmonious spaces where light is distributed efficiently and aesthetically. The implications of this work extend beyond mere aesthetic considerations, touching upon crucial aspects such as energy conservation, ecological impact, and the psychological effects of lighting on human occupants [9].

This paper aims to bridge the gap between traditional lighting design practices and the potential offered by AR and VR technologies. By proposing a Unity-based framework (Fig. 1) for the understanding of lighting scenarios, we delve into a comprehensive analysis aimed at redefining the standards of lighting simulation and application. Our research is grounded in the belief that the future of interior design and architecture can be significantly enhanced through the intelligent application of these advanced technologies, thus paving the way for more sustainable, efficient, and user-centered design solutions.

This work seeks not only to enhance the precision and adaptability of lighting design through AR and VR but also to underscore the transformative impact of these technologies on the field. By addressing the challenges and opportunities inherent in the visualization of complex lighting data, our work contributes to a broader understanding of the interplay between technology and design, ultimately aiming to improve the quality of living spaces and the experiences of those who inhabit them.

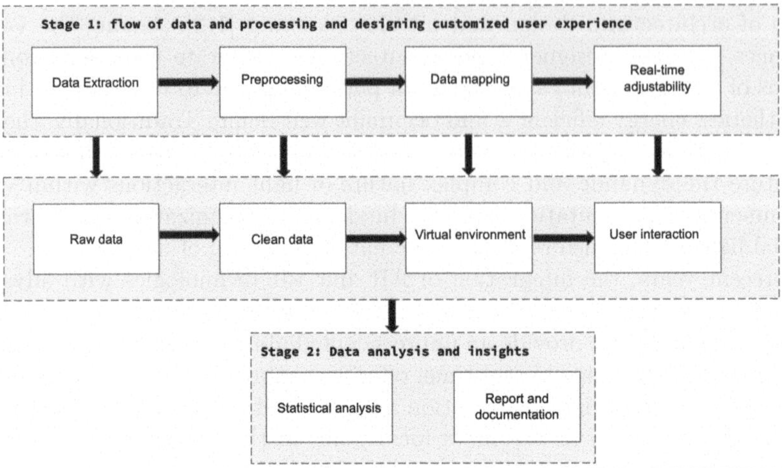

Fig. 1. A flowchart demonstrating framework.

2 Methods

We propose a custom-developed framework within the Unity 3D engine, designed specifically for the dynamic visualization and analysis of lighting within virtual environments. The framework utilizes Unity's advanced light probe technology, which allows for the detailed sampling of lighting information at numerous spatial locations within a scene. The development phase involved the creation of a virtual environment replicating a standard interior space, followed by the strategic placement of light probes throughout the area to ensure comprehensive coverage and data collection.

2.1 Light Probes

To enhance precision and adaptability, we integrate Unity's light probes as a foundational component. These probes, operating on the principle of sampling lighting information at specific positions, capture detailed lighting data, including reflections, surpassing the limitations of traditional lightmaps.

The basic principle of light probe is that light information is sampled at the location of a certain light probe, then light information is sampled from the positions of other light probes adjacent to that light probe. By interpolating these sampled light information, the light information at a position between these light probes can be calculated Fig. 2.

Unity's light probes play a crucial role in identifying areas within a room that lack sufficient light. By strategically placing these probes, we capture nuanced lighting details, enabling the analysis of light volumes and pinpointing sections requiring additional illumination.

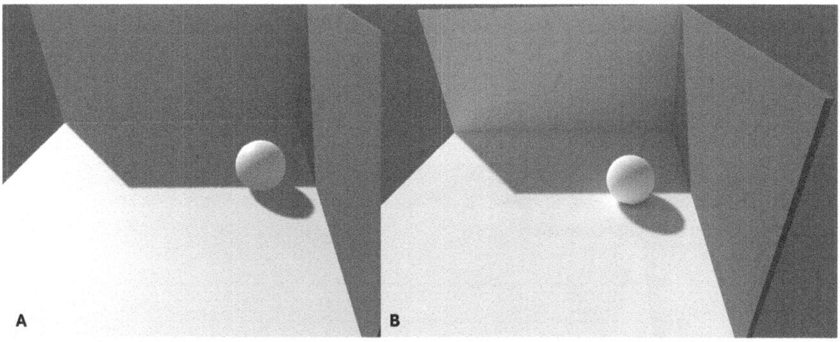

Fig. 2. A) Not added light probes. B) After adding light probes

The dynamic analysis of lighting conditions is made possible by the adaptability of Unity's light probes. Setting up these probes involves strategically placing them throughout the virtual environment (Fig. 3), considering the specific requirements of the interior space being analyzed. Once placed, the light probes can be moved dynamically within the AR/VR environment, capturing real-time lighting settings for different areas. This dynamic movement allows for a comprehensive examination of lighting conditions, ensuring that every corner of the room is analyzed for optimal illumination.

2.2 Calculation of Lighting Details

The basic principle of light probes involves the sampling of lighting information at the position of a specific probe. This information is then extrapolated from neighboring probes, and by interpolating these sampled lighting details, the illumination specifics at any given position between the probes can be accurately calculated [10]. In essence, light probes store "baked" information about the passage of light through empty space, providing a richer understanding of lighting conditions beyond what traditional lightmaps can offer.

2.3 Categorization

The gathered data is systematically categorized based on predefined criteria, facilitating the identification of areas with insufficient lighting. This categorization process not only helps pinpoint regions in need of additional illumination but also serves as the foundation for a comprehensive color scheme representing various lighting conditions.

Through the seamless integration of Unity's light probes and the dynamic adjustment of their positions, our methodology establishes a robust framework for analyzing, categorizing, and visualizing lighting conditions in an AR/VR environment. This meticulous approach not only enhances the precision of our framework but also introduces a user-friendly and interactive experience. The incorporation of a color scheme further enriches the visualization, providing a nuanced representation of lighting nuances that is valuable for researchers, healthcare professionals, and interior designers alike.

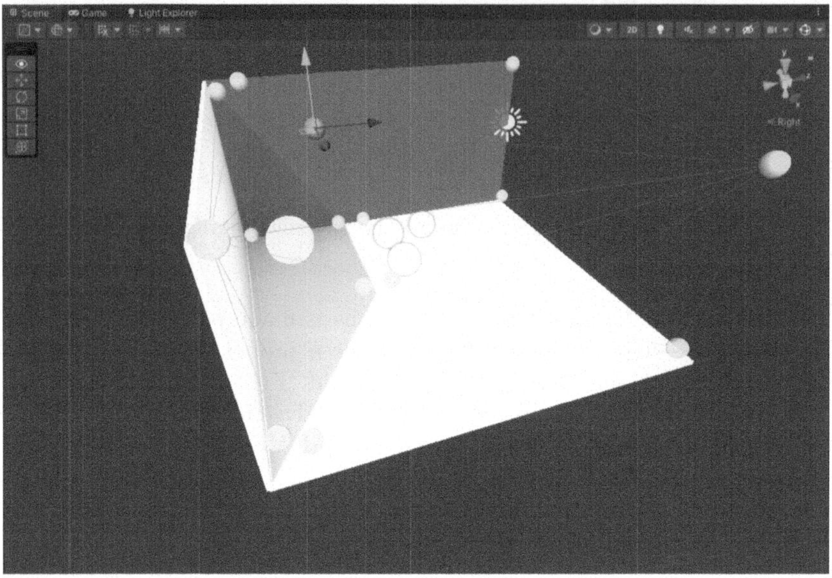

Fig. 3. Adding light probes to the scene.

3 Results

Light probes were arranged within the virtual environment according to a grid pattern to optimize the balance between spatial resolution and computational efficiency. Each probe's placement was determined based on a set of predefined criteria, including proximity to critical design elements (e.g., furniture, windows) and areas known to experience significant lighting variation (e.g., corners, near large objects). This systematic approach ensured that the probes could effectively capture a wide range of lighting conditions, from direct sunlight to subtle reflections.

To capture data, we simulated various lighting scenarios within Unity, reflecting different times of day and weather conditions. For each scenario, the light probes collected data on light intensity, color, and direction. This information was then processed and visualized within the framework to provide an interactive, real-time representation of lighting distribution across the environment.

3.1 Dynamic Analysis and Adjustment

A critical feature of our methodology is the dynamic adjustability of the light probes within the virtual environment. This capability allowed us to conduct iterative analyses, moving probes in response to initial findings to further refine our understanding of lighting conditions in specific areas. This iterative process was essential for identifying zones with insufficient lighting and for evaluating potential design modifications.

3.2 Data Processing and Visualization

The lighting data collected by the light probes were subjected to a comprehensive analysis to identify patterns and anomalies. We employed statistical techniques to categorize the lighting conditions into distinct levels, ranging from 'insufficient' to 'optimal' lighting, based on predefined thresholds. These categorizations were then visualized within the Unity environment using a color-coded scheme, facilitating an intuitive understanding of the spatial distribution of lighting quality.

3.3 Preliminary Evaluation

To assess the framework's effectiveness and user-friendliness, we conducted a pilot study. Feedback collected from this pilot study highlighted several key areas: ease of use, interpretability of data, and overall user experience. Participants appreciated the intuitive nature of the interface but noted challenges in navigation controls and a need for more straightforward data interpretation aids. While the immersive quality of the AR/VR environment was generally praised, reports of motion sickness and technical glitches were noted, underscoring the need for further refinement.

4 Discussion

The integration of AR and VR technologies using Unity's light probes into the field of interior design represents a significant advancement in our ability to visualize and analyze complex lighting data. The results demonstrate the potential of this approach to transform traditional practices by providing a more nuanced and dynamic understanding of lighting within interior spaces.

4.1 Implications for Design Practice

The application of our Unity-based framework has profound implications for interior design practice. By enabling real-time visualization and analysis of lighting conditions, designers can make informed decisions that significantly improve the aesthetics and functionality of a space. The ability to identify and rectify areas of insufficient lighting before the implementation phase can lead to more efficient design processes and cost savings. Furthermore, the framework's adaptability to different design scenarios enhances its utility across a range of projects, from residential to commercial spaces.

4.2 Technological Advancements and Limitations

While the results highlight the advantages of using AR/VR technologies in lighting analysis, they also underscore the importance of continuous technological refinement. The accuracy of light probes in capturing detailed lighting information is contingent on their placement and density within the environment. Therefore, developing algorithms for optimal probe placement and exploring the potential for automated adjustments based on real-time data could further enhance the framework's precision and user-friendliness.

Moreover, despite the promising outcomes, there are inherent limitations given the current state of AR/VR technology, such as hardware requirements and the potential for user discomfort during prolonged use. Addressing these challenges through hardware improvements and user interface design will be crucial for the widespread adoption of this technology in design practices.

4.3 User Engagement and Experience

The positive user feedback underscores the value of an intuitive and interactive approach to lighting analysis. The engagement of users with the AR/VR framework suggests that such tools can significantly enhance the understanding and communication of complex design concepts, making them accessible to a broader audience, including clients and stakeholders with no technical background. However, the user experience can vary based on individual familiarity with AR/VR technology, indicating the need for tailored training programs or guidance to maximize the framework's accessibility and effectiveness.

4.4 Future Research Directions

The findings open several avenues for future research. Investigating the integration of machine learning techniques for predictive lighting analysis could provide insights into the most effective design interventions. Additionally, exploring the application of the framework in outdoor settings or in the context of natural lighting could further expand its utility. Collaborative studies involving designers, architects, and healthcare professionals could also yield comprehensive guidelines for optimizing lighting in spaces according to different needs and functions.

5 Conclusion

This work showcases the use of AR and VR in interior design, specifically for dynamic lighting analysis, marking a shift from static methods to interactive, user-focused experiences. By employing Unity's light probes, we assessed lighting in interior spaces, revealing how these technologies can enhance lighting understanding and design. This method offers a significant improvement by allowing real-time design adjustments and better lighting visualization, beneficial for designers, architects, and non-professionals alike.

Despite its benefits, challenges such as hardware limitations, user comfort, and probe placement need addressing. Future work should expand the technology's use to more design scenarios and conditions.

Finally, integrating AR and VR in lighting design offers a revolutionary approach, making the design process more immersive, accurate, and user-friendly. This advancement has the potential to significantly impact the aesthetics, functionality, and comfort of spaces, pushing us towards better-designed environments.

References

1. Mohammadrezaei, E., Giovannelli, A., Lane, L., Gracanin, D.: A digital twin based approach to smart lighting design. In: 2022 Winter Simulation Conference (2022)
2. Mohammadrezaei, E., Gračanin, D.: Extended reality for smart built environments design: smart lighting design testbed. In: Streitz, N.A., Konomi, S. (eds.) International Conference on Human-Computer Interaction, pp. 181–192. Springer, Cham (2022). https://doi.org/10.1007/978-3-031-05463-1_13
3. Mohammadrezaei, E., Ghasemi, S., Dongre, P., Gračanin, D., Zhang, H.: Systematic review of extended reality for smart built environments lighting design simulations. IEEE Access **12**, 17058–17089 (2024)
4. Birt, J., Manyuru, P., Nelson, J.: Using virtual and augmented reality to study architectural lighting. **17**, 21 (2017)
5. Post, F.H., Nielson, G., Bonneau, G.P. (eds.) Data Visualization: The State of the Art. Springer, Science & Business Media, New York (2003)
6. Ng, E.Y.Y., Poh, L.K., Wei, W., Nagakura, T.: Advanced lighting simulation in architectural design in the tropics. Autom. Construct. **10**(3), 365–379 (2001)
7. Aparicio, M., Costa, C.J.: Data visualization. Commun. Des. Q. Rev. **3**(1), 7–11 (2015)
8. Baloch, A.A., Shaikh, P.H., Shaikh, F., Leghari, Z.H., Mirjat, N.H., Uqaili, M.A.: Simulation tools application for artificial lighting in buildings. Renew. Sustain. Energy Rev. **82**, 3007–3026 (2018)
9. Ochoa, C.E., Aries, M.B., Hensen, J.L.: State of the art in lighting simulation for building science: a literature review. J. Build. Perform. Simul. **5**(4), 209–233 (2012)
10. Mardaljevic, J.: Validation of a lighting simulation program under real sky conditions. Int. J. Light. Res. Technol. **27**(4), 181–188 (1995)

Why Social Media Users Are Hesitant to Embrace the Metaverse: Technology Acceptance, Perceived Risks and Mitigations

Haoran Qiu(✉), Dion Hoe-Lian Goh, Albert Ong, Shiming Jin, and Shuyu Wang

Wee Kim Wee School of Communication and Information, Nanyang Technological University, Singapore 637718, Singapore
{haoran004,w220019,jins0009,swang041}@e.ntu.edu.sg, ashlgoh@ntu.edu.sg

Abstract. This study investigated why social media users are hesitant to use the metaverse, along with their perceived risks and proposed mitigations. We conducted semi-structured interviews with 16 adult social media users who had not used and were not interested in the metaverse. Guided by the Technology Acceptance Model (TAM) and its extended frameworks, a theory-driven thematic analysis was conducted. We constructed five dimensions for social media users' metaverse acceptance, including perceived usefulness, perceived ease of use, perceived enjoyment, perceived connectedness, and perceived risks. The key influential factors included in each dimension were also revealed, which helped in understanding why people were hesitant to use the metaverse. In addition, we further identified four major perceived risks, encompassing data security, abuse or misuse, overuse, and health issues. Given these perceived risks, a set of corresponding mitigations were uncovered: data security protection, governance and management, access control and restriction, and user education. Based on the findings, we discussed theoretical contributions and practical implications.

Keywords: Metaverse · Social Media · Technology Acceptance · User Perception · Mitigations

1 Introduction

Originating from Neal Stephenson's [22] science fiction, *Snow Crash,* the metaverse was first conceptualized as an immersive virtual environment where users are interconnected through avatars. In recent years, empowered by advanced technologies like artificial intelligence (AI), virtual reality (VR), and blockchain, this fictional concept has gradually been realized [6, 20, 21]. The metaverse is commonly considered a "post-reality universe", a multi-user online environment that merges reality and virtuality [14, 18]. Regarded as an ultimate form of digital media [26], it has garnered significant attention upon its introduction. Numerous technology companies have developed publicly accessible metaverse platforms, such as *Horizon Worlds, Microsoft Mesh, Decentraland*, and *Sandbox* [13]. Currently, these platforms have attracted a total of 400 million users all

C. Stephanidis et al. (Eds.): HCII 2024, CCIS 2319, pp. 206–214, 2025.
https://doi.org/10.1007/978-3-031-78516-0_21

over the world, and are increasingly permeating various facets of human life, including work, education, and entertainment [5, 17, 26].

While a large number of users embraced this emerging technology with excitement and anticipation, a surge of criticism and skepticism swiftly followed [16]. With increasing reported cases of harassment and attacks in the metaverse [12, 19], some professionals, such as psychologists, lawyers, and journalists, have critiqued and warned about its negative' impacts, primarily focusing on three aspects: mental health, the amplifying of crime, and privacy security [10]. Numerous mainstream news outlets have also conveyed pessimistic perspectives on the metaverse, which influenced users' attitudes [8]. Consequently, people have reportedly refused or are hesitant to access the metaverse [15, 16].

However, there is insufficient research on the factors that influence people, especially social media users, to embrace or resist using the metaverse. It is crucial to delve into this topic from the user's perspective as it will help further academic contributions to technology acceptance research. Additionally, it also facilitates a deeper understanding of people's perceived risks and concerns, benefiting practitioners in platform regulation and product development.

Hence, this paper is organized around the following research questions: (1) Why are social media users hesitant about using the metaverse? (2) What are their perceived risks and concerns about the metaverse? (3) How can these risks and concerns be mitigated, according to them?

2 Methodology

To address these research questions, we conducted semi-structured interviews with 16 adult social media users who had not used and were not interested in the metaverse. Participants were recruited through convenience and snowball sampling in Singapore. They comprised 9 females and 7 males with an average age of 28. All of them use social media daily. The platforms they use most frequently are Instagram (50%), WeChat (31.25%), Facebook (25%), and X (former Twitter; 25%).

2.1 Data Collection

Three trained researchers in information studies conducted interviews either in person or online. The average length of each interview was approximately one hour. The interviews were divided into four sections. We first collected information about their demographics and social media usage. Participants were then asked about their perceptions of the metaverse and why they did not want to access it. After that, they were guided to share their perceived risks and concerns about this emerging technology. Subsequent questions delved deeper into their perspectives regarding potential mitigations for risks that were mentioned.

2.2 Data Analysis

All interviews were recorded and subsequently transcribed for follow-up analysis. We conducted a theory-driven thematic analysis adapted from Fereday and Muir-Cochrane's hybrid approach [11], which consists of six steps of inductive and deductive coding (see Fig. 1).

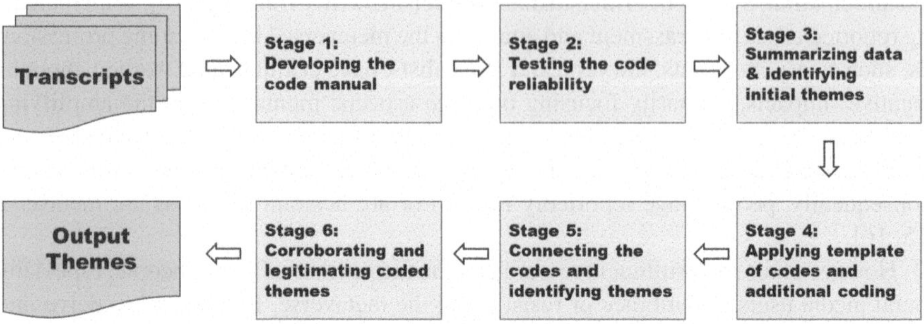

Fig. 1. Fereday and Muir-Cochrane's Hybrid Approach of Thematic Analysis

The Technology Acceptance Model (TAM) is a widely used theoretical model for examining user attitudes towards emerging technologies [7]. Guided by TAM and its extended frameworks [1, 24, 25, 27], two trained coders first developed an initial coding manual with five themes, including Perceived Usefulness, Perceived Ease of Use, Perceived Enjoyment, Perceived Connectedness, and Perceived Risks. They then independently analyzed transcripts line by line and tested the codes' reliability. Next, they summarized the transcribed data until initial themes in each category were identified. After that, they discussed with each other. Subsequently, they refined the codes, and added additional themes until code saturation was reached. In the last stage, codes with less than three occurrences were removed or merged, and final coded themes were named and defined [2–4, 23].

3 Findings

3.1 Dimensions and Key Factors Influencing Metaverse Acceptance

In constructing the five dimensions for social media users' metaverse acceptance, key influential factors included in each dimension were also revealed. This helped in the understanding of why people were hesitant to use the metaverse.

Perceived Usefulness. Most participants reported that the metaverse still lacked usefulness at present, which reduced their willingness to use it. Firstly, this emerging technology was still in the early stage and was not yet mature. Secondly, the metaverse did not enhance user productivity, such as improving efficiency at work or in school. Moreover, most metaverse platforms were not rewarding for the average person. Many expressed that they would try the metaverse if more rewards were offered. Additionally, there was a lack of necessity for users to engage with the metaverse. Current social media platforms already satisfied their online needs, so there was no pressing reason for them to seek additional social platforms that may increase their information load.

Perceived Ease of Use. Another key reason deterring some social media users from embracing the metaverse was its lack of ease of use, primarily in terms of affordability and accessibility. As mentioned by numerous participants, some devices or equipment required to access the metaverse, such as VR glasses and head-mounted displays (HMDs), were costly and beyond what they could afford. Additionally, while numerous metaverse platforms have been developed, accessing them was not convenient. Most users expected metaverse platforms to be compatible with mobile devices and be accessed conveniently at any time and from any location.

Perceived Enjoyment. Perceived enjoyment was a significant driver of users' metaverse acceptance. The metaverse is largely viewed as an entertainment platform. Participants who were gamers indicated that they would be more willing to try the metaverse if it were compatible with more mainstream video games. In addition, although many current metaverse platforms offered immersive experiences, participants indicated that the average performance fell short of their expectations, especially in terms of multisensory integration.

Perceived Connectedness. Social media users were also concerned with connectedness in the metaverse, including both social and spatial dimensions. Currently, metaverse platforms still face the challenge of insufficient social connectedness for users. Many participants expressed that they did not consider adopting the metaverse in the short term primarily because very few of their friends used these platforms. In addition, some were looking forward to the time when the metaverse would truly transcend spatial limitations, enabling them to engage in activities that are inconvenient in real life. For instance, individuals could engage in immersive travel from their homes without physically being there.

Perceived Risks. Almost all participants pointed out that the current metaverse environment was too risky, which was a key reason behind their hesitation to use it. Participants perceived four key potential risks, encompassing data security, abuse or misuse, overuse, and health issues. First, there were data security risks that excessive data uploaded could lead to unauthorized access, resulting in loss of individual privacy or organizational confidentiality. Besides, malicious actors might abuse or misuse the platform, such as spreading scams and harassing or attacking others. Additionally, participants worried that users might inevitably overuse the metaverse, leading to addiction and a consequent escape from reality. Moreover, heavy usage of the metaverse might also result in both physical and psychological health issues.

Figure 2 illustrates the dimensions and key factors influencing metaverse acceptance among our participants.

3.2 Mitigations for Perceived Risk of the Metaverse

Given the perceived risks mentioned, we further investigated the corresponding mitigations from our participants' perspectives.

Data Security Protection (DSP). Most participants believed that effective DSP measures need to be implemented. Firstly, metaverse companies could enhance both software and hardware protections, such as deploying anti-spyware and firewalls, to ensure data security. Additionally, the data transmission within these platforms could incorporate more secure encryption protocols. User verification, including real-name

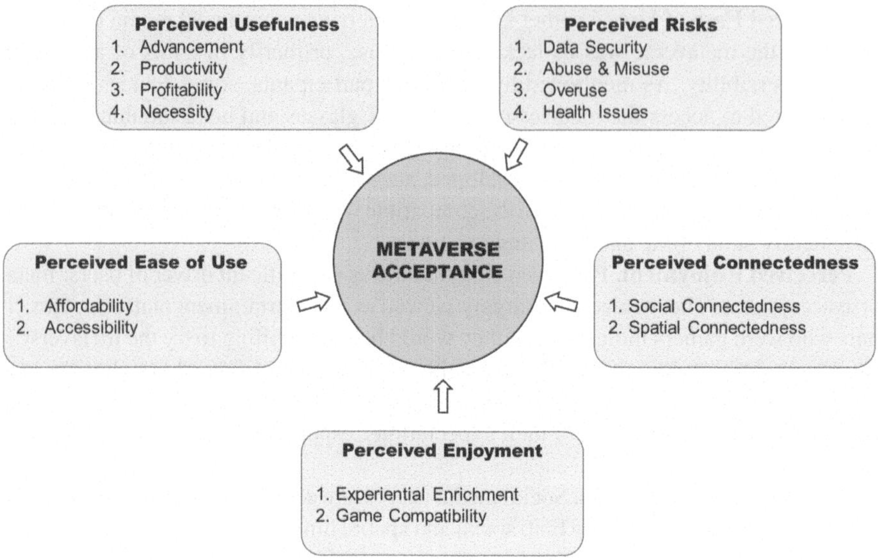

Fig. 2. Dimensions and Key Factors Influencing Metaverse Acceptance

authentication and biometric identification, was essential to prevent the unauthorized use of accounts.

Governance and Management. The metaverse is currently undergoing rapid development, yet it suffers from governance and management deficiencies, leading to frequent instances of harassment and attacks. Many participants advocated for authorities to strengthen legislative measures, thereby providing legal authorization for regulation mechanisms of the metaverse. Moreover, governments should take more responsibility for platform monitoring, to combat abuse or misuse behaviors, and foster a more harmonious metaverse media environment.

Access Control and Restriction. The implementation of access controls and restrictions by platform operators was deemed necessary. Many participants indicated that anti-addiction mechanisms could be useful, for example, limiting user's total weekly login duration or automatically logging out individuals who remain online for prolonged periods. Furthermore, deploying minimum age restrictions for account registration was essential. These measures might mitigate risks associated with overuse and health, particularly for vulnerable users like minors.

User Education. In addition, user education was also indispensable. Many participants proposed that more public education programs, such as online courses or community lectures, could be launched to improve users' metaverse literacy, thereby cultivating their self-awareness of risk prevention. Additionally, the rise of the metaverse will foster a new type of independent practitioners, such as meta-anchors or content creators. Governments and platform operators could provide training for these individuals to regularize their practices, thereby reducing the risk of them misleading or harming the public.

Figure 3 shows the correspondence between mitigations and perceived risks.

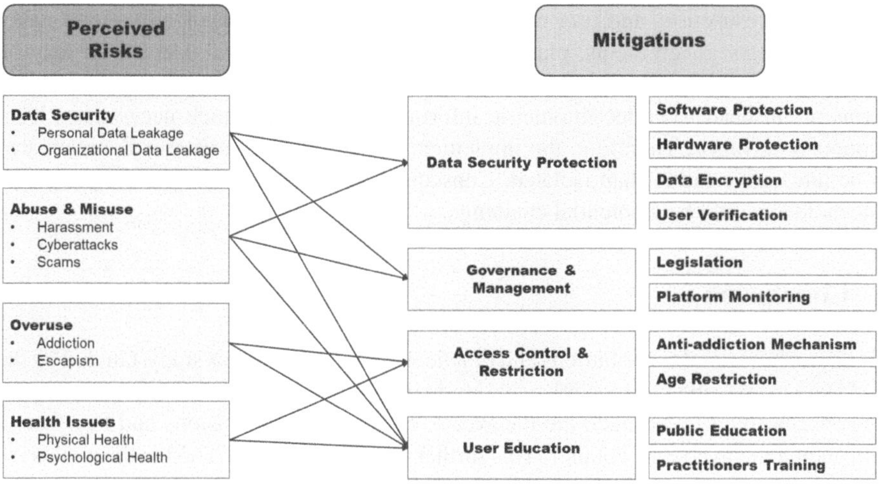

Fig. 3. Correspondence between Mitigations and Perceived Risks

4 Discussion

In this study, we constructed five dimensions to conceptualize social media users' metaverse acceptance, including perceived usefulness, perceived ease of use, perceived enjoyment, perceived connectedness, and perceived risks. We further identified key influential factors in each dimension, illuminating why social media users were hesitant to engage with the metaverse. It is worth noting that the five dimensions and key factors influencing metaverse acceptance are not mutually independent. They might be intricately connected in many instances. This reflects complex perceptions based on diverse user expectations, which could be divided into hedonic and utilitarian dimensions [9]. On the one hand, individuals expected a safe, useful, and user-friendly metaverse platform that facilitates the seamless fulfillment of practical needs, such as enhancing work efficiency or generating profit. On the other hand, they expected a metaverse that is oriented towards socializing and entertainment, providing them with enjoyment and social empowerment. When these prior expectations did not align with the existing perceptions, social media users were less likely to adopt the metaverse.

Moreover, four perceived risks were identified and categorized, encompassing data security, abuse or misuse, overuse, and health issues. Due to developmental immaturity and reported negative incidents, many participants perceived a high level of risk associated with current metaverse platforms. Consequently, they were inclined to adopt a defensive mindset, making it challenging for them to trust and embrace this emerging technology in the short term. However, surprisingly, many individuals were still optimistic about its subsequent development and were open to using it in the future. This suggested that the metaverse holds substantial growth potential, with social media users, our participants, representing a significant prospective user group.

Given these perceived risks, a set of corresponding mitigations were proposed by participants, including data security protection, governance and management, access control and restriction, and user education. These mitigations involved various stakeholders such as governments, platform operators, and individual users, who may be closely interconnected during mitigation implementation. For example, metaverse platforms might need to collect biometric information for DSP, which necessitates legal support in advance. Therefore, the implementation of these mitigations is anticipated to be integrative rather than isolated. Consequently, the coordination among multiple stakeholders could be a potential challenge.

5 Conclusion

There are theoretical contributions and practical implications in this study. Guided by the TAM and its extended frameworks, this study investigates the reasons why social media users are hesitant to embrace the metaverse, constructing dimensions and key factors influencing metaverse acceptance. This further expands the use of TAM in the metaverse context, and which could both be a theoretical and empirical basis for subsequent studies.

Based on our preliminary findings, the following practical implications can be drawn. First, the metaverse can integrate more practical functions that are closely related to work or commerce settings to enhance its productivity and profitability. Second, developers can further explore the compatibility with lower-cost devices to improve affordability and user accessibility. Third, gaming and social scenarios can be key focus areas for subsequent product research and development, where immersive experiences with multisensory modal interactions can be embedded. Meanwhile, the perceived risks and the corresponding mitigations outlined may inform practitioners to develop a safer metaverse ecosystem.

There are limitations in this study that may point to directions for future work. First, the qualitative method used limits the generalizability of findings. However, our findings can inform future quantitative research in the metaverse and its derived technologies. Second, the effectiveness of the mitigations proposed can be further verified through experiments or longitudinal cross-sectional studies.

Acknowledgments. This study was funded by Meta Platforms, Inc., grant number: INB2681518.

Disclosure of Interests. The authors have no competing interests to declare that are relevant to the content of this article.

References

1. Al-Qaysi, N., et al.: Employing the technology acceptance model in social media: a systematic review. Educ. Inf. Technol. **25**(6), 4961–5002 (2020). https://doi.org/10.1007/s10639-020-10197-1
2. Braun, V., Clarke, V.: Reflecting on reflexive thematic analysis. Qual. Res. Sport Exerc. Health **11**(4), 589–597 (2019). https://doi.org/10.1080/2159676X.2019.1628806

3. Braun, V., Clarke, V.: Thematic analysis. In: APA Handbook of Research Methods in Psychology, Vol 2: Research designs: Quantitative, Qualitative, Neuropsychological, and Biological, pp. 57–71 American Psychological Association, Washington, DC, US (2012). https://doi.org/10.1037/13620-004
4. Braun, V., Clarke, V.: Using thematic analysis in psychology. Qual. Res. Psychol. **3**(2), 77–101 (2006). https://doi.org/10.1191/1478088706qp063oa
5. Buana, I.M.W.: Metaverse: threat or opportunity for our social world? In understanding metaverse on sociological context. JMv. **3**(1), 28–33 (2023). https://doi.org/10.57019/jmv.1144470
6. Cao, L.: Decentralized AI: edge intelligence and smart Blockchain, metaverse, Web3, and DeSci. IEEE Intell. Syst. **37**(3), 6–19 (2022). https://doi.org/10.1109/MIS.2022.3181504
7. Davis, F.D.: A technology acceptance model for empirically testing new end-user information systems: theory and results. Massachusetts Institute of Technology (1985)
8. Deng, R., Matthes, J.: Utopian or dystopian? The portrayal of the metaverse in popular news on social media. Heliyon. **9**(4), e14509 (2023). https://doi.org/10.1016/j.heliyon.2023.e14509
9. Dhar, R., Wertenbroch, K.: Consumer choice between hedonic and utilitarian goods. J. Mark. Res. **37**(1), 60–71 (2000). https://doi.org/10.1509/jmkr.37.1.60.18718
10. Dolata, M., Schwabe, G.: What is the metaverse and who seeks to define it? Mapping the site of social construction. J. Inf. Technol. **38**(3), 239–266 (2023). https://doi.org/10.1177/02683962231159927
11. Fereday, J., Muir-Cochrane, E.: Demonstrating rigor using thematic analysis: a hybrid approach of inductive and deductive coding and theme development. Int J Qual Methods **5**(1), 80–92 (2006). https://doi.org/10.1177/160940690600500107
12. Frenkel, S., Browning, K.: The metaverse's dark side: here come harassment and assaults (2021). https://www.nytimes.com/2021/12/30/technology/metaverse-harassment-assaults.html
13. Law, M.: Top 10 best metaverse platforms to look out for in 2023 (2023). https://technologymagazine.com/articles/top-10-best-metaverse-platforms-to-look-out-for-in-2023
14. Lim, W.Y.B. et al.: Realizing the metaverse with edge intelligence: a match made in heaven (2022). http://arxiv.org/abs/2201.01634
15. MacDonald, K.: I've seen the metaverse – and I don't want it (2022). https://www.theguardian.com/games/2022/jan/25/ive-seen-the-metaverse-and-i-dont-want-it,
16. Martin, L.: Why everybody hates the metaverse. https://medium.com/@itslizmartin/why-everybody-hates-the-metaverse-ab46edba5ec8. Accessed 4 Oct 2023
17. Mileva, G.: 48 Metaverse Statistics | Market size & growth (2023). https://influencermarketinghub.com/metaverse-stats/. Accessed 27 Oct 2023
18. Mystakidis, S.: Metaverse. Encyclopedia **2**(1), 486–497 (2022). https://doi.org/10.3390/encyclopedia2010031
19. Nix, N.: Attacks in the metaverse are booming. Police are starting to pay attention (2024). https://www.washingtonpost.com/technology/2024/02/04/metaverse-sexual-assault-prosecution/
20. Oh, H.J., et al.: Social benefits of living in the metaverse: the relationships among social presence, supportive interaction, social self-efficacy, and feelings of loneliness. Comput. Hum. Behav. **139**, 107498 (2023). https://doi.org/10.1016/j.chb.2022.107498
21. Ritterbusch, G.D., Teichmann, M.R.: Defining the metaverse: a systematic literature review. IEEE Access. **11**, 12368–12377 (2023). https://doi.org/10.1109/ACCESS.2023.3241809
22. Stephenson, N.: Snow Crash. Penguin UK (1994)
23. Tracy, S.J.: Qualitative Research Methods. Wiley-Blackwell Chichester (2013)
24. Venkatesh, V., Bala, H.: Technology acceptance model 3 and a research agenda on interventions. Decis. Sci. **39**(2), 273–315 (2008). https://doi.org/10.1111/j.1540-5915.2008.00192.x

25. Venkatesh, V., Davis, F.D.: A theoretical extension of the technology acceptance model: four longitudinal field studies. Manage. Sci. **46**(2), 186–204 (2000). https://doi.org/10.1287/mnsc.46.2.186.11926
26. Wang, H., et al.: A survey on the metaverse: the state-of-the-art, technologies, applications, and challenges. IEEE Internet Things J. **10**(16), 14671–14688 (2023). https://doi.org/10.1109/JIOT.2023.3278329
27. Wu, R., Yu, Z.: Investigating users' acceptance of the metaverse with an extended technology acceptance model. Int. J. Hum. Comput. Interact., 1–17 (2023). https://doi.org/10.1080/10447318.2023.2241295

Moving Beyond SUS and Other Lazy Metrics: Redefining Usability of Cloud Solutions

Vanshika Sanghi, Sparshad Kasote(✉), and Santhosh Rao(✉)

SAP Labs Bangalore, Whitefield, India
sparshad501@gmail.com, santhosh.rao@sap.com

Abstract. The paper critiques the use of traditional usability metrics like System Usability Scale (SUS) and Net Promoter Score (NPS) in evaluating enterprise cloud solutions, highlighting their inadequacies in capturing the complexity of user experience. It introduces an alternative framework called System Usability Matrix (SUM) tailored for enterprise cloud contexts. SUM emphasizes the importance of considering both objective and subjective metrics to assess usability effectively. SUM highlights the need to move towards context-driven and user-centric approaches to measure usability in the enterprise cloud industry.

Keywords: Usability Metrics · Enterprise Cloud Solutions · System Usability Matrix · SUS · NPS

1 Introduction

Evaluation of usability of any tool, system or solution should consider the context in which it is used and its appropriateness to that context, as usability is defined as a measure of how well a specific user in a specific context can use a product to achieve or define a goal effectively, efficiently, and satisfactorily [1].

Overtime, many metrics have been introduced to measure usability - SUS and NPS are such general usability metrics which have been widely accepted as industry standard measures for digital products, including enterprise cloud solutions. John Brooke, the creator of SUS defined SUS on the idea that measuring usability can be generalised based on metrics released by some basic classes of usability measures such as ISO 9241-11, but he also believed that the context-specificity of usability makes it very difficult to make comparisons across different systems [2]. Usability measures are often general and created to account for all industries. In business contexts, due to this, often similar objective and subjective usability metrics are shared between business-to-consumer (B2C) and business-to-business (B2B) industries [3], neglecting the difference in objectives through which usability is measured for B2C solutions versus B2B. For the B2C sector, there is a strong correlation between the measure of the mass consumers usability and business growth. Whereas, in the B2B context, especially for enterprise cloud solutions, it is trickier to measure usability as the context changes from catering to the general consumer to hyper-specific, role-based professionals who perform complex tasks often involving multiple business processes.

C. Stephanidis et al. (Eds.): HCII 2024, CCIS 2319, pp. 215–226, 2025.
https://doi.org/10.1007/978-3-031-78516-0_22

With time, technology has become more interactive with the user and therefore, the approach to measuring usability needs to adapt to keep up. Research on usability models have been extensively focused in the B2C market [4]. Over the last three decades, digital products have heavily evolved even in B2B scenarios. Newer technologies have been adopted and products are being disseminated through various mediums, for example the cloud over on-premise solutions. The origins of popular usability measures often overlook this progression in the enterprise cloud context.

SUS is detached from the user experience, from the experience journey, from the layers and facets of how users experience products. Organisations can't explain what contributes to variations in customer experience metrics as SUS does not provide actionable insights [5]. At some level, SUS has become an arbitrary checklist item as per traditional protocol but upon further reflection, one can ask - what value does it bring to the process, the designed applications or to the customers? Since SUS is so homogenized for all contexts, it has lost the essence of what a true usability metric should do.

2 The Gaps of System Usability Scale and Other Lazy Metrics

2.1 System Usability Scale (SUS)

SUS is a ten item Likert scale measuring usability addressing aspects like support, training, and complexity [6]. However, for enterprise cloud solutions that handle complex tasks requiring training and support, end-users often bypass the traditional learning curve making SUS questions less relevant. Usability issues are often reported by users despite having above-average, sometimes even near-perfect SUS score. An incongruence many have faced as practitioners in the domain as well.

Usability Evaluation study was conducted for a cloud enterprise product, where SUS was used as the benchmark metric to measure the usability of the designed user experience, as is the industry norm. The study was for Configuration Management Software-as-a-Service (SaaS) capability where Configuration Managers create 'baselines' to store complex product data related to the entire lifecycle of the product. During the study with 12 participants, key shortcomings of using SUS were identified-

End-users Prefer Assistance. End-users of Configuration Management software prefer assistance due to its complexity, often relying on training or support documentation. A common SUS statement, "I think I would need the support of a technical person to use this system," becomes irrelevant for enterprise software, where support is expected. The study participant clarified the same by asking what assistance meant – whether it is training or day to day assistance. SUS in its calculations inaccurately categorizes the need for assistance as a negative usability trait, which is unsuitable for the enterprise context.

End-Users Require Clarifications. SUS, often used unmoderated, faces challenges due to imprecise and outdated terms [6]. In the study, 5 of 12 participants struggled with certain words due to geographical, language, and socio-cultural differences, necessitating multiple clarifications. This emphasised that as a metric SUS is inaccessible and heavily dependent on being used during a moderated session. This makes it not a 'quick and dirty tool' as intended by John Brooke. Often in the enterprise industry, SUS is unmoderated which poses the question of whether the results are heavily biased, lack true understanding of the system and provide any actionable insights?

End-Users Have Subjective Opinions. SUS results are often biased due to its subjective nature. In the study, 50% of participants gave average ratings of 4 for most statements despite difficulties, influenced by monetary rewards and misconceptions about SUS measuring their performance. This often leads to artificially high scores of products with many usability issues. While subjective assessments can help provide background on user biases, dispositions, and contexts to better understand user feedback, SUS's abstract statements provide only superficial insights, lacking the granularity needed for actionable feedback.

This put into perspective that in work contexts learnability, memorability, engagement, interest is not core factors contributing to a successful experience [7] and SUS used by itself is not an accurate measure of usability for the enterprise cloud context. What truly matters to the end-user and the business is task efficiency, quick response time, reliability, speed and seamlessness.

2.2 Net Promoter Score (NPS) and Other Lazy Metrics

NPS is a common metric used to measure customer experience. An NPS score measures user loyalty by looking at customer likelihood of recommending a given business [8]. While the end-user gets a nudge to fill the NPS survey, the typical user of a cloud solution is not given the agency of choice. They use the product because it was chosen for them by a person in a higher position of authority. Judging loyalty or recommendation is an irrelevant metric to the usability of the product as the end-users are solely aiming to do their tasks seamlessly.

Satisfaction metrics (NPS, Effort Score etc.) don't tell product teams how to improve their offerings. Hence, a lot of these subjective scores induce biases and when considered as sole usability measures become lazy metrics. Responding to a push survey (like NPS) while in the middle of a business process takes the user away from their primary task. NPS is influenced by the product's price, safety, and overall customer satisfaction apart from user experience. This makes NPS unsuitable to measure true user experience for enterprise contexts [3].

The inadequacy of metrics such as NPS and SUS are an industry-wide issue. There are many unbiased and objective metrics which can give a more accurate insight without themselves hindering user experience. Seeing the gaps of accurate usability metrics in the B2B market, companies have been forced to come up with metrics of their own to measure usability in their particular contexts [9], however there is still potential to have a universal model to measure usability of enterprise cloud products. As an industry at the intersection of business and user experience, metrics are what unite stakeholders since they provide a universally understandable, simple measure of progress and a benchmark which is why this paper presents an alternative system for measuring usability which is tailor made for B2B SaaS contexts.

3 Introducing System Usability Matrix (SUM)

Research on usability models has focused extensively on the B2C market, while the B2B industry needs metrics for more thorough usability analysis. Reliable metrics are needed for evaluating cloud solutions in a B2B context effectively [10]. As subjective assessments alone are insufficient, there's a greater need for objective metrics. To comprehensively quantify user experience, companies like Google, Alipay, and Alibaba use both subjective and objective data, with models like Google's HEART and GSM Framework, Alipay's PTECH Model, and Alibaba Cloud's USE Model [3].

Enterprise cloud solutions require combined usability measures to refine their end-user experiences. Existing models often lack relevant metrics for enterprises or are tailored by companies to their specific scenarios, highlighting the need and potential for a universal measure. Such is the approach of System Usability Matrix (referred to as SUM henceforth). The heart of usability for an enterprise product is how efficiently and effectively end-users can perform their tasks. The productivity of the tool and the user are both of equal importance. SUM proposes that usability i.e., productivity, requires both the user and the product (or tool) to be evaluated. Inspired from the Four Factor Model and the GSM Framework, SUM provides a context-accurate way to define relevant metrics to measure usability taking into account behavioural and attitudinal user experience metrics for enterprise cloud solutions.

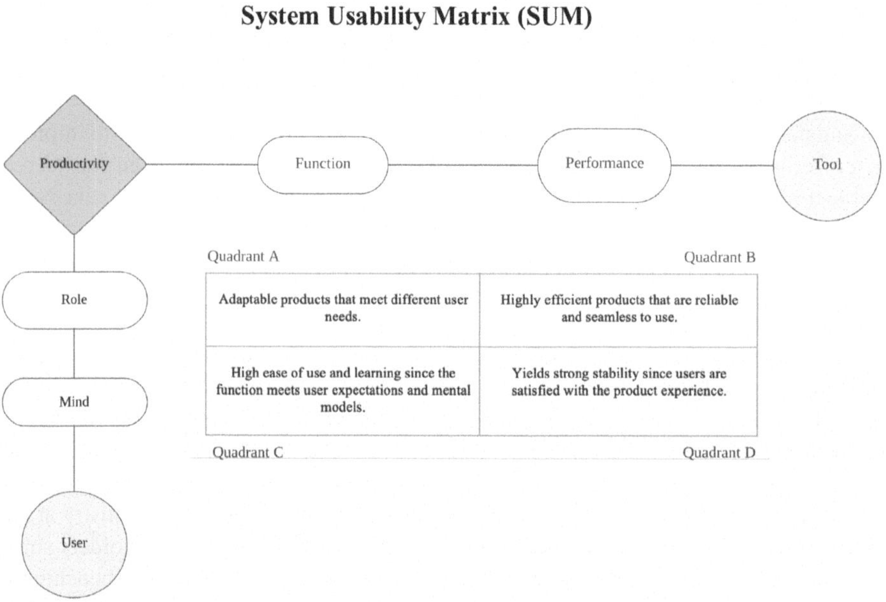

Fig. 1. The SUM visualised. To achieve productivity, both the user and the tool are needed. These two components lay the foundation of SUM. Two factors make up the 'user' component—the user's role and mind. The 'tool' component is made up of tool's function and performance. Together, these four factors form a matrix suitable to measure usability of enterprise cloud solutions.

SUM comprises of four quadrants as depicted in Fig. 1. It uses the term 'tool' as most enterprise SaaS products are tools which enable the user to perform their tasks. Let's dive into each quadrant of the matrix.

3.1 Role of the User and Function of the Tool

Enterprise business users perform highly role dependent tasks. Their goal is to get their job done through the tool provided to them. When the tool contains the capabilities to enable the user to do their tasks, the end result is adaptable products that meet different user needs.

This can be calculated through various usability metrics, some of them being customer and end user feedback. The data can be collected through qualitative methods that map the needs, tasks, and workflows of the end user to the affordances of the tool.

3.2 Mind of the User and Function of the Tool

A key user experience criteria is that the workings of the tool are intuitive and the interactions with the product fit into the existing mental models of the user, thereby reducing the learning curve and resulting in easy-to-use products that meet user expectations, with minimal deviation from their ideal path.

Usability metrics for evaluation would be end-user completion time or task time (time it takes to complete a task end-to-end) and various clickstream analytics (such as navigation data and general usage analytics) of the end user. These metrics provide an overall objective understanding of where the user is in their task flow, how easily they are performing their tasks and provide a better understanding of their pain-points based on where they spend excessive time in their process.

3.3 Role of the User and Performance of the Tool

When the performance of the tool does not hinder the end user tasks and the quality standards of the tools are upheld to satisfy user needs, the end result is reliable tools that are seamless to use. Such tools result in higher efficiency and output since the user faces no challenges in their workflow.

Tool response and load times provide valuable insight to measure efficiency. This metric will aid in understanding how well tools operate with respect to the expectations of the business role.

3.4 Role of the Mind and Performance of the Tool

Users are satisfied with their product experience when the products uphold all performance standards required for an enterprise cloud solution. Some subjective measures of usability such as user generated error reports and objective metrics such as application refreshes could be some ways to understand users' satisfaction with the overall product experience.

SUM is a model to measure the evolving usability of an enterprise cloud solution. The metrics mentioned above act as probes and starting points that are relevant to map and implement, to get a holistic understanding of usability. Depending on end-user goals and business objectives, different metrics can be added or substituted in the SUM. Employing all the four quadrants of SUM (not in any order) is imperative to measure usability that has considered multiple perspectives.

4 Validating the System Usability Matrix (SUM)

To achieve a deeper understanding of how SUM works, a usability study was conducted where usability metrics were derived from the different quadrants of SUM. These subjective and objective usability metrics informed various observations and insights for an enterprise cloud application.

4.1 The Study

The objective of the study was to test the same application mentioned in Sect. 2.1 with the aim to understand how efficient and seamless the experience was for end-users to perform their tasks successfully. It was also a priority to grasp the adaptability of the application due to it being a new addition to the product.

Defining Metrics. The product team was handed the SUM after they had performed a usability evaluation on using SUS as a benchmark previously. The average SUS score from the validation was 90.5 which is considered to be excellent and a sign of great user experience, but there were key shortcomings (refer to Sect. 2.1) and even with a high overall score there was lack of clarity on actionable areas of improvement to outline a future roadmap. This is where SUM helped as it allowed the product team to pinpoint exact quadrants that aligned with business objectives and utilise existing usability metrics within those to better understand the overall user experience of the enterprise cloud application. There were three quadrants A, B and C (Fig. 1.) that stood out along which key metrics for this study were chosen to measure usability. SUS was the metric of choice under Quadrant A, Task Success Rate, Number of Actions, Time on Task were usability measures under Quadrant C and System Response Time, Time Based Efficiency under Quadrant B.

Measuring Usability. The test was conducted with 9 out of the previous 12 participants who were part of the SUS validations. There were 7 tasks total, and the method was remote, moderated task-based interviews. In a span of 60 min, the participants navigated through the Configuration Management application and as each unique user performed their tasks, specific metrics were recorded and then analysed. The findings were as follows -

Task Success Rate. It is a metric to measure percentage of tasks accomplished successfully by participants. For an enterprise cloud application, it's important to identify pain points for users as this helps in realising where tasks are hindering the user-function relationship (Table 1).

Task 5 required the user to discover a feature and with the lowest success rate it proved to be pain-point (Table 2). This was a valuable, granular, task specific finding which would otherwise have gone unnoticed.

Table 1. Task Performance (1 is task completed, 0.5 is task attempted, 0 is task failed)

Participants	Task 1	Task 2	Task 3	Task 4	Task 5	Task 6	Task 7
1	1	1	1	1	1	0.5	1
2	1	1	1	1	0	1	1
3	1	1	1	1	1	1	0.5
4	1	1	0.5	1	1	1	1
5	1	1	1	1	0	1	1
6	1	1	1	1	1	1	1
7	1	1	1	1	1	1	1
8	1	1	1	1	1	1	1
9	1	1	1	1	0.5	1	1

Table 2. Task Success Rate per Participant vs Task Success Rate per Task (in %)

Participants	Task Success Rate (%)	Tasks	Task Success Rate (%)
1	92.86	1	100.00
2	85.71	2	100.00
3	92.86	3	94.44
4	92.86	4	100.00
5	**85.71**	**5**	**72.22**
6	100.00	6	94.44
7	100.00	7	94.44
8	100.00		
9	92.86		
Average	93.65		

Number of Actions. The total number of steps a user takes to accomplish a task. It is measured by mapping the active steps taken by a participant from the moment they start on a task up until it's completed. The aim is always to reduce this number to make the user journey as productive as possible which is the goal of an enterprise cloud solution.

For a business user, the number of actions taken to complete a task is imperative to understand how seamless the tool is, even more than qualitative feedback. Even though tasks 2 and 11 were completed by the participants (Table 3), the actions taken were not as per the ideal navigation path and provided a tangible insight into how users navigate the tool currently and there is potential to improve the flow.

Time on Task. It is the total time spent on a specific task. This metric is used to understand how much time users are holistically spending on their tasks to further understand task's efficiency as this metric also accounts for system performance.

Table 3. Number of Actions per task per participant. (Ideal number of steps are in brackets)

Participants	Task 1 (12)	Task 2 (13)	Task 3 (6)	Task 4 (4)	Task 5 (2)	Task 6 (11)	Task 7 (10)
1	15	20	8	6	2	20	10
2	18	17	8	6	Failed	15	10
3	12	19	6	6	2	16	15
4	12	15	12	6	5	17	10
5	16	18	6	6	Failed	17	10
6	18	20	8	6	4	15	11
7	12	17	6	6	5	14	10
8	13	13	6	5	2	17	10
9	15	13	6	6	5	20	11

Table 4. Time taken for each task per participant (in seconds.)

Participants	Task 1	Task 2	Task 3	Task 4	Task 5	Task 6	Task 7
1	126	140	72	30	19	145	97
2	132	125	56	34	154	113	110
3	112	141	45	36	21	109	135
4	115	118	98	32	62	123	89
5	120	136	44	33	120	121	94
6	136	140	65	34	23	112	121
7	114	123	44	32	20	110	125
8	119	110	43	29	24	117	92
9	125	112	40	33	76	136	112

Using the times above (Table 4), the average time taken per task was calculated. The average system response time, i.e., the time taken by the cloud enterprise product to respond to the user when they interact with the application UI for them to perform their task was also recorded to map System Response Efficiency.

From the Table 5 above it is highlighted that system performance plays a role in the user experience of a product and longer response times (for e.g., in task 6) result in lower system efficiency which could become a major pain point for users with prolonged usage of the application. From Table 3 and Table 4, it can be synthesised that even though task 5 was ideally a two-step task, it took users much longer to complete and 2/9 users failed to complete the task. A learning here was that designing an experience with less clicks might not always result in the best user experience.

Table 5. The System Response Efficiency for the Configuration Management application

Tasks	Average Time on Task / Participant *t* (s)	Average System Response Time / Participant *s* (s)	System Response Efficiency (t-s/t) *100%
1	122	15	87.70
2	127	19	85.03
3	56	6	89.28
4	33	3	90.90
5	53	6	88.68
6	121	21	82.64
7	108	10	90.70
Average			87.85

Time Based Efficiency. A metric to calculate how efficiently a user can complete a task within a specific time frame in an enterprise cloud application [11]. From Table 6 below it can be inferred that efficiency varies with complexity. Although Task 4 introduced a new feature, it was the most efficient task highlighting that the tool and user were in harmony (as shown in Fig. 2. Below).

4.2 Inference

SUM is a foundational approach to map product requirements, business objectives and user goals through usability metrics as it provides a holistic understanding of end-to-end usability of an enterprise cloud application. From the study, it is clearly observed that for B2B products SUS quantifies user feedback but falls short of assisting in identifying insights. Good SUS score might not translate to good usability of a B2B solution, especially when the usability for B2B scenario is a function of the user's skill and tool's efficiency. SUM assisted product teams with granular, actionable insights that measure evolving usability of capabilities and products.

While presenting the SUM model to industry design practitioners and researchers, many advantages and some disadvantages of SUM came to light. SUM is highly customizable and provides a framework to fit apt, existing, and potential metrics into, the matrix layout helps pinpoint precise areas of improvement. It is comprehensive since it relies on both subjective and objective metrics for a well-rounded set of actionable insights. It allows business and product teams to scope usability tests better since they need not approach all product and user problems at once but can pick a combination of tests and metrics basis the current problem at hand. SUM can therefore result in better prioritization of product timelines with deeper focus on specific areas of work. It is also adaptable to any enterprise cloud business context, product, and end-user. Some potential pain points of SUM that were highlighted are that it has the potential to be extensive at first, but with time SUM would provide better clarity of product evolution w.r.t user

Table 6. Time based Efficiency per task

Tasks	Time based Efficiency (tasks/sec)
1	0.0082
2	0.0079
3	0.0181
4	0.0308
5	0.0279
6	0.0076
7	0.0086
Average	**0.0156**

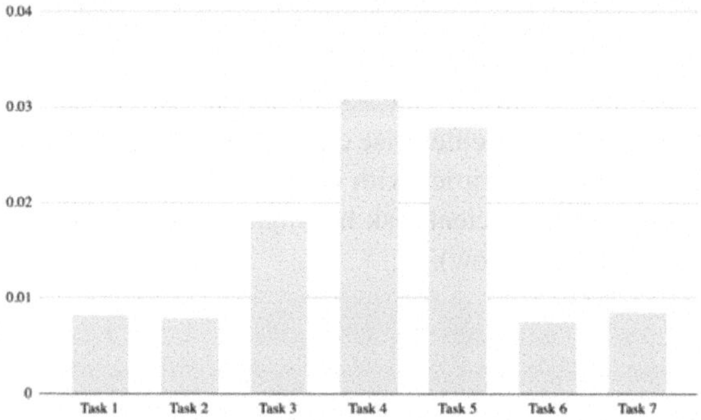

Fig. 2. Time Based Efficiency per task visualised where the y axis is the efficiency in tasks/sec.

experience, it is not a quick and dirty model and requires more thought from the business or practitioner implementing it.

5 Conclusion

The enterprise cloud industry is vastly different from a B2C business, the products are not comparable, and the objective of their usage is unalike. SUS and other lazy metrics have become the industry norm for measuring usability, but such subjective results are too inadequate, skewed and biased to truly quantify user experience. Organizations are unable to explain why customer experience metrics are going up or down as subjective assessment tools do not provide actionable insights. They do not motivate specific changes in product because design and research teams are unable to attribute issues to a specific problem area, which is why combined measures (both objective and subjective [12]) are needed to understand the true usability of an enterprise cloud product. SUM is a model aimed at rectifying the same. It is a novel approach and an alternative system for measuring usability which is tailor made for enterprise cloud solutions. SUM defines measuring usability as achieving productivity, i.e., how efficiently and effectively users can perform their tasks. It highlights that to achieve productivity, both the user and the tool (the product) are needed. It outlines multiple metrics beyond SUS that one must consider while measuring usability for cloud solutions. The impact of exploring usability through SUM will present us with a more accurate measure of how our products perform, prioritise end-user needs, provide actionable insights across product teams while upholding the measurable contribution of customer experience to the functioning of a business.

6 Discussion

The long-term ripple effect of such an approach to usability in the industry will be welcomed with resistance as it's intended to challenge already established models and deem them suboptimal, but the need to examine further is of the essence. This paper emphasizes that using SUS as the only standard usability measure for enterprise cloud solutions is not enough. This paper recognises the requirement for an effective model that upholds the standards of the industry and the consequence it could potentially create however, given the novelty of SUM it would require some time and more testing to guarantee its success. The paper is a call to action to enterprise businesses and product teams to recognise gaps of current industry usability standards and to welcome novel models aiming to redefine usability in their contexts. The aim is that this paper acts as a tangible starting point to move away from lazy metrics and move towards context driven, business relevant and truly user-first standards of usability measures for enterprise cloud industries.

Acknowledgments. This paper would not have taken full form had it not been for Rashi Balachandran and Sai Saran Patibanda. Thank you for being constant shoulders I could lean on through the entire process.

References

1. What is usability - The ultimate guide. The interaction design foundation (2023). https://www.interaction-design.org/literature/topics/usability
2. John brooke and usability professionals' association. 2013. SUS: a retrospective. https://uxpajournal.org/wp-content/uploads/sites/7/pdf/JUS_Brooke_February_2013.pdf
3. How to measure user experience of B2B products? Medium. https://medium.com/orientalreview/how-to-measure-user-experience-of-b2b-products-7dfd4a836074. Accessed 22 March 2024
4. Cooiman, G.M.: University of Twente. Output vs. Outcome: measuring usability in a business-to-business context. University of Twente, Faculty of electrical engineering, mathematics and computer science (2019). https://essay.utwente.nl/79179/1/Cooiman_BA_BMS.pdf
5. Anders, O.: Pros and cons of the system usability scale (SUS) -. Research collective (2023). https://research-collective.com/sus/
6. Brooke, J.: Redhatch consulting Ltd. (n.d.). SUS - A quick and dirty usability scale. https://digital.ahrq.gov/sites/default/files/docs/survey/systemusabilityscale%2528sus%2529_comp%255B1%255D.pdf

7. Bratati, C., Sharmistha, R., Prasant Kumar P.: User satisfaction metrics for cloud computing environment. Eur. J. Acad. Essays **1–3**, 63–69 (2014). https://cloud.report/Resources/Whitepapers/49e582c8-8054-4cc2-a5ab-f9b12bd4f9c4_User%20Satisfaction%20Metrics%20for%20Cloud%20Computing%20Environment.pdfLNCS
8. Net promoter score (NPS): the ultimate guide - Qualtrics. Qualtrics (2024). https://www.qualtrics.com/experience-management/customer/net-promoter-score/?rid=cookie&prevsite=au&newsite=en&geo=&geomatch=
9. Google's HEART framework for measuring UX. The interaction design foundation (2024). https://www.interaction-design.org/literature/article/google-s-heart-framework-for-measuring-uxLNCS
10. Cooiman, G.M.: University of Twente. Output vs. Outcome: measuring usability in a business-to-business context. University of Twente, Faculty of electrical engineering, mathematics and computer science. Retrieved LNCS Homepage. http://www.springer.com/lncs. Accessed 2 Oct 2023
11. Mifsud, J.: Usability metrics - a guide to quantify the usability of any system. In: Usability Geek (2019). https://usabilitygeek.com/usability-metrics-a-guide-to-quantify-system-usability/. Accessed 16 Apr 2024
12. Gabriela, L.L.: Case study: UX Metrics for a B2B product - Bootcamp. Medium (2023). https://bootcamp.uxdesign.cc/case-study-ux-metrics-for-a-b2b-product-9e99a7ed8beb#:~:text=One%20thing%20I%20can%20say,satisfaction%20or%20Error%2Drate%20reduction. Accessed 25 Oct 2023

Innovative Technologies and Human-Centered Solutions

Social Behaviors on Sharing Expenses in Saudi Arabia

Saif Alshammari[1,2(✉)] and Munira Alenzi[1,2]

[1] Neoleap (urpay) Company, Riyadh, Saudi Arabia
salshammari@neoleap.com.sa
[2] HCI International 2024, Washington, DC, USA

Abstract. This study explores the evolving landscape of expense sharing among Saudi nationals, highlighting the significant influence of financial technology (Fintech) adoption on social and financial practices. With the rapid growth of Fintech in Saudi Arabia, mobile payment applications and peer-to-peer (P2P) money transfer platforms have emerged as pivotal tools in facilitating new forms of expense sharing among individuals, friends, and families. Through qualitative research, including semi-structured interviews with residents across Saudi Arabia, this paper explores the social dimensions of expense sharing, distinguishing between periodic and non-periodic expenses, and identifies a comprehensive five-stage process of shared financial activities. The findings indicate a generally positive attitude towards expense sharing, emphasizing benefits such as mutual aid and efficient budget management. However, challenges such as increased personal costs due to collective decisions and the complexity of managing diverse preferences also surface.

Keywords: Sharing expenses · Fintech Adoption · Social Behaviors

1 Introduction

Financial technology (fintech) innovations are transforming financial services globally, with significant implications for emerging markets like Saudi Arabia. Saudi Arabia's fintech sector has seen a significant rise in recent years. Since 2018, the number of companies has grown by 14.7 times [1]. In particular, the rise has been in mobile payment platforms and peer-to-peer (P2P) money transfer applications, as Albarrak and Alokley note, more than any other category in fintech [2] which serves the central bank's strategy of moving toward a cashless society [2]. As the kingdom moves toward a cashless society these types of applications have to consider already existing social norms in dealing with cash (like lending and splitting an expense) and how can technology facilitate and enable new forms of financial collaboration among individuals, friends, and families. However, as cashless transactions continue to grow exponentially in Saudi Arabia [3], research into how fintech can complement social norms and behaviors surrounding collaborative financial management is still limited, especially in the Saudi context.

This paper explores the social dimensions of expense-sharing practices in Saudi Arabia, using traditional methods like cash or bank transfers or mobile payment platforms,

C. Stephanidis et al. (Eds.): HCII 2024, CCIS 2319, pp. 229–236, 2025.
https://doi.org/10.1007/978-3-031-78516-0_23

and what benefits and challenges arise from these practices. The goal of this paper is to help fintech companies increase their customer adoption by exploring social norms around shared expenses to be able to design convenient and easy-to-use products. As Albarrak and Alokley (2021) note, "Customers are interested in new products that are convenient and easy to use" when it comes to fintech adoption in Saudi Arabia [2].

Given high mobile penetration and fintech adoption rates among Saudi consumers, changing social dynamics facilitated by innovative services warrant attention. This study collects qualitative insights from Saudi fintech users through interviews regarding their expense-sharing experiences and sheds light on their utilization of digital solutions. New technologies like mobile wallets and money transfer apps have created innovative ways for people to share costs [4]. By documenting social behaviors and attitudes related to financial management and shared expenses, findings can inform an understudied area regarding social behaviors that can be facilitated by fintech solutions in Saudi Arabia. Results may also guide future fintech developments to better align with local social contexts and behaviors.

2 Related Work

The problem of splitting expenses and utilizing fintech products has been explored in many different aspects of literature. In fintech, researchers have utilized technology acceptance models to study and measure the factors that influence users to accept fintech solutions. On the other hand, researchers have explored various social norms when it comes to sharing an expense. Utilizing game theory, Natalie and Bernardo discussed how group member's preferences in terms of acting selfishly or cooperating with the other members at a dinner table (Natalie S. Glance and Bernardo A. Huberman) While another paper by Gneezy, Haruvy, & Yafe tested the member's preferences in an environment close to real-life experiences [5].

One notable meta-analysis paper led by Bommer concluded that Hedonic motivation comes second with a high weight as a factor (19.65% after the price-value of 21.73%) which aligns with the value we are proposing for splitting expenses solutions in this study [6].

3 Method

The study employed a qualitative research approach, utilizing semi-structured interviews, to enable in-depth exploration of participants' experiences and viewpoints, as the primary data collection method. The data were analyzed through thematic analysis to allow for flexibility in exploring socio-cultural behaviors and identify recurring themes and patterns in the collected qualitative data following the guidelines of Braun, V. and Clarke, V. [8].

3.1 Participants

A vast amount of research, including articles, book chapters, and books, suggests a participant range of 5 to 50 for qualitative studies [7]. However, we settled for 12 interviews after reaching data saturation as per Dworkin [9]. The 12 residents of Saudi Arabia were selected randomly to represent diverse regions, nationalities, genders, and age groups.

This diverse sample ensured a comprehensive understanding of the cultural nuances and societal norms influencing expense-sharing practices within the Saudi context. Participants across Saudi Arabia (diverse regions) were interviewed in person (rapport, non-verbal cues) or online (wider participation) to meet preferences and logistics.

3.2 The Interviews

Participants were voluntarily asked to join the study, and then, given a structured questionnaire designed to delve deeper into their experiences and perspectives on sharing expenses. The questionnaire elicited concise responses about participants' feelings, experiences, and management of shared expenses, as well as two exercises: designing a hypothetical mobile app for expense splitting and identifying and prioritizing occasions for splitting expenses. This structured approach complemented the qualitative depth obtained from interviews, providing a comprehensive view of attitudes, behaviors, and challenges associated with expense sharing, particularly among Saudis. The combined data from interviews and questionnaires were analyzed through thematic analysis, yielding insights into social behaviors regarding expense splitting in Saudi Arabia.

4 Results

This comprehensive study delves into the intricacies of sharing expenses, known as Qatta, among Saudis, providing valuable insights into their perceptions, practices, and the challenges they face in this process. Through analyzing participants' feedback, we categorize their experiences under three main subheadings: Perception, Types of Expenses, and The Stages of Sharing Expenses. Each category offers a deep dive into different aspects of expense sharing—from the general attitudes and feelings towards splitting costs to the specific types of expenses encountered, and finally, the distinct phases that groups navigate through when managing shared financial responsibilities. This structured approach allows for a nuanced understanding of the social dynamics at play in the practice of Qatta, highlighting its complexities and the potential areas for innovation in facilitating smoother shared expense transactions.

4.1 Perception

Mainly participants had a positive impression when they were asked about splitting expenses with others (known as Qatta in Saudi Arabia). When they were asked to express their opinion about splitting expenses with others in one word, their answers were: Fair, helping others, Cheaper, no one is in debt to anyone else, saving money, controlling spending, and better allocation.

Participants also had few negative responses, like effort, money loss, and displeasure. Customers mentioned that when they decide to split the bill for dinner, some of the group members may lean toward more expensive choices. A general assumption of negative externalities states that "economic agents equate individual marginal costs and marginal benefits with complete disregard for the costs imposed on others or for social efficiency." [5] as Ernan Haruvy and Hadas Yafe of Uri Gneezy explain.

When customers were asked whether they would like to be in charge of the shared payment, most customers said no. When they were asked why, their answers can be summarized in three main reasons, the payment is not fulfilled, "It takes effort, I want to enjoy the trip" Saad says, and it ruins the occasion for them.

All the reason to believe that any solution for splitting expenses has to address these concerns by adopting three main values: Fulfillment, Effortless, and Fun.

4.2 Types of Expenses

Participants ranked activities that necessitate shared expenses based on their perceived importance and popularity. From the participant's answers, we found that parting, traveling and dinners are the most popular occasions where people prefer to share the expenses while Estiraha (a rented place where a group of people meet up almost every night) is the most important for males mostly [see the Fig. 1 below].

Periodic Expenses. These are recurring expenses that occur at regular intervals, such as monthly, quarterly, or annually. They can be predictable in nature and often include:

Fixed Amounts. Expenses that remain constant in each period, such as rent, subscription services, or scheduled loan repayments. "Three customers mentioned that they and their friends share the same expenses every month for Estraha." (Mansour/Alwaleed/Zakaria)

Variable Amounts. Costs that can fluctuate from one period to another but still occur regularly, such as utility bills. Ali mentioned, "I split the amount of my father's house bills every month with my brothers." Additionally, Ashjan mentioned they wait for the bill owner to give them the amount: "We wait for my mother to tell us the amount of her phone bill before we transfer money to her," including grocery expenses or fuel for shared vehicles.

Non-periodic Expenses. These expenses arise irregularly and are not tied to a specific schedule. They can be unpredictable and vary significantly in amount, including:

Planned. Costs that are anticipated but don't occur regularly, such as vacations, major purchases (like electronics or furniture), or special events (weddings, major celebrations).

Unplanned. Unexpected expenses can arise without warning, including emergency repairs, sudden healthcare costs, or last-minute travel. Alwaleed mentioned, "Paying for someone's expenses to help them when they have an accident."

4.3 The Stages of Sharing Expenses

Through all types and occasions shared by our participants, we identified 5 main stages that splitting expenses activities go through. After a group of customers agrees on a shared goal, the life cycle of Qatta goes through five main stages: Intentions, Splitting Intentions, Payment, Fulfilling Qatta, and the Occasion itself. These stages can be in a different order depending on the occasion's circumstances.

Intentions. In this stage, customers identify the requirements for conducting an event in terms of budget and responsibilities. Sometimes, they skip this part and rely

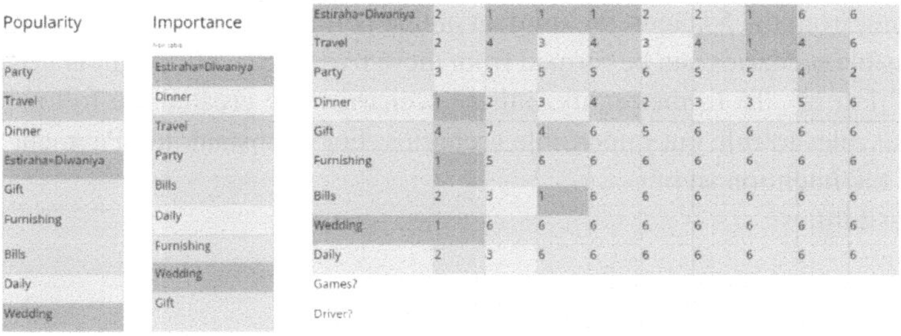

Fig. 1. Participants identified two primary categories of expenses relevant to their shared financial practices.

on the shared goal to start collecting the money. For example, when a family wants to renovate their house, they usually begin collecting money and working on the house without knowing how much they would spend renovating it.

Ways of Splitting the Intentions. At this stage, the customers decide how much each group member has to pay. This stage has to be done naturally before the Qattah is fulfilled. Customers mentioned that they might split the requirements in multiple ways, tasks, budgets, and in rotations.

The decision to use one way over another relies mostly on the amount, the familiarity among the group members, and the nature of the occasion.

Payment. In this stage, the group must pay for the occasion's cost. This stage happens only after having intentions to buy what's needed. This stage doesn't occur before the intentions stage.

Fulfilling Qatta. For this stage, group members must pay their shares or settle their amounts. Although sharing expenses is typical social behavior, it can also be a sensitive topic to bring up. The facilitators of Qatta often find themselves in an "awkward" situation when they have to remind the group's members to settle their amounts. Many customers' express disappointment when their Qatta is not fulfilled, which is one of the main reasons they don't enjoy being in charge of Qatta. They avoid reminding the other member, and the Qatta is abandoned and never fulfilled. One customer mentioned that they only tell the group about the total cost and never ask the members to pay or tell them how much their share is. "I can't. I am shy. I told them the total cost. They should figure out how much they should pay by themselves. However, sometimes, they pay less, and other times they don't pay at all. I never remind them." Rana said. When the group knows each other, they tend to be flexible, "we know when someone doesn't have money at the moment to settle their amount, so we remind them at the end of the month [when they get their salary]." Mansour said.

Event (The Occasion Itself). The occasion is an essential part of Qatta. This is when the event takes place. People try to avoid talking about the costs during the occasion to maintain a light mood. However, the occasion's nature plays a pivotal role in the process. For example, when a group plans to camp, they usually split tasks between the members. When they want to have dinner in a fine restaurant, one of the groups would pay the amount, split the payment afterward, and so on.

Drawing from the 5 stages, we used an online permutations calculator to know how many possible scenarios can be formed from these five stages. The result is 120 possible scenarios [Fig. 2]. To further analyze these scenarios, we created the following basic and logical rules to rule out impossible scenarios. For an instant, the Payment step can be before the Intention step:

Impossibilities:

- Intention cannot be the last step
- Payment cannot come before intention
- Splitting Intentions then Qatta is meaningless
- Advance Qatta (Qatta before intention) cannot be after the event

Less Likely Scenarios:

- Dinners and Uber are exceptions to payment after the event
- Separation between Splitting and Qatta is less likely
- Qatta before Splitting is less likely except for Advanced Qatta
- Splitting can be skipped in some cases (Pay what you can)
- Splitting can come before Intention but it would be estimated

	Qatta steps	I=Intentions	S=Splitting Amount	Q=Qatta	P=Payment	E=Event
In which scenario Qatta is less likely to happen or be fulfilled						
Start with						
Goal	No Qatta starts without a goal					
Intentions	Usually qatta starts with stating the needs	ISQPE	ISQEP	ISPQE	ISPEQ	ISEQP
		ISEPQ	IQSPE	IQSEP	IQPSE	IQPES
		IQESP	IQEPS	IPSQE	IPSEQ	IPQSE
		IPQES	IPESQ	IPEQS	IESQP	IESPQ
		IEQSP	IEQPS	IEPSQ	IEPQS	SIQPE
Splitting Amount / Splitting tasks	Advanced Qatta usually for fixed amounts	SIQEP	SIPQE	SIPEQ	SIEQP	SIEPQ
		SQIPE	SQIEP	SQPIE	SQPEI	SQEIP
		SQEPI	SPIQE	SPIEQ	SPQIE	SPQEI
		SPEIQ	SPEQI	SEIQP	SEIPQ	SEQIP
		SEQPI	SEPIQ	SEPQI	QISPE	QISEP
Qatta	Saving / Pay what you can	QIPSE	QIPES	QIESP	QIEPS	QSIPE
		QSIEP	QSPIE	QSPEI	QSEIP	QSEPI
		QPISE	QPIES	QPSIE	QPSEI	QPEIS
		QPESI	QEISP	QEIPS	QESIP	QESPI
		QEPIS	QEPSI	PISQE	PISEQ	PIQSE
Payment	When Qatta starts witth someone paying the amount in advance, it increases the risk of not fulfilling the amount with Qatta	PIQES	PIESQ	PIEQS	PSIQE	PSIEQ
		PSQIE	PSQEI	PSEIQ	PSEQI	PQISE
		PQIES	PQSIE	PQSEI	PQEIS	PQESI
		PEISQ	PEIQS	PESIQ	PESQI	PEQIS
		PEQSI	EISQP	EISPQ	EIQSP	EIQPS
Event	Emergencies like surgeruies car accidents	EIPSQ	EIPQS	ESIQP	ESIPQ	ESQIP
		ESQPI	ESPIQ	ESPQI	EQISP	EQIPS
		EQSIP	EQSPI	EQPIS	EQPSI	EPISQ
		EPIQS	EPSIQ	EPSQI	EPQIS	EPQSI

Fig. 2. Scenarios = green, Impossibilities = red, and Less Likely Scenarios = yellow. (Color figure online)

From the customer's interviews, we found that the (ISQPE) is the most satisfying scenario for the person who manages Qatta, greatly increasing the chances of everyone paying their shares.

5 Conclusion

In Saudi Arabia, financial technology (Fintech) is revolutionizing expense sharing, with a ripple effect on social customs and financial practices. This study dives into this evolving landscape. Drawing on qualitative insights from 12 interviews, the study highlights a predominantly positive reception towards expense sharing in general. Despite the advantages identified, the research also points out challenges, such as the potential for increased personal costs due to group decisions and the difficulties in managing varying preferences. Furthermore, when it comes to managing the expense-sharing experience, participants expressed their concerns in three words, unsettled amounts, takes effort, and unpleasant. The paper also highlights the involvement of technology in the experience of sharing expenses between families and friends, starting from planning for an occasion to settling the expenses.

The distinction between different types of expense-sharing, like periodic and non-periodic expenses, along with an in-depth analysis of 120 payment scenarios, offers a thorough understanding of the intricate behaviors and preferences associated with shared financial activities.

This research unveils a five-stage model for expense-sharing activities. After a group of customers agrees on a shared goal, the life cycle of Qatta goes through five main stages: Intentions, Splitting Intentions, Payment, and Fulfilling Qatta. This cycle is flexible, with the order of stages adapting to the specific circumstances of each situation.

References

1. Saudi fintech annual report. (2022). https://www.sama.gov.sa/en-US/Documents/AFR22_en.pdf
2. Albarrak, M.S., Alokley, S.A.: FinTech: ecosystem, opportunities and challenges in Saudi Arabia (2021). https://www.mdpi.com/1911-8074/14/10/460
3. Khan, R.: Digital payments: Barrier or boon for entrepreneurs' success - A case study of Saudi Arabia. College of Business Administration, Department of Finance and Banking, Jazan University (2023). https://ijaem.net/issue_dcp/Digital%20Payments%20Barrier%20or%20Boon%20for%20Entrepreneurs%20Success%20A%20Case%20Study%20of%20Saudi%20Arabia.pdf
4. Huarng, K.-H., Yu, T. H.-K.: Causal complexity analysis for fintech adoption at the country level. ScienceDirect Causal complexity analysis for fintech adoption at the country level – ScienceDirect (2022)
5. Gneezy, U., Haruvy, E., Yafe, H.: The inefficiency of splitting the bill (2004). https://rady.ucsd.edu/_files/faculty-research/uri-gneezy/splitting-bill.pdf
6. Bommer, W.H., Rana, S., Milevoj, E.: A meta-analysis of eWallet adoption using the UTAUT model. Department of Management, Department of Accountancy, California State University Fresno, Fresno, California, USA (2022). https://www.researchgate.net/publication/359239341_A_meta_analysis_of_eWallet_adoption_using_the_UTAUT_model

7. Guest, G., Bunce, A., Johnson, L.: How many interviews are enough? An experiment with data saturation and variability. Field Methods, **18**(1), 59–82 (2006). https://journals.sagepub.com/doi/10.1177/1525822X05279903
8. Braun, V., Clarke, V.: Using thematic analysis in psychology. Qual. Res. Psychol. **3**(2), 77–101 (2006). (27) Braun & Clarke 2006-thematic analysis | Uda Mok De - Academia.ed.
9. Dworkin, S.L.: Sample size policy for qualitative studies using in-depth interviews. Springer Science + Business Media, LLC (2012). https://doi.org/10.1007/s10508-012-0016-6,https://link.springer.com/article/10.1007/s10508-012-0016-6
10. Glance, N. S., Huberman, B.A.: The dynamics of social dilemmas: Individuals in groups must often choose between acting selfishly or cooperating for the common good. Social models explain how group cooperation arises—and why that behavior can suddenly change (1994). https://www.academia.edu/33459817/The_Dynamics_of_Social_Dilemmas

"Cerésbox: Development of an Innovative Platform for the Commercialization of Green Products Through 4.0 Technologies"

Heidy Bravo(✉) and Jairo Narváez

Institución Universitaria de Barranquilla, Cra. 45 #48-31, Barranquilla, Colombia
hbravob@unibarranquilla.edu.co

Abstract. The strategic and financial feasibility of a platform directed to the market for eco-friendly cosmetics and personal hygiene items is investigated in this article. In order to do this, the firm's commercial and financial objectives have been evaluated using a combined quantitative and qualitative analysis method. Financial estimates have been made using discounted cash flow models and corporate financial data has been gathered. A sensitivity analysis is also carried out to assess the ways in which different factors influence the project's financial outcomes. With a positive contribution margin and positive cash flow projections, the results show that a platform of this kind would be profitable. The Net Present Value and the Internal Rate of Return indicate that the project would produce positive returns with a 10% discount rate. Furthermore, a thorough understanding of this sustainable platform's strategic potential and market obstacles is offered by the Canvas model and SWOT analysis. The organization is able to create efficient plans to capitalize on its competitive advantages and advance through the assessment of strengths, weaknesses, opportunities, and threats. Conversely, the platform's business plan is outlined in detail by the Canvas model, which also highlights its customer categories, distribution channels, and value propositions. But it turns out that the project's profitability might vary a lot depending on the circumstances, especially when it comes to subscriber growth and sales expenses. These findings highlight how crucial it is to effectively manage crucial factors in order to enhance the proposed platform's long-term success and profitability in a market that is becoming more demanding and competitive.

Keywords: Business model · SWOT · Feasibility · Eco-friendly · Sensitivity analysis

1 Introduction

Within the contemporary context of increased environmental consciousness and a never-ending quest for healthier and more sustainable products, the market for beauty and personal care products has experienced a dramatic shift. Products that improve both the environment and the well-being of the consumer are becoming more and more appealing [1]. This is the setting for the launch of a sustainable platform directed to the market

C. Stephanidis et al. (Eds.): HCII 2024, CCIS 2319, pp. 237–243, 2025.
https://doi.org/10.1007/978-3-031-78516-0_24

for eco-friendly cosmetics and personal hygiene items, an inventive idea that aims to transform the market by providing a premium range of environmentally friendly and fully sustainable beauty and personal care goods.

For customers who are dedicated to leading more environmentally friendly and sustainable lives, a platform as the one described previously would be positioned as a complete solution. The platform would sell monthly subscription boxes that would be filled with a carefully chosen assortment of beauty and personal care items that are only created with natural, organic, and cruelty-free materials. These boxes would support ethical and environmentally friendly business practices in the sector in addition to providing a distinctive customer experience [2].

This article's goal was to conduct a thorough analysis of the strategic and financial feasibility of a sustainable platform for the current beauty and personal care market. In order to accomplish this, a thorough assessment encompassing everything from the business model analysis to the financial results prediction was conducted. To get a comprehensive understanding of the project's condition and its prospects going forward, a blended approach combining qualitative and quantitative methodologies was employed [3].

The company's value proposition, client categories, distribution routes, revenue streams, and critical resources, among other pertinent information, has been identified during the development of this research [4]. The performance of this platform could be influenced by both internal and external factors, so it was important to identify these factors in order to help define the best strategies for maximizing the platform's opportunities and minimizing its risks. These factors included consumer trends, market competition, government regulations, and growth opportunities [5].

A thorough financial analysis was completed after the company's operational and strategic environment was determined [6]. As part of this analysis, the project's economic viability was assessed. Projected revenues and expenses were calculated over a specified time period using discounted cash flow models, and the project's profitability was assessed using a suitable discount rate. Furthermore, a sensitivity analysis was carried out to assess the potential impact of various variables, including subscriber growth and sales expenses, on the project's financial outcomes [7].

Synthesizing all the presented ideas, the goal of this research was to present a thorough evaluation of a sustainable platform's strategic and commercial feasibility in the current market for eco-friendly cosmetics and personal hygiene products. The researchers believe that it is necessary to look for possibilities and difficulties facing the project and establish plans for its long-term development, and have attacked this subject through the thorough financial analysis, the strategic assessment utilizing the SWOT matrix, and the complete review of the business model developed in this research.

2 Materials and Methods

Through a hybrid approach that combined qualitative and quantitative methods, the study's methodology was created to offer a thorough and rigorous analysis of the economic viability of the platform proposal—dubbed Céresbox by the researchers—in the market for sustainable beauty and personal care products, enabling a thorough assessment of the project's financial and strategic elements [8].

In order to guarantee Céresbox's financial success, data on market trends, opportunities, and obstacles was first gathered from secondary sources. This process produced insightful knowledge on the business environment and best practices [9]. Financial information on the industry was gathered in addition to market trends. The financial projection for this idea was seen in depth thanks to the financial reports, income statements, balance sheets, and other pertinent papers that were collected. Understanding the cost structure, revenue, and cash flows that this platform would provide at the corporate level was made possible by this data, which was also crucial for identifying potential growth areas and places for development.

Discounted cash flow models were used to create financial estimates based on the financial data that was gathered [10]. It was feasible to project the company's future revenue using this method, together with the expenses related to corporate growth and the introduction of new products [11, 12]. To represent the uncertainty present in the business environment, various scenarios and hypotheses were considered, yielding a more accurate evaluation of Céresbox's long-term economic sustainability.

A sensitivity analysis was performed in addition to the financial predictions to assess the impact of various variables on the project's financial outcomes. The project's risks and possibilities were discovered by identifying key variables, including subscriber growth, sales costs, and discount rates, and analyzing how changes in these variables could affect Céresbox's profitability. The company's strengths, weaknesses, opportunities, and threats in the market were also understood through the use of SWOT analysis, and the Canvas model offered a thorough understanding of its business strategy, yielding important data for strategic decision-making [13, 14].

To sum up, the suggested platform has the ability to establish itself as a standard in the industry for environmentally friendly cosmetics and personal hygiene items. Its creative approach, along with a sound plan backed by financial and strategic analysis, might help it stand out from the competition and draw in customers who are becoming more environmentally conscious. But aggressive risk management and quick response to market shifts are essential components that ensure "Céresbox" and related projects remain viable for the long run.

3 Results

3.1 Strategic Analysis

The creation of the Canvas Model and the SWOT matrix serve as a foundation and offer a greater understanding of the business's structure and important internal and external elements.

The Céresbox Canvas Model highlights the essential components that lead to the project's success by providing a visual depiction of the nine core business sectors (Fig. 1).

The core ideas of Céresbox's business strategy are outlined in the Canvas Model, along with how it is intended to provide value to clients in a lucrative and sustainable manner.

The project's strengths, weaknesses, opportunities, and threats were then analyzed using Céresbox's SWOT analysis, yielding a thorough evaluation of the internal and external environments in which the platform would function (Fig. 2)

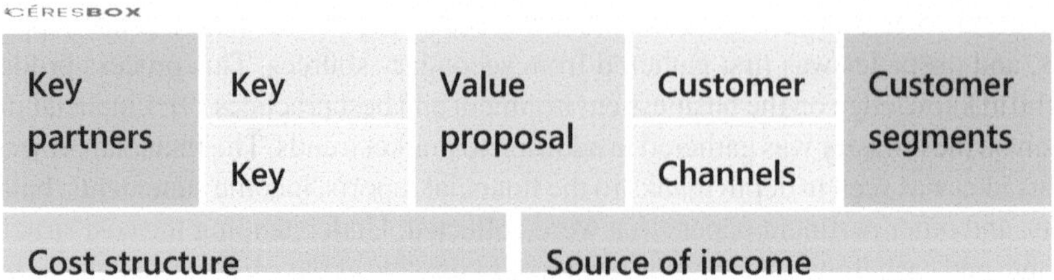

Fig. 1. Céresbox Canvas Model

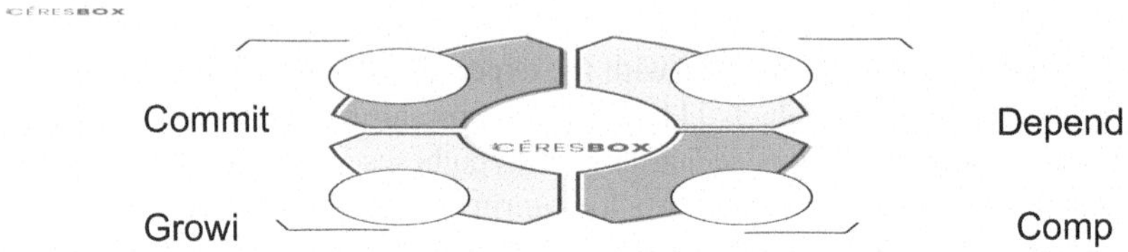

Fig. 2. SWOT Analysis

This SWOT analysis highlights the internal and external factors that can influence the future success of Céresbox and provides a solid foundation for strategy formulation and business decision-making.

3.2 Financial Analysis

According to the financial analysis, Céresbox shows a positive contribution margin in each of the anticipated years, indicating the project's sound financial standing. Over the anticipated years, this contribution margin—which represents the gap between revenue and variable costs—gradually rises, demonstrating a rise in the company's profitability. This data is summarized in the table below (Table 1).

Table 1. Potential cash flows for a sustainable platform directed to the market for eco-friendly cosmetics and personal hygiene items

Year	Contribution Margin (COP)	% Contribution	Flujo de Efectivo (COP)
1	$17,792,000	16.17%	$16,174,545
2	$36,272,400	19.98%	$29,977,190
3	$56,593,224	23.62%	$42,519,327

Source: own elaboration (2024)

These figures demonstrate Céresbox's ability to produce positive cash flows, which may be used to pay operational expenses and possibly reinvested in the expansion and improvement of the company.

The Internal Rate of Return (IRR) and Net Present Value (NPV) are crucial metrics for assessing an investment project's profitability. The findings for Céresbox indicate that, with a 10% discount rate, the project would yield positive returns. The project would add value and produce a positive return on the initial investment, as indicated by the calculated positive net present value (NPV). In addition, the project appears to give a competitive return when considering the applied discount rate, as indicated by the IRR of 8.15%. A table summarizing these findings is shown below (Table 2):

Table 2. Project financial indicators

Indicator	Value (COP)
Net Present Value (NPV)	$88,671,062
Internal Rate of Return (IRR)	8.15%

Source: own elaboration (2024)

These findings bolster Céresbox's financial sustainability and indicate that the initiative may yield profitable returns for investors.

3.3 Sensitivity Analysis

Even though the baseline financial analysis produced positive results, the sensitivity analysis shows that the project's profitability can vary dramatically depending on several situations. Subscription growth and sales expenses were shown to be the two main factors influencing the project's financial outcomes. The sensitivity scenarios and corresponding outcomes are listed below:

Sensitivity Scenario 1. Reduced subscriber growth to 40% in Year 2.

The second-year subscriber growth in this scenario is lowered to 40%. Sales and the contribution margin are therefore less than in the base situation. A negative impact on cash flow also results in an IRR of 5.53% and an NPV of $83,837,961.

Sensitivity Scenario 2. Increased subscriber growth to 60% in Year 2.

In this case, the number of subscribers grows by 60% in the second year. Sales and the contribution margin are therefore higher than in the base situation. Higher cash flow and an NPV of $164,392,313 with an IRR of 41.88% are indicators of this.

Sensitivity Scenario 3. Decrease in cost of sales by 5% in Year 2.

In this case, the second year's cost of sales is lowered by 5%. Cash flow and the contribution margin both rise significantly as a result of this. With an IRR of 25.04%, the final NPV is $125,041,611.

Sensitivity Scenario 4. Increased cost of sales by 10% in Year 2.

In this case, the cost of sales rises by 10% in the second year. In comparison to the base case, this lowers the cash flow and contribution margin. $75,795,888 is the final NPV, with an IRR of 0.95%.

These results from the sensitivity scenario highlight how crucial it is to effectively manage crucial factors like subscriber growth and sales costs in order to guarantee the project's long-term viability.

4 Conclusions and Discussions

The proposed project has a good contribution margin and favorable cash flow estimates, showing significant profitability potential, according to the mixed approach results. The project's long-term financial feasibility is validated by the examination of the Internal Rate of Return and Net Present Value, which show that it would generate positive returns at a 10% discount rate.

The sensitivity analysis, however, emphasizes how crucial it is to take into account various scenarios and significant factors that may have an impact on the financial outcomes of a sustainable platform targeted at the market for environmentally friendly cosmetics and personal hygiene products. In particular, it is noted that subscriber growth and sales expenses can have a substantial impact on the project's profitability. This implies that in order to enhance revenue and reduce the risks related to these aspects, careful and strategic management is required.

A comprehensive understanding of this platform's market potential and strategic difficulties is also offered by the SWOT analysis and Canvas model. By recognizing its advantages over competitors and addressing areas for improvement, the organization may create plans that effectively address risks, opportunities, weaknesses, and strengths. Conversely, the Canvas model provides a well-defined framework for comprehending the business model of a sustainable platform of this kind, emphasizing its value propositions, distribution channels, and client segmentation, among other important elements.

In conclusion, the proposed platform has the potential to position itself as a benchmark in the market for sustainable beauty and personal care products. Its innovative approach, combined with a solid strategy supported by financial and strategic analysis, could allow it to differentiate itself and capture the attention of an increasingly sustainability-conscious market. However, proactive risk management and agile adaptation to changes in the business environment are key elements to guarantee the long-term sustainability of "Céresbox" and other similar projects.

Furthermore, it is expected that this work will serve as a basis for the development of future commercial proposals similar to the platform presented. The methodology used, as well as the financial and strategic analyzes carried out, can serve as models for entrepreneurs and companies that wish to enter the sustainable products market. Likewise, the lessons learned during the development and implementation of the "Céresbox" platform can provide valuable insights to address similar challenges in the future. In this sense, this work not only contributes to the success of "Céresbox", but can also inspire and guide other market players in the creation and management of sustainable initiatives in the beauty and personal care sector.

References

1. Arevalo, O., Parra, M., García-Tirado, J., Ramírez, J., Ballestas, M., Rondón Rodríguez, C.: Dynamic adaptive capacity of metalworking companies in barranquilla-colombia: analysis from the export process in the 4.0 era. In: International Conference on Computer Information Systems and Industrial Management, pp. 127–138. Springer Nature Switzerland, Cham (2023). https://doi.org/10.1007/978-3-031-42823-4_10
2. Borre, J.R., Romero, G.C., Gutiérrez, J.M., Ramírez, J.: Discussion of the aspects of the cultural and creative industries that impact on sustainable development: a systematic review. Procedia Comput. Sci. **224**, 532–537 (2023). https://doi.org/10.1016/j.procs.2023.09.077
3. Musonda, I., Okoro, C.S.: A hermeneutic research on project management approaches applied in a business process re-engineering project. Bus. Process. Manag. J. **28**(8), 66–89 (2022). https://doi.org/10.1108/BPMJ-11-2021-0694
4. Rintamäki, T., Saarijärvi, H.: An integrative framework for managing customer value propositions. J. Bus. Res. **134**, 754–764 (2022). https://doi.org/10.1016/j.jbusres.2021.05.030
5. Bazaluk, O., Yatsenko, O., Zakharchuk, O., Ovcharenko, A., Khrystenko, O., Nitsenko, V.: Dynamic development of the global organic food market and opportunities for Ukraine. Sustainability **12**(17), 6963 (2020). https://doi.org/10.3390/su12176963
6. Bartolacci, F., Caputo, A., Soverchia, M.: Sustainability and financial performance of small and medium sized enterprises: a bibliometric and systematic literature review. Bus. Strateg. Environ. **29**(3), 1297–1309 (2020). https://doi.org/10.1002/bse.2434
7. Tsvetkova, O., Ouarda, T.B.: A review of sensitivity analysis practices in wind resource assessment. Energy Conver. Manage. **238**, 114112 (2021). https://doi.org/10.1016/j.enconman.2021.114112
8. Gemino, A., Horner Reich, B., Serrador, P.M.: Agile, traditional, and hybrid approaches to project success: is hybrid a poor second choice? Proj. Manag. J. **52**(2), 161–175 (2021). https://doi.org/10.1177/8756972820973082
9. Khan, O., Daddi, T., Iraldo, F.: Microfoundations of dynamic capabilities: Insights from circular economy business cases. Bus. Strateg. Environ. **29**(3), 1479–1493 (2020). https://doi.org/10.1002/bse.2447
10. Johnson, C., Nobler, E., Eudy, L., Jeffers, M.: Financial analysis of battery electric transit buses (No. NREL/TP-5400-74832). National Renewable Energy Lab. (NREL). Golden, CO (United States) (2020). https://doi.org/10.2172/1659784
11. Ellram, L.M., Tate, W.L., Choi, T.Y.: The conflicted role of purchasing in new product development costing. J. Supply Chain Manag. **56**(1), 3–32 (2020). https://doi.org/10.1111/jscm.12217
12. Samper, M. G., Florez, D. G., Borre, J. R., Ramirez, J.: Industry 4.0 for sustainable supply chain management: drivers and barriers. Procedia Comput. Sci. **203**, 644–650 (2022). https://doi.org/10.1016/j.procs.2022.07.094
13. Ismal, R., Sanrego, Y.D.: Business strategy analysis for spin-off and islamic banking growth: canvas business model approach. Int. J. Educat. Res. Soc. Sci. **3**(1), 225–237 (2022). https://n9.cl/p6xaw
14. Puyt, R.W., Lie, F.B., Wilderom, C.P.: The origins of SWOT analysis. Long Range Plan. **56**(3), 102304 (2023). https://doi.org/10.1016/j.lrp.2023.102304

Versatile Video Coding (VVC) Applied to Mobile Screen Content

Anderson V. C. de Oliveira(✉), Paulo S. S. Farias, and Emerson S. Domingos

Sidia Instituto de Ciência e Tecnologia - Sidia Amazon Innovation - SW Solutions, Avenue Torquato Tapajós, 6770 Novo Israel, 69039-125 Manaus, Brazil
{anderson.oliveira,paulo.farias,emerson.domingos}@sidia.com
http://www.sidia.com

Abstract. In this work, we carried out a case study of the new video codec standard established by the ITU/ISO (H.266/VVC) for a specific video category, "mobile screen content". To accomplish it, we created four uncompressed video sequences consisting of some of the most common mobile usages, and compared the new codec performance with both the previous H.265/HEVC standard and its extensions for desktop screen content (SCC). The results show that the new codec performs better than the previous codec for all video sequences tested, reducing the bitrate almost 40%, and outperforms the SCC extension for three of four video sequences, but the processing time increases exponentially when tested under the same conditions.

Keywords: VVC · H.266 · HEVC · H.265 · Mobile screen content

1 Introduction

About every ten years, a new video codec standard is established by entities such as ITU and ISO in order to increase the encoding performance, since the produced videos increase resolutions, and therefore it also increases the size amount to storage and transmit them. When a new codec is established as the current standard, it is generally capable of achieving half the previous codec bitrate, maintaining the same visual quality. However, that performance improvement is achieved by adding more and better tools, leading to a greater computational cost. Moreover, video codec standards are applied to a very wide range of usages and devices. In the same way, along the period between the release of two codec standards, the hardware used to run these tools has also been improved. Since the codec standard must works also in old devices, it is common an old standard codec remains in force for some years while the most recent one will be slowly adopted by video services. Even H.264/AVC codec [5] was established in 2003, it is yet the most used format for recording, compressing and distributing video content [8], while H.265/HEVC standard has been gradually adopted by video platforms as Youtube and Netflix.

C. Stephanidis et al. (Eds.): HCII 2024, CCIS 2319, pp. 244–252, 2025.
https://doi.org/10.1007/978-3-031-78516-0_25

H.266 Versatile Video Coding (VVC) [10] is the new video codec, established in 2020. It presents many features to improve video compression efficiency over its predecessor H.265 (HEVC) [4], however, the implementation and adoption of H.266 in devices and services may take some time.

The H.265/HEVC standard has some extensions designed to specifically encode different types of content. In particular, the screen content coding (SCC) extension [3] provides improvements in compression of content as screen sharing instead of camera-captured video scenes. Screen content images and videos may present particular characteristics such as computer-generated regions (which can be completely noise-free), and it can show graphics, icons, texts, and mixed of artificial and natural images, providing multiple types of content. In general, computer-generated regions present sharp edges, high contrast level, and large smooth regions.

The joint video experts team (JVET) has defined test conditions together with some test videos to be used to evaluate the performance of codecs [7]. Among them, class F defines four screen content video sequences between games and office screen capture. However, they are all from computers; no mobile content is defined.

A class of video that is not so tested in codecs is the "mobile screen content". Since people use more mobile than computer nowadays [9], one important application for video codec must be its ability to encode that kind of content. Moreover, as it is already common in computers, users can use services where it is needed to share its mobile screen through a broadcast channel. Due to channel bandwidth limits, it is not recommended to share the screen frame by frame, so a codec must be used.

In this work, we create a dataset consisting of four totally uncompressed sequences captured on the mobile screen. They represent common mobile usages. Then we used them to perform a performance study of the new video codec H.266 VVC and compared it to its predecessor H.265 (HEVC) with and without the SCC extension. In Sect. 2, we describe the created dataset. In Sect. 3 we present experimental results of the codecs tested on the created dataset, and Sect. 4 shows the conclusions.

2 Building a Mobile Screen Content Dataset

In order to evaluate the new video codec H.266 VVC, we built a dataset consisting of four uncompressed sequences of mobile screen content in common mobile usages. All sequences are in raw YUV format with a 4:2:0 pixel sample.

First sequence is a mobile tour, swiping through some applications. Although this sequence presents many different patterns, as home screen, music player and web browser, all frames are artificial, i.e. computer-generated, but sometimes mixed with real-word images. Moreover, it presents many text regions, and the content is scroll down and up along the sequence. It has 1,396 frames with a resolution of 720×1480 at 50 frames per second.

Second sequence is a video conference meeting using Zoom App. Although this sequence is also a mobile screen content, it is not computer-generated, but

Fig. 1. Mobile tour sequence.

the content is camera-captured, inside of large black uniform regions. It has 313 frames with a resolution of 1080×2340 at 30 fps.

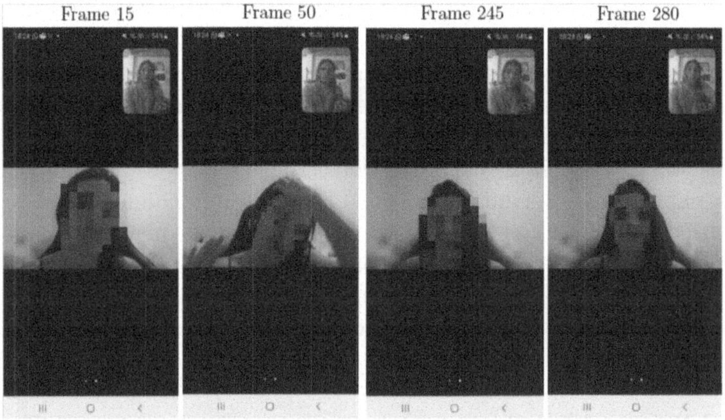

Fig. 2. Zoom meeting sequence.

Third sequence is a variant of a "tetris" game, called "candy crush", whose objective is fitting geometric shapes. It is a totally computer-generated artificial sequence. It has a fixed position with no scroll movement and has 608 frames with 1080×2340 pixels at 60 frames per second.

The fourth sequence is a mobile soccer game called "Football 2023". The adjustable position scene is automatically defined along the sequence. It has 740 frames with 2340×1080 pixels at 60 frames per second.

Technical information about the four created sequences is summarized in Table 1, and selected frames from each of the sequences are shown in

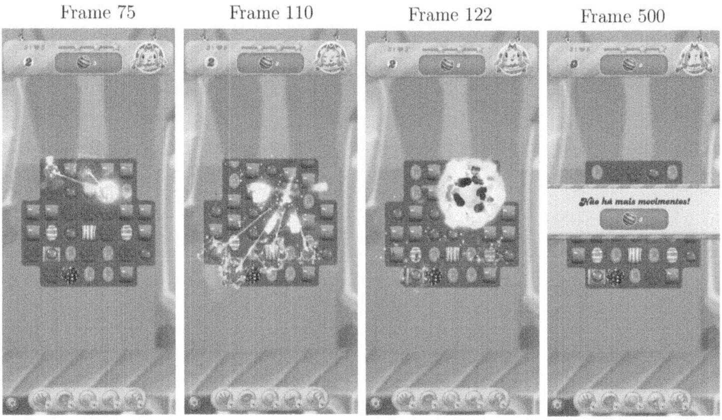

Fig. 3. Candy Crush sequence.

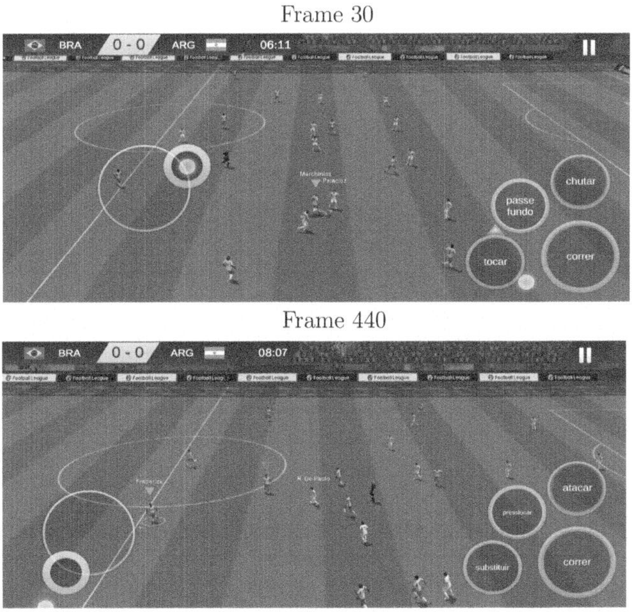

Fig. 4. Football2023 sequence.

Figs. 1, 2, 3 and 4. Note that even these are short period sequences, with from 10 to 27 s, all they have size of more than 1 GB in their uncompressed form, showing the need to use a video codec.

Table 1. YUV 4:2:0 raw sequence specifications.

Sequence	Resolution	Frames	FPS	Duration	Size (Bytes)
S9 Tour	720 × 1480	1396	50	27.55 s	2231366400 (2.1 GB)
Zoom Meeting	1080 × 2340	313	30	10.25 s	1186520400 (1.1 GB)
Candy Crush	1080 × 2340	608	60	10.07 s	2304806400 (2.1 GB)
Football 2023	2340 × 1080	740	60	12.20 s	2805192000 (2.6 GB)

3 Results

By investigating the performance of the new video codec H.266 VVC to encoding mobile screen contents, we use the reference software [6] over the four sequences described in Sect. 2, and we compare it with the reference software of its predecessor H.265/HEVC HM-16.13 [1], with and without the screen content module SCM-8.3. In both codecs, we use the "High Main" profile.

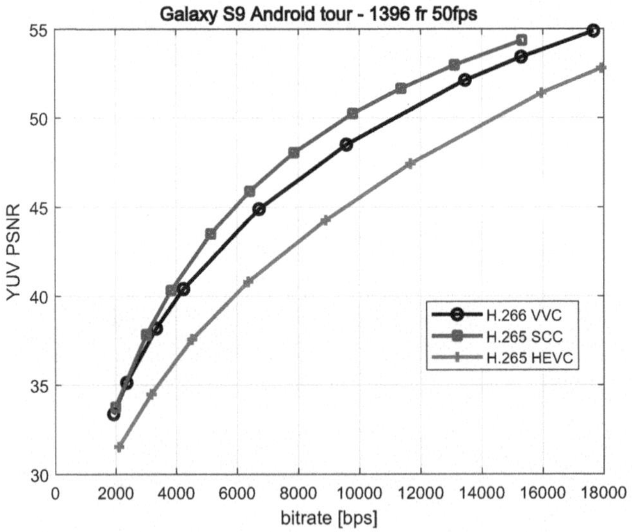

Fig. 5. Galaxy S9 tour sequence.

The plots from Figs. 5, 6, 7 and 8 show the behavior of the rate distortion (RD) curves over the sequences.

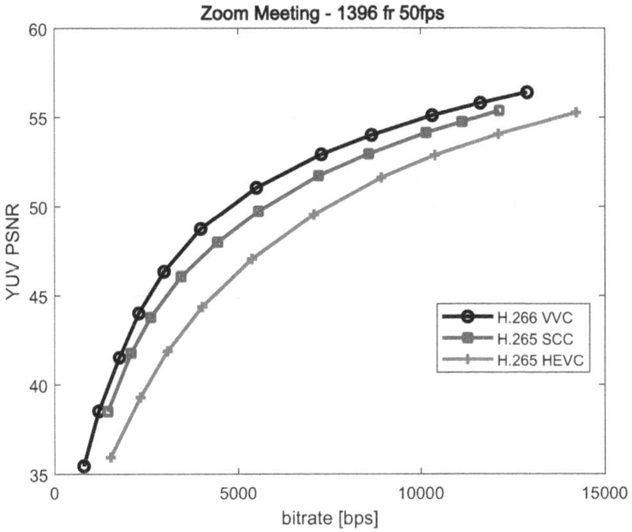

Fig. 6. Zoom meeting sequence.

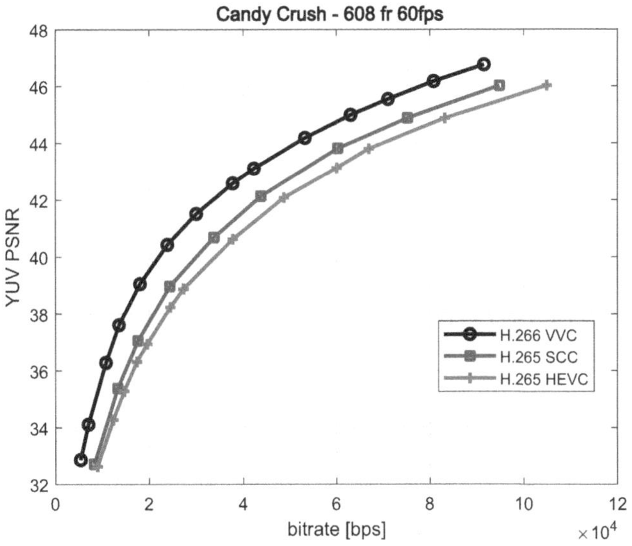

Fig. 7. Candy Crush sequence.

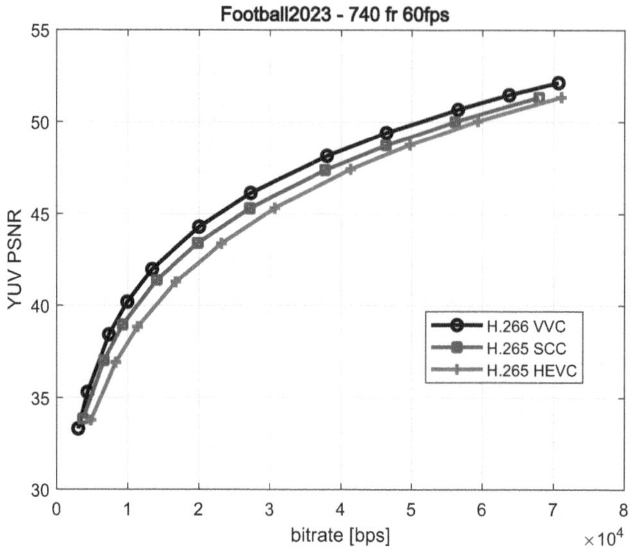

Fig. 8. Football2023 sequence.

We can clearly see that H.266 VVC overlaps H.265/HEVC without screen content coding (SCC) for all sequences. In general, it shows gains over 3 dB for some bitrate ranges, especially the middle ones, with a average reducing of 28% of bitrate. When SCC extention is enable, H.266 VVC codec is better for three of the four sequences. The exception is for "mobile tour sequence", which presents a mix of patterns between the Android home screen, music player, and web browser. As it presents many text regions along the sequence, these regions have many details and sharp edges in the outline of the letters, making it more difficult for a generic codec to encode these regions efficiently, so that the SCM extension increases the performance of H.265 to overlap H.266 / VVC along all rates, with an average of $\sim$ 11% less bitrate and 1dB more PSNR, as in Table 3.

Zoom meeting sequence has the greatest gain, with almost 4 dB in some ranges, and it shows the greatest reduction in bitrate, with about 38%, as in Table 2, since that sequence is a camera-captured scene with no computer-generated content, so that SCM does not make a significant difference, and a generic codec can efficiently encode it.

Table 2 summarizes the results for H.266/VVC versus H.265/HEVC, and Table 3 the results for H.266/VVC versus H.265/SCM. Values were obtained by using Bjontegaard delta [2], that represents the average of PSNR (Peak Signal-to-Noise Ratio) and bitrate along the RD curves.

In Table 2 we see that candy crush tetris game sequence has a gain average of 2.15 dB and a bitrate of 34. 87% lower on average. "Football 2023" sequence shows the minors gains, with average of 1.77 dB and 24.63% of bitrate reduction, since this sequence shows more uniform regions that can be coded by large blocks, and without many complex details for the players characters in the game. Note that sequence "zoom meeting" also presents many uniform regions, but there the details consist of natural faces, while in the football sequence it is an artificial video representation. Table 3 shows the H.266/VVC codec consistently overlaps its predecessor for the sequences "zoom meeting", "candy crush" and "Football 2023", even with screen content module enable.

Table 2. Bjontegaard results: H.266/VVC versus H.265/HEVC

Sequence	BD-BR (%)	BD-PSNR (dB)
S9 Tour	−28.05	3.21
Zoom Meeting	−38.49	3.84
Candy Crush	−34.88	2.15
Football 2023	−25.28	1.77

Table 3. Bjontegaard results: H.266/VVC versus H.265/SCM

Sequence	BD-BR (%)	BD-PSNR (dB)
S9 Tour	10.98	−1.03
Zoom Meeting	−15.55	1.30
Candy Crush	−26.80	1.53
Football 2023	−12.10	0.77

4 Conclusions

In this work, we successfully created a mobile screen content dataset with four uncompressed sequences consisting of common mobile usage. It is a class of video content that is not so tested in codecs yet, and they can be used to test the efficiency performance of a lot of other video codecs. We also tested them using the new H.266/VVC video codec standard and compared it with its predecessor H.265/HEVC with and without its mobile screen content module (SCM). The results show that H.266 beats H.265 for all sequences when SCM is disabled, by reducing the bitrate from 24% to 38%, and providing gains of almost 4 dB. When SCM is enabled, H.266 shows better results for three of four images, even being a codec for generic content. In fact, the only sequence for which H.266 did not overcome SCM is a computer generated content with many tesxts along the sequence.

As a suggestion for future investigations into this issue, we quote including the third-party codec AV1 over this kind of content and compare it to the standards.

Also we quote perform a real-time broadcast of the full screen of a mobile, investigating bandwidth size limitations and necessary adjustments of the codecs.

Acknowledgment. This work was presented as part of the results of the Harp Plataform 2.0 Project, carried out by Sidia Instituto de Ciência e Tecnologia in partnership with Samsung Eletrônica da Amazônia LTDA, according to IT Law n.8387/91, article 39, Decree 10.521/2020.

References

1. ITU-T: Reference software for ITU-T H.265 high efficiency video coding (2016). https://handle.itu.int/11.1002/1000/12947
2. Bjontegaard, G.: Calculation of average PSNR differences between RD-curves. ITU-T/SG16/Q6, Austin, Texas, USA (2001). document VCEG-M33
3. ITU-T: The SCM reference software for HEVC SCC development, version 8.8. https://hevc.hhi.fraunhofer.de/svn/svn_HEVCSoftware/tags/HM-16.19+SCM-8.8
4. ITU-T: Conformance specification for ITU-T H.265 High efficiency video coding. joint collaborative team on video coding, Rec. ITU-T H.265, ISO/IEC 23008-2 (2018)
5. ITU-T: Recommendation ITU-T H.264. H-Series: audiovisual and multimedia systems. advanced video coding v.14, ISO/IEC 14496-10 (2021)
6. ITU-T: Reference software for ITU-T H.266 versatile video coding (2022). https://handle.itu.int/11.1002/1000/14970
7. ITU-T, ISO-IEC: JVET common test conditions and software reference configurations. Document: JVET-J1010-v1 (2018)
8. Lopez, L.M.: Why H.264 is the most popular video compression standard (2022). https://www.videomaker.com/how-to/shooting/files-and-formats/h-264-the-most-popular-video-compression-standard. Accessed 13 Aug 2023
9. Petrov, C.: 51 Mobile vs. Desktop usage statistics for 2023 (2023). https://techjury.net/blog/mobile-vs-desktop-usage. Accessed 16 Aug 2023
10. ITU-T: Conformance specification for ITU-T H.266 Versatile video coding. joint collaborative team on video coding, Rec. ITU-T H.266, ISO/IEC 23090-3 (2023)

Exploiting American Patriotism in Influence Operations

April Edwards[1](✉), Peter Antonaros[2], Meyer Levy[3], and Dana Weinberg[3]

[1] Cyber Science Department, United States Naval Academy, Annapolis, MD 21402, USA
aedwards@usna.edu

[2] Applied Physics and Applied Mathematics Department, Columbia University, New York, NY, USA

[3] Sociology Department, Queens College, City University of New York, Queens, NY 11367, USA

Abstract. There is growing concern that mis/disinformation is used in social media campaigns to alter public opinion on important topics with broad societal implications. In this article, we explore the use of patriotic themes, defined in an American context, in social media for four recent politically charged events: the 2016 United States (U.S.) presidential election – which was subject to an influence campaign from foreign (Russian) sources, the 2020 U.S. presential election, the COVID-19 pandemic, and the 2022 U.S. mid-term elections. We demonstrate a clear negative bias through simple keyword analysis in the Russian influence operation and 2022 mid-term elections. The bigram analysis on the 2020 elections and COVID data did not show a similar bias in either a positive or negative direction. Thus, we use narrative extraction to perform a deeper dive into these corpora and identify the narratives that are prevalent. We conclude that keyword analysis is not sufficient in all circumstances, and that narrative analysis can fill the gaps. We further conclude that replies in social media can substantially reinforce negative discourse, but do not show a bias effect when the discourse is generally neutral.

Keywords: Social Media Analysis · Narrative Extraction · Influence Operations

1 Introduction

One of the purposes of disinformation campaigns is manipulation of public opinion. This can be done with tacit approval or direct involvement of state actors as with the widely recognized and often studied "Russian Influence Operation" and its involvement in the 2016 US Presidential Election (Zannettou et al. 2019; Consentino & Consentino 2020; Linvill et al. 2019; among many others). These influence operations often involve development of personas that add legitimacy, such as development of profiles or content that purports to be from members of the military (Weinberg et al. 2023) or other trusted groups (Couretas 2022).

In this article, we examine the appropriation of a deeply held concepts or values for use in influence operations. Specifically, we study the use of patriotic themes as

C. Stephanidis et al. (Eds.): HCII 2024, CCIS 2319, pp. 253–262, 2025.
https://doi.org/10.1007/978-3-031-78516-0_26

both an influencer and a "call to arms" in social media identity, particularly in times of political unrest. Although there is disagreement on how patriotism is measured (Huddy & Khatib 2007), there is consensus in the academic community that it can be defined as a "deeply felt affective attachment to the nation" (Conover & Feldman 1987) such as in the American National Election Studies (ANES). America is widely recognized for its patriotic nature, with 67% of Americans responding "Extremely" or "Very" to the question "How proud are you to be an American?" (Statista Research Department 2024).

Four major U.S. political events have played out in a social media context within the last decade: The 2016 Presidential Election (Trump vs. H. Clinton), the 2020 Presidential Election (Trump vs. Biden), the COVID-19 Pandemic (2020–2021), and the 2022 mid-year election cycle. Our study provides insight into the frequency with which patriotism appears as a theme in politically charged social media activity. We use a data science approach to understanding the context of these references.

2 Methodology

2.1 Data Sources

This study used social media activity on Twitter (now X™) from each of the four political events of interest. These data were collected in real time as events were unfolding, with the exception of the 2016 data, which was released by Twitter after the troll accounts that participated in the campaign were identified and removed (Twitter Moderation Research Consortium 2021). Table 1 describes the collection methodology.

2.2 Term Analysis

From the data described in Table 1, the project team extracted all tweets with the terms from a list of "patriotic themes", which included "patriot" or its variations – patriotic, patriotism, etc. (references to the New England Patriots football team were excluded), "oath", "constitution" – including references to constitutional amendments, "freedom" and it's variations, and explicit references to the "United States" (including U.S., USA, America, American, etc.).

Pre-processing. Before conducting the term and bigram extraction, special characters and emojis were removed, and the text was converted to lowercase. @mentions, hashtags, and links were also removed. Standard English and Spanish stop word lists from Python's *nltk* library (Bird et al. 2009) were applied to remove common words. Lemmatization using the *nltk WordNetLemmatizer* was also applied to reduce similar words to a common root. Remaining terms with fewer than three characters were removed.

Tweet Categorization. Tweets in each of the four datasets were separated into three categories: original posts, retweets, and replies to other tweets. In previous work, replies have correlated better with current events and appear to be "real opinions" as opposed to posts from "corporatized" accounts (Edwards, et al. 2023). Table 2 shows the distribution of data across the four corpora. Retweets were not used for this analysis as they tend to skew word counts without adding information about content. The density of tweets with patriotic themes was more prevalent in election related content, as would be expected. The density in replies is higher for all datasets except for the COVID-19 collection.

Table 1. Summary of Corpora

Corpus	Methodology
Russian Influence Operations	Retrieved from the Twitter Moderation Research Consortium
COVID	Huang et al. (2020) collected and posted COVID-related tweet IDs. We collected and rehydrated a random sample of 100,000 tweets per month from these data from Feb 2020-January 2022
2020 Election	Tweets were collected daily from the Twitter API using *Tweepy* (Roesslein 2020) in real-time based on a keyword search of *trump OR biden OR election OR 2020* from August 31, 2020 to March 20, 2021, multiple times per day until rate limits were exceeded. Tweets were subsequently rehydrated to obtain all data fields
2022 Election	Tweets were collected daily from the Twitter API using *Tweepy* in real-time based on a keyword search of *election OR midterm OR mid-term OR fraud OR stolen OR oath OR constitution* from August 31, 2022, to October 31, 2022, multiple times per day until rate limits were exceeded. Tweets were subsequently rehydrated to obtain all data fields. Additional data was collected for November/December 2022 but was not usable for this project because it was not rehydrated before the Twitter API for educators was discontinued. For this purpose of this project, only tweets containing *election OR midterm OR mid-term* were used for analysis

Table 2. Summary of Tweets with Patriotic Themes

Corpus	Num Tweets*	Num Replies	Density of Terms in Tweets*	Density of Terms in Replies
Russian Influence Operations	383,511	49,134	2.00%	3.43%
COVID	790,502	308,278	3.52%	2.41%
2020 Election	727,346	392,500	5.68%	5.75%
2022 Election	5,462,778	3,545,445	4.51%	4.60%

* Includes replies but not retweets

2.3 Narrative Analysis

To analyze the narrative content of the COVID-19 and 2020 Election corpora, we use a character-based model (Shahsavari et al. 2022; Tangherlini et al. 2020) which focuses on the actions and experiences of subjects and objects within a document. Following Chambers and Jurafsky (2009), we operationalize our character-based narratives as a "a tuple of an event (most simply a verb) and its participants" (p. 791). This approach allows us to look at all the actions which are taken by or toward any one actor, giving us the set of their interactions with other, and thus outlining the nature of their role within a corpus.

Preprocessing. All tweets were pre-processed by removing hashtags, web links, leading Twitter handles (@mentions), and unicode characters. Tweets were then segmented into sentences, which are delineated following typical sentence boundaries as well as new-line characters.

Feature Generation. In the feature generation step, we conduct sematic role labeling and generate BERT embeddings for each sentence. Semantic role labeling is a natural language processing technique which assigns roles to terms and phrases in text. These roles, which in our case follow the PropBank convention (Palmer et al. 2005), identify relationships between subjects, objects, verbs, and adverb modifiers, thus revealing the latent structure of a sentence. We perform this labeling using a neural network model provided by Gardner et al. (2018). BERT embeddings are generated by passing each sentence through a pre-trained neural network intended for text classification and retrieving the values of the final hidden layer before the output step. These values can be used as semantic features which richly represent something close to the underlying meaning of a statement. BERT embeddings are generated for each word or word-section, in the sentence. These embeddings are then matched to the phrases identified by the semantic role labeling step. Our pre-trained BERT model, "bert-base-uncased," was provided through the *transformers* python package (Wolf et al. 2019).

Relationship Clustering. Finally, we cluster the relationships from the semantic role labeling process in terms of our BERT embeddings. This clustering process consists of measuring the cosine similarity between the BERT embeddings representing each phrase representing a subject or object, building a network graph in terms of these similarities, and then performing Louvain community detection (Blondel et al. 2008) on this graph. We then recursively perform this process on each resulting cluster until all node-pairings within the clusters meet a cosine similarity of at least 0.9. After clustering subjects and objects, we perform the same process on the relationships themselves, which gives us our narrative families.

3 Results

3.1 Term Analysis

The results of the bigram analysis for the four datasets based on the patriotic theme filtering appear in Tables 3 (posts and replies, no retweets) and 4 (replies only). The bigrams for the 2020 Election and COVID datasets are about what would anticipate, with references to relevant topics, in a neutral tone. By contrast the results for the Russian Twitter Influence and 2022 Election data are markedly different.

Keeping in mind that the purpose of the Russian influence operation was to disrupt the normal election discourse for the 2016 US presidential election, with a noticeable preference for the election of one candidate (Trump) over the other (H. Clinton). The shaded terms include subtle and not so subtle racist comments, as well as calls to join a "U.S. Freedom Army," also referred to as the "Patriot Army," which has subsequently been suspended from Twitter (Schwartz & Ross 2019). The *usfreedomarmy.com* url also no longer references the same organization.

Table 3. Bigram Analysis (Original Posts and Replies, No Retweets) – Top 20 Terms

Russian Twitter Influence	2020 Election	COVID	2022 Election
patriot army	american people	american died	2020 election
enlist patriot	donald trump	american people	american people
america great	president trump	million american	midterm election
make america	united state	covid vaccine	fair election
president trump	president biden	died covid	election denier
african american	trump america	american covid	presidential election
trump make	million american	covid relief	election fraud
american fall	state america	covid death	election stolen
join patriot	25th amendment	american dead	election result
native american	white house	every american	free fair
american people	america great	coronavirus pandemic	overturn election
american dream	trump supporter	dead american	american election
united state	america first	many american	next election
donald trump	make america	wear mask	lost election
american pharoah	vice president	donald trump	election american
america enlist	american history	thousand american	steal election
stand america	america trump	american life	donald trump
first african	biden america	covid case	stolen election

The results for the 2022 US midterm elections were surprising. Typically, non-presidential elections in the US do not general much public discourse; however, after the hotly contested 2020 election, the reluctance of the losing candidate (Trump) to concede to the winner (Biden) caused an unprecedented series of events. These events culminated in an attack on the US Capital on January 6, 2021, in an attempt to prevent certification of the election results. The results of the 2020 election, and subsequent events, resulted in much higher engagement during the 2022 mid-term elections. It is telling the top bigram

Table 4. Bigram Analysis (Replies Only) – Top 20 terms

Russian Twitter Influence	2020 Election	COVID	2022 Election
hate america	american people	american people	2020 election
america hate	donald trump	million american	american people
native american	president trump	american covid	fair election
pocahontas awful	united state	american died	election fraud
awful senator	trump america	died covid	election stolen
senator racist	million american	covid relief	election denier
racist fraud	president biden	covid death	presidential election
fraud native	state america	many american	election result
america schumer	trump supporter	covid vaccine	free fair
schumer hate	america great	thousand american	overturn election
american crazy	dead american	dying covid	lost election
crazy bitch	25th amendment	donald trump	american election
america great	america trump	american dead	next election
make america	america first	american dying	steal election
american need	american dead	wear mask	stolen election
black people	make america	american citizen	election american
american people	american trump	america covid	every election
keeping america	american president	covid case	midterm election

in 2022 was "2020 Election" and there were multiple references to election fraud, an election being stolen, etc. (see shaded terms in Table 3).

We further analyzed the bigrams for replies only. As noted above, replies tend to track better with current events (Edwards et al. 2023) and are frequently from individuals rather than organizational news sources. As shown in Table 4 (shaded terms), the results within the replies were even more negative in the 2022 Election and Russian Twitter Influence data. The results for the COVID and 2020 election were neutral - similar to the all tweets (no retweets) results shown in Table 3.

3.2 Narrative Analysis

The topics of discourse from the patriotic themed filters for the 2022 Election and 2016 Russian Influence Operation were readily apparent from the bigram analysis. To determine the patriotic narratives used during the COVID-19 pandemic and 2020 election, we need to explore the interactions in the text more deeply. Using the methodology described in Sect. 2.2, we extracted subject-verb-object triads from the text. For the most frequently occurring themes that were not mere duplication of the same tweet (retweets were removed but there were multiple instances of individual(s) reposting the same tweet), we extracted the narrative as well as sample data to identify topics of discussion. The results were both interesting and surprising. In Tables 5 and 6 we show the narrative, frequency of occurrence, and a tweet which represents the "most central" example of the narrative in the data for the COVID and 2020 Election data, respectively.

COVID Data. The top three most frequently occurring narratives that are not mere repeats of a single tweet appear in Table 5, along with the number of times the narrative appears and sample text. In these data, we see that two of the three examples are presenting negative/snarky perspectives, directly attacking specific individuals. The third is more neutral, although still clearly directed at Vice President Pence. Unlike the bigram analysis for the Russian influence operations and 2022 election, the patriotic themes are treated in a disparaging manner – implying that those who hide behind "patriotism" are not considering what is best for the whole of the American population, but rather specific subgroups, often with conservative political leanings.

2020 Election Data. As with the COVID data, the top three most frequently occurring narratives for the 2020 election appear in Table 6, along with the number of times the narrative appears and sample text. Similar to the COVID data, we see more nuanced messaging and opposition to one party/candidate. However, it is also clear that the process for narrative extraction worked as expected, allowing us to summarize major themes in the patriotic extract from the corpus.

Table 5. COVID Tweets – Narrative Extraction – Top 3 Narratives

Narrative (Subject Verb Object)	Example Tweet (date/time)
You get COVID (n = 222)	@RepHarshbarger Other names considered: -the Just Get COVID and You'll Be Fine Act -the Real Patriots Aren't Afraid of a Virus but We Carry Guns Everywhere Act -the Vaccines are for Pussies Act -the Whatever Trump Said is Scripture Act Not sure why these didn't get any traction (2021-10-18 18:24:10)
The people lost loved ones (n = 134)	@IvankaTrump Congratulations to the small percentage of Americans who own stock and the wealthy that got the Trump tax cut. To the people who have lost loved ones to covid who are sick with covid lost their jobs/homes or who are standing in food lines not so much #TraitorBarbie. (2020-11-24 18:04:35)
We wear masks (n = 70)	@Mikeyvp Unfortunately masks are political. It's like guns for certain people… just extremely passionate about not infringing on their freedom of choice. Plus, if you believe COVID is overblown then masks have no purpose (2020-08-20 06:06:28)

Table 6. 2020 Election Tweets – Narrative Extraction – Top 3 Narratives

Narrative (Subject Verb Object)	Example Tweet (date/time)
tRump did what (n = 130)	@Katier1964 @bigbearzeus @StephenKing I won't say that everything Trump has done is wrong but I would like to see more valid accomplishments that helped all Americans and not just some Americans either way thanks for your response hope you have a good day (2020-09-09 14:59:44)
President Biden done more (n = 84)	@peterbakernyt @farhip @POTUS has done more in his limited time in Office than many Presidents in the Past! Please don t instigate trouble when he is doing everything Possible to help Americans and Undo Trump s Miserable Failure of the last 4 years! ENOUGH! (2021-03-14 18:59:37)
They do that (n = 77)	@mwr_dbm wow… they just flat out declared the intention to burn the Constitution. The GOP is in a panic. Trump must be dying for them to get this desperate. (2020-10-08 14:00:00)

4 Discussion and Conclusions

In this article we describe two approaches to deriving a greater understanding of patriotic themes in politically charged social media discourse. We have shown that simple bigram analysis can be a valuable tool for understanding the overall tone or demeanor in some cases but is insufficient in others. Narrative extract holds promise for the development of a more nuanced understanding when the discourse appears to be neutral or general.

We have further demonstrated that replies in social media posts appear to reinforce and perpetuate negative content, resulting in an even more combative environment. However, when the content is initially neutral, replies do not appear do skew the data in either a positive or negative direction.

Acknowledgments. This study was funded by Air Force Research Labs (AFRL award FA8650-22-2-6469). The views expressed are those of the authors and do not reflect the official policy or position of the United States Naval Academy, United States Navy, United States Air Force, United States Marine Corps, the Department of Defense or the United States Government.

Disclosure of Interests. The authors have no competing interests to declare that are relevant to the content of this article.

References

Bird, S., Klein, E., Loper, E.: Natural language processing with Python: analyzing text with the natural language toolkit. O'Reilly Media, Inc. (2009)

Blondel, V.D., Guillaume, J.L., Lambiotte, R., Lefebvre, E.: Fast unfolding of communities in large networks. J. Stat. Mech: Theory Exp. **2008**(10), P10008 (2008)

Chambers, N., Jurafsky, D.: Unsupervised learning of narrative schemas and their participants. In: Proceedings of the Joint Conference of the 47th Annual Meeting of the ACL and the 4th International Joint Conference on Natural Language Processing of the AFNLP, pp. 602–610 (2009)

Conover, P.J., Feldman, S.: Measuring patriotism and nationalism. ANES Pilot Study Report, No. nes002263 (1987)

Cosentino, G., Cosentino, G.: Polarize and conquer: Russian influence operations in the United States. Social Media and the Post-Truth World Order: The Global Dynamics of Disinformation, pp. 33–57 (2020)

Couretas, J.M.: Cyber influence operations. In: An Introduction to Cyber Analysis and Targeting, pp. 57–89. Springer International Publishing, Cham (2022)

Edwards, A., Metcalf, L., Casey, W.A., Chatterjee, S., Janwa, H., Battifarano, E.: Getting local and personal: toward building a predictive model for COVID in three united states cities. In: Latifi, S. (eds.) ITNG 2023 20th International Conference on Information Technology-New Generations. ITNG 2023. AISC, vol. 1445. Springer, Cham (2023). https://doi.org/10.1007/978-3-031-28332-1_2

Gardner, M., et al.: Allennlp: A deep semantic natural language processing platform. arXiv preprint arXiv:1803.07640 (2018)

Huang, X., Jamison, A., Broniatowski, D., Quinn, S., Dredze, M.: Coronavirus Twitter Data: A collection of COVID-19 tweets with automated annotations (2020). http://twitterdata.covid19dataresources.org/index

Huddy, L., Khatib, N.: American patriotism, national identity, and political involvement. Am. J. Politic. Sci. **51**(1), 63–77 (2007)

Linvill, D.L., Boatwright, B.C., Grant, W.J., Warren, P.L.: "THE RUSSIANS ARE HACKING MY BRAIN!" investigating Russia's internet research agency twitter tactics during the 2016 United States presidential campaign. Comput. Hum. Behav. **99**, 292–300 (2019)

Palmer, M., Gildea, D., Kingsbury, P.: The proposition bank: an annotated corpus of semantic roles. Comput. Linguist. **31**(1), 71–106 (2005)

Roesslein, J.: Tweepy: Twitter for Python! (2020). https://Github.Com/Tweepy/Tweepy

Schwartz, R., Ross, B.: Exclusive: Twitter Suspends 'US Freedom Army' Accounts After Alleged Connections to Russian Bots (2019). https://lawandcrime.com/exclusive/exclusive-twitter-suspends-us-freedom-army-accounts-after-alleged-connections-to-russian-bots/. Accessed May 2024

Shahsavari, S.: Automated conspiracy theory detection and narrative consensus tracking in social media. University of California, Los Angeles (2022)

Statista Research Department. U.S. level of pride to be an American 2023 (2024). https://www.statista.com/statistics/261561/proud-to-be-american/#:~:text=67%20percent%20of%20the%20American,branding%20patriotic%20imagery%20or%20symbols

Tangherlini, T.R., Shahsavari, S., Shahbazi, B., Ebrahimzadeh, E., Roychowdhury, V.: An automated pipeline for the discovery of conspiracy and conspiracy theory narrative frameworks: Bridgegate, Pizzagate and storytelling on the web. PLoS ONE **15**(6), e0233879 (2020)

Twitter Moderation Research Consortium (2021). https://transparency.x.com/en/reports/moderation-research.html. Accessed 29 March 2024

Weinberg, D., Dawson, J., Edwards, A.: How the russian influence operation on twitter weaponized military narratives. In: International Conference on Cyber Warfare and Security, vol. 18, no. 1, pp. 431–439 (2023)

Wolf, T., et al.: Huggingface's transformers: State-of-the-art natural language processing. arXiv preprint arXiv:1910.03771. https://arxiv.org/pdf/1910.03771 (2019)

Zannettou, S., Caulfield, T., De Cristofaro, E., Sirivianos, M., Stringhini, G., Blackburn, J.: Disinformation warfare: Understanding state-sponsored trolls on Twitter and their influence on the web. In: Companion Proceedings of the 2019 World Wide Web Conference pp. 218–226 (2019)

Effect of a Movement Imagery-Based Fashion Model Walking Program Using Kinect on EEG Activity and Cognitive Function

SungHee Hong(✉), SunHee Park, and SunOk Jung

Dongduk Women's University, 60 Hwarang-ro 13-gil, Seongbuk-gu, Seoul, South Korea
hongsungh22@hanmail.net

Abstract. The purpose of the study is to investigate changes and differences in brain wave activity and cognitive function between fashion model walking movement programs based on movement imagery using Kinect. The purpose of this study is to investigate changes and differences in brain wave activity and cognitive function between fashion model walking movement programs based on movement videos using Kinect. The subjects of the study were elderly women, and the program was conducted 10 times per session. As a result of the study, first, significant differences were found in brain wave activity. It has been shown to improve cognitive skills related to attention and problem solving. Second, in the case of cognitive function tests, it was found that there was a significant positive effect based on the rhythm of the steps. In the walking learning program using Kinect, the activity effect according to EEG measurement was found to be higher in the 4-beat step and 2-beat step exercise programs than the pose movement.

Keywords: Kinect · Movement Imagery · Fashion model walking · EEG Activity · Cognitive Function

Laban (1974) analyzed walking, the most basic human activity, as effort, one of the movement analysis (LMA) categories, and analyzed the space required to create internal emotions and attitudes about how to move as a qualitative aspect of movement.), weight, time, and flow are used in walking movements. The fashion model's walking movements are complex with the flow and intensity of time-continuous energy from the stage appearance to the end of the stage exit, and present internal expressions such as the relationship between the stage and the audience. The body image of a model walking on the runway is expressed as confidence, with movements that indicate correct posture and body balance. A fashion model's walking is an individual's unique body movement expression that effectively utilizes body shape, muscle movement, and energy utilization. In other words, temporal elements of movement energy such as strength, speed, and rhythm, rhythmic elements of music, and spatial elements related to body movement are needed. Fashion model walking is a comprehensive art of movement that aesthetically expresses body relaxation and movement through posture correction and practice. Relaxation and movement movements are differentiated from general simple walking, which is expressed with continuity, and show the effect of correcting the body's posture and body shape. Several recent studies have suggested that cerebral cortical activity

C. Stephanidis et al. (Eds.): HCII 2024, CCIS 2319, pp. 263–271, 2025.
https://doi.org/10.1007/978-3-031-78516-0_27

is involved in human walking. Through a study using positron emission tomography, the motor cortex and including sensory cortex several brain regions Reports has been activated. However, the brain imaging technique has low temporal resolution and has limitations in observing dynamic changes in cerebral cortical activity according to the gait cycle. Human walking involves input and feedback from the cerebellum, motor cortex, and basal ganglia, as well as feedback from visual, vestibular, and proprioceptive sensors. It is a complex non-linear process that integrates (Harsdorf 2007). This means that walking relies on high-level cognitive function (Ambani, Bar one & Harsdorf 2013), and cognitive function and gait pattern can be seen as closely reflecting brain function (Watson et al. 2010). In cross-sectional studies, slow walking speed is associated with cognitive decline (Ver linden, van der Geset, Hoffman & Ikram 2014), mild cognitive impairment (Varghese, Wang, Lipton, Holzer & Xue 2007), and dementia (Munoz et al. 2010), and longitudinal studies have shown that people with slower walking speeds have faster cognitive decline (Mielke et al. 2013; Calisaya et al. 2015). Various characteristics appear in the walking speed and behavior patterns of elderly people. In general, walking speed tends to decrease due to a decrease in muscle strength and balance ability due to aging. Additionally, it is observed that the stride length decreases when walking and the movement of the knee joint and ankle joint decreases. Unstable walking patterns increase the risk of falls, which poses a major threat to the independent living and health of the elderly. Safe walking occurs when the body's center of gravity is well established. Gait and body alignment are both important issues for health and safety.

As you age, flexibility decreases and muscle strength weakens, which can lead to problems with gait. Elderly people need to practice walking safely in various places through a walking program. Body alignment required for walking is a way to maintain posture and balance in the elderly. Elderly people may lose posture as their strength and flexibility decrease due to aging. To prevent this, you must maintain balance and correct your posture through body alignment exercises. Gait is related to brain function, and the area that integrates the automatic and voluntary movements required for walking exists in the frontal lobe (Nielsen 2003; Morton & Bastian 2004). In addition to being responsible for executive functions including attention and working memory (Erickson & Barnes 2003), the prefrontal cortex is functionally connected to the hippocampus and influences walking (Mangas et al. 2005). Since this kind of gait is completed through the appropriate interaction of various cognitive areas, it shows a clearer correlation in tests such as the MMSE (Mini Mental State Examination) total score, which measures the degree of the overall cognitive area rather than individual cognitive areas (Han Jeong-hoon, Seongwook Lee, Geonwoo Park 2013). Game online exercise training is a technology that is attracting attention in the fields of modern cognitive science and rehabilitation. This method can assess an individual's cognitive and motor skills by measuring brain activity and functional connectivity. Game-based training can also help you improve your motor skills in a fun way. By analyzing the measured data, you can design a customized cognitive training program by identifying the individual's cognitive function, attention, memory, and executive ability. Kinect's depth sensor and motion tracking capabilities allow you to capture your movements with precision. By connecting this with the Unity 3D engine, you can simulate the user's walking in a virtual environment in real time. Combining Kinect's accurate motion data with Unity3D's lifelike graphical rendering can create highly realistic and immersive gait images that can be used in a variety of applications, including balancing and gait analysis. By combining Kinect's high-resolution depth sensor and Unity3D's photorealistic graphics rendering, we can deliver a realistic virtual walking experience. Game-based exercise training is a method of improving exercise ability using fun game content. By combining various sensors and virtual reality technology, it monitors the user's movements in real time and provides feedback. Through this, users can gradually improve their exercise abilities while having fun exercising. It was found that simple game forms that repeat static, similar patterns are suitable for the elderly, and games that increase interest and restore confidence through comparison with others are suitable. Motion detection technology using the Kinect sensor has recently been used in various fields. The goal of this study is to capture the natural walking movements of fashion models with Kinect and analyze how walking training in a virtual environment changes brain waves and cognitive functions based on this. It is known to be particularly effective in exercise rehabilitation and cognitive ability improvement. In this study, we sought to determine whether a Kinect-based movement training program could be used to improve brain wave activity and cognitive function. In addition, the goal is to create a walking learning model using deep learning through walking practice to make walking possible regardless of place and time. Through this, we will be able to develop innovative content that can be used in various fields such as games, animation, and medical rehabilitation.

1 Methods

1.1 Fashion Model Walking Posture Program Production

Walking posture recognition is extracted after comparing the specific color area of the skeleton of the input image generated through the Kinect motion camera with the color information. Calculate the angle and slope between the extracted areas to determine whether to walk. This is a character created with the Unity 3D program. The movement of the character along the angle and slope calculated through the character makes it easier to understand the content. This process was expressed more realistically by using the humanoid control function tool. Following Kinect, the official name of the program used for production is 'Unity'. Among them, we are creating in the 'Unity URP 3D' environment. The Universal Render Pipeline (URP) is a pre-built scriptable render pipeline created by Unity. URP helps you quickly and easily implement optimized graphics on various platforms such as mobile, high-end consoles, and PC through an artist-friendly workflow. Issuetracker.unity3d.com Unity was used. Unity is a program used when developing games, and it has good interoperability with the current program, C#. The animation function of was used. In the currently produced program, a program was developed that detects human motion and displays motions that humans can imitate in front of their eyes so that users can follow them while watching them on the screen.

1.2 Research Design

The progress of the program design was determined as the concept of the game. One doctor of dance (movement analysis), two doctors of model studies (Kinect walking video demonstrators are two PhDs majoring in modeling and have worked as domestic and foreign models for many years. Fashion Show has had experiences such as Louis Vuitton, Celine, YSL, Valentino, Gucci, Prada, Fendi 2002 Bazaar of the Year Award, 2002 Modeling in Paris Fashion Shows – CHANEL, HERMES fashion show, and one dance movement analyst participated.), and Kinect program technicians participated in setting up the fashion model walking motion. Participants were asked to follow the movements of their avatars on the game screen. At the same time as the walking action avatar appears, the participant's appearance is also projected on the screen as an avatar. When adjusted to a certain level of motion, the score of the motion ratio increases, and a 'ding-dong' sound is heard and the next walking motion proceeds. This was set for the adaptability and motivation of the game, and the values of the skeleton's joints and axes were assigned to each action according to the recognition of the walking action.

Participants were seated on a Bio Steps tepper(Biodex Medical Systems Inc., Shirley, NY). While wearing a 64-channel EEG electrode cap, stepper walking was performed consistently at a gait cycle of 10 times per minute using a stepper monitor, and the electrodes were placed according to the traditional 10 to 20 electrode placement method. In this study, a 19-channel (F7, Fp1, Fp2, F8, F3, Fz, C3, Cz, P8, P7, Pz, P4, T3, P3, O1, O2, C4, T4) headset EEG device (Q20r, CGX) was used. Ltd., USA) was used to collect data 10 times from senior women. During the experiment, auditory stimulation was provided every 4 s to enable one movement to be performed within 3 s, and the measurement was performed at a sampling frequency of 500 Hz per second. The range of analysis frequencies is the alpha, beta, and sub-gamma regions were designated as 8 to 80 Hz (Fig. 1).

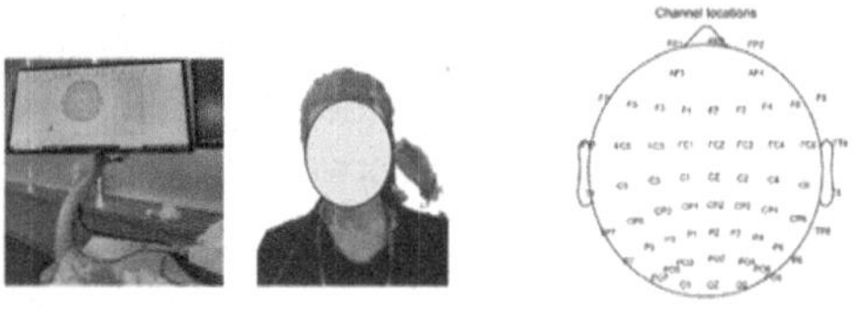

Fig. 1. Experimental setup and location of EEG electrodes

1.3 Azure Kinect

Kinect depth sensor and motion tracking capabilities allow it to precisely capture the user's movements. By linking this to the Unity 3D engine, you can simulate the user's walking in a virtual environment in real time. When Kinect's accurate motion data and Unity3D's vivid graphic rendering are combined, very realistic and immersive walking images can be created, which can be used in various application fields such as balancing and gait analysis. Combining Kinect's high-resolution depth sensor and Unity3D's realistic graphic rendering can provide a realistic virtual walking experience. Through this, innovative content that can be used in various fields such as games, animation, and medical rehabilitation can be developed (see Fig. 2).

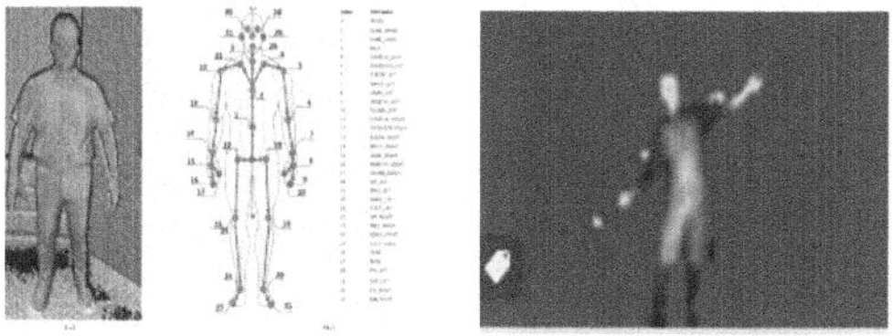

Fig. 2. Main components of the frame (https: azure.microsoft.com)

1.4 Motion Recognition Program Progress

The first scene of the walking motion calculates the spinal axis and joint values for by recording the individual's brief name, gender, and date of birth (see Fig. 3).

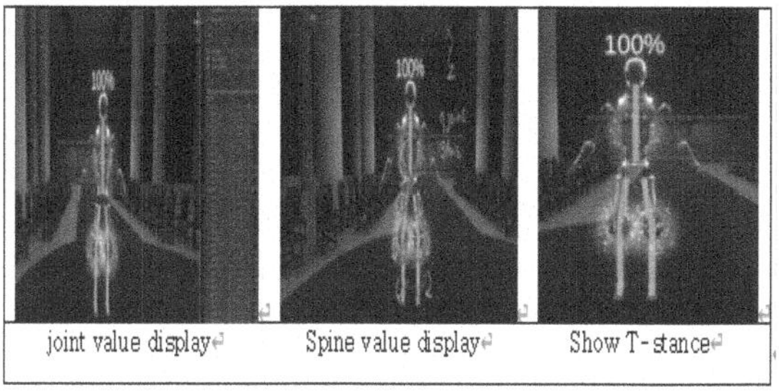

Fig. 3. Program motion recognition progress.

The humanoid is manipulated using a humanoid control function called Human Pose within the Unity3D program (name of model and each joint). Just as a real person makes a specific motion by contracting and relaxing muscles, posture is controlled by bending and extending muscles related to each joint. The amount of error is calculated by comparing the triaxial contraction values of each muscle. Spine error. thigh error, knee error, and ankle error are added and averaged. The match rate is indicated as a minimum of 0% and a maximum of 100%. In case of mismatch, it is displayed in red, and in case of agreement, it is displayed in green. When the match rate is 60% or higher, glitter is displayed to indicate match. Calculate the relative position of the pelvis based on the position of the two legs of the model. The position of the pelvis of the user's two legs reference model is display ed as a blue cylinder and a red line to visually indicate how distorted the position of the user's pelvis is. 4 Fashion model walking posture measurement (see Fig. 4).

The standing pose, walking pose, and turn pose were photographed as separate motions. Walking and turn animations were filmed in real time. This data is utilized for comparison with the user's working data is. Model walking was divided into 4 steps. (See Fig. 5).

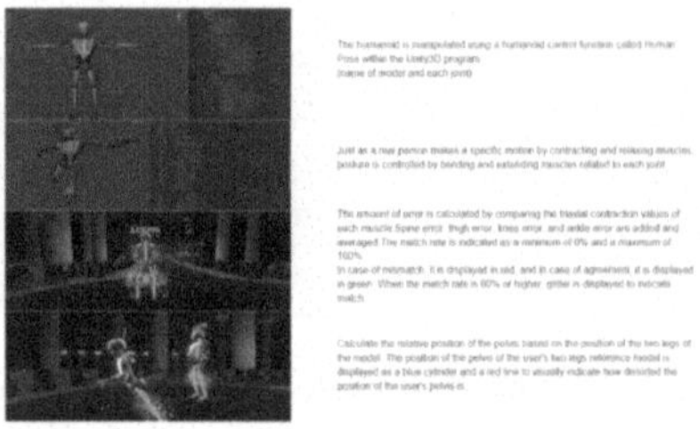

Fig. 4. Humanoid model and names of each joint and axis

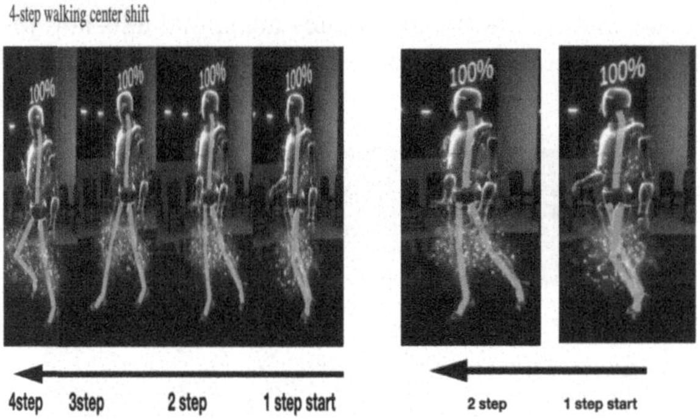

Fig. 5. Walking 4-step, 2-step centering process

2 Result

Motions are scored as a percentage of the skeleton based on the player's ability to perform the motion. A bell and percentage score were added if the movement exactly matched the picture of the Kinect skeleton displayed on the screen. Data on motion performance during and after participation in the motion game were evaluated. For each motion calculation, Unity 3D's Human Pose library was used to record 3 axes: pose data for a total of 7 joints (see Fig. 6), and 21 of the 95 joint values of the model pose skeleton.

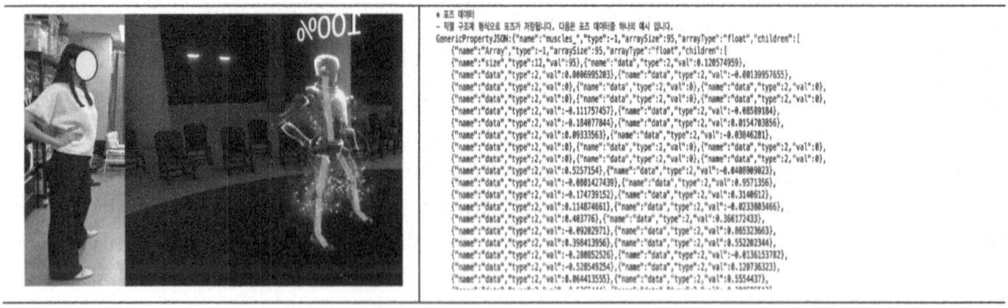

Fig. 6. Pose data processing.

A visual effect appeared on the screen to help participants perceive changes in scores. When walking motion matches the skeleton, it changes to a green color and a percentage number appears. If the skeletons do not match, a red color appears, and the colors change in order of red-yellow-green until the center movement is aligned (see Fig. 7).

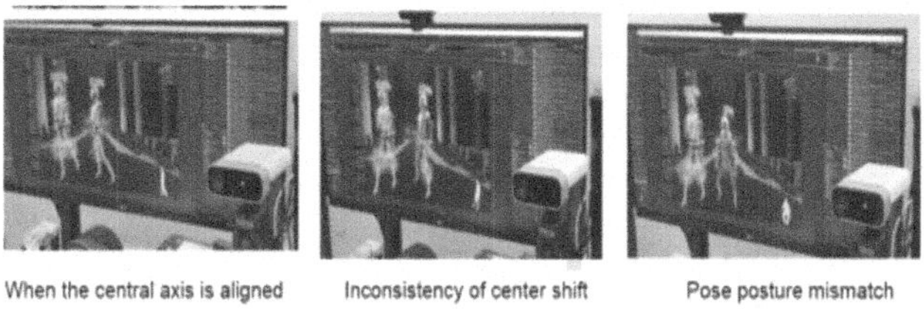

Fig. 7. Skeleton central axis, walking joint position, appearance in case of congruence and mismatch of posture.

3 Conclusion

As a result of running this study's program, participants were found to have good body center of gravity balance in the pose-motion posture, and the agreement rate increased as they participated in Kinect practice. The walking movement appeared at normal speed only up to the two stages (see Fig. 8).

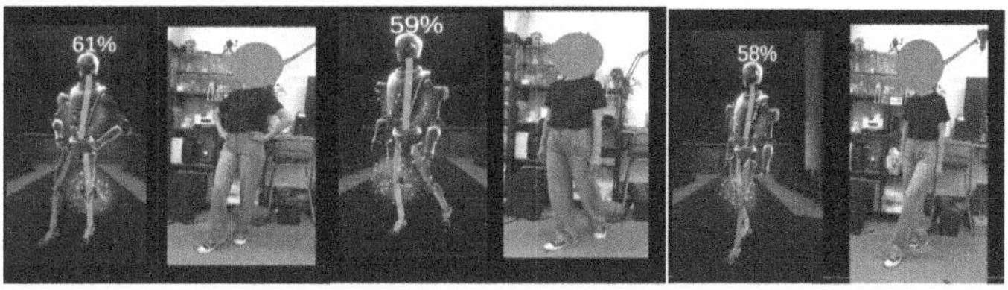

Fig. 8. Working program implementation.

In this study, walking and three poses were selected as case studies and ratios were measured. To organize the data, data was collected through the posture of the movement according to the game movement, and when the movement matched the program, a ding-dong sound feedback was given to increase the score. On the other hand, the ratio is lower in scenes where the participant's posture represents inconsistent behavior. He expressed himself on the screen and confirmed his movements through it. Testers received a sparkling visual effect when the bones matched. 4-beat step walking showed relatively low classification accuracy. Relatively low classification accuracy was derived between 4-beat step walking and 2-beat step walking. To test the effectiveness of the walking learning program implemented in this study, participants were given 10 learning sessions divided into before and after walking. This study was conducted to examine the effects of brain wave training on brain wave activity and cognitive function because of physical exercise enhancement.

First, the effect of exercise through the walking learning program, and second, analyzing the effect on brain wave activity and cognitive function through the walking learning program, 67% to 86% in the 4 steps before implementation of the walking learning program, and 70% in the 2 steps before implementation. Showed a high score of 75% after implementation, and in pose movement, a high score of 81% before implementation was shown and 92% after implementation (see Fig. 9).

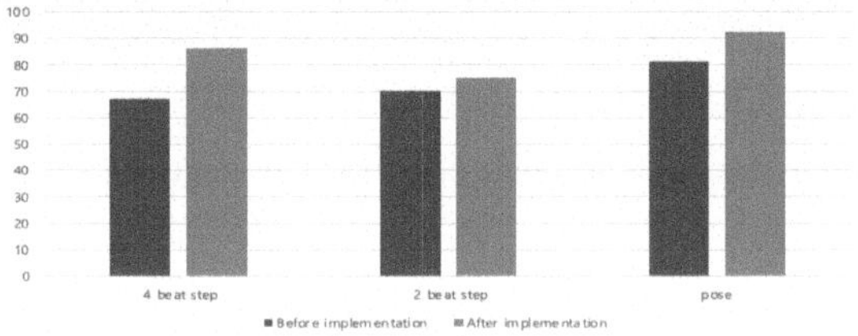

Fig. 9. Working program implementation.

4 Suggestions

In this study, we were able to measure brain wave activity while participants walked.It is expected that it can be used to observe changes in gait-related cortical activity and its functional recovery in brain disease patients. Kinect walking learning can classify walking patterns from actual brain wave motion recognition. Through this, we were able to confirm the applicability of actual motor brain waves in the field of walking assistance and rehabilitation, and it is expected that it will be able to increase the walking stability of patients by playing an assistive role appropriate for cognition.

Changes in beta wave (β wave) activity showed changes in cognitive activities such as alertness, concentration, and problem solving, and an increase in beta wave activity was observed before and after the program. This suggests that participants' cognitive function improved. Brain activation and efficiency are improved through regular training.

Changes in alpha wave (α wave) activity are related to a comfortable state of alertness, stability of mind, and creativity. After participating in the program, alpha wave activity tended to increase. This can be interpreted as the participants' psychological stability and positive emotional state improving, and regular participation in activities contributing to the improvement of brain-psychological health.

Changes in theta wave (θ wave) activity A significant increase in theta wave activity was observed after the program. This can be seen as a result that reflects the participants' psychological relaxation, improved concentration, and improved memory. It can be suggested that regular participation in activities helped improve the overall cognitive function and psychological state of elderly women.

Overall, this program is judged to have had a positive effect on brain activation, cognitive ability improvement, and psychological well-being in elderly women, and it is expected that the quality of life in old age will improve through continued participation in the program.

By analyzing measured data, you can understand an individual's cognitive function, attention, memory, executive ability, etc. This allows you to build an individual's cognitive profile, which can be used in a variety of fields. This study can be used in the field of education to evaluate students' learning abilities and develop customized educational programs. Additionally, in the medical field, it can help detect cognitive decline in patients early and develop appropriate treatment plans. In this way, cognitive function evaluation can be said to be an important field that can contribute to improving the quality of life of individuals and the development of society. Overall, this program is judged to have had a positive effect on the brain activation, cognitive ability improvement, and psychological well-being of elderly women, and it is expected that the quality of life in old age will improve through continued participation in the program.

References

Laban: Effort Economy of Human Movement: Laban, Rudolf, Lawrence, F. C.: Amazon.co.uk: Books (1974)

Harsdorf, M.: The role of emotional intelligence in leadership effectiveness. Unpublished doctoral dissertation, University of Southern California, Los Angeles (2007)

Ambani, P., Bar-One, L., Harsdorf, M.: Exploring the relationship between emotional intelligence and leadership effectiveness. J. Manag. Psychol. **28**(7/8), 755–770 (2013)

Watson, A.J., Lovelock, J.E., Margulis, L.: Biological homeostasis of the global environment: the parable of daisyworld. Tellus B: Chem. Phys. Meteorol. **35**(4), 284–289 (2010)

Verlinden, V.J., van der Geest, J.N., Hofman, A., Ikram, M.A.: Cognition and gait show a distinct pattern of association in the general population. Alzheimers Dement. **10**(3), 328–335 (2014). https://doi.org/10.1016/j.jalz.2013.03.009

Munoz, R.I., Lauzen, M.M., Real, M.R.: Influences of ethnic diversity and gender on students' multicultural competence. J. Educ. Media Library Sci. **48**(1), 21–42 (2010)

Mielke, J., Vermaas, P.E., Zwart, S.D., Mulder, B.: Competitive renewable electricity market designs in an agent-based model. Compet. Regul. Network Indust. **14**(2), 112–146 (2013)

Calisaya, P., Garcia, H.A., Hooijmans, C.M., Brdjanovic, D.: Assessment of current wastewater treatment plants in Bolivia. J. Water Sanitat. Hygiene Develop. **5**(3), 426–437 (2015)

Nielsen, J.: Usability 101: Introduction to usability. Nielsen Norman Group (2003). https://www.nngroup.com/articles/usability-101-introduction-to-usability

Morton, H., Bastian, J.: Assessing the switch from face-to-face to online learning. Int. J. E-Learn. **3**(3), 27–38 (2004)

Erickson, L.D., Barnes, G.M.: The relationship between the gender context of adolescent friendship groups and their drug use. Adolescence **38**(149), 59–78 (2003)

Han, J.H., Lee, S., Park, G.: The impact of interoperability on BPMS performance in the health insurance industry. Inf. Syst. Front. **15**(3), 1–14 (2013)

Habit Instigation vs Execution Related Behavior Change Techniques (BCT) in Mobile Intervention for Physical Activity: A Systematic Review and a z-curve Analysis

Hyun Seon Kim and Alison L. Phillips(✉)

Iowa State University, Ames, IA 50011, USA
estherk@iastate.edu

Abstract. This is a work-in-progress report on the systematic review and a z-curve analysis on mobile interventions for physical activity. We outline the primary and secondary goals and details of the methods for this review in this presentation. The current literature does not fully explain why certain behavior change techniques (BCTs) work and do not work in mobile interventions. We use the habit instigation vs execution processes in attempt to explain the effectiveness of the BCTs.

Keywords: Digital Health · Physical Activity · Habits · Mobile Interventions · Systematic Review

1 Introduction

Physical activity is crucial to living a healthy lifestyle, but many have trouble keeping physical activity consistent over long-term or find it difficult to even initiate such routines in their daily lives. One of the ways to maintain behavior change is by developing habits. Recent literature has identified several ways a habit could develop - through habit instigation, habit execution or both [1]. For many years, researchers have used technology (e.g. mobile applications, wearables, etc.) to promote physical activity and maintain the behavior change [2]. Some of the typical manipulations are – priming participants with certain concepts, asking participants to set goals and many others that will either help overcome barriers to behavior change or strengthening existing cognitive pathways to maintain behavior change [3].

The current literature does not fully capture the mechanism behind the behavior change and maintenance. Therefore, we propose that the behavior change techniques that contribute to behavior change and maintenance are related to either habit instigation or execution. We suggest that outlining the theoretical frameworks in behavior change and identifying what types of interventions were most effective will help future researchers to develop more successful and effective interventions. Medical professionals, health psychologists and application developers can work together to build more relevant and effective intervention to promote physical activity.

C. Stephanidis et al. (Eds.): HCII 2024, CCIS 2319, pp. 272–275, 2025.
https://doi.org/10.1007/978-3-031-78516-0_28

The primary goal of this review is to identify effective behavior change techniques that are used in mobile interventions to promote physical activity among adults (18–65 years old) and compare the effectiveness of the different accounts of habit formation (habit instigation, habit execution or both). The secondary objectives of this work would include: (1) To review the ways physical activity has been measured, (2) To review the ways habit has been measured, (3) To review the ways mobile interventions have been delivered, (4) To evaluate the possible presence of publication bias or questionable research practices in this area of research, (5) To evaluate the quality of the primary studies that have investigated this research question, (6) To evaluate the use of open science practices among researchers in this area.

2 Methods

To ensure the quality of the systematic review, the guidelines given by Preferred Reporting Items for Systematic Reviews and Meta-Analysis (PRISMA) were used [4].

To be included in this review, the study must be an intervention study aiming to test the effectiveness of the mobile intervention to promote physical activity. Only experimental study design (with a proper control group) will be considered for inclusion. One of the outcome variables must be reporting levels of physical activity (whether frequency, volume or other forms) or any form of habit related to physical activity. The study must use a mobile application or wearable device to be considered for inclusion. A mixed approach (using both mobile application and texting) will be considered for inclusion. Studies that are published and peer-reviewed or unpublished studies in the forms of dissertation or thesis will be considered for this review. The first mobile application was introduced by the Apple app store in 2008. Therefore, only studies from 2008 and onwards will be eligible for this review. Only studies written in the English language will be considered for this review.

Study participants in the reviewed articles must be legally old enough to sign their own informed consent without parental guidance (above 18) and participants who are considered under the category of adults (18–65 years old) as defined by the APA will be eligible. Younger children will not be eligible as they are under supervision of older adults and such supervision may affect the intervention and the outcomes. Participants from all countries and of all races are considered for this review. Older adults will not be considered for this review because older aged participants may have other unreported health or physical complications that may affect the outcome of the intervention. Participants mean age for each study will be coded. Participants with reported mental or physical health complications will be eligible for the review but this group of participants will be coded separately. Some studies that may contain participants with age range of 50–80 years old. For such studies, we will include their data as long as the mean age of the participants are within the 18–65 years old range.

If it is evident from the paper that they exclusively present statistically significant results, the paper will not be considered for the review. This could manifest in various ways. For instance, authors may provide a correlation matrix that excludes non-significant correlations. Alternatively, they may present multiple statistical findings, with some being statistically significant and others not, without explicitly reporting the non-significant results (e.g., by stating that the analysis yielded non-significant results). Another approach could involve an explicit statement from the authors indicating their intention to only report significant effects, among other possibilities.

The search term we used are as follows: abstract("intervention" OR "interventions" OR "experiment" OR "experiments" OR "RCT" OR "randomized controlled trial" OR "randomized controlled trials" "controlled trial" OR "controlled trials") AND abstract ("mobile" OR "fitbit" OR "smartphone" OR "smart" OR "app" OR "application" OR "mhealth" OR "wearable" OR "digital") AND abstract (("physical activities" OR "physical activity") OR "exercis*" OR "weight change" OR "weight loss" OR "weight maintenance" OR "fitness"). The database we used were PsychInfo and PubMed. Out initial search gave us 894 articles.

After searching through the mentioned databases, the first author will gather all the studies into Endnote. The other coders and the first author will then screen these articles based on their title and abstract to remove articles that do not fit into the eligible criteria. The included articles will be collected in a shared online drive folder. Then the other coders and first author will read these articles in full text and code the variables indicated below. Each coder will be assigned to equal amounts of articles but different articles. After the first round of coding has been completed, one coder will be assigned to code random 25% of the articles coded by another coder. If the coding agreements are above 90% for the two coders, double-coding will stop there. If it's below 90% agreement, the second coder would have to code all of the articles coded by the first coder. Coders will always refer to the first author is they want to clarify any part of the process. After the coding process, the first author and the supervisor (the last author) will review the behavior change techniques used in each study and code them for habit instigation, habit execution, both or none.

Data collection will be completed by two coders. The first coder will enter data and the data will be double-checked by the second coder. Disputes will be resolved through discussion between the two coders and the lead author. Both coders will use the same coding scheme, constructed in Qualtrics survey. Effect size computation for mean differences will be done using the Campbell Collaboration calculator, which is available online. The coding requires some training to understand the exact protocol and criteria. This training will be during a lab meeting where I will explain the process to the other members involved. Meanwhile, the last author (who is an expert in habit research) will work on labeling which behavior change techniques in the official taxonomy relate to habitual instigation, habitual execution, both or none. After data has been extracted from the study reports, lead author and supervisor (last author) will address the variable "behavior change techniques" and use the official taxonomy of behavior change techniques to label the type of intervention used.

Firstly, a z-curve will be used to estimate predicted replicability, power, and publication bias of the selected literature and select literature that are "certain" and reliable. The z-curve will also tell us what kind of effect sizes to look out for to label the intervention as "effective". Next, we will perform meta-analysis on the effectiveness of the intervention by habitual instigation vs habitual execution vs both vs none. Random-effects meta-analysis will be used, and the standard deviation of rho will be used to assess heterogeneity. Other methodological data will be presented descriptively in tables.

3 Results

Currently, this project is a work-in-progress. We are at the stage of screening the 894 articles on Endnote and Qualtrics. Further analysis is pending at the moment. You can view the progress of the project on Open Science Framework (OSF) (link).

References

1. Gardner, B., Phillips, L.A., Judah, G.: Habitual instigation and habitual execution: definition, measurement, and effects on behaviour frequency. Br. J. Health. Psychol. **21**(3), 613–630 (2016). https://doi.org/10.1111/bjhp.12189
2. Zhu, Y., Long, Y., Wang, H., Lee, K.P., Zhang, L., Wang, S.J.: Digital behavior change intervention designs for habit formation: systematic review. J. Med. Internet Res. **26**, e54375 (2024). https://doi.org/10.2196/54375
3. Han, M., Lee, E.: Effectiveness of mobile health application use to improve health behavior changes: a systematic review of randomized controlled trials. Healthcare Inform. Res. **24**(3), 207 (2018). https://doi.org/10.4258/hir.2018.24.3.207
4. Moher, D., et al. PRISMA-P Group: Preferred reporting items for systematic review and meta-analysis protocols (PRISMA-P) 2015 statement. System. Rev. **4**(1), 1 (2015). https://doi.org/10.1186/2046-4053-4-1

Development of a Virtual Human Based Interactive Kiosk

Jae-Hwi Kwon and Chang Joo Lim(✉)

Tech University of Korea, Siheung City, Gyeonggi-do 15073, Republic of Korea
scjlim@tukorea.ac.kr

Abstract. While kiosk usage has been increasing since the spread of COVID-19, the usage rate of the elderly has been only about half. In order to replace the menu-based touch-type kiosk, an interactive kiosk using virtual humans was proposed and implemented in this study.

For the efficiency of implementation, the VHTK (Virtual Human Toolkit) developed by the USC (University of Southern California) is used to create virtual humans, and interactive voice synthesis and recognition functions for ordering and payment are implemented.

We used Kakao's voice synthesis API as a voice input/output function. We also used the 'Meta's Oculus Lip-sync' to replace the existing character-based lip-sync function with a voice analysis-based lip-sync for the virtual human lip-sync animation. Using the developed program, we applied it to a kiosk that responds to customers at cafes.

A preliminary experiment was conducted for usability evaluation. In the future, through this experiment, in-depth usability study is needed on the low-aged and elderly people who are uncomfortable using menu-based touch-type kiosks.

Keywords: voice recognition · virtual human · interactive kiosk · lip-sync

1 Introduction

As the contact-less era continues after the spread of COVID-19 in 2019, the use rate of kiosks which can be ordered and paid non-face-to-face is increasing (Table 1) [1]. However, unlike the increase in kiosk penetration, only half of the people prefer to buy kiosks. Among them, it was found that the proportion of people in their 50s and older prefer direct orders was higher (Fig. 1) [2]. As the proportion of the elderly in Korea is increasing, it is necessary to increase the demand of the elderly to increase the use rate of kiosks [3]. According to the results of a survey on the inconvenience of kiosks, it was found that the highest percentage of people aged 60 or older had difficulty reading the screen [2]. To solve this problem, we develop a system that adds a voice recognition-based ordering method to the kiosk. Through this, we hope to expect the result of increasing kiosk accessibility to the elderly and groups that are difficult to use lettering means.

C. Stephanidis et al. (Eds.): HCII 2024, CCIS 2319, pp. 276–280, 2025.
https://doi.org/10.1007/978-3-031-78516-0_29

Table 1. Usability Assessment Questionnaire

year	Increase rate kiosk (%)
2019	66.7
2020	106.7
2021	45.2

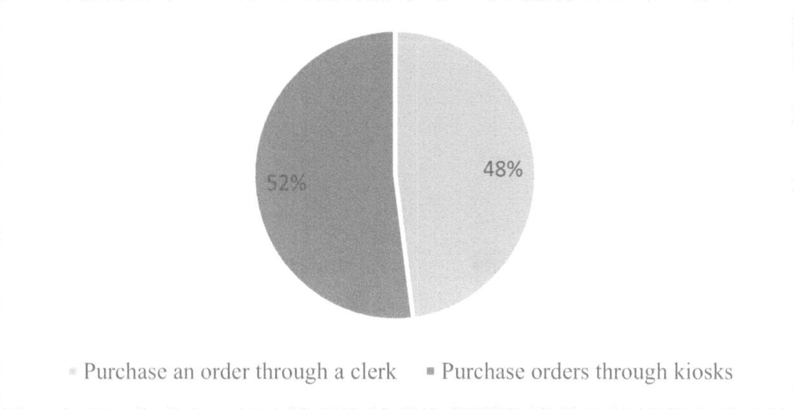

Fig. 1. Investigate order purchase preferences through kiosks

2 Development

It was aimed to develop kiosks that take orders from ordinary cafes. It consists of order request-menu (Fig. 2), selection-payment method (Fig. 3) and selection-payment order. And you can ask questions about anything other than the order by using a dialog button or voice before ordering. All orders can be received through voice recognition, and it is possible to simply click the button to order.

It was developed to operate in a Korean environment while maintaining the basic form of the Virtual Human Tool Kit (VHTK). VHTK is components that support the creation of virtual human conversation characters developed by USC (University of Southern California) [4]. When a command is input through voice recognition, it finds the most appropriate answer and action in a pre-written dialogue, outputs the voice to TTS (Text to Speech), and the character takes the appropriate action on the screen operated by Unity 3D.

The voice part operates using Kakao API [5]. After sending a mic-recorded voice file to the API through REST to obtain a text sentence, the recognized sentence uses CLOVA Chatbot to find and print the appropriate answer according to the pre-written dialogues [6]. When processing Chatbot's API, a server was created and connected with Python [7].

Since the existing VHTK lip-sync is designed to be played based on English text, it was necessary to implement a new lip-sync system to implement lip-sync of Korean characters. Accordingly, Oculus' OVRLipsync plug-in was used to change from a text-based lip-sync system to a voice file-based lip-sync system.

The newly implemented lip-sync system adds a Shape Key corresponding to each pronunciation supported by the face part of the modeling, analyzes the voice file being played, and lip-sync is performed through a combination of Shape Keys [8].

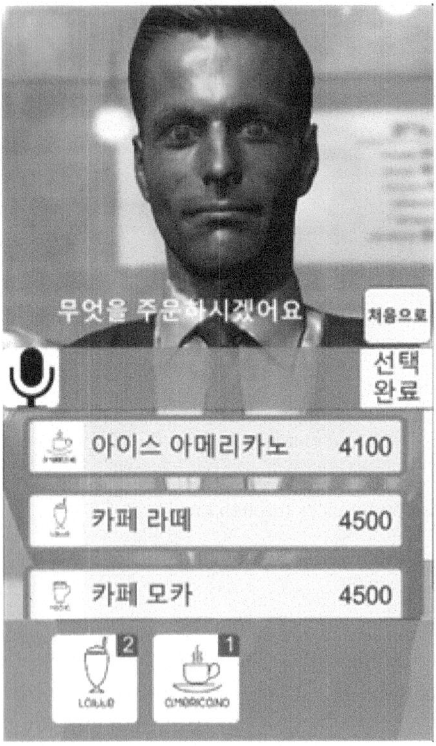

Fig. 2. Menu Selection Page

Fig. 3. Select payment method page

3 Pilot Test

Before conducting this experiment on a prototype of an interactive kiosk, we conducted a pilot test with two people who developed the corresponding interactive kiosk. To verify the validity of the developed interactive kiosk, we compared usability for two methods: ordering using voice and ordering using button.

3.1 Test Environments

Experiment Scenario. The experiment was conducted in two ways, voice, and button, respectively (Fig. 4).

Fig. 4. Order scenario of the experiment

Evaluation. The evaluation criteria for the test were evaluated as a total of 15 points, 5 points for each of the following three questions, and the comparison was conducted with the total score of the results (Table 2). Questions 1 to 3 were used as indicators of the ease of understanding, flexibility, and efficiency of kiosks, respectively.

Table 2. Usability Assessment Questionnaire

1. The process of ordering was not difficult	1~5
2. Even if the ordering system changes, it would be easy to order	1~5
3. It would be easy to order in the current way even if it is a complicate order	1~5

3.2 Result

As a result of the pilot test, there was no difference in ease of understanding and efficiency, but there was a meaningful difference in flexibility, with a difference of 1 point and 2 points, respectively (Tables 3 and 4).

Table 3. Results from a test through button

Q1	Q2	Q3
4	4	3
5	3	3

Table 4. Results from a test through voice

Q1	Q2	Q3
5	5	3
5	5	3

4 Conclusion

The reason why the virtual human based interactive kiosk is better than the existing kiosk is that it is expected to be available to people who cannot read or feel uncomfortable. What is missing is that simply receiving orders in the voice recognition section is easy to recognize, but it is as difficult to get out of context or answer questions as much as people. The pattern of dialogue was insufficient to call it a conversation with an actual person. This could be improved in the future by replacing AI, which processes natural language, with OpenAI's ChatGPT or Naver's Hyper CLOVA X, which is scheduled to be released soon. In addition, it is difficult to see the same conversation with voice and simple movements, supplementary measures such as eye contact using a camera are needed.

This paper was supported by Korea Institute for Advancement of Technology (KIAT) grant funded by the Korea Government (MOTIE) (N00012725, The Competency Development Program for Industry Specialist).

References

1. Ministry of Agriculture, Food and Rural Affairs of Korea., A Survey on the Management of Restaurant Companies., 2021, 2023.03.22, Force terminals and unmanned ordering machines (kiosks) are used
2. Lee, D.H.: Hankook research weekly report, vol. 92–93, pp. 5–6. Hankook Research (2020)
3. KOSTAT. Statistics of the elderly in 2021, pp. 16–19 (2022)
4. Hartholt, A., et al.: All together now: introducing the virtual human toolkit. In: International Conference on Intelligent Virtual Humans (2013)
5. Kakao Corp. Kakao Voice API. https://developers.kakao.com/docs/latest/ko/voice/rest-api
6. Naver Corp. Clova Chatbot. https://api.ncloud-docs.com/docs/ai-application-service-chatbot
7. Unity3D Python Communication. https://github.com/off99555/Unity3D-Python-Communica tion
8. 2022 Meta. Oculus Lipsync for Unity Development. https://developer.oculus.com/documenta tion/unity/audio-ovrlipsync-unity/?locale=ko_KR

Revitalizing Community Identity Through Interactive Art Installations: A Case Study of Gan Zhu Tan Hydropower Station in Zuotan Village

Jie Ling[1], Ran Wang[1], and Li Ou Yang[2(✉)]

[1] Zhongkai University of Agriculture and Engineering, Guangzhou 510220, Guangdong, China
[2] The Guangzhou Academy of Fine Arts, Guangzhou 510261, Guangdong, China
oylee@163.com

Abstract. Community cultural construction significantly enriches the spiritual lives of residents and plays an irreplaceable role in promoting mutual understanding and unity among community members. The Ganzhutan Hydropower Station in Zuotan Village is a significant memory for the residents there. Due to its avant-garde and interactive nature, the interactive art installation has attracted both residents and tourists, serving as a vital medium for them to engage with local history and culture. Having been abandoned for many years, the Ganzhutan Hydropower Station once made a remarkable contribution to the Foshan Shunde area and remains a historical memory cherished by the older generation. However, as time passes, this historical and cultural knowledge has faded, with limited awareness among the younger generation and even less among tourists. Thus, this study aims to strengthen community historical and cultural construction through interactive art installations, which plays a critical role in promoting the historical and cultural significance of the Ganzhutan Hydropower Station and enhancing residents' cultural identity. This research utilized observational methods to identify the main activity nodes of residents and tourists, and interview methods to gauge their interest in local history and culture. The historical culture of the Ganzhutan Hydropower Station in Zuotan Village was selected as the subject for designing the interactive art installation. This installation uses light and sound to allow residents and tourists ($n = 42$) to simulate the electricity generation process of the hydropower station, enabling local residents to revisit memories of the hydropower station and educating tourists about its historical and cultural background. The study demonstrates that the introduction of interactive art installations significantly propels community cultural construction. This innovative artistic form not only deepens the residents' understanding and experience of the local hydropower station's historical culture but also stimulates their sense of community identity and pride. Moreover, these installations enrich tourists' visiting experiences, promoting the historical culture of the Ganzhutan Hydropower Station and the spiritual culture of Zuotan Village. These findings hold significant implications for the role of artistic interventions in cultural construction. In the discussion, we explore the positive impacts of interactive art installations on community historical and cultural construction, offering guidance for further exploration of artistic interventions in community cultural development.

C. Stephanidis et al. (Eds.): HCII 2024, CCIS 2319, pp. 281–291, 2025.
https://doi.org/10.1007/978-3-031-78516-0_30

Keywords: Installation art · Community environment · Community culture

1 Introduction

1.1 Relevant Policies

Nationally, the "Thousand Villages Demonstration, Ten Thousand Villages Renovation" [1] initiative aims to comprehensively rejuvenate rural areas. For Zuotan Village, this initiative not only supports cultural development but also lays a foundation for long-term growth.

In response, Guangdong Province launched the "High-Quality Development Project for Hundreds of Counties, Thousands of Towns, and Ten Thousand Villages." [2] This project selects exemplary counties, towns, and villages to lead rural development province-wide. Zuotan Village, with its unique geographical benefits, rich culture, and proactive governance, has been chosen as a prime example.

Locally, Zuotan Village prioritizes the preservation and inheritance of its culture through various activities, facility development, and talent nurturing, enriching its cultural life and enhancing its image externally. This cultural advancement has not only propelled economic development but also bolstered the villagers' cultural confidence and identity, revitalizing the rural community.

Under these policies, Zuotan Village actively enhances its cultural landscape, preserving and promoting its rich local heritage and contributing to sustainable development.

1.2 Problem Statement

This study introduces interactive art installations at the Ganzhutan Hydropower Station in Zuotan Village to deepen visitors' and residents' understanding of its historical culture. These installations go beyond mere displays; they combine creative design with technological interaction, plunging participants into the area's rich historical narratives. Residents revisit their storied past, while tourists gain firsthand experiences of the area's unique history and culture, boosting their knowledge and emotional ties to the region. This approach not only creates a new channel for conveying historical culture but also fosters cultural exchange among community members and tourists.

1.3 Research Purpose

As interactive art evolves, it extends beyond traditional settings like galleries, becoming a versatile contemporary art form in various spaces. Its growing popularity brings art closer to the public and amplifies its impact significantly.

The project aims to enhance understanding of the Ganzhutan Hydropower Station's history through artistic installations, offering immersive sensory and interactive experiences that boost the village's cultural vitality and communicate its historical essence to a wider audience. By leveraging interactive and experiential elements, these installations not only reinforce community pride but also enrich visitors' experiences, providing a fuller appreciation of the station's historical context.

1.4 Research Significance

Practical Significance. Implementing interactive art installations in Zuotan Village enriches local culture and attracts tourists. These installations enable deeper exploration of the village's history, enhancing visitors' connections with the area. This innovative approach not only enriches the village's cultural narrative but also reshapes its spatial and cultural identity.

Interactive installations integrate the locale's spatial and historical essence, becoming a key exploratory tool. By enhancing the area's cultural fabric and displaying its heritage, these installations elevate the village's cultural profile, especially as the Ganzhutan Hydropower Station becomes a pivotal cultural feature.

Academic Significance. The introduction of interactive installations is crucial for advancing research in community history. These installations open new research avenues and revitalize historical preservation efforts. By vividly presenting Zuotan Village's history through practical applications, they enhance public understanding of the Ganzhutan Hydropower Station's past, facilitating the preservation and development of community history while providing valuable insights for academic inquiry.

2 Literature Review and Related Work

2.1 Literature Review

Interactive art installations are a dynamic and evolving art form, recognized for their diverse interpretations across various academic fields. Scholars contribute their unique perspectives based on their backgrounds and expertise, enhancing the depth and breadth of this art form. Lin Yonglian (2018) highlights the interactive nature of these installations, noting how they engage audiences and stimulate their senses, allowing for personal interpretation and intellectual exchange that generate new meanings.[3] Du Chengwei (2019) elaborates on the contemporary aspects, emphasizing the integration of computer technology and interactive media that transform public spaces with innovative display methods.[4].

Fan Zijie (2022) expands on the inclusivity of interactive installation art, which merges traditional cultural elements with modern expressions to create experiences that resonate with contemporary and traditional audiences alike. She stresses that this is not simply replication but a sophisticated design process that blends cultural insight with technological innovation.[5].

Recent contributions from Li Xiaojia and Zhang Yi (2023) discuss how interactive installations break conventional boundaries by fostering a direct, intuitive connection between the artwork and the viewer, enhancing the accessibility of the artist's concepts.[6].

Guo Dayao (2018) discusses the use of regional cultural symbols—like Shaanbei's paper-cutting, Luoyang's peonies, and Beijing's sugar figurines—as a means to enrich the cultural identity of spaces, making them more recognizable and distinct.[7] Dai Yongbing, Xu Xiaon, and Chu Haifeng (2021) also emphasize the importance of deeply integrating local cultural elements into design to showcase regional uniqueness and enhance artistic and cultural value.[8].

Yu Zhi (2023) sees interactive art installations as a form of avant-garde public art that can significantly influence community engagement and cultural development, particularly in historic districts.[9] Xie Yaping and Lu Feng (2023) highlight the role of these installations in revitalizing rural culture by facilitating a deeper connection with and reflection on one's cultural roots, which is essential for fostering local cultural identity and invigorating rural communities.[10].

Through comprehensive research, it is evident that interactive art installations serve as more than just art; they are pivotal in cultural transmission and innovation. By combining regional cultural symbols with modern technology and sophisticated design, these installations provide new aesthetic experiences and ways for audiences to engage with culture, thereby playing a critical role in cultural dissemination, community engagement, and the revitalization of public spaces.

2.2 Conclusion

This study advocates for the innovative use of interactive art installations in community cultural construction, aiming to infuse Zuotan Village with new energy. Inspired by the rich history of the Ganzhutan Hydropower Station, this initiative seeks to deepen the village's cultural heritage. The goal is for the interactive installations to not only evoke cherished memories among residents but also to boost their cultural pride and identity. These installations will enable both residents and tourists to forge a deeper connection with the village's land and history. For tourists, the installations provide a vivid portrayal of the hydropower station's development and its impact on local socio-economic growth, enriching their cultural appreciation of Zuotan Village.

3 Methodology

3.1 Introduction

This study utilizes observational and interview methods to accurately identify key activity areas within Zuotan Village and to understand the local interest in the history and culture deeply. The Ganzhutan Hydropower Station's historical culture was chosen as the primary focus, with the aim to develop interactive art installations that enhance this experience.

3.2 Research Design

The design of this study is structured to deepen our understanding of how residents and visitors of Zuotan Village perceive and engage with the Ganzhutan Hydropower Station's historical heritage and interactive art installations. The methodology includes conducting telephone interviews with selected residents and distributing electronic surveys via alumni networks and social media platforms, such as Xiaohongshu (Little Red Book). These tools collect diverse viewpoints on the historical importance and cultural impact of the installations, helping tailor the project to community and tourist expectations more effectively.

The multi-channel approach of this study ensures a comprehensive collection of authentic viewpoints from both community members and tourists, providing a robust foundation for the design of interactive installations and enhancing our understanding of cultural construction needs within the community.

3.3 Data Collection Techniques

Interview Method. Interviews are conducted either face-to-face or over the phone to collect detailed insights into individuals' perceptions of the Ganzhutan Hydropower Station. Questions are open-ended, such as inquiries about the station's history and its cultural impact, prompting respondents to share personal views and experiences. This method not only gathers rich qualitative data but also helps gauge the emotional and cultural resonance of the hydropower station within the community.

Observational Method. Observations focus on understanding why certain areas in Zuotan Village, like the riverbank, are popular among both residents and tourists. This method assesses the area's role as a transport hub, its recreational offerings, and its function as a social gathering spot. Observations help clarify how these spaces serve the community's needs and highlight the riverbank's importance as a vibrant center of daily life and interaction.

3.4 Presentation of Results

Interviews reveal a deep respect for the Ganzhutan Hydropower Station among the residents, who view it as a symbol of local pride. However, generational differences in knowledge about the station's history are evident, with older residents possessing more detailed memories and emotional connections, often involved in its construction. Younger residents, while less informed, show enthusiasm for learning through proposed interactive art installations, which are also seen as a means to engage more deeply with their heritage.

Furthermore, observational data provide insights into the strategic importance of the riverbank area, confirming its role as a hub for transport, tourism, and social interaction. This comprehensive understanding of how different areas are utilized assists in further refining the focus and placement of interactive installations to maximize their impact and accessibility.

These methodologies together paint a detailed picture of how the Ganzhutan Hydropower Station is interwoven with the community's fabric, guiding future efforts to enhance local engagement and cultural preservation through art and interaction.

4 Preliminary Analysis and Design Presentation

4.1 Project Overview

Site History. The Ganzhutan Hydropower Station, a testament to Shunde's manufacturing prowess, was entirely produced locally—from screws to generators and turbine blades. This embodies Shunde's spirit of intelligent manufacturing. The station's history is marked by challenging conditions, as captured in a local rhyme describing the perilous Ganzhutan waters that once caused frequent drownings. On January 1, 1971, a transformative project began to tame these waters, culminating in the construction of the Ganzhutan Tidal Power Station—a project that unified the community and took over three years to complete. Early attempts to establish the station date back to 1934, but it was not until 1970 that efforts materialized, reflecting a commitment to self-reliance. Upon completion, the station enhanced navigation, controlled flooding, and integrated power, navigation, and water management, drawing global expertise for study. Although no longer operational, the station now serves as an educational base, continuing its legacy by educating Party members on leadership and perseverance.

4.2 Survey of the Audience

A survey conducted among 50 participants, with 42 effective responses (11 from residents and 31 from tourists), assessed familiarity and interest in the Ganzhutan Hydropower Station's history and the desired features of interactive installations. The findings reveal a general lack of awareness but a strong interest in learning more about the station, particularly through interactive installations involving light and sound, which were favored for enhancing the visitor experience (Fig. 1).

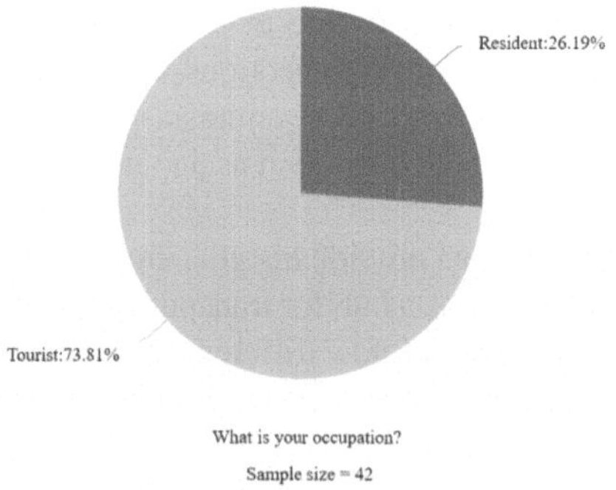

Fig. 1. Identity (n = 42)

In the conducted survey, the findings revealed that a significant majority of respondents (52.38%) are entirely unaware of the historical and cultural background of the Ganzhutan Hydropower Station. Only a small fraction (4.76%) reported having a comprehensive understanding of the station, while 26.19% possessed some basic knowledge, and 16.67% had heard of the station but lacked a detailed understanding. Overall,

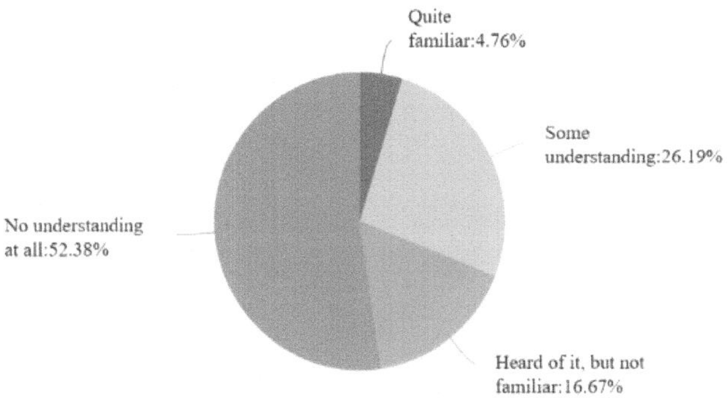

Fig. 2. Distribution Map of the Understanding of the Historical and Cultural Knowledge of the Ganzhutan Hydropower Station in Zuotan Village. (n = 42)

these results indicate a prevalent lack of familiarity with the history and culture of the Ganzhutan Hydropower Station among the participants (Fig. 2).

Analysis of the data extracted from the graphical representation indicates a strong inclination among the majority towards learning about the historical and cultural aspects of the Ganzhutan Hydropower Station. Specifically, 46.15% of respondents expressed a high level of interest, an identical percentage (46.15%) showed interest, while none of the respondents were neutral. Only a small minority of 7.69% displayed disinterest. These statistics underscore a general enthusiasm among participants to engage with the history and culture of the Ganzhutan Hydropower Station (Fig. 3).

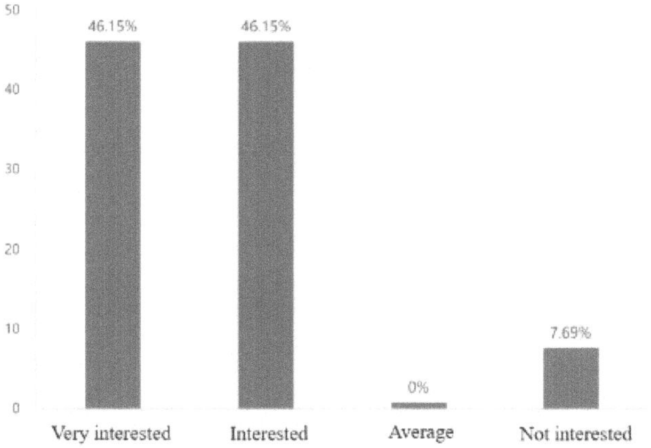

Fig. 3. Statistical Chart of Audience Perceptions of the Historical and Cultural Significance of the Ganzhutan Hydropower Station. (n = 42)

In the survey, this was a multiple-choice question. The final results show that respondents believe interactive art installations reflecting the history and culture of the Ganzhutan Hydropower Station, particularly those involving light and sound, would be the most captivating (Fig. 4).

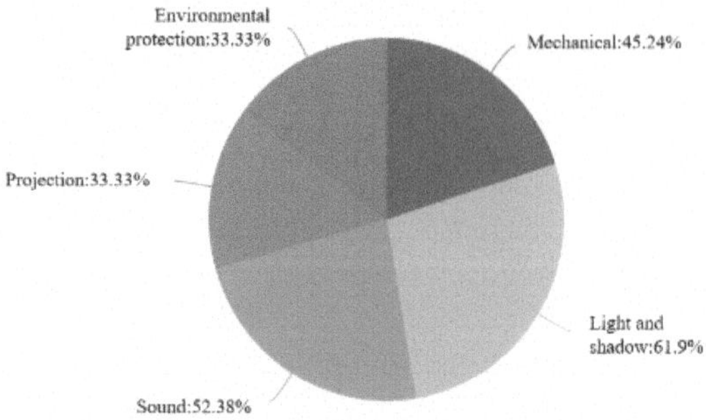

Fig. 4. Statistical Chart of Audience Preferences for Art Installations. (n = 42)

The final results indicate that people believe interactive art installations reflecting the history and culture of the Ganzhutan Hydropower Station would enhance public understanding of the local history and culture, as well as enrich their tourism experience (Fig. 5).

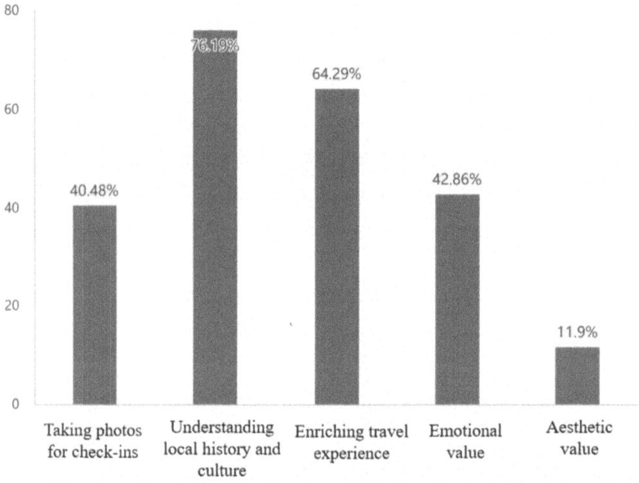

Fig. 5. Statistical Chart of Audience Expectations from Interactive Installations. (n = 42)

These insights are instrumental in designing installations that effectively convey the historical significance of the Ganzhutan Hydropower Station and engage both residents and tourists in meaningful ways, thereby enriching their cultural and educational experience at the site.

4.3 Presentation of Results

The survey results have been pivotal in shaping the design of the interactive installations. Named "Era of Endeavors," the installation aims to immerse visitors in the transformative history of the Ganzhutan Hydropower Station. It uses modern technology to create an interactive environment where movements trigger auditory and visual effects that simulate the hydropower generation process. The installation's design features mirror materials and flower-shaped lights made from laser-cut acrylic, which reflect colorful patterns and adjust in brightness in response to visitor interactions, enhancing the dynamic and engaging nature of the exhibit (Figs. 6 and 7).

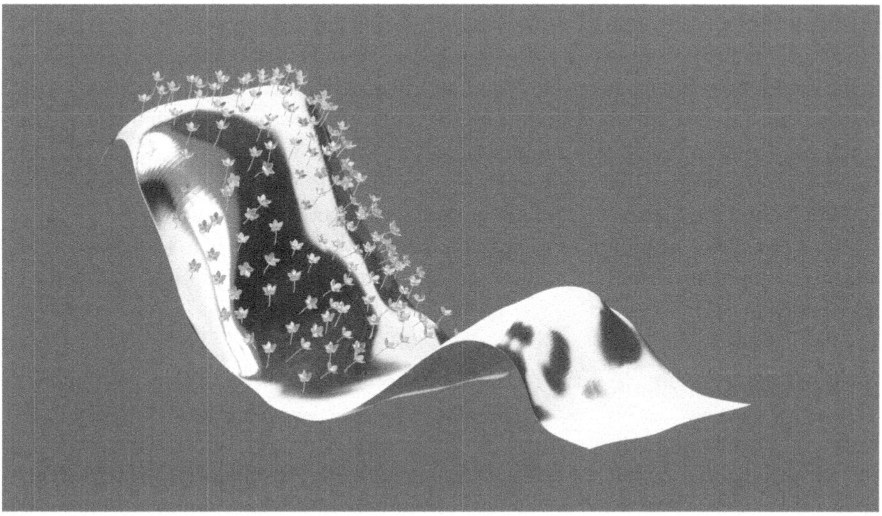

Fig. 6. Interactive Art Installation Renderings. Source: Designed by Ran wang

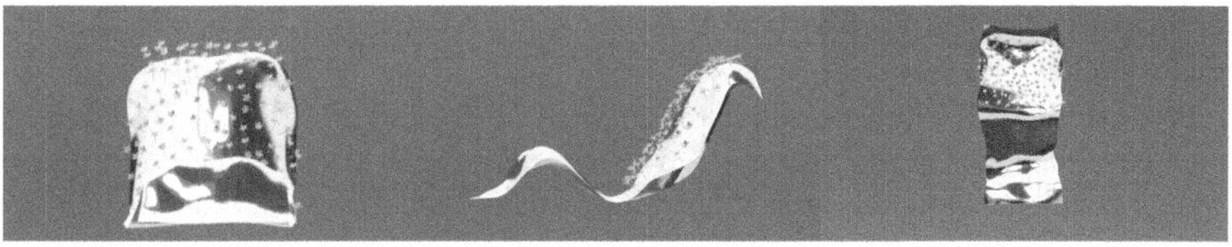

Fig. 7. Front view, side view, and top view of the interactive installation. Source: Designed by Ran wang

4.4 Summary

The "Era of Endeavors" installation not only commemorates the historical impact of the Ganzhutan Hydropower Station but also celebrates the collective memory and resilience of Zuotan Village. By facilitating an exploratory and interactive experience, it connects visitors with the village's cultural heritage and inspires community pride and future development. This project exemplifies how art and technology can merge to preserve history and stimulate cultural engagement.

5 Conclusion and Outlook

5.1 Main Conclusions

This study underscores the transformative impact of interactive art installations in community cultural development. These installations do more than educate; they enhance the local community's connection to their heritage, significantly boosting their pride and sense of belonging. For tourists, these installations offer a deep, immersive experience of the Ganzhutan Hydropower Station's rich history and culture, effectively broadcasting the distinctive cultural identity of Zuotan Village. Interactive installations serve as a dynamic interface, vividly bringing to life the community's historical and cultural narratives and fostering meaningful interactions between residents and visitors. This approach not only revitalizes the community but also enriches tourists' cultural experiences, allowing them to engage more directly with the local heritage.

Moreover, these installations contribute innovative approaches to sustainable community development, ensuring cultural preservation and introducing new pathways for future growth.

5.2 Research Contributions

The findings from this study are crucial for integrating art into cultural development. The research detailed the beneficial impacts of interactive art installations on both historical awareness and cultural enhancement, offering insights that support further artistic endeavors within community development. This study has bridged theory and practice effectively, showcasing how these concepts are realized in Zuotan Village through practical application. The blend of theoretical insights and practical application outlined in this research provides a replicable model for using artistic interventions to aid rural revitalization.

Furthermore, the study highlights the role of interactive installations in boosting community engagement. By interacting with these art pieces, tourists gain a vivid understanding of the Ganzhutan Hydropower Station's history and the broader cultural heritage of the area, while residents are encouraged to engage more actively in community life. This increased engagement is essential for strengthening community ties and building cultural confidence, pivotal for the ongoing cultural and communal development.

Acknowledgments. This study was supported by several projects:the Provincial-Level Top-Tier Offline Course (KA24YY044,6040324137), the 2024 Guangdong Provincial Graduate Education Innovation Plan (2024SFKC_054), the New Agricultural Science Teaching Research and Reform Practice Project at Zhongkai University of Agriculture and Engineering (PX-44231059), and the Design Fundamentals Virtual Teaching and Research Office (ZG2023011).Their generous support greatly facilitated the research.

Disclosure of Interests. The authors have no competing interests to declare that are relevant to the content of this article.

References

1. Opinions of the Central Committee of the Communist Party of China and the State Council on learning and applying the experience of the "Thousand Villages Demonstration and Ten Thousand Villages Improvement" project to effectively and effectively promote the comprehensive revitalization of rural areas. https://www.gov.cn/zhengce/202402/content_6929934.htm. Accessed 25 May 2024
2. Decision of the Guangdong Provincial Committee of the Communist Party of China on implementing the "High-Quality Development Project of Hundreds of Counties, Thousands of Towns and Thousands of Villages" to promote the coordinated development of urban and rural areas. http://www.gd.gov.cn/zzzq/gdyw/content/post_4101012.html. Accessed 25 May 2024
3. Lin, Y.: Research on installation art forms in urban public product design. Art Panorama, pp. 120–121 (2018)
4. Du, C.: Research on the design application of interactive installation art in urban commercial space (2019). https://kns.cnki.net/kcms2/article/abstract?v=s5eXW7nWjw3xRQ8P4l70dRyYzNICUOSpavKcciIaVwAxaa9gDKBfwAcBksC0AOMCl9_PdN_HM0lCqu3vIgLIRraXPbO7NOyWKTiimvUE3RCgQ5kR2GcFHg==&uniplatform=NZKPT&language=gb
5. Fan, Z.: Research on the design of Tianshui Fuxi cultural interactive installation under multi-sensory interaction (2023). https://kns.cnki.net/kcms2/article/abstract?v=s5eXW7nWjw1a6wEIpk4E8uyx58SsvpQGsx_88VQWJgD3MPKOcp-2p9Oe8TWhFi5qEWSl6GcN2LxvY6Dj_v2MEx4gnDPXjilIqBjscLB3Jk0soBmdaiTH-A==&uniplatform=NZKPT&language=gb
6. Li, X., Zhang, Y.: Exploring the ways of integrating interactive installation art into university leisure spaces under the influence of traditional culture. Architect. Cult. 258–260 (2023). https://doi.org/10.19875/j.cnki.jzywh.2023.02.082
7. Guo, D.: Integration of regional cultural symbols in the design of urban public facilities. Packag. Eng. **39**, 252–255 (2018). https://doi.org/10.19554/j.cnki.1001-3563.2018.16.043
8. Xu, X., Dai, Y.: The application and dissemination of Jinxiu Yao cultural elements in ceramic interactive installation art. Ceramic Sci. Art **55**, 55–56 (2021). https://doi.org/10.13212/j.cnki.csa.2021.05.026
9. Yu, Z.: Research on the design application of interactive installation art in historical districts (2024). https://kns.cnki.net/kcms2/article/abstract?v=LGlPPz-4LgENlVpNgWJv9kDOXdAJ8jVF2hT4f4amPinGHHxMMYViSMeJjwkCUuU3ENRZigHjVRizyvGDz5b2tyNSw4jyj0_D5SybiiJSFjC3cL1hH0UcrQ==&uniplatform=NZKPT&language=gb
10. Xie, Y., Lu, F.: Design is a culture of practice - thinking based on the sustainable development of a traditional handmade papermaking village. Decorate 26–31 (2023). https://doi.org/10.16272/j.cnki.cn11-1392/j.2023.10.004

Offline Indoor Navigation via QR Codes

Robert Modic(✉), Matevž Ogrinc, Andraž Simčič, Bojan Blažica, and Drago Torkar

Jožef Stefan Institute, Jamova Cesta 39, 1000 Ljubljana, Slovenia
{robert.modic,matevz.ogrinc,andraz.simcic,bojan.blazica, drago.torkar}@ijs.si

Abstract. This paper introduces a novel, cost-effective system for indoor navigation and localization that operates independently of satellite positioning services and data communication networks. The proposed solution leverages QR codes affixed within building interiors and an accompanying smartphone application, which, through integration with the device's inertial motion unit (IMU) sensors and the application of the Pedestrian Dead Reckoning (PDR) algorithm [1], accurately determines the user's position. This position data is then utilized by the Dijkstra navigation algorithm [2] to facilitate user navigation to their desired destination. Beyond navigation, this system offers significant utility in healthcare logistics, enabling efficient collection and transmission of triage decisions in emergency situations, even in the absence of a communication network.

Keywords: Indoor Navigation · QR Codes · Offline Navigation · First Response

1 Introduction

The primary goal was to create a proof of concept demonstrating the feasibility of indoor navigation and localization using only passive tags. To achieve this, a smartphone navigation app was developed for use inside buildings, which operates without relying on satellite positioning services or communication networks. Satellite navigation systems (GPS, GLONASS, Galileo, BeiDou, QZSS, IRNSS) typically fail to function accurately inside buildings, particularly on lower floors, in basements, central areas, and away from windows due to a limited number of visible satellites. Similarly, communication networks (WiFi, LTE, 5G) may be unavailable in certain situations, such as during catastrophic incidents, power outages, or other emergencies, rendering localization systems based on these networks ineffective.

The smartphone app serves two main purposes. First, it aims to provide a reliable, user-friendly, and cost-effective indoor navigation system suitable for large buildings like hospitals, shopping malls, trade centers, and fairs where other positioning services are unavailable. Second, it aims to offer an indoor position reporting system for use in emergencies and mass-casualty incidents to report triage decisions to a server. Both functionalities rely on QR codes containing all the necessary information [3].

C. Stephanidis et al. (Eds.): HCII 2024, CCIS 2319, pp. 292–296, 2025.
https://doi.org/10.1007/978-3-031-78516-0_31

2 Methodology

To ensure comprehensive navigation data, two types of QR codes were created, each containing all necessary information.

1. Floor QR Codes placed at the entrance to each floor. These include:
    - A compressed floor plan presented as an edge list (Fig. 1). A Python script was developed to automatically generate these edge lists from raster images of floor plans.
    - The navigation graph, which includes the coordinates of destinations and navigation points, along with descriptive labels for all destinations (Fig. 2).

These QR codes are very dense [4], which can slow down the recognition process. If printed too small, the rows and columns are too close together, and under normal lighting conditions, the smartphone camera may not capture an image that the decoding routine, even with machine learning support, can robustly recognize. Experiments indicated that printing on A3 paper size is appropriate for these dense QR codes.

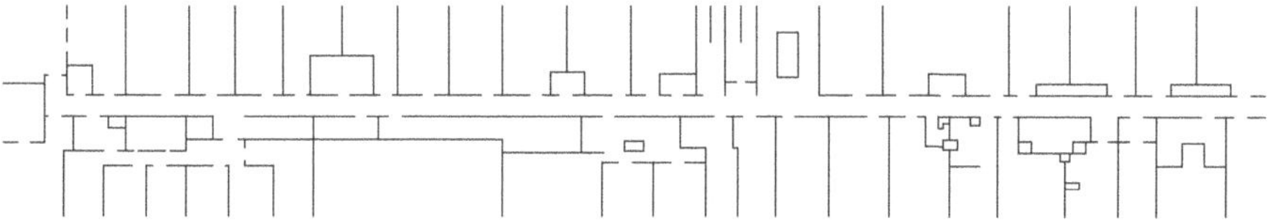

Fig. 1. A test floor plan saved in the floor QR after reconstruction.

2. Location QR Codes placed at destinations, intersections, and other navigation points. These codes include the location in GPS (latitude, longitude) and metric UTM (northing, easting) coordinates, as well as additional data about the location (room label, residents, etc.). The data size of these codes is much smaller—3 to 4 times smaller than the floor QR codes—making them less dense. Experiments showed that they can be printed on A4 or even A5 paper size for robust recognition.

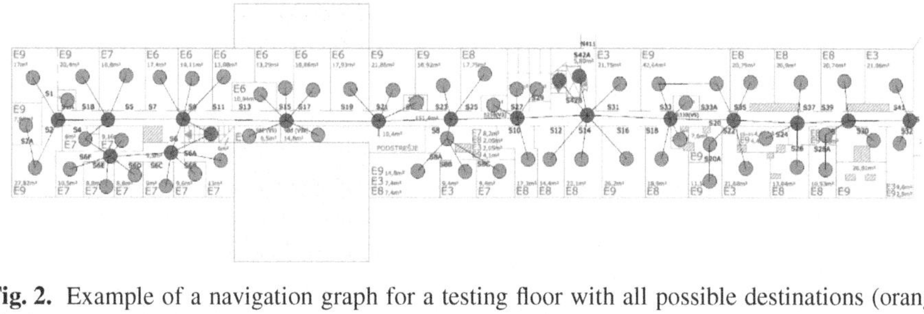

Fig. 2. Example of a navigation graph for a testing floor with all possible destinations (orange circles) and navigation points (blue circles) depicted on the original floor plan raster image. (Color figure online)

3 Navigation and Localization

Upon scanning a Floor QR code, users select their destination, and the app calculates the optimal route, visually represented on the device (Fig. 3). The app continuously updates the user's position using PDR, factoring in stride length and direction from IMU sensors. This system is not only effective for guiding users but also ensures that localization is aligned with global coordinate standards, facilitating integration with widely-used mapping services.

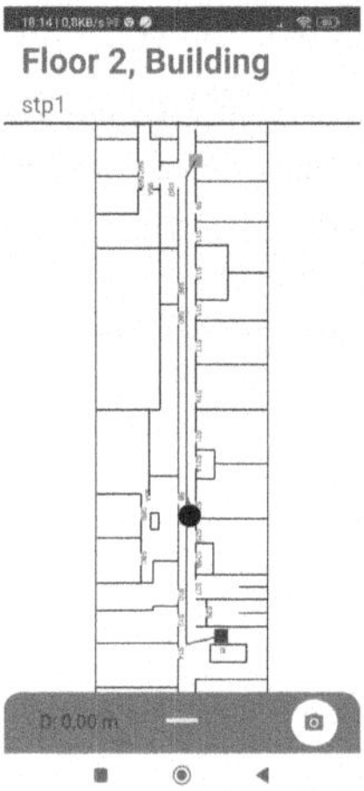

Fig. 3. Visualized path from the starting point (blue square) to the destination (green square), showing the user's current location and orientation (black circle with red pointer). (Color figure online)

4 Healthcare Logistics and Triage Support

A significant application of our system is in healthcare logistics, where it aids first responders in reporting triage decisions during mass-casualty incidents. By associating triage decisions with precise location data, the app enables efficient communication with emergency services, even in the absence of a reliable communication network. This feature is particularly valuable in disaster scenarios, ensuring that critical information is conveyed without delay.

The app supports the following triage scenario: First responders locate each casualty, determine the emergency level, and then use the app's menu to select the triage decision. This decision, along with the GPS coordinates of the location, is sent to the server using a REST API interface and GeoJSON data format (Fig. 4). If the communication network is unavailable, the data is saved to a local JSON-based database. Once communication is restored, the data is automatically sent to the cloud, and the user is notified, as shown in Fig. 5.

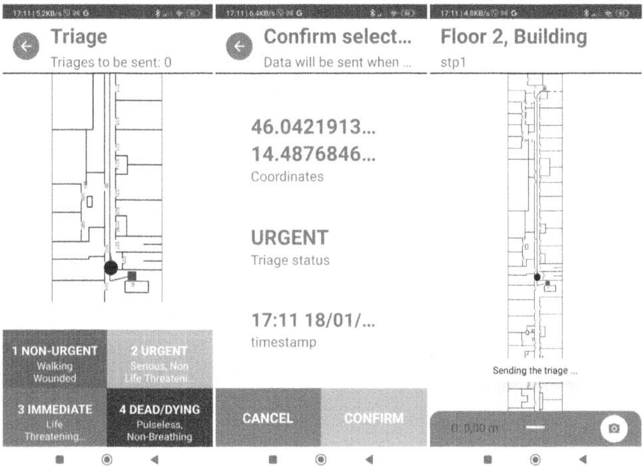

Fig. 4. The app's screens for triage decisions: selecting the triage decision (left), confirming the data to be sent (middle), and sending the data to the server (right).

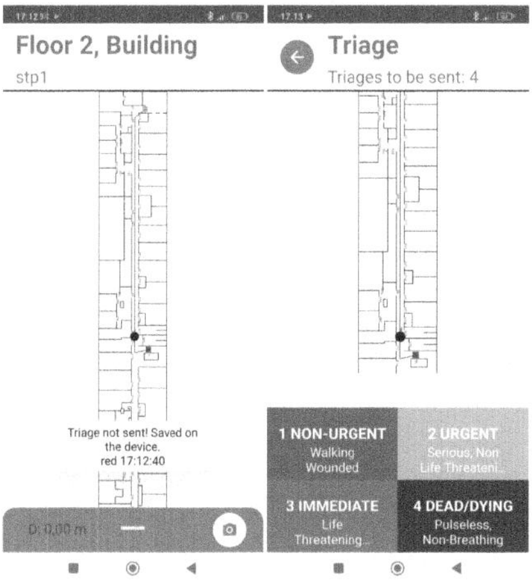

Fig. 5. If the triage message is not successfully sent (left), the status of unsent messages is displayed on the triage selection screen (right).

5 Future Work

Future developments will focus on improving the system's ease of use and efficiency by pre-loading navigation data onto smartphones, eliminating the need for QR code scanning. This approach will provide users with immediate access to comprehensive maps and directions for entire buildings, ensuring a seamless navigation experience from the outset. Additionally, the system will incorporate real-time updates and dynamic route adjustments to enhance user guidance and adaptability. Enhanced user interface features will also be developed to provide a more intuitive and user-friendly experience.

6 Conclusions

We have successfully developed and tested an innovative indoor navigation and localization system that circumvents the limitations of conventional satellite and network-based solutions. By utilizing QR codes and smartphone technology, our system demonstrates a viable alternative for indoor navigation, with substantial implications for emergency response and healthcare logistics. Our findings suggest significant potential for further development and integration with existing technological infrastructures, promising to enhance indoor navigation capabilities substantially.

Acknowledgments. This work has been supported in part by the Slovenian Research Agency (research core funding No. P2-0098) and in part by ECSEL Joint Undertaking (JU) InSecTT under grant agreement No 876038.

References

1. Hou, X., Bergmann, J.: Pedestrian dead reckoning with wearable sensors: a systematic review. IEEE Sens. J. **21**(1), 143–152 (2021). https://doi.org/10.1109/JSEN.2020.3014955
2. Dijkstra, E.W.: A note on two problems in connexion with graphs. Numer. Math. **1**(1), 269–271 (1959). https://doi.org/10.1007/BF01386390.S2CID123284777
3. Aayushi, M., Manish, M.: A review on QR code. Int. J. Comput. Appl. **164**, 17–19 (2017). https://doi.org/10.5120/ijca2017913739
4. Umaria, M.M., Jethava, G.B.: Enhancing the data storage capacity in QR Code using compression algorithm and achieving security and further data storage capacity improvement using multiplexing, In: Proceedings of the International Conference on Computational Intelligence and Communication Networks (CICN), pp. 1094–1096. Jabalpur, India (2015). https://doi.org/10.1109/CICN.2015.215

Government Management and Inventory System

Jose Ricardo Mondragon Regalado[1](✉), Grimaldo Heredia Pérez[2], Jaime Mundaca Araujo[3], Alexander Huaman Monteza[1], Willam Suárez Peña[1], Nancy Saldaña Mendoza[4], Orestes Daniel Adrianzén Guerrero[1], John Smith Rodríguez Estacio[1], and Wesley Olano Chuquihuanga[3]

[1] University National of Jaen, Cajamarca, Peru
jose.mondragon@unj.edu.pe
[2] University Catholic of Trujillo Benedict XVI, La Libertad, Peru
[3] University Cesar Vallejo, Lambayeque, Peru
[4] Institution Educative Agropecuary "TRM" of Bagua, Amazonas, Peru

Abstract. The purpose of the study was to evaluate the effectiveness and identify benefits and analyze challenges offered by information systems in the public sector, there-fore, the objective was to determine the impact of inventory control systems in the management a local government the Cajamarca region. The study presented a non-experimental design with a quantitative approach, the population was made up of 5 collaborators from the logistics department. The results allowed us to determine that the use of information systems in the control of assets of the public entity is essential. Allowing to improve transparency and accountability, prevention of losses and misappropriations, optimization of inventory management, agility in decision making, regulatory compliance and operational efficiency.

Keywords: Inventory · system · internal control · government management

1 Introduction

The influencing factors are varied, ranging from political will to the absence of the application of more effective strategies for controlling and distributing resources. According to Milan et al. (2022), government effectiveness is determined by the new management methodologies that each government adopts, as well as by the resources available for adequate control. In the same line of argument, it is argued that the internal management dynamics of government leaders influence the creation of good practices in their performance (Distor and Khaltar 2022). On the other hand, Rambe et al. (2022) state that a government is considered efficient if it has control programs and plans aimed at improving the quality of life of its citizens.

Organizations must have effective internal control to ensure transparency, reduce risks and prevent fraud, thus protecting the assets and interests of the entity (Putri et al. 2023). However, problems associated with inventory management, such as discrepancies between physical and digital records, product damage, and expiration of goods, are

C. Stephanidis et al. (Eds.): HCII 2024, CCIS 2319, pp. 297–302, 2025.
https://doi.org/10.1007/978-3-031-78516-0_32

common and can lead to considerable financial losses; therefore, both internal and external control is essential to ensure efficiency and regularity in administrative operations (Tritto 2022). Effective inventory management is of utmost importance and involves addressing distribution challenges and applying proper storage practices to optimize stock, reduce costs and prevent fraudulent activities. In addition, various strategies need to be implemented to improve efficiency in this aspect (Ye et al. 2020).

Inventory management in Latin America has undergone significant changes, which has generated the need for specific solutions both in terms of storage and software to ensure reliable control. Technologies have also made it possible to integrate different areas and share information using established standards and various data structures (Singh and Kumar 2023). A study conducted in Mexico points to a growing interest in the adoption of technologies, especially the Internet, for more effective inventory management, with potential benefits such as the implementation of tracking systems to monitor the movement and circulation of products. In addition, it is argued that technology facilitates formal control over assets belonging to companies and organizations (Robles and Corzo 2021).

According to Ismail et al. (2023), the importance of internal control lies in its ability to promote independence and objectivity. In the same vein, Abd et al. (2022) point out that internal control systems have faced significant challenges in several areas due to the impact of globalization and the advancement of information technologies. Xie and Zhang (2022) argue that the integration of internal control systems, such as those related to inventories, contributes to improving the effectiveness of audits in various contexts. On the other hand, Yang et al. (2021) argue that internal control capabilities related to investment and sustainability play a crucial role in improving internal governance and sustainable development of companies and organizations. Furthermore, Villarreal et al. (2021) highlight the importance of internal monitoring and efficiency in the management of public goods and assets.

However, Sagat et al. (2021) points out in their study that the implementation of external and internal control systems in the public management of many local, regional and national governments is limited. In this context, Radovic et al. (2021) highlights the existing differences in the implementation of internal controls of goods and products between utilities and other entities, as well as in their performance and approach to customer service optimization.

Local governments often face problems in inventory control due to lack of adequate technology, outdated procedures, and insufficient staff training. This can result in loss of resources, embezzlement and lack of transparency, complicating planning and decision-making. Furthermore, genres suspicions of corruption and mismanagement; Therefore, it is important to implement advanced inventory control systems to improve efficiency and confidence in government administration.

According to the aforementioned problematic, the following research question is posed: What is the impact of inventory control systems on the management of a local government in the Cajamarca region?

In accordance with the research question, the following objective has been formulated: Determine the impact of inventory control systems on the management of a local government in the Cajamarca region.

Information systems play a fundamental role in the administration of resources; in short, this will have a positive impact on the provision of public services and the satisfaction of the needs of the population through more efficient and responsible inventory management in the government entities.

2 Methodology

The materials used were paper, pencil, corrector, laptop and processing software, including Microsoft Excel and SPSS version 23. The population and sample were made up of 5 collaborators from the logistics area of a municipality in the Cajamarca region, and a non-probabilistic statistical method to select the sample. The study design was non-experimental and cross-sectional, with a correlational descriptive level. To collect the information, a questionnaire on "Information systems and government management" was applied, which was validated by experts and also demonstrated statistical feasibility.

The variables under study were: information systems and government management. The study began with the request for permission from the competent authorities of a municipality in the Cajamarca region. Subsequently, informed consent was obtained from each participant. Then, the sample information was collected using the instrument "Information systems and government management", which was subsequently systematized and processed. Finally, the analysis and interpretation of the findings was carried out, which allowed us to reach the general conclusions of the study.

3 Results

The data in Table 1 shed light on the application of information systems in inventory control in this municipality. The results show that 3 informants rate the use of these systems as good, while 2 consider their contribution to be regular, which suggests that there are other factors that influence good resource management.

Table 1. Use of information systems in inventory control

Variable	Good	Bad	Regular
Information systems	3	0	2

Similarly, Table 2 presents an evaluation of different dimensions related to information systems in government management. The results show that the majority of respondents consider that information systems improve transparency and accountability, although a smaller segment suggests areas for improvement in this dimension. They also maintain that the systems contribute to the prevention of losses and embezzlement, highlighting their effectiveness in this regard. Furthermore, information systems are seen by the majority of respondents as effective in optimizing inventory management. It stands out that the majority believes that information systems improve decision making. However, although the majority believes that the systems help with regulatory compliance, there is a segment that points out gaps that must be corrected in this dimension.

Table 2. Information systems in government management by dimensions

Dimensions	Good	Regular	Bad
Transparency and accountability	3	1	1
Loss and embezzlement prevention	4	0	1
Inventory Management Optimization	3	1	1
Agility in decision making	3	1	1
Normative compliance	3	2	0
Operating efficiency	3	2	0

The value of 0.875 indicates a strong positive relationship between the implementation of information systems and the effectiveness of government management. This suggests that as the use of information systems improves, the quality of government management also tends to improve significantly. From another point of view, it is stated that information systems have a positive impact on government management .

Table 3. Correlation between information systems and government management

			Information systems	Government management
Rho de Spearman	Information systems	Correlation coefficient	0,875	0,905
		Sig. (bilateral)	–	0,000
		N	5	5
	Government management	Correlation coefficient	0,905	0,875
		Sig. (bilateral)	0,000	–
		N	5	5

The results bear some similarity to those presented by Milan et al. (2022) and Rambe et al. (2022); who highlight the importance of political will and the adoption of new management methodologies to improve effectiveness. Our results also indicate that information systems, as a management tool, significantly improve the quality of government management. This coincidence underlines the relevance of innovation and political support in the effective implementation of information technologies.

While our results indicate that information systems have a positive impact on several dimensions of government management, areas for improvement have also been identified, especially in regulatory compliance compliance and operational efficiency. This means that, although information systems are beneficial, there are specific barriers and challenges that must be addressed to maximize their effectiveness.

Regarding systems as a means of security and control, it is also consistent with those proposed by Putri et al. (2023) and Tritto (2022) who emphasize the need for effective internal control to guarantee transparency and prevent fraud, is an aspect also reflected in our findings. The evidence presented by the study indicates that information systems are effective in preventing losses and embezzlements, which agrees with the literature that highlights the importance of control for operational integrity and efficiency.

Although our results show a strong positive correlation (0.875) between the implementation of information systems and the effectiveness of government management, some studies, such as that of Villarreal et al. (2021), emphasize the need for constant monitoring and continuous adjustment of systems to maintain their effectiveness. That is to say, although our findings are positive, the effectiveness of information systems may vary depending on how they are managed and integrated into the organizational context; it is possible that other factors intervene, such as: staff training, access to technology. Through which other studies are needed to determine this problem in more depth.

The results of Singh and Kumar (2023) and Robles and Corzo (2021) highlight technology as an important tool to improve inventory management and government management. Our results confirm that the adoption of information systems optimizes inventory management and improves decision making, supporting the conclusion that technology facilitates control and efficiency.

However, Distor and Khaltar (2022) argue that the internal management dynamics of government leaders influence the creation of good practices. The results of this study reflect that while the majority of respondents view information systems as beneficial, there is a minority who perceive areas for improvement. This could indicate that differences in management and leadership can affect the perception and effectiveness of information systems, which constitutes an alternative for further research.

4 Conclusions

The analysis concludes that information systems for inventory control have a positive impact on government management, mainly improving transparency and accountability. These systems also help prevent losses and embezzlement, and optimize inventory management by providing real-time reports, which favors decision making. In addition, it contributes to regulatory compliance and generates operational efficiency for the benefit of citizens.

Furthermore, it has been statistically proven that information systems have a direct relationship with government management. This suggests that as the use of information systems improves, the quality of government management also tends to improve significantly. From another point of view, it is stated that information systems have a positive impact on government management.

References

Abd, W.H., Kareem, A.D., Jassim, E.E.: The role of the modern COSO framework in evaluating the internal control system through the mediating role of the internal auditor: (Al-Muthanna State University as a model). Res Militaris **12**(2), 4376–4391 (2022). https://www.scopus.com/inward/record.uri?eid=2-s2.0-85142130058&partnerID=40&md5=be62bf1fbf7a69a00ea72f8ee6cc1dae

Distor, C.B., Khaltar, O.: What motivates local governments to be efficient? Evidence from philippine cities. Sustainability (Switzerland) **14**(15) (2022). https://doi.org/10.3390/su14159426

Ismail, M.D., Kathim, A.M., Al-Kanani, M.M.: Corporate governance and its impact on the efficiency of internal control on non-profit government institutions: an exploratory study. Int. J. Profess. Bus. Rev. **8**(1) (2023). https://doi.org/10.26668/businessreview/2023.v8i1.1155

Milán-García, J., Rueda-López, N., De Pablo-Valenciano, J.: Local government efficiency: reviewing determinants and setting new trends. Int. Trans. Oper. Res. **29**(5), 2871–2898 (2022). https://doi.org/10.1111/itor.13032

Putri, C.M., Argilés-Bosch, J.M., Ravenda, D.: Creating good village governance: an effort to prevent village corruption in Indonesia. J. Finan. Crime (2023). https://doi.org/10.1108/JFC-11-2022-0266

Radovic, M., Vitomir, J., Popovic, S.: Impact of internal control in enterprises founded by local self-government units: The case of Republic of Serbia. Eng. Econ. **32**(1), 82–90 (2021). https://doi.org/10.5755/j01.ee.32.1.23243

Rambe, R.A., Purmini, P., Armelly, A., Alfansi, L., Febriani, R.E.: Efficiency comparison of pro-growth poverty reduction spending before and during the COVID-19 Pandemic: a study of regional governments in indonesia. Economies **10**(6) (2022). https://doi.org/10.3390/economies10060150

Robles, M.A.G., Corzo, R.F.M.: Inventory control and the use of technology in businesses: a survey study of micro-companies in Mexico. In: Entrepreneurial Innovation for Securing Long-Term Growth in a Short-Term Economy, pp. 1–15. IGI Global (2021). https://doi.org/10.4018/978-1-7998-3568-4.ch001

Sagat, V., Krapek, M., Nemec, J.: Efficiency of control in regional self-government of the Slovak republic. Administ. Si Manage. Public **37**, 6–26 (2021). https://doi.org/10.24818/amp/2021.37-01

Singh Nain, P.K., Kumar, A.: Intelligent agent-based supply chain management using service-oriented architecture. In: Contemporary Studies of Risks in Emerging Technology, Part A, pp. 111–126. Emerald Group Publishing Ltd (2023). https://doi.org/10.1108/978-1-80455-562-020231008

Tritto, D.N.M.: The system of regional internal controls: critical issues and prospects for reforms. Federalismi.it **2022**(11), 200–217 (2022). https://www.scopus.com/inward/record.uri?eid=2-s2.0-85141712532&partnerID=40&md5=3073a3150a727fe5c7612b875978d630

Villarreal-Flores, A.G., Carrera-Sánchez, M.M., Villarreal Villarreal, L.A., Tamez-Garza, S.: Public management factors that affect the efficient use of financial resources in the municipalities of the monterrey metropolitan area fuzzy regression analysis. Fuzzy Econ. Rev. **26**(2), 15–31 (2021). https://doi.org/10.25102/fer.2021.02.02

Xie, T., Zhang, J.: Data-driven intelligent risk system in the process of financial audit. Math. Probl. Eng. **2022** (2022). https://doi.org/10.1155/2022/9054209

Yang, L., et al.: Resource slack, environmental management maturity and enterprise environmental protection investment: An enterprise life cycle adjustment perspective. J. Clean. Prod. **309** (2021). https://doi.org/10.1016/j.jclepro.2021.127339

Ye, B., Chen, Y., Zhang, B., Liang, Q., Zhu, L.: Research on multi-echelon coordinated inventory control model of tobacco industry enterprises. Acta Tabacaria Sinica **26**(4), 117–123 (2020)

Movement Characteristics During Directional Change in Wheelchair Badminton

Hiroyuki Ohshima(✉), Akinori Sasaki, Hitoshi Ishido, and Shigenobu Shimada

Tokyo Metropolitan Industrial Technology Research Institute, Tokyo, Japan
ohshima.hiroyuki@iri-tokyo.jp

Abstract. Wheelchair badminton was a new event at the Tokyo 2021 Summer Paralympic Games. To develop a motor-learning support system, this study aimed to quantify the motion of a world-class wheelchair badminton player. For this purpose, static and dynamic posture analyses were conducted. An ex-member of the Japanese national wheelchair badminton team volunteered for this study. Three-dimensional scanning was used for static posture analysis, and the deformation of the lower side of a wheelchair seat during shuttle hitting was quantified. The wheelchair customized for the participant demonstrated less change in the maximum deformation and its position in different postures. Next, inertial sensors were used for the dynamic posture analysis. The relative angle between the upper and lower trunk was recorded. The participant moved back and forth five times over a distance of 3 m. During the forward-to-backward transition, the first trunk flexion acts as a brake for forward movement, while the second trunk flexion acts as an accelerator for backward movement. During the backward-to-forward transition, the first trunk extension acts as a brake for backward movement, while the second trunk extension acts as an accelerator for forward movement. Based on these results, we will develop a feedback system utilizing visual, auditory, and tactile modalities to guide new wheelchair badminton players toward these propulsion patterns. We aim to promote sports for disabled individuals.

Keywords: motion analysis · 3D scan · shot posture

1 Introduction

Wheelchair badminton was a new event at the Tokyo 2021 Summer Paralympic Games [1]. The matches are played on a regular badminton half-court for singles and full-court for doubles. Badminton is accessible at most local leisure centers with a sports hall. These sports halls commonly have badminton court markings, nets, and posts, and courts can be booked by the general public. It is highly likely that individuals with disability who enjoy playing sports, but are not athletes, can enjoy wheelchair badminton.

Two important factors will increase its popularity: improving the equipment and increasing the number of players. First, wheelchairs specifically designed for badminton are still under development. Several playing tools are the same in regular and wheelchair badminton; however, the wheelchair is the most distinct playing tool. A

C. Stephanidis et al. (Eds.): HCII 2024, CCIS 2319, pp. 303–311, 2025.
https://doi.org/10.1007/978-3-031-78516-0_33

considerable amount of knowledge has been accumulated during the development of ordinary wheelchairs and other wheelchair sports by addressing various user needs. The primary difference between using an ordinary wheelchair for daily use and a para-badminton wheelchair is the dynamic posture change during play. Based on the advice of the world's top-level wheelchair badminton players, we developed a wheelchair specifically for wheelchair badminton (Fig. 1); the players who used it won gold medals at the Tokyo 2021 Paralympics. This study focuses on the second point: an important factor in new players continuing the sport is whether they experience an improvement in their skills. Although several motor-learning support systems have been developed for able-bodied individuals, only a few such systems have been developed for individuals with disabilities [2, 3], and none at all for wheelchair badminton. The system has not been developed due to an absence of sufficient knowledge about the movement characteristics of wheelchair badminton. The inclusion of biomechanical analysis would enhance our understanding of wheelchair badminton, particularly concerning performance. To develop a motor-learning support system for wheelchair badminton players, this study aimed to analyze the motion characteristics of a world-class wheelchair badminton player. The results of this study will contribute to the increase of wheelchair badminton players in the future.

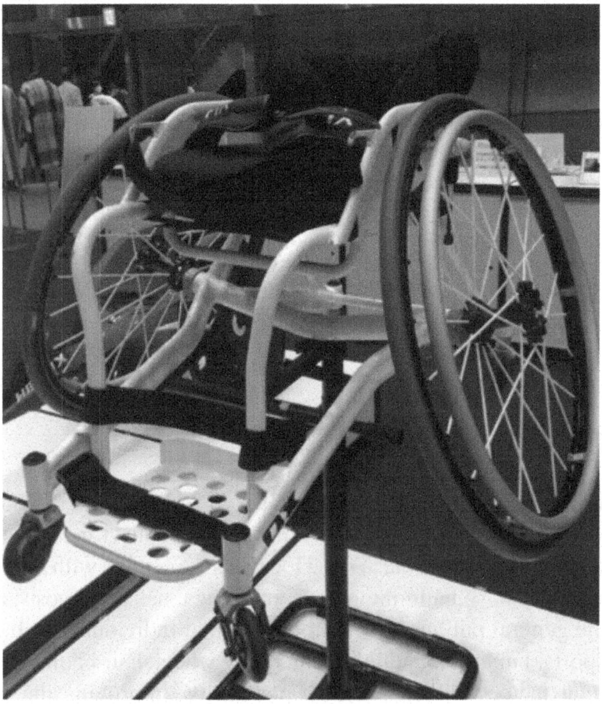

Fig. 1. Wheelchair specially designed for badminton.

2 Static Posture Analysis

Wheelchair badminton is characterized by discontinuous forward and backward movement propulsion with little or no lateral movement on the court. However, it requires various postural changes depending on the direction of the shuttle. Trunk movements are fundamental for generating force in high-resistance propulsion [4]. Ideally, the wheelchair suitable for the dynamic motion characteristics of wheelchair badminton should respond flexibly and desirably to the players. It is important to quantify the contact surface between the player and the wheelchair. However, measuring this using sensor is difficult. Therefore, this study focused on the deformation of the lower side of the chair seat.

2.1 Participant

An ex-member of the Japanese national wheelchair badminton team volunteered for this study. Per institutional requirements, they provided prior written informed consent. The Tokyo Metropolitan Industrial Technology Research Institute's ethics committee approved the experimental procedure (ES2021-11).

2.2 Apparatus and Experimental Setup

An optical three-dimensional scanner (ATOS 5, Carl Zeiss GOM Metrology, Germany) was used to collect information about the height, breadth, and depth of a wheelchair with a person seated. It is a non-contact, non-destructive digital device that uses a light source to accurately capture the shape of a physical object into computer-aided design data. It generates a point cloud in a geometric framework that accurately depicts a physical object's size and shape. The wheelchair was placed on a pallet. The size of the pallet was 1 square meter. The lower side of the chair seat could be measured in a single scan (Fig. 2 left). Two wheelchairs were used in this study: a customized wheelchair and a generalized wheelchair. The customized wheelchair was specifically designed for the participant in this study. The generalized wheelchair was a badminton wheelchair suitable for the typical body size. To compare the deformation behaviors of different wheelchairs, it was necessary to set up a common geometric framework. However, the two wheelchairs used in this study were of different sizes and had different seat and back inclinations. Therefore, it is inappropriate to refer to the frame members of the wheelchair, as differences in shape are likely to affect the amount of deformation. Thus, each wheelchair, without a person sitting in it, was scanned 360 degrees using a rotating platform. The geometric frameworks were set by the symmetry of the floor surface, the center of the tire, and the wheelchair (Fig. 2 right).

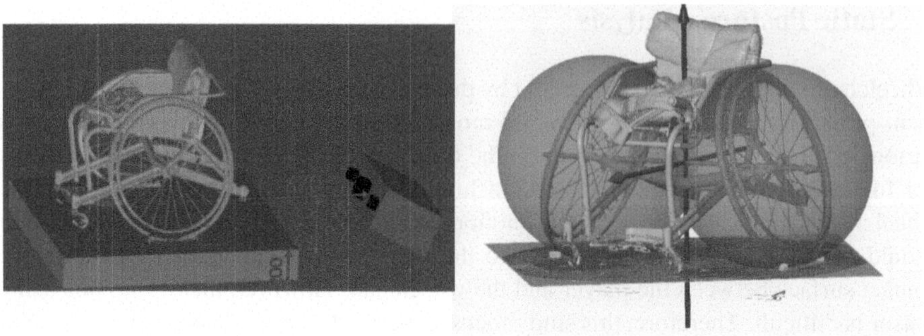

Fig. 2. Experimental setup. Left: location of the wheelchair and 3D scanner. Right: geometric framework defined from prior 3D scan data (red: X-axis, green: Y-axis, blue: Z-axis).

2.3 Procedure

Five postures of each wheelchair were scanned. These were a static sitting posture and four-shot postures (right-back, right-front, center-back, and left-front) frequently observed in wheelchair badminton games. For drives, smashes, and net shots that demand greater postural control, wheelchair badminton players necessitate either significant trunk flexion or extension. The obtained 3D scan data showed that the deformation of the wheelchair frame was sufficiently small compared to the deformation of the lower side of the chair seat. Thus, the scan data of the wheelchair without a participant sitting in it was used as a reference, and the scan data of the wheelchair with the participant sitting in it was aligned to minimize the frame deformation. The maximum deformation of the lower seat surface and its position were calculated for the customized wheelchair and the general wheelchair in each posture. The contact between the buttocks and the seat was then quantified by it.

2.4 Results

Figure 3 and Table 1 list the maximum displacement and its position in the five postures for the customized and generalized wheelchairs. The maximum deformation of the generalized wheelchair ranged from 7.44 mm to 11.64 mm, resulting in a difference of 4.20 mm among the five postural conditions. The maximum deformation of the customized wheelchair ranged from 13.68 mm to 15.74 mm, with a difference of 2.06 mm among the five postural conditions. The maximum deformation position of the generalized wheelchair in the anterior-posterior (x-coordinate) direction varied significantly from -37.26 mm (right-back shot posture) to 212 mm (left-front shot posture). The variation for the customized wheelchair was smaller, ranging from −1.4 mm (left-front shot posture) to −9.94 mm (right-back shot posture). The lateral-medial (y-coordinate) variation of the maximum deformation position for the generalized wheelchair was 57.91 mm, ranging from -30.14 mm (center-back shot posture) to 27.77 mm (right-back shot posture). For the customized wheelchair, the variation was 14.03 mm, ranging from −0.13 mm (right-front shot posture) to 13.90 mm (center-back shot posture).

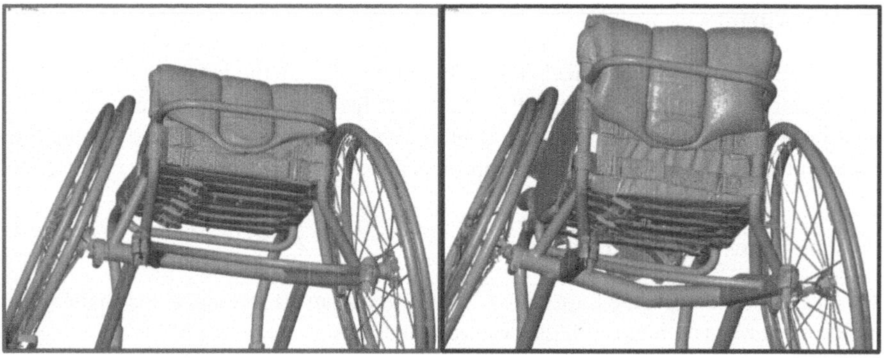

Fig. 3. The maximum deformation and its position of the lower side of the chair seat in five postures is indicated by a vector in green (left: generalized wheelchair, right: customized wheelchair).

Table 1. The maximum deformation and its position of the lower side of the chair seat under two wheelchairs and five posture conditions.

Wheelchair	Posture	deformation (mm)	x-coordinate (mm)	y-coordinate (mm)
General	static sitting	10.71	−13.06	24.72
	right-back	11.64	−37.26	27.77
	right-front	7.81	−9.68	−27.60
	center-back	11.54	−34.03	−30.14
	left-front	7.44	212.10	−5.62
Custom	static sitting	15.74	−6.86	9.17
	right-back	15.22	−9.94	10.23
	right-front	15.09	−4.65	−0.13
	center-back	14.55	−4.75	13.90
	left-front	13.68	−1.40	0.99

3 Dynamic Posture Analysis

A typical poor posture in wheelchairs used for daily living is a sitting posture in which the pelvis is tilted backward, resulting in kyphosis. Pressure and misalignment forces are generated in the sacral area, which may cause bedsores. The risk is particularly high for wheelchair badminton players. As described earlier, trunk movements are fundamental for generating force in high-resistance propulsion [4]. This study focused on the trunk movements during continuous back-and-forth turning movements, simulating a real game.

3.1 Participant

The aforementioned former wheelchair badminton player on the Japanese national team also volunteered as a participant in this study. Per institutional requirements, they provided prior written informed consent. The Tokyo Metropolitan Industrial Technology Research Institute's ethics committee approved the experimental procedure (ES2022-2).

3.2 Apparatus and Experimental Setup

Two inertial sensors (Angle Lab, Zero C Seven, Inc., Japan) were attached to the upper and lower trunk. The relative angles between the sensors were recorded. Zero degrees means that the upper and lower trunks are vertical. A positive angle indicates trunk flexion and a negative angle indicates trunk extension. Two phases were analyzed: forward-to-backward transition and backward-to-forward transition.

3.3 Procedure

The participant moved back and forth five times over a distance of 3 m (Fig. 4). The customized wheelchair was used. The participant was asked to complete the task as quickly as possible.

3.4 Results

During the forward-to-backward transition, five bimodal peaks of angular displacement of the trunk flexion, opposite to the direction of movement, were observed (Fig. 5). The first trunk flexion acts as a brake for forward movement, and the second trunk flexion acts as an accelerator for backward movement. During the backward-to-forward transition, five bimodal peaks of angular displacement of the trunk extension, opposite to the direction of movement, were observed. The first trunk extension acts as a brake for backward movement, the second trunk extension acts as an accelerator for forward movement.

Fig. 4. Movement task. The participant moved back and forth five times over a distance of 3 m.

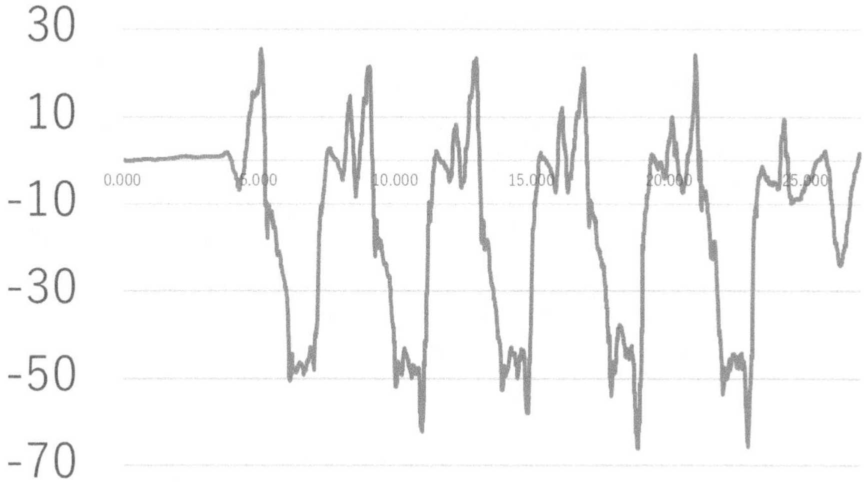

Fig. 5. Relative angle (deg) between upper and lower trunk.

4 Discussion and Conclusion

The absence of biomechanical data is a significant limitation in understanding a sporting discipline. Previous studies in wheelchair sports such as wheelchair racing, basketball, and rugby have conducted biomechanical analyses [5]. They have contributed significantly to our understanding of the kinematic and kinetic aspects of propulsion, which are essential for assessing athlete performance and identifying injury risk. Nevertheless, wheelchair badminton remains a relatively nascent and expanding sport. Research on the kinematic characteristics of wheelchair badminton has not progressed. Therefore, this study examined wheelchair badminton movements from two perspectives: static and dynamic posture analysis.

For static posture analysis, the maximum deformation and its position on the lower side of the chair seat of the wheelchairs were quantified. The chair seat of the badminton wheelchairs consists of five fiber belts connecting the left and right wheelchair frames and a cushion placed on top of the belts. In the generalized wheelchair, the maximum deformation was located on the fourth belt from the front in four posture conditions, including the static sitting posture. However, in the left-front condition, the maximum deformation was located on the first belt. This position is considered to be the optimal position where the pelvis is fixed. By adjusting the belt so that the fourth belt deforms the most when the posture changes, this fourth belt becomes the fulcrum. This belt is expected to have a support function for trunk retention in wheelchair badminton, which is characterized by back-and-forth movement.

For dynamic posture analysis, the relative angles between the upper and lower trunk were recorded during the forward and backward turning movements. During the forward-to-backward transition, the first trunk flexion acts as a brake for forward movement, and the second trunk flexion acts as an accelerator for backward movement. During the backward-to-forward transition, the first trunk extension acts as a brake for backward movement, and the second trunk extension acts as an accelerator for forward movement. Based on these results, we will develop an efficient motor-learning support system for wheelchair badminton players. Feedback for visual, auditory, and tactile modalities would be appropriate to guide new wheelchair badminton players toward these propulsion patterns. It can indicate the ideal timing of trunk flexion and extension and their angular displacement.

There are several limitations of this study. The use of the racket is a distinctive aspect of wheelchair badminton, and athletes cannot avoid it. Previous studies in wheelchair tennis have shown a reduction in the performance of athletes due to changes in their kinetics, kinematics, and spatiotemporal parameters when using a racket [6, 7]. Therefore, even in wheelchair badminton, it is necessary to evaluate the influence of the badminton racket on their propulsion. Alberca et al. focused on examining the effects of using a badminton racket on the propulsion kinetics [8]. Their results on the kinetic parameters of propulsion reveal that the use of the racket changes the way the forces are applied to the handrim, increasing the force generated while decreasing the propulsive efficiency. The gripping motion of the handrim while grasping the racket forces the players to adapt to propulsive motion. The next step is to examine how trunk motion in propulsion is changed while holding the racket. In addition, the issue of laboratory testing has been extensively explored in physiological studies [9]. Due to limitations of laboratory tests, field tests have become a preferred solution for wheelchair players. Therefore, further research is needed to explore other perspectives on wheelchair badminton and to promote wheelchair badminton.

Acknowledgments. This work was carried out partly under cooperative research with OX Engineering Co., ltd. The authors express their appreciation. We would like to thank Editage (www.editage.jp) for English language editing.

Disclosure of Interests. The authors have no competing interests to declare that are relevant to the content of this article.

References

1. Para-badminton (Official website of the paralympic movement). https://www.paralympic.org/badminton. Retrieved 17 May 2024
2. Kobayashi, M.: Blind bowling support system which detects a number of remaining pins and a ball trajectory. In: Miesenberger, K., Fels, D., Archambault, D., Peňáz, P., Zagler, W. (eds.) Computers Helping People with Special Needs. ICCHP 2014. LNCS, vol. 8547, pp. 283–288. Springer, Cham (2014). https://doi.org/10.1007/978-3-319-08596-8_45
3. Ohshima, H., Kobayashi, M., Shimada, S.: Development of blind football play-by-play system for visually impaired spectators: Tangible Sports. In: Extended Abstracts of the 2021 CHI Conference on Human Factors in Computing Systems (CHI EA 2021), vol. 209, pp. 1–6. Association for Computing Machinery, New York (2021). https://doi.org/10.1145/3411763.3451737
4. Vanlandewijck, Y., Theisen, D., Daly, D.: Wheelchair propulsion biomechanics. Sports Med. **31**, 339–367 (2001). https://doi.org/10.2165/00007256-200131050-00005

5. Astier, M., Weissland, T., Vallier, J.M., Pradon, D., Watelain, E., Faupin, A.: Effects of synchronous versus asynchronous push modes on performance and biomechanical parameters in elite wheelchair basketball. Sports Eng. **21**, 43–51 (2018). https://doi.org/10.1007/s12283-017-0245-y
6. Goosey-Tolfrey, V.L., Moss, A.D.: Wheelchair velocity of tennis players during propulsion with and without the use of racquets. Adapt. Phys. Activ. Q. **22**(3), 291–301 (2005). https://doi.org/10.1123/apaq.22.3.291
7. Alberca, I., et al.: Sprint performance and force application of tennis players during manual wheelchair propulsion with and without holding a tennis racket. Plos One **17**(2), e0263392 (2022). https://doi.org/10.1371/journal.pone.0263392
8. Alberca, I., et al.: Impact of holding a badminton racket on spatio-temporal and kinetic parameters during manual wheelchair propulsion. Front. Sports Act. Living **4**, 862760 (2022). https://doi.org/10.3389/fspor.2022.862760
9. Goosey-Tolfrey, V.L., Leicht, C.A.: Field-based physiological testing of wheelchair athletes. Sports Med. **43**, 77–91 (2013). https://doi.org/10.1007/s40279-012-0009-6

Contrastive Learning with Multi-level Embeddings for Speech-Based Emotion Recognition

Mei Si(✉)

Rensselaer Polytechnic Institute, NY, Troy, USA
sim@rpi.edu

Abstract. This study investigates the use of contrastive learning to improve speech emotion recognition. Our method captures temporal features at various resolutions, ensuring the model generates consistent predictions with these features during contrastive learning. We further enhance our approach by integrating contrastive learning directly into the supervised training phase, rather than merely using it for pretraining. This integration allows for delicate adjustments to the neural network weights, steering the model past local optima and enhancing classification performance. Our results indicate that this integrated strategy outperforms current leading techniques.

Keywords: Speech Emotion Recognition · Contrastive Learning

1 Introduction

Recent advancements in emotion detection through speech have opened up new possibilities in human-computer interactions and mental health monitoring. Traditional methods primarily used hand-picked features from audio signals, but the advent of deep learning has shifted the focus to automatically extracting complex patterns from raw audio, significantly enhancing detection capabilities [10].

Our research expands on pioneering efforts by introducing a unique contrastive learning approach, specially designed for speech-based emotion detection purposes. Speech provides a deep insight into an individual's emotions, differing notably from facial expressions and text. While a single phrase or facial cue might directly reveal emotions, vocal cues need a broader analysis. Factors like tone variations, emphasis on specific words, and prosody changes across different time intervals all play a crucial role.

Building on the insights from studies like [17], which emphasize the importance of capturing temporal features at varying scales for improved accuracy, our work explores how contrastive learning can be effectively applied to distinguish different emotions by examining temporal information from multiple time scales.

C. Stephanidis et al. (Eds.): HCII 2024, CCIS 2319, pp. 312–321, 2025.
https://doi.org/10.1007/978-3-031-78516-0_34

Furthermore, we investigate how contrastive learning can be integrated with supervised learning, especially in limited data scenarios where supervised methods already show strong results. Our approach involves using contrastive learning not just as a pre-training step, but as a means to fine-tune neural network weights during supervised training, aiming to help the network break free from potential local optima, and unlike random perturbations, it does so in a manner conducive to improved classification outcomes.

2 Related Work

2.1 Speech-Based Emotion Recognition

Early efforts in speech-based emotion recognition focused primarily on handcrafted features such as prosodic, spectral, and voice quality parameters, capturing emotion-specific characteristics. Features such as Mel-frequency cepstral coefficients (MFCCs), pitch, energy, and formants were widely used [11,14].

The advent of machine learning, particularly deep learning, significantly transformed this field. Models such as deep neural networks (DNNs), convolutional neural networks (CNNs), and recurring neural networks (RNNs) became prominent, offering automated hierarchical feature extraction from raw or minimally processed audio signals [6,7,10]. This shift led to the development of end-to-end systems that learn directly from data, moving away from reliance on handcrafted features.

Concurrently, the integration of contextual and linguistic information through multi-modal frameworks gained traction. Combining Natural Language Processing (NLP) techniques with audio-based emotion recognition systems facilitated a more comprehensive understanding of emotional expressions [16,18].

2.2 Contrastive Learning

Recently, there has been a growing interest in leveraging unsupervised and self-supervised learning techniques, especially contrastive learning [4]. The power of these methods lies in harnessing large unlabeled datasets, which are abundantly available in the speech domain. By contrasting positive and negative samples, these techniques learn rich and discriminative representations, enhancing the performance of the model on emotion detection tasks [5]. Contrastive learning is performed by maximizing the similarity between pairs of data points considered to be similar and minimizing the similarity between pairs of data points considered dissimilar.

Given two data points x_i and x_j, a binary label y indicating if x_i and x_j are similar ($y = 1$ if similar, $y = 0$ if dissimilar), and D as the distance between the embeddings of x_i and x_j, the contrastive loss L is defined as:

$$L(x_i, x_j, y) = \frac{1}{2} y D^2 + \frac{1}{2}(1 - y) \max(0, m - D)^2$$

where m is a margin that specifies how far apart the embeddings of dissimilar items should be.

Contrastive learning has been shown to be effective for a variety of tasks, including speech recognition, speaker identification, and speech separation. In speech recognition, contrastive learning can be used to learn representations of speech features invariant to factors such as noise, reverberation, and speaker variability [5,12]. In speaker identification, contrastive learning can be used to learn representations of unique speech features of each speaker [2]. In speech separation, contrastive learning can be used to learn representations of speech features associated with different speakers or sound sources [8].

3 Contrastive Learning for Multi-scaled Features

When data can be sourced from multiple scales, such as speech features derived at varied time intervals, our goal is for all these channels to harmonize and learn cohesively. This unified learning process should promote the right decisions, and represent the input with a more meaningful embedding.

3.1 Multi-scale Contrastive Learning

Traditional contrastive learning focuses on bringing the representations of similar data points closer and pushing apart the representations of dissimilar data points in the embedding space. The proposed Multi-level Contrastive Learning (MCL) method enhances this idea by creating multiple embeddings for the same data using features computed at different temporal resolutions. It then trains these embeddings to agree with each other, allowing for a richer representation and improved discrimination in the embedding space. TIM-NET, with its unique architecture, serves as the encoder for this task [17].

3.2 TIM-NET Encoder

For automated feature extraction, we employ TIM-Net, which is a novel temporal emotional modeling approach for speech emotion recognition called Temporal-aware bi-direction Multi-scale Network (TIM-Net) [17]. The approach learns multi-scale contextual affective representations from various temporal resolutions. TIM-Net first employs temporal-aware blocks to learn temporal affective representation, then integrates complementary information from the past and the future to enrich contextual representations, and finally fuses multiple time scale features for emotion detection. The experimental results on six benchmark SER datasets demonstrate the superior performance of TIM-Net, gaining 2.34% and 2.61% improvements in the average UAR and WAR over the second best in each corpus.

The temporal-aware block is based on the Dilated Causal Convolution (DC Conv) and can enlarge and refine the receptive field of temporal patterns. The dilated convolution can capture long-term dependencies by increasing the dilation rate of the convolution kernel. In TIM-NET, a weighted layer is used to merge embeddings from different levels, yielding a singular embedding output, which is used for classification. Our proposed Multi-level Contrastive Learning (MCL) does not use this weighted layer. Instead, we train each embedding individually and force them to agree with each other with a consistency loss function.

TIM-NET stands out due to its unique capabilities in handling time-series data, making it especially suited for this task. Its structure inherently supports multi-level feature extraction. The different layers and stages in TIM-NET can be viewed as producing features of different granularity (Fig. 1).

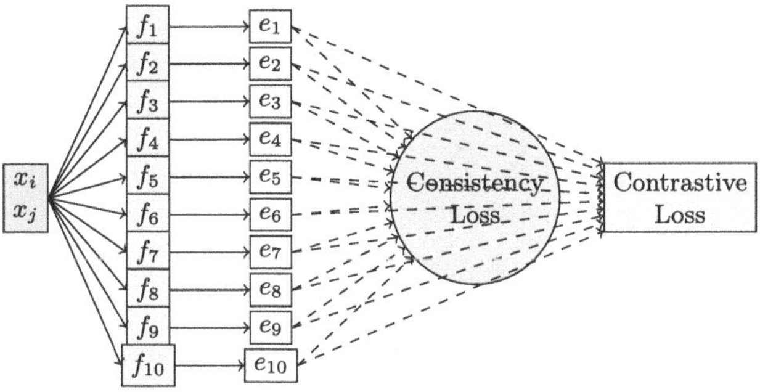

Fig. 1. Multi-Level Contrastive Learning

3.3 Multi-level Embeddings and Training

Utilizing TIM-NET, the Multi-level Contrastive Learning (MCL) approach diverges from traditional methods that obtain a singular representation for each data point. Instead, MCL generates multi-level embeddings. Each embedding level captures a distinct granularity or facet of the data, ensuring that both similarities and differences are perceived across various resolutions.

Given a data point x, its multi-level embeddings from TIM-NET are denoted as:

$$f_1(x), f_2(x), \ldots, f_n(x) \tag{1}$$

Here, f_i indicates the embedding function corresponding to the i-th level of dilation rates for TIM-NET's temporal-aware blocks, and n specifies the overall number of levels.

These multi-level embeddings offer a range, e.g., ten perspectives on the data. Through the learning process, a dialogue between these perspectives is fostered. This is manifested in the computation of contrastive loss, which takes place both within individual levels and between distinct levels. For example, a representation from a more detailed level might be contrasted against one from a broader level. Such cross-level interaction augments the learning experience, ensuring that each level complements the others. The primary losses utilized to quantify the relationships both across and within these levels are:

Intra-level Loss (Contrastive Loss): This is the loss within the same level, ensuring representations within a particular level are adequately contrasted. It is formulated as:

$$L_i = -\log\left(\frac{\exp(\langle f_i(x), f_i(x')\rangle/\tau)}{\sum_{k\neq i}\exp(\langle f_i(x), f_k(x')\rangle/\tau)}\right) \quad (2)$$

In this equation, x' denotes a positive augmentation of x, τ is a temperature parameter, and $\langle .,.\rangle$ symbolizes the dot product.

Inter-level Loss (Consistency Loss): This loss gauges the prediction differences across various levels, promoting cohesiveness among embeddings of each level while ensuring they contain unique information. Its formula is:

$$L_{\text{inter}} = \sum_{i=1}^{n-1}\sum_{j=i+1}^{n} |p(f_i(x)) - p(f_j(x))| \quad (3)$$

Here, $p(f_i(x))$ represents the prediction originating from the i-th level embedding.

For training, the total loss, a blend of intra-level and inter-level losses, is computed as:

$$L_{\text{total}} = \sum_{i=1}^{n} \alpha_i L_i + \beta L_{\text{inter}} \quad (4)$$

With α_i being the weights for each level's contrastive loss and β the weight for the inter-level loss.

3.4 Integrating Contrastive Learning with Supervised Learning

Our approach uniquely integrates contrastive learning within the supervised learning framework, serving as a strategic tool to help the classifier escape local optima. Traditional pre-training with contrastive learning may not always enhance supervised learning performance, at least when the datasets are small as in our case. In contrast, our approach directly incorporates it into the supervised training phase, effectively recalibrating neural network weights. This allows for subtle steering towards improved label differentiation, avoiding the pitfalls of conventional supervised techniques that often get trapped in local optima. Our method's refined adjustment of weights offers a more targeted and sophisticated approach than relying on random disturbances or abrupt changes like spikes in learning rate.

This adjustment aims to sharpen the differentiation between labels, ensuring a more effective starting point when supervised learning continues (Fig. 2).

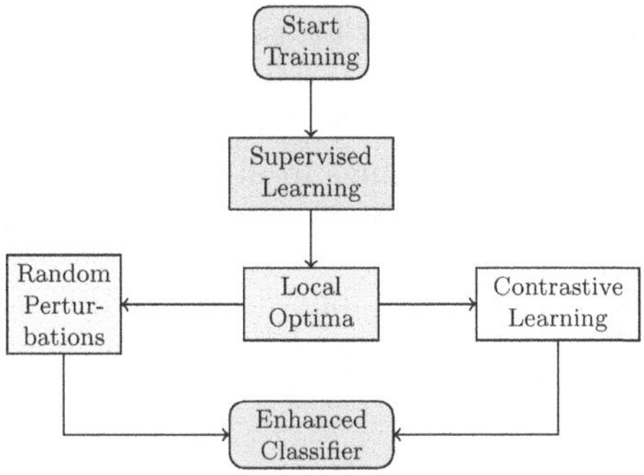

Fig. 2. Use Contrastive Learning in Supervised Learning

4 Evaluation

4.1 Datasets and Experiment Set Up

For our study, we utilized six publicly available and prominent speech emotion recognition datasets. EMODB is a German dataset featuring emotional sentences [15]. EMOVO, in Italian, comprises recordings of actors emoting in different contexts [3]. SAVEE is an audio-visual set with male actors portraying varied emotions [9]. CASIA, by the Chinese Academy of Sciences, includes Mandarin emotional speeches [19]. RAVDESS encompasses diverse emotional speech and song recordings [13]. IEMOCAP offers multi-modal English conversational interactions [1]. We prepared the data from these datasets by extracting Mel-Frequency Cepstral Coefficient (MFCC) features from the speech data, which were then used in all subsequent experiments.

Our evaluation contains two studies. The first study aimed to determine how contrastive learning might bolster the effectiveness of supervised learning. We established four training configurations:

1. **S1_MCL_S2**: Supervised learning, followed by Multi-level Contrastive Learning (MCL), and another round of supervised learning.
2. **MCL_S2**: Begins with MCL, then transitions to supervised learning.
3. **S1_S2**: Two consecutive stages of supervised learning.
4. **S2**: Solely employs supervised learning, i.e., the original TIM-NET training.

We used the default TIM-NET architect for supervised learning (S1 and S2). The initial round of supervised learning (S1) undergoes 60 epochs, often reaching or nearing local maxima. The MCL interlude is limited to 4 epochs. When MCL intervenes between two supervised sessions, we clip the gradient to mitigate drastic weight alterations. There's no gradient clipping for MCL if it's the initial training phase. The succeeding supervised learning (S2) is capped at 300 epochs but incorporates early stopping, the same as how TIM-NET was trained.

The second phase of our experiment focused on evaluating the efficiency of our proposed MCL against traditional contrastive learning. We directly used TIM-NET's model to get the embedding for standard contrastive learning, by using a weighted layer to combine embeddings from different levels, which produced a single embedding output. This introduced two more training configurations:

5. **S1_CL_S2**: Supervised learning, followed by traditional Contrastive Learning (CL), and another round of supervised learning.
6. **CL_S2**: Begins with CL and then transitions to supervised learning.

Similar to the first phase, when CL is positioned between two supervised sessions, gradient clipping is employed to stabilize learning. All other settings mirror those of the first experimental phase.

4.2 Results and Discussion

For evaluation, we conducted 10-fold cross-validation for all configurations, averaging the accuracies from each fold to determine the final accuracy. The experiments were conducted using an A100 GPU, with each dataset taking approximately one to three hours to evaluate.

Table 1. Contrastive Learning with Multi-Level Embedding. C1 stands for S1_MCL_S2 and C2 stands for MCL_S2.

	C1	C2	S1_S2	S2
EMODB	**92.91**	92.70	92.52	92.14
EMOVO	**88.59**	86.39	87.41	86.72
SAVEE	85.83	**86.67**	84.38	85.63
CASIA	**89.92**	88.58	89.67	88.25
RAVDE	**88.54**	87.50	87.64	87.22
IEMOCAP	**70.66**	69.66	69.66	70.06

We established two baselines for our experiment. Condition 4 – the $S2$ only condition serves as our primary baseline. This condition only uses supervised learning, which is how the original TIM-NET is trained. In [17], it is demonstrated that TIM-NET surpasses all other state-of-the-art models across each of these six datasets. Thus, enhancing this baseline positions our results at the forefront of current state-of-the-art results. The $S1\_S2$ condition, which incorporates two consecutive sessions of supervised learning, represents our secondary baseline. This was designed to gauge the impact of halting and then recommencing the learning process.

In Table 1, it becomes evident that interlacing contrastive learning between two supervised learning sessions generally enhances performance outcomes.

Notably, the MCL approach consistently excels, surpassing other methodologies in nearly all instances except for the SAVEE dataset. However, positioning MCL at the beginning of the training process yields mixed results. While in some cases, it matches or even outperforms pure supervised learning, in datasets like EMOVO and IEMOCAP, it marginally underperforms, indicating that the integration point of MCL within the training pipeline can significantly influence outcomes.

Table 2. Contrastive Learning with One Embedding

	S1_CL_S2	CL_S2
EMODB	**92.34**	90.28
EMOVO	**86.21**	86.05
SAVEE	**84.79**	84.38
CASIA	**89.75**	88.17
RAVDE	86.88	**88.06**
IEMOCAP	**70.11**	69.95

In Table 2, a recurring trend is observed: when contrastive learning (CL) is inserted between two supervised training sessions, it consistently yields better results compared to initiating the training process with CL. Cross-referencing the outcomes from both tables, it's evident that for none of the datasets does the S1_CL_S2 condition surpass its counterpart, the S1_MCL_S2 condition. Intriguingly, the CL_S2 condition and, in certain instances, even the S1_CL_S2 condition, underperform relative to the S2-only baseline in Table 1.

5 Conclusion

Our proposed Multi-level Contrastive Learning (MCL) training offers two benefits:

- **Richer Representations**: The multiple levels of embeddings facilitate a holistic representation of each data point.
- **Optimized Discrimination**: The model optimizes the discriminative capability of temporal-aware embeddings, achieving enhanced differentiation both within individual levels and across different levels.

Our empirical findings bolster our initial hypothesis: multi-level contrastive learning (MCL) possesses a distinct edge over the traditional contrastive learning (CL) methodology. Moreover, strategically positioning contrastive learning amidst supervised learning sessions can potentially improve the latter's efficacy.

6 Limitations and Future Work

This study has several limitations. Firstly, the datasets used are relatively small, with IEMOCAP, the largest, having fewer than 5000 data points, and smaller ones like EMODB only having hundreds. This size constraint may partly explain why contrastive learning is less effective as a pretraining approach in our context, and it's uncertain if this conclusion applies to larger datasets. However, our approach is demonstrated to be an effective approach for learning from small datasets.

Secondly, the datasets contain audio expressing fairly straightforward emotions. For instance, the RAVDE dataset involves 10 actors reading sentences in 7 emotions, where typically, the whole sentence conveys a clear emotion. This contrasts with real-life scenarios where different parts of a sentence can express varied emotions. Thus, our assumption that features extracted at different granularities should represent the same emotion might not be universally valid. In the future, we are interested in validating our approach with more types of data.

Lastly, our research only utilized features from the audio channel. We did not extend our multi-level contrastive learning technique to multimodal emotion recognition, an area we intend to explore in future work.

7 Ethical Consideration

In our research on emotion recognition using speech processing techniques, we recognize the potential for biases in speech data, which could lead to unfair or discriminatory outcomes.

We are also aware of the limitations inherent in current models, particularly their inability to fully grasp the subtleties of human language, potentially leading to incorrect decisions.

Additionally, we recognize the risk of emotion recognition technology being misused, for instance, in unauthorized surveillance or in ways that could violate individual privacy and autonomy. We strongly advocate for the responsible and ethical application of this technology, ensuring it is used in a manner that respects individual rights and brings positive contributions to society.

References

1. Busso, C., et al.: IEMOCAP: interactive emotional dyadic motion capture database. Lang. Resour. Eval. **42**, 335–359 (2008)
2. Chen, S., et al.: Unispeech-Sat: Universal speech representation learning with speaker aware pre-training. In: ICASSP 2022-2022 IEEE International Conference on Acoustics, Speech and Signal Processing (ICASSP), pp. 6152–6156. IEEE (2022)
3. Costantini, G., Iaderola, I., Paoloni, A., Todisco, M., et al.: EMOVO Corpus: an italian emotional speech database. In: Proceedings of the ninth international conference on language resources and evaluation (LREC 2014), pp. 3501–3504. European Language Resources Association (ELRA) (2014)

4. Dai, B., Lin, D.: Contrastive learning for image captioning. In: Advances in Neural Information Processing Systems, vol. 30 (2017)
5. Dhamyal, H., Elizalde, B., Deshmukh, S., Wang, H., Raj, B., Singh, R.: Describing emotions with acoustic property prompts for speech emotion recognition. arXiv preprint arXiv:2211.07737 (2022)
6. Fan, Y., Lu, X., Li, D., Liu, Y.: Video-based emotion recognition using CNN-RNN and C3D hybrid networks. In: Proceedings of the 18th ACM International Conference on Multimodal Interaction, pp. 445–450 (2016)
7. Huang, Z., Dong, M., Mao, Q., Zhan, Y.: Speech emotion recognition using CNN. In: Proceedings of the 22nd ACM international conference on Multimedia, pp. 801–804 (2014)
8. Huang, Z., Watanabe, S., Yang, S.w., García, P., Khudanpur, S.: Investigating self-supervised learning for speech enhancement and separation. In: ICASSP 2022-2022 IEEE International Conference on Acoustics, Speech and Signal Processing (ICASSP), pp. 6837–6841. IEEE (2022)
9. Jackson, P., Haq, S.: Surrey Audio-Visual Expressed Emotion (SAVEE) Database. University of Surrey, Guildford, UK (2014)
10. Khalil, R.A., Jones, E., Babar, M.I., Jan, T., Zafar, M.H., Alhussain, T.: Speech emotion recognition using deep learning techniques: a review. IEEE Access **7**, 117327–117345 (2019)
11. Kishore, K.K., Satish, P.K.: Emotion recognition in speech using MFCC and wavelet features. In: 2013 3rd IEEE International Advance Computing Conference (IACC), pp. 842–847. IEEE (2013)
12. Li, M., et al.: Contrastive unsupervised learning for speech emotion recognition. In: ICASSP 2021-2021 IEEE International Conference on Acoustics, Speech and Signal Processing (ICASSP), pp. 6329–6333. IEEE (2021)
13. Livingstone, S.R., Russo, F.A.: The Ryerson audio-visual database of emotional speech and song (RAVDESS): a dynamic, multimodal set of facial and vocal expressions in north American English. PLoS ONE **13**(5), e0196391 (2018)
14. Milton, A., Roy, S.S., Selvi, S.T.: SVM scheme for speech emotion recognition using MFCC feature. Int. J. Comput. Appl. **69**(9), 34–39 (2013)
15. Parlak, C., Diri, B., Gürgen, F.: A cross-corpus experiment in speech emotion recognition. In: SLAM@ INTERSPEECH, pp. 58–61 (2014)
16. Sailunaz, K., Dhaliwal, M., Rokne, J., Alhajj, R.: Emotion detection from text and speech: a survey. Soc. Netw. Anal. Min. **8**, 1–26 (2018)
17. Ye, J., Wen, X.C., Wei, Y., Xu, Y., Liu, K., Shan, H.: Temporal modeling matters: a novel temporal emotional modeling approach for speech emotion recognition. In: ICASSP 2023-2023 IEEE International Conference on Acoustics, Speech and Signal Processing (ICASSP), pp. 1–5. IEEE (2023)
18. Yoon, S., Byun, S., Jung, K.: Multimodal speech emotion recognition using audio and text. In: 2018 IEEE Spoken Language Technology Workshop (SLT), pp. 112–118. IEEE (2018)
19. Zhang, J., Jia, H.: Design of speech corpus for mandarin text to speech. In: The Blizzard Challenge 2008 Workshop (2008)

BrailleÉcran: A Tangible Braille Approach for Smartphone Text Entry

Fabrizzio Soares[1(✉)], Joyce Siqueira[4], Mateus M. Luna[1], Emilia A. Nogueira[1], Lillian Cristina dos Santos[2], Juliana G. Faria[2], Juliana Paula Felix[1], Joao Soares de Oliveira Neto[3], Afonso U. Fonseca[1], and Thamer Horbylon Nascimento[5]

[1] Instituto de Informática, Universidade Federal de Goiás, Goiânia/GO, Brazil
fabrizzio@inf.ufg.br, emilia@discente.ufg.br, {julianafelix,afonsoueslei}@ufg.br,mateus.m.luna@gmail.com

[2] Faculdade de Letras, Universidade Federal de Goiás, Goiânia/GO, Brazil
lilian_cristina@discente.ufg.br, julianagf@ufg.br

[3] Universidade Federal da Bahia, Camaçari/BA, Brazil
j-neto@ufba.br

[4] Universidade Católica de Brasília, Brasília/DF, Brazil

[5] Instituto Federal Goiano – Campus Iporá Federal, Iporá/GO, Brazil
thamer.nascimento@ifgoiano.edu.br

Abstract. Touch screens have made smartphones more dynamic but less accessible to visually impaired people due to the lack of a physical keyboard. This research aimed to develop a Braille-based text input method using a tactile interface on a touch screen, guided by W3C accessibility guidelines and input from a Braille-literate specialist. The result was BrailleÉcran, an Android app with a 3D-printable tactile interface, a customizable settings panel, and a spoken tutorial. Usability tests with ten volunteers showed a typing speed of 2.52 words per minute and an error rate of 2.68

Keywords: Blind · Braille Smartphone · Tactile interface · Text entry

1 Introduction

In today's society, smartphones are part of daily life and have become essential to carry out various activities, of which communication potential stands out. It's use is so expressive, that research [1] predict in the next five years an increase of one billion smartphone users. However the touch screen still represents a barrier for blind users usability. To promote smartphone use among the 39 million visually impaired people globally [2], accessibility solutions like VoiceOver and TalkBack have been developed. However, these solutions still limit text entry by relying on a difficult-to-use virtual QWERTY keyboard, voice typing which is ineffective in noisy environments and lacks privacy, and external devices like

C. Stephanidis et al. (Eds.): HCII 2024, CCIS 2319, pp. 322–331, 2025.
https://doi.org/10.1007/978-3-031-78516-0_35

Braille keyboards, which are impractical. This research aims to develop a low-cost, Braille-based text entry method for smartphones that ensures privacy and usability. Leveraging touch and auditory feedback, the application uses sound and vibrations, supported by a tactile interface on the touch screen, to create a comfortable and pleasant tool for visually impaired users.

This paper is organized in: Sect. 2, Related Work, Sect. 3, Conceptual Aspects; Sect. 4, Materials and Methods; Sect. 5, Prototypes; Sect. 6, Results and lastly, in Sect. 7, the Conclusion.

2 Related Work

Over the year, many researches have been conducted to provide better text input for the Blind. BrailleType [3] provided a touch screen text-entry method using the Braille alphabet, while BrailleKey presented a comparative study of a simplified Braille to existing methods like Apple's VoiceOver for iOS [4] In BrailleTouch [5] was developed a touchscreen text entry system for proficient braille users who achieved typing speeds of up to 32.1 wpm on smartphones. LêBraille [6] [7] provides a virtual Braille keyboard for touchscreen devices and compare to alphanumeric virtual keyboards. The evaluation of nonvisual text entry methods, focusing on Perkinput's performance compared to VoiceOver for blind users is discussed in Perkinput [8]. TypeinBraille [9] introduces a Braille-based typing technique focused in typing efficiency and accuracy for visually impaired users on smartphones. EdgeBraille [10] researched a Braille-based text input method for visually impaired users on touchscreens, showing comparable performance to talking keyboards with potential for further improvements. In [11] [12] evaluates the SingleTapBraille keyboard for blind users, comparing its performance with the QWERTY keyboard and highlighting its advantages in speed and accuracy. A Braille slate soft keyboard prototype aimed at enhancing accessibility for visually impaired individuals by leveraging their Braille writing experience for input on touch-enabled devices is explored in H-Slate [13]. BrailleSketch [14] provides a gesture-based text input method that enables visually impaired users to input Braille code efficiently on touch screens with promising typing speeds and low error rates. Moreover, HoliBraille [15] introduces a multipoint vibrotactile device that enhances Braille character discrimination on mobile devices through localized feedback using six vibrotactile motors and springs. Finally, [16] discusses the development of a wireless smartphone keyboard for visually challenged users, highlighting the need for user-friendly and cost-effective solutions to improve text input accessibility. A Systematic Literature Review (SLR) is provided in [17] with a more comprehensive description of those works.

3 Conceptual Aspects

BrailleÉcran is a proposed Assistive Technology (AT) for visually impaired individuals, designed to enhance their autonomy, independence, quality of life, and social inclusion [18]. This prototype concept was introduced in 2016 [19], and has evolved over the years. This AT encompasses products, resources, methodologies, strategies, practices, and services. The target audience includes both blind and low-vision individuals, as defined by Brazilian Federal Decree n. 3298/99 [20], which specifies blindness as a visual acuity of 0.05 or less and low vision as a visual acuity between 0.3 and 0.05, both in the best eye with optimal correction.

4 Materials and Methods

4.1 Material

Prototypes were tested in a Motorola Moto G 2nd, with a 5" screen (70.7 *mm* x 141.5 *mm*), running Android 6.0 (Lollipop). The software was developed in IDE (*Integrated Development Environment*) Android Studio 2.0.0 with API 23, along with Android's *TextToSpeech* library. The tactile surface was modeled with OpenScad version 2015.03–2 and printed in white translucent Polylactic Acid (PLA) in a Prusa Mendel i3 3D printer.

4.2 Method

The authors collaborated with the PixelLab research group at the Federal University of Goiás to develop prototypes, evaluated with a 38-year-old congenitally blind Braille-literate specialist. These prototypes' interfaces align with Mobile Accessibility guidelines from the W3C [21], focusing on Perceivable, Operable, Understandable, and Robust principles.

Eight out of 17 guidelines were used, omitting those for hybrid applications. These selected guidelines address issues like screen size, contrast, keyboard control, touch target size, gestures, grouping elements, providing actionable indications, and offering instructions for device manipulation. The application of these guidelines is elaborated in the study's Results section. For Evaluation Metrics were used: Speed [22]: Words per Minute - WPM; Error rate [22,23]: Total Error Rate - TER, Not Corrected Error Rate - NCER and Corrected Error Rate - CER.

Experimental Study. The experiments involved 10 volunteers proficient in Braille. They used text sourced from Vertanen and Kristensson (2011) [24]. Different texts were employed to prevent memorization. The text was dictated and repeated as needed. If a volunteer forgot, didn't understand, or stopped typing without valid reason, the data was discarded, and the iteration restarted. Each experiment phase was conducted individually within a single session.

The procedure was divided into stages, listed below:

1. Braille System review: optional step, a participant can review a paper Braille written.
2. Training: (1) presentation of BrailleÉcran; (2) "Help Center" use by user (3) free training and (4) dictated training with 6 letters and 5 aleatory words. Duration limit: 45 min.

3. Speed test: (1) words typed: 5 random words from a set of 16. Each word was repeated 6 times to check the progression of text input speed [25]. The results were normalized to show the time taken to type 18 Braille points, the smallest word typed by the volunteers. Each volunteer typed 3 identical phrases. Mistakes were allowed to be ignored, except for accent, punctuation, and capitalization.
4. Error test: each voluntary typed 3 phrases, the same for all of them. The volunteers should edit and use accent, punctuation and capital letters.

5 BrailleÉcran Prototype

The BrailleÉcran, Fig. 1a, is a combination of the application and tactile interface. In this section, it is presented the characteristics and layout of each one. A video demonstrating the working prototype is submitted with this paper.

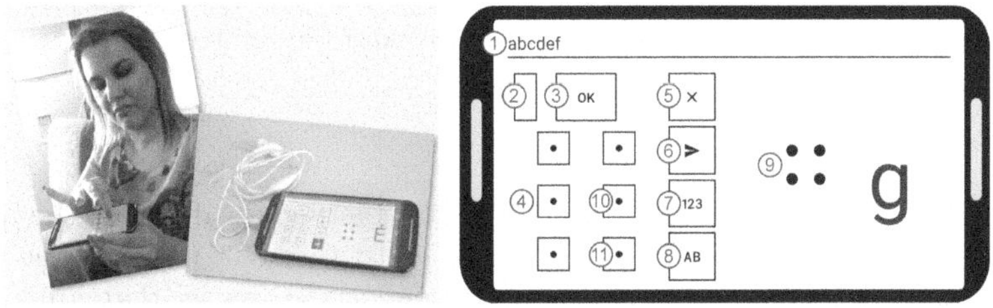

(a) Specialist Evaluation (b) App Interface

Fig. 1. BrailleÉcran Evalution and Prototype

5.1 Application

The app prototype provides (Fig. 1b):

1. **Text Box:** shows the message that is being typed at the top.
2. **Unlock Button:** app starts with buttons disabled, then user can explore it without accidental taps. A simple tap in "OK" button unlocks it.
3. **Confirm:** "OK" button is always activated by a single tap and act as confirming typed letter, "Help Center" and "Settings Panel", and inserting space.
4. **Braille Cells:**: each dot is activated/deactivated by single tap. Many dots can be activated simultaneously and it is no necessary follow the any sequence. All buttons are deactivated when a letter is confirmed.
5. **Delete:** also has two functions: short tap deletes letters, and long tap, deactivate all Braille cells.
6. **Send:** single tap reads the message out loud, long tap sends a message, a new single tap cancels sending and returns to typing mode.

7. **Number:** in Braille, the number is represented by symbol 3456 before a letter. On BrailleÉcran, for reducing the number of taps, a specific button was created, enabled and disabled by a simple tap. However, it is possible to insert the symbol by Braille cells. In this case, only the first character entered will be a number.
8. **Uppercase:** for capital letters, in Braille, it is used the symbol 46 before the letter. As with the numbers, a specific button is available, however, the Braille symbol too can still be typed in Braille cells.
9. **Display:** shows the Braille dots typed and the letter being formed on the right side of the interface.
10. **Settings Panel:** allows to configure some features. To maintain layout simplicity, "Settings Panel"is activated with a shortcut, using existing buttons "Numbers" and "fifth dot" followed by the confirmation.

Initial tests, performed with the expert user, showed the importance to offer a visual experience for those who can assist the blind people in some moments and even for those with low vision. Thus, this layout was developed joining two different realities, for blind, introduced above, and for sighted, bellow.

5.2 Tactile Interface

The tactile interface was created for bring the tactile sensation for the app. It was 3D printed with translucent material to assist the sight users. In the tactile interface, all buttons were highlighted. Beyond these, paths that guide users between menu buttons and delimit application boundaries were added. It acts as tactile floor, used for directing people in open environments, Fig. 2.

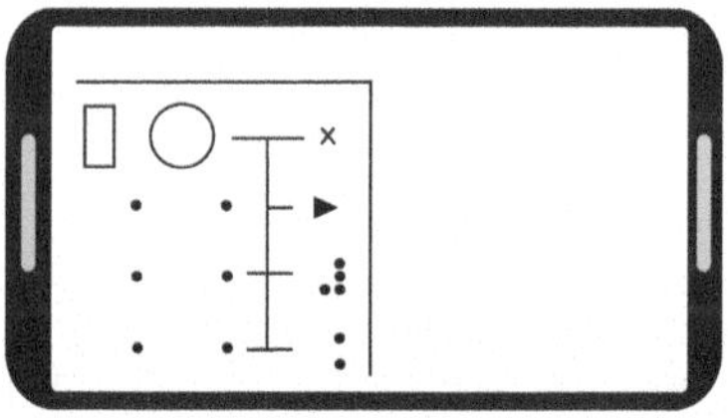

Fig. 2. Tactile Interface

The Braille symbol was created using the Braille font and a text generator function. The symbol size was defined empirically. The measures are presented in Table 1.

Table 1. Tactile Interface Measurements

Shield	height	63 mm
	width	110 mm
	thickness	0.2 mm
Braille symbols	buttons	0.4 mm
	dots	0.6 mm^2
Buttons size	height	0.4 mm
	radius	0.8 mm
Other relays	height	0.2 mm

6 User Study and Results

The experiments results were described. First, shows the volunteers profile, followed the speed, error rate, user satisfaction and user experience.

6.1 Volunteers

The volunteers were recruited with the assistance of Braille teachers from CEMAD - Centro Municipal de Apoio ao Deficiente, in the city of Anápolis - GO. At the end, 10 volunteers, 6 women and 4 men, aged between 21 and 56, accepted to participate in the experiments. Table 2 displays the general profile of the group.

Table 2. Volunteers Profile

Visual impairment	10% low vision	90% blind
Level of education	10% Elementary	20% High
	40% University	30% Master's
Computer experience	50% basic	50% intermediary
	0% advanced	0% never used
Cellphone experience	30% basic	40% intermediary
	20% advanced	10% never used
Smartphone with physical keyboard experience	20% basic	60% intermediary
	20% advanced	0% never used
Smartphone with virtual keyboard experience	20% basic	70% intermediary
	10% advanced	0% never used

6.2 Speed and Error Rate

The speed tests were done in two steps: words repetition and phrases. The group behavior is presented in Table 3, with time average (μ) and standard deviation (ρ) for each word. The result presents the gradual decrease in typed speed, demonstrating that the training is relevant for the user purchase most agility.

Table 3. Evolution of volunteers in typing 18 braille dots, in minutes

Evolution	01	02	03	04	05
μ	46.031	39.899	38.045	35.360	37.271
ρ	16.114	12.682	12.800	12.010	12.899

Table 4. Words per minutes typed by volunteers group

Phrase	1	2	3	μ
WPS	2.40	2.59	2.58	2.52

Each voluntary typed 3 phrases, with 21, 19 and 20 characters, respectively. The group behavior is presented in Table 4.

Finally, the volunteers typed 3 phrases, characters and braille dots were analyzed. The group behavior are presented in Table 5. For typing characters, the Total Error Rate (TER) average was 2,68%, that is, 97.32% accuracy. Before characters are confirmed, users type on braille dots, in this phase, the TER average was greater, 5.36%, that is, 94,64% accuracy.

Table 5. Error rate (%), per phrases, considering characters and braille dots

	Characters			Braille dots			Result[1]
	TER	NCER	CER	TER	NCER	CER	
01[2]	1.80	0.71	1.08	5.34	0.00	5.34	90%
02[3]	2.11	0.29	1.82	4.53	0.00	4.53	90%
03[4]	4.13	1.46	2.67	6.20	0.00	6.20	70%

[1] % correct phrase.
[2] 26 characters e 72 braille dots.
[3] 31 characters e 78 braille dots.
[4] 30 characters e 73 braille dots.

These data show that analyzing only the characters is not enough for checking the error rate, because the error may have occurred before characters confirmation. Beyond that, errors of the braille symbol also affects the time spent, even resulting in correct characters.

7 Conclusions and Future Works

BrailleÉcran was developed to provide an efficient tool for Braille text entry on smartphones for the blind and low vision community. Three key challenges were addressed: identifying necessary elements for smartphone Braille entry, ensuring efficiency and user experience, and achieving affordability. To address the first challenge, a systematic literature review and collaboration with a blind specialist guided the method's development, adhering to mobile accessibility guidelines.

Volunteers conducted experimental tests to assess efficiency and user experience, informing iterative improvements. The proposed method is low-cost, with the Android app available for free and a low-cost tactile interface, though challenges remain with 3D printer accessibility. BrailleÉcran contributes significantly to Human-Computer Interaction, prioritizing efficiency and user experience. Notable features include its open-source nature, adherence to W3C mobile accessibility guidelines, tactile interface, customizable settings panel, and a help center.

Future improvements aim to enhance integration with smartphone features like TalkBack and incorporate user feedback. Continued studies aim to provide a practical technological solution that fosters greater independence for the visually impaired community.

Acknowledgments. The authors of this study would like to acknowledge the support provided by CAPES (Coordenação de Aperfeiçoamento de Pessoal de Nível Superior) Call 17/2023 – Graduate Development Operation (PDPG) – Affirmative Policies and Diversity (3156 – 88887.914010/2023-00 and 88881.914011/2023-01), and Financing Code #001.

References

1. The Statistics Portal, Number of smartphone users worldwide from 2014 to 2020 (in millions) (2016). URL: https://www.statista.com/statistics/330695/number-of-smartphone-users-worldwide/ (visited on 11/15/2016)
2. World Health Organization, World Health Organization. Visual Impairment and Blindness (2014). URL: http://www.who.int/mediacentre/factsheets/fs282/en/ (visited on 12/13/2015)
3. Oliveira, J., Guerreiro, T., Nicolau, H., Jorge, J., Gonçalves, D.: BrailleType: unleashing braille over touch screen mobile phones. In: Campos, P., Graham, N., Jorge, J., Nunes, N., Palanque, P., Winckler, M. (eds.) INTERACT 2011. LNCS, vol. 6946, pp. 100–107. Springer, Heidelberg (2011). https://doi.org/10.1007/978-3-642-23774-4_10
4. Subash, N.S., Nambiar, S., Kumar. V.: BrailleKey: an alternative braille text input system: comparative study of an innovative simplified text input system for the visually impaired. In: Intelligent Human Computer Interaction (IHCI), 2012 4th International Conference on, pp. 1–4 (2012). https://doi.org/10.1109/IHCI.2012.6481790
5. Southern, C., et al.: An Evaluation of BrailleTouch: mobile touchscreen text entry for the visually impaired. In: Proceedings of the 14th International Conference on Human-computer Interaction with Mobile Devices and Services. MobileHCI '12. San Francisco, California, USA: ACM, pp. 317–326 (2012). ISBN: 978-1-4503-1105-2. https://doi.org/10.1145/2371574.2371623.
6. Façanha, A.R., et al.: LêbrailleTWT: providing visual accessibility to twitter on touchscreen devices. In: Proceedings of the 18th Brazilian Symposium on Multimedia and the Web. WebMedia '12. São Paulo/SP, Brazil: ACM, pp. 313–320 (2012). ISBN: 978-1-4503-1706-1. https://doi.org/10.1145/2382636.2382703.

7. Façanha, A.R., et al.: Touchscreen mobile phones virtual keyboarding for people with visual disabilities. English. In: Human-Computer Interaction. Applications and Services. Ed. by Masaaki Kurosu. Vol. 8512. Lecture Notes in Computer Science. Springer International Publishing, pp. 134–145 (2014). ISBN: 978-3-319-07226-5. https://doi.org/10.1007/978-3-319-07227-2_14.
8. Azenkot, S., et al.: Input finger detection for nonvisual touch screen text entry in perkinput. In: Proceedings of Graphics Interface 2012. GI '12. Toronto, Ontario, Canada: Canadian Information Processing Society, pp. 121–129 (2012). ISBN: 978-1-4503-1420-6. URL: http://dl.acm.org/citation.cfm?id=2305276.2305297
9. Mascetti, S., Bernareggi, C., Belotti, M.: "TypeInBraille: quick eyes-free typing on smartphones". English. In: Computers Helping People with Special Needs. Ed. by Klaus Miesenberger et al. Vol. 7383. Lecture Notes in Computer Science. Springer Berlin Heidelberg, pp. 615–622 (2012). ISBN: 978-3-642-31533-6. https://doi.org/10.1007/978-3-642-31534-3_90.URL: http://dx.doi.org/10.1007/978-3-642-31534-3_90
10. Mattheiss, E., et al.: "Dots and Letters: accessible braille-based text input for visually impaired people on mobile touchscreen devices". English. In: Computers Helping People with Special Needs. Ed. by Klaus Miesenberger et al. Lecture Notes in Computer Science. Springer International Publishing. vol. 8547, pp. 650–657 (2014). ISBN: 978-3-319-08595-1. https://doi.org/10.1007/978-3-319-08596-8_100.URL
11. Alnfiai, M., Sampalli, S.:"An evaluation of singletapbraille keyboard: a text entry method that utilizes braille patterns on touchscreen devices". In: Proceedings of the 18th International ACM SIGACCESS Conference on Computers and Accessibility. ASSETS '16. Reno, Nevada, USA: ACM, pp. 161–169 (2016) . ISBN: 978-1-4503-4124-0. https://doi.org/10.1145/2982142.2982161.
12. Alnfiai, M., Sampalli, S.: SingleTapBraille: developing a text entry method based on braille patterns using a single tap. Proce. Comput. Sci. **94**, 248–255 (2016)
13. Cavazos Quero, L., et al.: "H-Slate: a hybrid braille slate soft keyboard for touchscreen devices". In: Companion of the 2017 ACM Conference on Computer Supported Cooperative Work and Social Computing. CSCW '17 Companion. Portland, Oregon, USA: ACM, pp. 159–162 (2017). ISBN: 978- 1-4503-4688-7. https://doi.org/10.1145/3022198.3026340.
14. Li, M., Fan, M., Truong, K.N.: "BrailleSketch: a gesturebased text input method for people with visual impairments". In: Proceedings of the 19th International ACM SIGACCESS Conference on Computers and Accessibility. ASSETS '17. Baltimore, Maryland, USA: ACM, pp. 12–21 (2017). ISBN: 978-1-4503-4926-0. https://doi.org/10.1145/3132525.3132528.
15. Nicolau, H., et al.: "HoliBraille: multipoint vibrotactile feedback on mobile devices". In: Proceedings of the 12th Web for All Conference. W4A '15. Florence, Italy: ACM, pp. 301–304 (2015). ISBN: 978-1-4503-3342-9. https://doi.org/10.1145/2745555.2746643.
16. D'silva, C., Parthasarathy, V., Rao, S.N.: "Wireless smartphone keyboard for visually challenged users". In: Proceedings of the 2016 Workshop on Wearable Systems and Applications. WearSys '16. Singapore, Singapore: ACM, pp. 13–17 (2016). ISBN: 978-1-4503-4326-8. https://doi.org/10.1145/2935643.2935648.
17. Siqueira, J., et al.: "Braille text entry on smartphones: a systematic review of the literature". In: 2016 IEEE 40th annual computer software and applications conference (COMPSAC). vol. 2. IEEE, pp. 521–526 (2016)
18. Comitê de Ajudas Técnicas. "Tecnologia assistiva". In: Brasılia: CORDE (2009)

19. Siqueira, J., et al.: "BrailleÉcran: a braille approach to text entry on smartphones". In: 2016 IEEE 40th Annual Computer Software and Applications Conference (COMPSAC). vol. 2. IEEE, pp. 608–609 (2016)
20. Brasil. "Decreto no 3.298, de 20 de dezembro de 1999. Regulamenta a Lei no 7.853, de 24 de outubro de 1989, dispõe sobre a Polıtica Nacional para a Integração da Pessoa Portadora de Deficiência, consolida as normas de proteção, e dá outras providências". In: Diário Oficial da União (1999)
21. World Wide Web Consortium. Mobile Accessibility: How WCAG 2.0 and Other W3C/WAI Guidelines Apply to Mobile (2015). URL: https://www.w3.org/TR/mobile-accessibility-mapping/ (visited on 11/17/2016)
22. Arif, A.S., Stuerzlinger, W.: "Analysis of text entry performance metrics". In: 2009 IEEE Toronto International Conference Science and Technology for Humanity (TIC-STH), pp. 100–105 (2009). https://doi.org/10.1109/TIC-STH.2009.5444533
23. Koivisto, M., Urbaczewski, A.:"Accuracy metrics in mobile text entry". In: Proceedings 1st IASTED Conference on Human-Computer Interaction (2005)
24. Vertanen, K., Kristensson, P.O.: "A versatile dataset for text entry evaluations based on genuine mobile emails". In: Proceedings of the 13th International Conference on Human Computer Interaction with Mobile Devices and Services. MobileHCI '11. Stockholm, Sweden: ACM, pp. 295–298 (2011). ISBN: 978-1-4503-0541-9. https://doi.org/10.1145/2037373.2037418.
25. Wang, C.Y., et al.: "PalmType: using palms as keyboards for smart glasses". In: Proceedings of the 17th International Conference on Human- Computer Interaction with Mobile Devices and Services. MobileHCI '15. Copenhagen, Denmark: ACM, pp. 153–160 (2015). ISBN: 978-1-4503-3652-9. https://doi.org/10.1145/2785830.2785886.

ChatGPT, Machine Learning and AI Killed My Password. Building Next Generation Authentication Systems

Afamefuna P. Umejiaku and Victor Sheng(✉)

Texas Tech University, Lubbock, TX 79415, USA
victor.sheng@ttu.edu

Abstract. The urgency to retrofit password authentication systems has grown significantly with the rise of computational power and the integration of advanced Artificial Intelligence (AI) and machine learning models in password guessing tools. As these tools become more sophisticated, creating passwords that are both strong enough to withstand such challenges and memorable has become increasingly difficult. This difficulty often leads users to adopt unsafe practices, such as reusing passwords or creating weak passwords. The RoseCliff Algorithm offers a promising solution by introducing a dual authentication mechanism that not only fortifies systems against sophisticated guessing techniques but also dynamically updates stored passwords. Our research demonstrates that this algorithm significantly increases the time required for a hacker to decipher a user's password using current dominant hacking techniques. Additionally, we show that large language models (LLMs) can assist in generating stronger memorable passwords and creating more effective honey tokens. We propose that leveraging LLMs, such as ChatGPT, in conjunction with the RoseCliff Algorithm, could pave the way for the next generation of robust and dynamic authentication systems, offering enhanced security and usability for users.

Keywords: Passwords · Machine learning · ChatGPT · RoseCliff

1 Introduction

Digital interactions have become ubiquitous, making it paramount to secure these interactions. With passwords remaining the most dominant form of digital authentication, it is integral to ensure that they are robust enough to withstand potential attacks. Users are often encouraged to use strong passwords, which are checked to see if they meet certain requirements with the aim of increasing password strength [1]. Password strength is a measure of how resistant a password is to guessing and cracking attempts. It is influenced by factors such as the length of the password and the variety of characters used [2]. Users have devised various techniques to create passwords. One such technique involves the manipulation of characters using "leet" speak, where letters are replaced with

C. Stephanidis et al. (Eds.): HCII 2024, CCIS 2319, pp. 332–340, 2025.
https://doi.org/10.1007/978-3-031-78516-0_36

similar-looking numbers or symbols, such as replacing "e" with "3" or "o" with "0". Another approach is the utilization of keyboard patterns, where users create passwords by typing sequences of characters that form geometric shapes or easily remembered patterns on a standard keyboard layout. Additionally, some users incorporate personal dates or significant numbers into their passwords, leveraging meaningful associations to aid in recall. Mnemonics, or memory aids, are also commonly employed, wherein users create passwords based on phrases or sentences that are easy to remember but difficult for others to guess. Some users combine multiple techniques to enhance security. For example, they might use a mnemonic phrase with leet speak and a keyboard pattern. An example could be turning the phrase "I love New York!" into "I<3N3wY0rk!". While some users rely on password managers or random password generators to create highly secure passwords that are difficult to crack, memorizing these passwords tends to be difficult for the average user [3,4]. Increasing developments in password guessing attacks facilitated by machine learning models underscore the critical need for robust security measures. As computational power continues to rise, it is imperative that password authentication systems are further strengthened. The RoseCliff Algorithm aims to enhance password authentication systems and has shown promising results. Additionally, ChatGPT has proven effective in generating strong and memorable passwords as well as developing more effective honey tokens. We explore the impact the RoseCliff Algorithm could have on mitigating password guessing attacks and the potential benefits of integrating both the RoseCliff Algorithm and large language models (LLMs) in password authentication systems. This integration could lead to more secure and resilient authentication methods, addressing the challenges posed by modern guessing techniques.

2 Password Cracking

Passwords are hashed using encryption techniques to produce hash values that are difficult to crack. Consequently, hackers tend to use guessing attacks to decipher these passwords. The resilience of a password to such guessing attacks is considered to be the password strength. Password entropy is a quantifiable measure of a password's unpredictability, with higher entropy indicating a more secure password. Entropy is calculated based on the number of possible combinations that could be used to generate the password [6]. Password entropy H for a character set of size N and length of the password L, expressed in bits, is calculated as:

$$H = \log_2(N^L) \tag{1}$$

2.1 Brute Force

A brute force guess attack is a method used by attackers to gain unauthorized access to a system by systematically attempting all possible combinations of passwords or encryption keys until the correct one is found. if T is the time it would take to crack a password, the time to crack a password using brute force T_b(time using brute-force) in seconds would be the Password entropy H divided by the number of guesses per second G.

$$T_b = \frac{H}{G} = \frac{\log_2(N^L)}{G} \tag{2}$$

2.2 Dictionary Attacks

John the Ripper and similar tools improved the time complexity by using dictionary attacks. Instead of trying every possible combination, they use a list of common passwords, words from dictionaries, or previously leaked passwords, drastically reducing the search space. A dictionary attack is successful only if the password is within the dictionary. Thus, hybrid attacks, which combine dictionary attacks with brute-force methods, were developed. These attacks first try variations of dictionary words (e.g., appending numbers or special characters) before resorting to a full brute-force search. This optimizes the attack by focusing computational resources on the most likely password patterns first [6]. Mathematically, the time for a hybrid attack T_h with dictionary size D and the complexity of Hybridization C_h where C_h is 1 if the password is in the dictionary and increase with the more number of variations needed to crack the password and α where α tend to be zero if the password can be cracked using a dictionary or its variations can be represented as:

$$T_h = \frac{D \times C_h}{G} + \alpha \tag{3}$$

2.3 Markov Model

To further improve dictionary attack time complexity, Narayanan A. and Shmatikov V proposed the use of a Markov model [7]. Wang et al. [8] explained that a Markov model assumes that each character is only related to the first x characters in front of it irrespective of other characters, where $x(= n + 1)$ is the order of the Markov model. The conditional probability for character c_i following the string $c_1c_2 \ldots c_{i-1}$ is

$$\Pr(c_i \mid c_1c_2 \cdots c_{i-2}c_{i-1}) = \Pr(c_i \mid c_{i-x} \cdots c_{i-1}) = \frac{Count(c_{i-x} \cdots c_{i-1}c_i)}{Count(c_{i-x} \cdots c_{i-1}\cdot)}, \tag{4}$$

where $Count(c_{i-x} \cdots c_{i-1}c_i)$ denotes the number of occurrences of the string $c_{i-x} \cdots c_{i-1}c_i$, and $Count(c_{i-x} \cdots c_{i-1}\cdot)$ denotes the number of occurrences of the string $c_{i-d} \cdots c_{i-1}$ where it is followed by an undetermined character (i.e., where it is not at the end of a string). Then the probability of the string $s = c_1c_2 \cdots c_n$ is given by:

$$\Pr(s) = \Pr(c_1)\Pr(c_2 \mid c_1) \cdots \Pr(c_n \mid c_{n-1}c_{n-2} \cdots c_1) = \prod_{i=1}^{n} \Pr(c_i \mid c_{i-x} \cdots c_{i-1}). \tag{5}$$

The time complexity of generating passwords using a Markov model can be described using Big O notation, where the character set size N, the order of the Markov model n, and the length of the password L. The Big O time complexity $O(T_m)$ of generating passwords using a Markov model is given by:

$$O(T_m) = O(N^n \times L) \tag{6}$$

Inference time complexity depends on the specific algorithm used. For simple models like first-order Markov chains, it's typically $O(N)$ or $O(1)$ if transition probabilities are precomputed. This approach allows for faster attacks by leveraging a time-space trade-off based on the probability of characters in a sequence and is called Markovian dictionary. Similarly, techniques like Rainbow tables enable faster attacks by precomputing a larger number of passwords. However, for higher-order models or more complex algorithms, the inference time complexity can increase. The time complexity T_m of generating passwords using a Markov model, where N is the size of the character set, n is the order of the Markov model (the number of previous characters considered), T_t is the average time taken to transition between states and L is the length of the password being generated can be expressed as:

$$T_m = S^n \times T_t \times L \tag{7}$$

2.4 Probabilistic Context-Free Grammars

Michael Collins [9] proposed Probabilistic Context-Free Grammars (PCFGs) which can be used to model the structure of passwords, including common patterns, character combinations, and other linguistic features. The PCFG assigns probabilities to different rules or productions that generate passwords and the probability of a password can be computed as the product of the probabilities of the individual rules or productions used to generate it. Variants of PCFG like the Template-based Probabilistic Context-Free Grammar (PCFG) leverages the concept of templates, which are predefined structures or patterns commonly found in passwords, to generate candidate passwords probabilistically. Given a set of templates and associated probabilities, the probability of a password generated from a template PCFG can be calculated as the product of the probabilities of the individual components used to generate it. Let t represent the set of templates, $\pi(t)$ signify the probability of template t, and $\pi(c)$ represent the probability of character c. The probability $\pi(p)$ of a password p generated from a template t is calculated as:

$$\pi(p) = \pi(t) \times \prod_{c \in p} \pi(c) \tag{8}$$

where c represents characters in the password generated from the template t. hence calculating the time (T) to using a Template-based Probabilistic Context-Free Grammar (PCFG) depends on several factors, including the size of the template space, the length of generated passwords, and the specific implementation of the PCFG generation algorithm [2,10,11].

2.5 Machine Learning and Artificial Intelligence

Using machine learning and AI in password cracking diverge from rule-based or probability-based approaches by disregarding assumptions about password structures. Machine learning models autonomously encode a wide range of password information, surpassing human-generated rules and Markovian methods. Melicher et al. [12] pioneered RNN utilization for extracting and predicting password features, introducing the Fast, Lean, Accurate (FLA) model. FLA integrates transfer learning, demonstrating improved guessing efficacy, particularly for complex or longer password policies. Zhang et al. [13] presented Structure Partition and BiLSTM Recurrent Neural Network (SPRNN), a hybrid technique combining structure partitioning using Probabilistic Context-Free Grammar (PCFG) and Bidirectional LSTM (BiLSTM). SPRNN outperforms traditional models like Markov Models and PCFG in both cross-site and one-site scenarios. Building on SPRNN, Liu et al. [14] introduced GENPass, a model suitable for cross-site attacks. GENPass preprocesses passwords using PCFG-based tagging, followed by LSTM-based password generation. Attention-based models, such as BERT, ELMO, and GPT, enhance deep neural network architectures by prioritizing tokens during processing with Li et al. curated a deep neural network architecture and refined it using BERT, showcasing significant performance improvements through the tutoring process.

3 RoseCliff Algorithm and Password Cracking

The RoseCliff algorithm [5], designed to enhance the security of password authentication systems, operates as follows:

1. **Password Structure**: Users are required to have two passwords:
   - A standard password P_L which is preferably long and complex. Users may use a password manager.
   - A shorter, main password P_s that the user needs to remember and is derived from the longer standard password.
2. **Authentication Process**:
   - When authentication is initiated, the server sends a one-time number O_{tp} to the client's system.
   - The user either types the standard password P_L manually or retrieves it from a password manager but must manually type the shorter password P_s separately.
   - The shorter password is subtracted from the longer password generating a value V.

$$(V = P_L - P_s) \tag{9}$$

   - The value V is combined with the one-time number O_{tp} generating a temporary value K.

$$(K = V \ \& \ O_{tp} = (P_L - P_s) \ \& \ O_{tp}) \tag{10}$$

- The temporary value K is then encrypted and sent to the server.
- The temporary value K is also combined with the shorter password P_s to create a dynamic password P_d, which is then encrypted and sent to the server.

$$(P_d = P_s \,\&\, V \,\&\, O_{tp} = (P_L - P_s) \,\&\, O_{tp} \,\&\, P_s). \tag{11}$$

3. **Server-side Verification**:
   - Upon decryption at the server, the temporary value K is deducted from the dynamic password P_d, producing the shorter password P_s.
   - The previously stored dynamic password P_d and temporary value K are also decrypted similarly, and if the same short password P_s is obtained, the user is verified.

3.1 RoseCliff Algorithm and Brute Force

The time T it would take to crack a password authentication system implementing the RoseCliff Algorithm can be calculated by determining the time required to crack the dynamic password P_d. We assume that the dynamic password P_d is longer than the temporary value K. By replacing the length of the password L in equation (2), we get:

$$T_b = \frac{\log_2(N^{(P_L - P_s) \,\&\, O_{tp} \,\&\, P_s})}{G} \tag{12}$$

3.2 RoseCliff Algorithm and Dictionary Attacks

Traditional dictionaries can be expected to struggle with the introduction of randomness by the RoseCliff Algorithm. However, hybrid attacks may be possible with increased complexity, depending on how the RoseCliff Algorithm is implemented and the value of the One-time Number used. Hence, the complexity of hybridization C_h is multiplied by a factor of K. As shown in equation (3), the time for a hybrid attack can be represented as:

$$T_h = \frac{D \times (C_h \, * K)}{G} + \alpha \tag{13}$$

3.3 RoseCliff Algorithm and Markov Models

With the introduction of randomness by the RoseCliff Algorithm, when implemented correctly, the dynamic password P_d and the temporary value K become independent of regular grammar. Consequently, the conditional probability c_i following the string $c_1 c_2 \ldots c_{i-1}$, as expressed in equation (4), takes on a random value. As a result, the effectiveness of Markov Models and its variations in password prediction and generation may diminish. It is anticipated that these traditional techniques will struggle to adapt to the unpredictability introduced by the RoseCliff Algorithm. However, further experimentation is necessary to confirm this hypothesis.

3.4 RoseCliff Algorithm and PCFG

It would be intriguing to investigate the performance of Probabilistic Context-Free Grammar (PCFG) models in authentication systems secured using the RoseCliff algorithm as the dynamic password (P_d) and a temporary value (K) that have no discernible relationship with regular grammars. Leveraging PCFGs within the context of the RoseCliff algorithm could lead to the development of more robust and secure authentication systems. Experimentation with this integrated approach could yield valuable insights into the effectiveness of PCFGs.

3.5 RoseCliff Algorithm and Machine Learning

Given that the dynamic password (P_d) and temporary value (K) generated by the RoseCliff algorithm exhibit no discernible relationship with regular grammars, and machine learning models have not been exposed to similar information, there arises a compelling opportunity to investigate their performance in experimentation. Experimentation with this integrated approach holds the potential to yield significant advancements in password security and authentication. By evaluating the performance of PCFGs, machine learning models, and the RoseCliff algorithm in tandem, researchers can gain a deeper understanding of their strengths, weaknesses, and potential synergies. Such experimentation not only contributes to the advancement of password security but also sheds light on the broader intersection of linguistics, cryptography, and machine learning.

4 Large Language Models

With the success of using machine learning models to develop tools for password cracking, Umejiaku A. & Sheng V. [15] explored whether Large Language Models (LLMs) could effectively generate passwords and if passwords generated by ChatGPT are superior to user-generated passwords. McKee et al. [16] used ChatGPT as a unique tool for honeypots and demonstrated that it can delay an attacker's access to critical network assets. Similarly, Reti et al. [17] utilized several LLMs to address scalability challenges in designing honeytoken, a key defense mechanism, and concluded that generic LLMs are capable of creating a wide array of honeytoken. Here, we analyze the potential of combining the RoseCliff algorithm and LLMs to enhance authentication system security.Below we discuss how we can integrate LLMs like ChatGPT in building secured systems -

- Passwords generated using ChatGPT tend to be robust enough to be considered secure against current cracking techniques and are also much more memorable than those generated by traditional password generators that do not use LLMs. The RoseCliff algorithm requires users to create two passwords, preferably with the shorter password derived from the longer one. Our experiments showed that the strength of the longer password and its relationship to the shorter password could significantly influence the overall strength of the authentication system. Teaching users how to create effective passwords can

be challenging compared to training LLMs to generate passwords. Allowing LLMs to handle password generation based on memorable words and numbers suggested by users could simplify the process and enhance security.
- Honeywords, a security concept first introduced by Bojinov et al. [18], involve using decoy passwords inserted alongside genuine ones in a system's database to confuse attackers. If an attacker breaches the system and selects a honeyword, it triggers an alarm, signaling a potential security breach. Essentially, honeywords serve as traps to detect unauthorized access attempts and enhance overall system security. Developing intelligent honeywords is challenging, as they need to resemble user passwords closely enough to deceive attackers while distinguishing genuine user errors.ChatGPT has demonstrated its capability in designing honeywords. Integrating the RoseCliff algorithm with an LLM like ChatGPT in the password creation process could further enhance this capability. For example, if a user asks ChatGPT to create a password using three words and a number, and then chooses one of the words as the short password, the other words and their variations could be immediately embedded as honeywords. This approach could produce more effective honeywords and improve overall system security.

5 Conclusion

This study provides an in-depth analysis of contemporary trends in password authentication systems, while also exploring the potential for enhancing the overall architecture of these systems through the integration of the RoseCliff Algorithm. Beyond merely focusing on password guessing, the research delves into leveraging the capabilities of machine learning. It demonstrates how the RoseCliff algorithm can fortify authentication systems against hacking attacks. Additionally, the study highlights the success of machine learning models in password guessing, underscoring their potential utility in password generation. By amalgamating the RoseCliff Algorithm with Large Language Models (LLMs), the study envisions the development of robust authentication systems capable of withstanding sophisticated cyber threats.

Disclosure of Interests. The authors have no competing interests to declare that are relevant to the content of this article.

References

1. Yu, F.: On deep learning in password guessing, a survey. In: Proceedings of ACM Conference (Conference 2017), p. 8. ACM, New York, NY, USA (2022). https://arxiv.org/pdf/2208.10413
2. Xu, M., Wang, C., Yu, J., Zhang, J., Zhang, K., Han, W.: Chunk-level password guessing: towards modeling refined password composition representations. In: Proceedings of the 2021 ACM SIGSAC Conference on Computer and Communications Security (CCS 2021), pp. 5–20. Association for Computing Machinery (2021). https://doi.org/10.1145/3460120.3484743

3. Li, W., Zeng, J.: Leet usage and its effect on password security. IEEE Trans. Inf. Forensics Secur. **16**, 2130–2143 (2021). https://doi.org/10.1109/TIFS.2021.3050066
4. Dong, Q., Jia, C., Duan, F., Wang, D.: RLS-PSM: A robust and accurate password strength meter based on reuse, LEET and separation. IEEE Trans. Inf. Forensics Secur. **16**, 4988–5002 (2021). https://doi.org/10.1109/TIFS.2021.3107147
5. Umejiaku, A.P., Sheng, V.S.: RoseCliff algorithm: making passwords dynamic. Appl. Sci. **14**(2), 723 (2024). https://doi.org/10.3390/app14020723
6. Chowdhury, N.: Analyzing password strength: A combinatorial entropy approach. In: Proceedings of ACM Conference (Conference 2017) (2024). https://doi.org/10.5281/zenodo.10487696
7. Narayanan, A., Shmatikov, V.: Fast dictionary attacks on passwords using time-space tradeoff. In: Proceedings of the 12th ACM Conference on Computer and Communications Security (2005). https://doi.org/10.1145/1102120.1102168
8. Wang, D., Zou, Y., Zhang, Z., Xiu, K.: Password guessing using random forest. In: 32nd USENIX Security Symposium (USENIX Security 23), pp. 965–982. USENIX Association (2023). https://www.usenix.org/conference/usenixsecurity23/presentation/wang-ding-password-guessing
9. Collins, M.: Probabilistic context-free grammars (PCFGs) (2011). http://www.cs.columbia.edu/~mcollins/courses/nlp2011/notes/pcfgs.pdf
10. Cheng, H., Li, W., Wang, P., Liang, K.: Improved probabilistic context-free grammars for passwords using word extraction. In: ICASSP 2021 - 2021 IEEE International Conference on Acoustics, Speech and Signal Processing (ICASSP), pp. 2690–2694. IEEE (2021). https://doi.org/10.1109/ICASSP39728.2021.9414886
11. Zhang, J., Glass, J., He, T.: PCFG-based natural language interface improves generalization for controlled text generation (2022). https://arxiv.org/abs/2210.07431
12. Melicher, W., et al.: Fast, lean, and accurate: Modeling password guessability using neural networks. In: 25th USENIX Security Symposium (USENIX Security 16), pp. 175–191. USENIX Association (2016). https://www.usenix.org/conference/usenixsecurity16/technical-sessions/presentation/melicher
13. Tang, G., Li, B., Dai, H.-N., Zheng, X.: SPRNN: A spatial-temporal recurrent neural network for crowd flow prediction. Inform. Sci. **614**, 19–34 (2022). https://doi.org/10.1016/j.ins.2022.09.053
14. Liu, Y., et al.: GENPass: A general deep learning model for password guessing with PCFG rules and adversarial generation. In 2018 IEEE International Conference on Communications (ICC), pp. 1–6 (2018). https://doi.org/10.1109/ICC.2018.8422243
15. Umejiaku, A.P., Dhakal, P., Sheng, V.S.: Balancing password security and user convenience: exploring the potential of prompt models for password generation. Electronics **12**(10), 2159 (2023)
16. McKee, F., Noever, D.: Chatbots in a honeypot world [Preprint]. arXiv. https://arxiv.org/abs/2301.03771 (2023)
17. Reti, D., et al.: Act as a honeytoken generator! an investigation into honeytoken generation with large language models . arXiv preprint arXiv:2404.16118 (2024)
18. Juels, A., Rivest, R.L.: Honeywords: Making password-cracking detectable. In: Proceedings of the 2013 ACM SIGSAC Conference on Computer & Communications Security, pp. 145–160. Association for Computing Machinery (2013). https://doi.org/10.1145/2508859.2516671

Cognitive Conflict Classification Depending on Background Auditive Environment Using Support Vector Machine Based on Near-Infrared Hemoencephalography

Kota Yokoyama[1], Keiichi Zempo[2], and Sandra Puentes[2](✉)

[1] Graduate School of Science and Technology, University of Tsukuba, Tsukuba, Japan

[2] Institute of Systems and Information Engineering, University of Tsukuba, Tsukuba, Japan

sandra@ccr.tsukuba.ac.jp

Abstract. The development of voice assistants and other interfaces offers the potential to enhance productivity through multitasking. However, this increase in the sources and types of environmental sounds (e.g., music, speech, and natural sounds) to which people are exposed daily raises, concerns about potential adverse effects, such as discomfort, altered cognitive function, and cognitive conflict induction. While previous studies have examined cognitive conflict using physiological data (e.g., electroencephalogram), this study proposes Near-InfraRed HemoEncephaloGraphy (NIR-HEG) as a low-cost, movement-resistant alternative. NIR-HEG enables the indirect evaluation of brain activity without restricting user movement and providing valuable feedback on interfaces used in daily life. This study investigates the feasibility of implementing NIR-HEG to classify and analyze cognitive conflict. Ten participants who passed the Ishihara Color Vision test completed two Stroop tasks under six environmental sound conditions designed to induce cognitive interference. Task performance metrics and NIR-HEG data from two prefrontal areas (FP1 and FP2, International 10–20 System) were used as input for a Support Vector Machine (SVM) classification model. While the classification performance for environmental sound conditions was suboptimal, achieving a maximum accuracy of 64.37 % the classification of task types showed improved performance with a maximum accuracy of 88.01 %. These findings suggest task types may influence brain activity patterns associated with cognitive conflict. They underscore the utility of NIR-HEG in elucidating the neural correlates of cognitive conflict and highlight its potential practical applications in interface design and implementation of user interfaces for real-world environments.

Keywords: Cognitive conflict · Near-Infrared Hemoencephalography · Support Vector Machine

C. Stephanidis et al. (Eds.): HCII 2024, CCIS 2319, pp. 341–353, 2025.
https://doi.org/10.1007/978-3-031-78516-0_37

1 Introduction

In recent times, portable players, voice assistants, and other interfaces have been developed, offering the possibility of increasing productivity by multitasking. This scenario increases the source and types of environmental sounds (e.g., music, speech, and natural sounds) to which people are exposed during daily tasks like driving, working, and studying [1–3]. While selected background sounds may increase user and worker satisfaction, concerns arise regarding potential adverse effects from selected and non-selected environmental sounds, such as discomfort, altered cognitive function, and cognitive conflict induction [1–3]. Cognitive conflict is recognized as a cause of unpleasant and negative states, often leading to cognitive dissonance, which involves both physiological and psychological discomfort [4–6]. Consequently, previous research has utilized physiological data to evaluate and classify cognitive conflict and dissonance objectively. This approach helps to avoid the bias associated with self-rating of psychological states. Some studies investigating the arousal and reduction of dissonance explored physiological data related to indirect emotional responses (e.g., skin conductance) [5]. Other approaches analyzed the underlying neural dynamics to provide a more straightforward insight into cognitive processes. They investigated how brain activity measured by electroencephalography (EEG) is affected by various factors, such as cognitive load, by examining front-central deflections (prominent deflections in electrical activity over the front-central regions of the frontal cortex), which are often associated with high-order cognitive processes including executive functions, attention, and conflict monitoring and resolution [7]. Other studies expanded this perspective by approaching cognitive conflict and brain activity regarding environmental noise [4]. Given the advantages of EEG recordings, providing the opportunity to directly capture event-related potentials associated with cognitive processes, including attention, memory, decision-making, and conflict resolution, these results are highly valuable for better understanding cognitive load in different scenarios. However, despite the versatility of EEG, equipment accessibility, data processing, and experiments requiring mobility may restrict its use. Such limitations constrain the performance evaluation and live feedback on the interfaces used in daily life and work, restricting EEG evaluations of cognitive conflict to laboratory setups. For this study, we propose using NearInfraRed-HemoEncephaloGraphy (NIR-HEG) for cognitive conflict evaluation. NIR-HEG is a noninvasive technique that measures the changes in blood oxygen levels accompanying brain activity. This method leverages the absorption characteristics of infrared and near-infrared light, allowing the detection of prefrontal activation by identifying peaks in metabolism linked to blood flow distribution in the brain [8]. The use of NIR-HEG presents advantages over other methods, such as EEG, heart rate variability, and skin conductance. It accommodates a wide range of individuals, is more cost-effective, operates quietly, and is robust to motion artifacts [8]. These advantages allow indirect and quiet measuring without restricting movements and are expected to provide valuable feedback on interfaces in daily life [9,10]. This research explores the feasibility of implementing NIR-HEG to establish the relationship between cognitive conflict levels and physiological indicators. For this purpose, a classification model of cognitive conflict levels using a Support Vector Machine (SVM) model was implemented. SVM was selected given its proven efficacy in previous studies on classifying brain dynamics, cognitive state, and cognitive load [11–13]. Considering the evidence supporting that substantial cognitive dissonance elicits more significant brain responses [7], our hypothesis posits that higher cognitive conflict levels induced by environmental noise, a scenario known to cause high cognitive load, will result in more significant NIR-HEG responses. Furthermore, given the demonstrated effects of environmental sounds on cognitive performance [14–16], we plan to explore the impact of such sounds on cognitive conflict levels, acknowledging previous research indicating both positive and negative effects linked to environmental sounds [17,18]. This approach is particularly relevant, as individuals regularly navigate noisy environments in various settings, such as workplaces, construction sites, restaurants, hospitals, and other public places [2,19]. Furthermore, activities that require concentration as work or study are performed away from ideal scenarios such as quiet rooms or offices, and more in wild environments where the background sounds cannot be controlled. Our investigation aims to shed light on the mechanisms of cognitive conflict prevalent in everyday experiences, focusing on scenarios where information overload and environmental noise may affect cognitive processing capacities.

2 Methods

Ten university students (9 men, one woman), ranging from 22 to 25 years (mean 23.2, Standard Deviation (SD) 1.14) participated in this experiment. All volunteers were native Japanese speakers who did not report any disease related to the central nervous system or sensory impairment related to visual or hearing status. It was ensured that the participants had normal color vision by performing the Ishihara Color Vision test before enrollment [16] since one of the tasks required color discrimination. All participants joined voluntarily and signed an informed consent form after receiving an explanation about the experiments. All

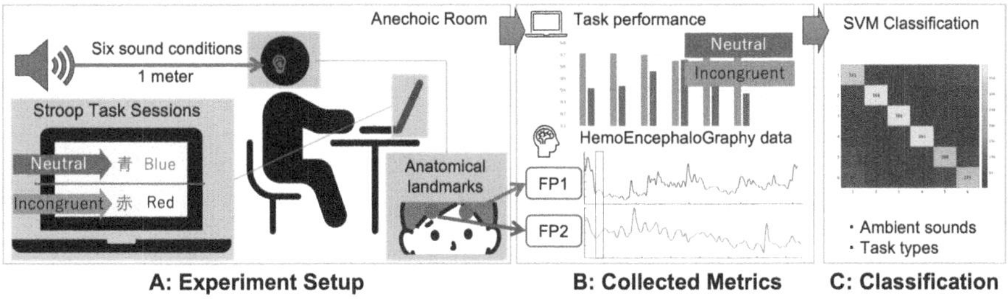

Fig. 1. Research protocol.

experiments were performed following the ethical principles of the Declaration of Helsinki and approved by the ethical committee of research implementation of the University of Tsukuba (Ethics approval number: 2023R839).

2.1 Procedure

Experiments were conducted in an anechoic room to eliminate unexpected environmental noise interference (Fig. 1). A participant was seated on a chair in front of a 15.6-inch laptop, and a speaker (TEAC S-300NEO) was located behind the participant at a distance of 1 m (Fig. 2A). A single-trial version of the color-word matching test known as the Stroop task, was employed to assess cognitive function [1,20], following the modified version used in previous research on cognitive

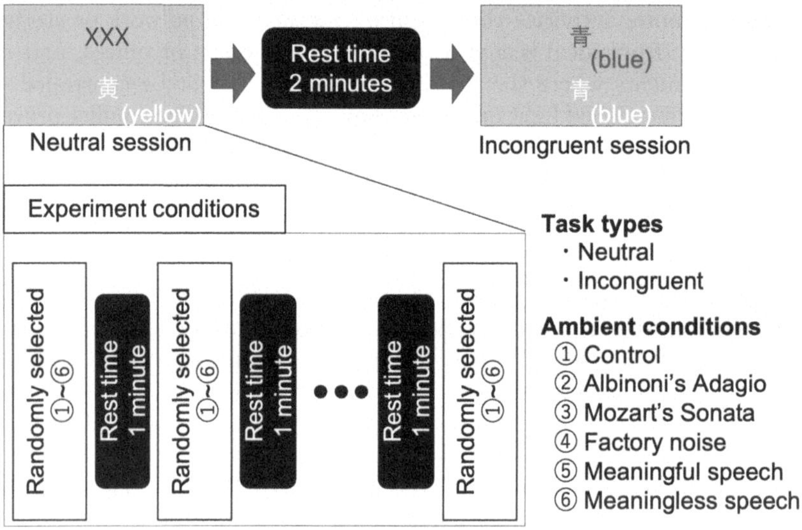

Fig. 2. Experimental diagram. Volunteers participated in two different sessions: neutral and incongruent. The experimental conditions were randomly selected for each session between six background sounds: control, Albinoni's Adagio, Mozart's Sonata, factory noise, meaningful speech, and meaningless speech. Once a volunteer was exposed to all conditions in the neutral session, the experiment was repeated for the incongruent session.

conflict [4,17]. The PsychoPy 3 software was used to construct a Japanese version of the test for the Stroop interference task. The participants then seated in front of the laptop, were asked to press keyboard keys depending on the correspondence of the written words and displayed colors, while being exposed to different types of environmental sounds (C1: Control (no sound), C2: Albinoni's Adagio, C3: Mozart's Sonata, C4: Factory noise, C5: Meaningful speech, and C6: Meaningless speech). A NIR-HEG headband was used to measure brain activity indirectly during the task. This device consisted of two optodes plugged into an eight-channel multi-modal encoder (ProComp Infiniti) and was placed on the regions denominated as FP1 and FP2 in the forehead (Fig. 1) according to the 10/20 international system to measure cognitive functions. The experiment consisted of two phases: neutral and incongruent sessions (Fig. 2). In both sessions, participants would encounter a gray screen displaying two rows of letters and be instructed to respond if the color of the top row corresponds to the color name written at the bottom row by using the keyboard's arrow keys. When an answer mismatch was encountered, the participant should press the left arrow key, and when the colors and word matched, the participant used the right arrow key. The setup used for the neutral session had two rows: the top row displayed "XXX" colored in red, blue, green, or yellow. On the other hand, in the incongruent session, the top row displayed colored Japanese kanji pictograms corresponding to "red", "blue", "green", and "yellow" in the Japanese language. In both sessions, the bottom row had the kanji corresponding to "red", "blue", "green", and "yellow" printed in Japanese language and colored white. The top row was shown 100 ms before the bottom row to prevent participants from focusing on the bottom row. Additionally, all color characters were randomly displayed on the screen to avoid bias by pattern guess by the participants. During the sessions, participants undertook the task while listening to one of six randomly selected environmental sounds chosen from prior research on noise and music effects during attention tasks [16,21]. The control condition (no noise condition) was conducted to be used as a baseline; the additional five environmental sounds included two classical music pieces (Mozart's Sonata for two Pianos in F Major, K. 448 and Albinoni's Adagio in G Minor for Organ and Strings) [21], two types of speech (meaningful speech and meaningless speech) [22] and factory noises [16]. The soundtrack used for "meaningful speech" was a recording of the early morning news of the day of experiments, and the one for "meaningless speech" was the same recording played backward. The strategy of the sound conditions was aimed to disturb or aid the performance of the Stroop task depending on the sound source. The volume was set at 65 dB and played through a speaker set 1 m behind the participants. Every session selected the environmental sounds randomly, and sessions were repeated until volunteers were exposed to all the experiment conditions. The participants conducted 150 trials in each condition and took one-minute rest between sessions. After finishing all conditions in the neutral session, a two-minute rest was provided before starting the incongruent session, where conditions were randomized as in the previous session. For the incongruent session, participants determined if the color name of the bottom row matched the colored characters of the top row in all conditions. The performance was evaluated in terms of success or failure, and response time for each trial. During each trial, data from NIR-HEG was recorded simultaneously.

2.2 Data Collection and Processing

The task performance was evaluated by calculating the mean value from accuracy and response time. The average accuracy and response time for each experimental condition were derived from the recorded task performance data. Regarding physiological indexes, activity from the frontal lobe (left and right sides, Fig. 1) was collected. The data was recorded with a 36 Hz sampling rate. To process NIR-HEG data, the Savitzky-Golay (SG) filter of 3rd order was applied, and a 121 frame length was selected for analysis. Next, the HEG ratio was calculated using the method described in previous research to assess brain function activity [9,23,24] as follows:

$$HEG\ ratio = 200 * \frac{Red\ light\ (variable)}{InfraRed\ light\ (unaffected)} \tag{1}$$

The preprocessed data was divided into 150 segments since the number of trials in each experiment was 150, and statistical features including mean, minimum peak (min), maximum peak (max), standard deviation (SD), skewness, and slope, were extracted for each segment. The Z-score method was used to normalize the statistical features of each measured experiment condition. The normalized data was used for statistical evaluation and as input data for the SVM model.

2.3 Support Vector Machine Model

The processed NIR-HEG data from FP1 and FP2 was used as input data for the SVM model. Statistical features validated by significant differences in statistical tests were employed as input data. For the model distinguishing between experimental conditions, input data comprised the mean, min, max, and SD of FP1, along with the mean, min, max, SD, and slope of FP2. Conversely, input data included the mean, min, and max values of FP1 and FP2, to build the model and differentiate between tasks. The characteristics obtained from different measure points were treated as features. K-Fold cross-validation (K = 5) was conducted in this research to evaluate the classification model. This study used the accuracy, precision, recall, and F1 values to assess model performance. Statistical analysis and the SVM model were performed using Matlab (R2023a).

3 Results

3.1 Task Performance Evaluation

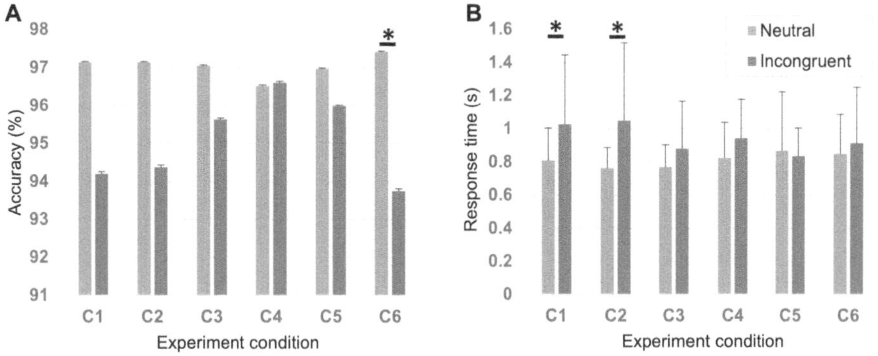

Fig. 3. Task performance between environmental sounds. The performance accuracy (A), expressed as a percentage, and the: response time (B), measured in seconds, were plotted for each experimental condition and compared between task types (neutral and incongruent sessions). Experiment conditions were set as C1: Control, C2: Albinoni's Adagio, C3: Mozart's Sonata, C4: Factory noise, C5: Meaningful speech, and C6: Meaningless speech. Errors bars correspond to the standard error (*P-value < 0.05).

The results of the task performance were derived as the mean values of accuracy and response time for the Stroop task, respectively, for each experimental condition. The accuracy and response time of the tasks performed in this experiment are shown in Fig. 3. The accuracy for each condition of the neutral session was above 96 %, with a response time close to 0.8 s (C1, control: 97.14 %, 0.81 s. C2, Albinoni's Adagio: 97.14 %, 0.76 s. C3, Mozart's Sonata: 97.05 %, 0.77 s. C4, Factory noise: 96.52 %, 0.82 s. C5, Meaningful speech: 96.98 %, 0.86 s. C6, Meaningless speech: 97.41 %, 0.85 s). On the other hand, the task performances of the incongruent session were lower, with an accuracy ranging between 93.5–96.5 % where the lowest accuracy corresponded to conditions C1, C2, and C6; and response times were close to 0.9 s (C1, control: 94.20 %, 1.03 s. C2, Albinoni's Adagio: 94.38 %, 1.05 s. C3, Mozart's Sonata: 95.63 %, 0.88 s. C4, Factory noise: 96.61 %, 0.94 s. C5, Meaningful speech: 95.98 %, 0.83 s. C6, Meaningless speech: 93.75 %, 0.91 s).

Table 1. The statistical test for NIR-HEG data features on FP1 and FP2 between task types (Wilcoxon signed-rank test) and between sound conditions (Friedman test).

	Wilcoxon Signed-Rank test		Friedman Test	
Statistical Feature	FP1	FP2	FP1	FP2
Mean	< 0.001	< 0.001	< 0.001	< 0.001
Min	< 0.001	< 0.001	< 0.001	< 0.001
Max	< 0.001	< 0.001	< 0.001	< 0.001
SD	0.13	0.12	< 0.001	< 0.001
Skewness	0.93	0.39	0.98	0.99
Slope	0.96	0.60	< 0.01	< 0.001

Statistical comparisons were initiated with the Shapiro-Wilk test ($\alpha = 0.05$) to assess data normality. Since the data didn't follow the normal distribution, non-parametric tests were used. Experimental conditions were initially evaluated with the Friedman test (reps = 2.0, $\alpha = 0.05$), and no statistical difference was found among the selected sound backgrounds. Following, the Wilcoxon signed-rank sum test ($\alpha = 0.05$) was used to compare the task types where significant differences were found between the neutral sessions and the incongruent sessions for both accuracy ($p < 0.01$) and response time ($p < 0.001$). For physiological data, the Shapiro-Wilk test ($\alpha = 0.05$) was performed for physiological data evaluation. Since NIR-HEG data was not normally distributed, the Friedman test (reps = 2.0, $\alpha = 0.05$) was performed for each statistical feature (mean, min, max, SD, skewness, and slope) of the HEG ratios from FP1 and FP2 for

Table 2. Bonferroni Post-hoc Test Results for Experimental Conditions. The P-value from comparisons is displayed, and features showing significance are highlighted in grey. The categories were abbreviated as follows; Albinoni: Albinoni's Adagio, Mozart: Mozart's Sonata, Meaningful: Meaningful speech, and Meaningless: Meaningless speech. The $\star$ indicates that the feature's average value is higher for the first condition listed in the comparison column.

Comparison	FP1					FP2				
	Mean	Min	Max	SD	Slope	Mean	Min	Max	SD	Slope
Control vs Albinoni	$< 0.001\star$	$< 0.001\star$	< 0.001	1.00	1.00	0.29	0.13	1.00	< 0.001	1.00
Control vs Mozart	$< 0.001\star$	< 0.001	< 0.001	1.00	1.00	$< 0.001\star$	< 0.001	$< 0.001\star$	< 0.001	1.00
Control vs Factory Noise	$< 0.001\star$	< 0.001	< 0.001	$< 0.001\star$	0.45	$< 0.001\star$	< 0.001	< 0.001	0.72	0.12
Control vs Meaningful	$< 0.001\star$	$< 0.001\star$	$< 0.001\star$	1.00	1.00	1.00	1.00	1.00	1.00	1.00
Control vs Meaningless	$< 0.001\star$	$< 0.001\star$	$< 0.001\star$	1.00	1.00	$< 0.001\star$	< 0.001	0.027	< 0.01	1.00
Albinoni vs Mozart	< 0.001	< 0.001	$< 0.001\star$	1.00	1.00	< 0.001	$< 0.001\star$	$< 0.001\star$	1.00	1.00
Albinoni vs Factory Noise	< 0.001	< 0.001	< 0.001	$< 0.001\star$	0.44	$0.037\star$	$0.031\star$	$0.043\star$	0.61	$0.033\star$
Albinoni vs Meaningful	< 0.001	$< 0.001\star$	$< 0.001\star$	1.00	1.00	0.24	0.098	0.20	$< 0.01\star$	1.00
Albinoni vs Meaningless	< 0.001	$< 0.001\star$	$< 0.001\star$	1.00	1.00	0.31	0.061	0.72	1.00	1.00
Mozart vs Factory Noise	1.00	1.00	1.00	< 0.001	0.21	$< 0.001\star$	$< 0.001\star$	< 0.001	$0.030\star$	$< 0.01\star$
Mozart vs Meaningful	0.027	$0.014\star$	0.13	1.00	1.00	$< 0.001\star$	< 0.001	< 0.001	$< 0.001\star$	1.00
Mozart vs Meaningless	1.00	1.00	1.00	1.00	1.00	$< 0.001\star$	< 0.001	< 0.001	1.00	1.00
Factory Noise vs Meaningful	0.90	0.057	1.00	< 0.001	0.80	$< 0.001\star$	< 0.001	$< 0.001\star$	1.00	0.033
Factory Noise vs Meaningless	1.00	1.00	1.00	$< 0.001\star$	0.21	1.00	1.00	1.00	0.75	0.17
Meaningful vs Meaningless	$0.031\star$	< 0.01	1.00	1.00	1.00	< 0.001	$< 0.001\star$	< 0.001	< 0.01	1.00

each task experimental condition. Statistically significant differences were found across features (mean, min, max, SD, and slope) for FP1 and FP2 (Table 1). The Wilcoxon Signed-Rank Test used to compare NIR-HEG features on FP1 and FP2 between task types showed significant differences for mean, min, and max features (P-value < 0.001). A post-hoc analysis using the Bonferroni correction method was performed after the Friedman test (Table 2). Varied results were found regarding significant differences between ambient conditions and physiological features (Table 2). Most significant differences were observed in the mean, min, and max values on FP1 when comparing no sound or monotonous sound with high-pace sounds such as Mozart's Sonata or speech. FP2 recordings also showed significant differences in mean, min, and max values, particularly when contrasting high-pace sound features like Mozart's Sonata, speech, or factory noise Table 2.

Table 3. SVM model classification results for experiment's conditions and task type

Experiment condition	Accuracy (%)	Precision	Recall	F1-score
Control	39.03	0.55	0.58	0.56
Albinoni's Adagio	48.12	0.67	0.63	0.65
Mozart's Sonata	63.01	0.80	0.75	0.77
Factory noise	64.37	0.78	0.79	0.78
Meaningful speech	41.29	0.57	0.61	0.58
Meaningless speech	49.42	0.67	0.65	0.66
Task Type				
Neutral	88.01	0.87	0.90	0.88
Incongruent	88.01	0.90	0.86	0.88

3.2 SVM Classification

After building and training two models, one for experimental conditions and another for task type classification, a K-Fold cross-validation ($K = 5$) was used to evaluate the models. The assessment included accuracy, precision, recall, and F1-score. The classification results for the model regarding experimental conditions are shown in Table 3. The accuracy and F1-scores were as follows; Control (Accuracy = 39.03 %, F1-score = 0.56), Albinoni's Adagio (Accuracy = 48.12 %, F1-score = 0.65), Mozart's Sonata (Accuracy = 63.01 %, F1-score = 0.77), Factory noise (Accuracy = 64.37 %, F1-score = 0.78), Meaningful speech (Accuracy = 41.29 %, F1-score = 0.58), Meaningless speech (Accuracy = 49.42 %, F1-score = 0.66). The lowest accuracy was 39.03 % for the control condition, while the highest accuracy was 64.37 % for the Factory noise condition Table 3. The performance of the SVM model for task type classification is shown in Table 3. The results for each task type were neutral session (Accuracy = 88.01 %, F1-score

= 0.88) and incongruent session (Accuracy = 88.01 %, F1-score = 0.88). The highest precision was 0.90 for the incongruent session, and the highest recall was 0.90 for the neutral session. From these classification results, the average accuracies were 50.87 % for ambient conditions and 88.01 % for task types.

4 Discussion and Conclusions

Cognitive conflict classification methods are techniques used to identify and categorize instances of cognitive conflict, where an individual experiences a clash between competing mental processes. Previous research has proven the usability of the Stroop task for inducing cognitive conflict [17] and the feasibility of implementing SVMs as a classification method for physiological measures [12,13]. Considering the beneficial impact of measuring brain activity in wild environments regarding background sounds and their influence on cognitive load, this research aimed to classify the level of cognitive conflict induced by environmental sounds using NIR-HEG data. In the present study, the accuracy and response times of volunteers performing cognitive tasks were collected while exposed to various environmental sound conditions that are known to affect task performance. During the tasks, NIR-HEG from the frontal lobe was collected and an SVM model was built using the HEG data and features from the task performance. The initial statistical assessment did not show a significant difference between the sound conditions. Opposite to our hypothesis, noisy environments and harmonic sounds, such as music, did not affect the task performance within different sound conditions (C1-C6, Fig. 3A). This result may reflect the participants' ability to filter out irrelevant sounds while focusing on the task, the nature of the noises used, individual differences in susceptibility to distraction, and specific experimental conditions. However, significant differences were found when task performances were compared between task types (neutral vs incongruent for each experimental condition) for accuracy while listening to meaningless speech (C6) and response time while performing in silence or listening to Albinon's Adagio (C1, C2, Fig. 3). Regarding accuracy, although significance was only found for meaningless speech, there is a trend for control and Albinoni's adagio conditions to be lower for incongruent sessions. As silence and monotone sounds such as the sound pattern provided by the Adagio may decrease frontal brain activity bilaterally, it may also have affected the attention level during the incongruent task impairing performance due to the increased challenging conditions. On the other hand, exposure to meaningless sounds activates the linguistic areas of the brain in search of sound patterns or non-semantic structures. Perhaps such activation interfered with the incongruent task where the required attention level is higher than in neutral conditions. NIR-HEG data analysis revealed significant disparities in the mean, min, and max values for Control, Albinoni, and Mozart for FP1, and Mozart, Factory Noise, Meaningful and Meaningless Speech for FP2 (Table 2). These variations likely reflect differences in brain activity in response to environmental sounds. In contrast, bilateral increased activity is triggered by exposure to sound sources such as music and meaningful speech.

However, in this case, the increase in brain activity is more pronounced in the left hemisphere, contrasting with the activation pattern from noise or meaningless speech exposure, which results in more marked activation of the right frontal lobe. Despite the lack of significance in most comparisons related to task performance, NIR-HEG may reveal variances in cognitive conflict induced by environmental sounds and their relationship to cognitive processes in the left or right frontal lobes. From this perspective, it was proposed to explore the feasibility of classification using NIR-HEG data. The SVM model built for the classification of environmental conditions achieved low accuracy performance, where the highest corresponded to 64.37 % (Factory Noise), and the lowest to 39.03 % (Control, Table 3). In contrast, the classification results between task types performed better, with accuracy of 88.01 % for the neutral session and 88.01 % for the incongruent session. The present study explored the effect of background sounds on cognitive overload and the feasibility of building a classifier for assessing mental status in daily activities via NIR-HEG. As previous research exploring EEG changes in the prefrontal cortex related to cognitive function showed response differences regarding background sounds [1–3,7], our results supported these findings by displaying different activation patterns when comparing brain activity under different environmental conditions while exposed to different levels of cognitive overload. However, the present study has limitations regarding the number of participants and the number of optodes used for collecting NIR-HEG data. By including a broader area encompassing the auditory cortex may be possible to improve the classification performance. Still, this initial approach leveraging NIR-HEG may be able to aid the classification of cognitive conflict by type rather than between experimental conditions. Moreover, the present findings underscore the NIR-HEG's utility in clarifying neural correlates of cognitive conflict and hint at its practical applications in interface design for real-world environments.

Acknowledgement. The authors are grateful to the volunteers who participated in the study. This research was supported by the Japanese Ministry of Education, Culture, Sports, Science and Technology Grant-in-Aid for Scientific Research (B) 23K24948.

References

1. Nadon, É., Tillmann, B., Saj, A., Gosselin, N.: The emotional effect of background music on selective attention of adults. Front. Psychol. **12**, 729037 (2021). https://doi.org/10.3389/fpsyg.2021.729037
2. Jeong, E., Ryu, H., Jo, G., Kim, J.: Cognitive load changes during music listening and its implication in earcon design in public environments: an fNIRS study. Int. J. Environ. Res. Public Health **15**(10), 2075 (2018)
3. Shih, Y.N., Huang, R.H., Chiang, H.Y.: Background music: effects on attention performance. Work (Reading, Mass.) **42**(4), 573–578 (2012). https://doi.org/10.3233/WOR-2012-1410
4. Sun, C.K., Harmon-Jones, E.: Supine body posture reduces cognitive conflict processing: evidence from N450 Stroop interference. Psychophysiology **58**(1), e13693 (2021)

5. Ploger, G.W., Dunaway, J., Fournier, P., Soroka, S.: The psychophysiological correlates of cognitive dissonance. Politics Life Sci. **40**(2), 202–212 (2021)
6. Barta, S., Gurrea, R., Flavián, C.: Using augmented reality to reduce cognitive dissonance and increase purchase intention. Comput. Hum. Behav. **140**, 107564 (2023)
7. Colosio, M., Shestakova, A., Nikulin, V.V., Blagovechtchenski, E., Klucharev, V.: Neural mechanisms of cognitive dissonance (revised): an EEG study. J. Neurosci. **37**(20), 5074–5083 (2017)
8. Pinti, P., Tachtsidis, I., Hamilton, A., Hirsch, J., Aichelburg, C., Gilbert, S., Burgess, P.W.: The present and future use of functional near-infrared spectroscopy (fNIRS) for cognitive neuroscience. Ann. N. Y. Acad. Sci. **1464**(1), 5–29 (2020)
9. Serra-Sala, M., Timoneda-Gallart, C., Pérez-Álvarez, F.: Evaluating prefrontal activation and its relationship with cognitive and emotional processes by means of hemoencephalography (HEG). J. Neurother. **16**(3), 183–195 (2012)
10. Weder, S., Shoushtarian, M., Olivares, V., Zhou, X., Innes-Brown, H., McKay, C.: Cortical fNIRS responses can be better explained by loudness percept than sound intensity. Ear Hear. **41**(5), 1187–1195 (2020)
11. Karmakar, S., et al.: Real time detection of cognitive load using fNIRS: a deep learning approach. Biomed. Signal Process. Control **80**, 104227 (2023)
12. Shin, J., Von Lühmann, A., Kim, D.W., Mehnert, J., Hwang, H.J., Müller, K.R.: Simultaneous acquisition of EEG and NIRS during cognitive tasks for an open access dataset. Sci. Data **5**(1), 1–16 (2018)
13. Ayman, S.U., Arrafuzzaman, A., Rahman, M.A.: Subject dependent cognitive load level classification from fNIRS signal using support vector machine. In Proceedings of International Conference on Information and Communication Technology for Development: ICICTD 2022, pp. 365–377. Springer Nature, Singapore (2023). https://doi.org/10.1007/978-981-19-7528-8_29
14. Urakami, J., Moriwaki, A., Nagao, S., Osumi, K., Yamamoto, E., Kanaoka, T.: Augmenting auditory attention and memory to reduce cognitive load in dual tasks: a wearable device to augment auditory attention and memory to improve performance in a duals task. In: Extended Abstracts of the 2023 CHI Conference on Human Factors in Computing Systems, pp. 1–6 (2023)
15. El Boghdady, M., Ewalds-Kvist, B.M.: The influence of music on the surgical task performance: a systematic review. Int. J. Surgery (London, England) **73**, 101–112 (2020). https://doi.org/10.1016/j.ijsu.2019.11.012
16. Liu, T., Lin, C., Huang, K., Chen, Y.: Effects of noise type, noise intensity, and illumination intensity on reading performance. Appl. Acoust. **120**, 70–74 (2017)
17. Masataka, N., Perlovsky, L.: Cognitive interference can be mitigated by consonant music and facilitated by dissonant music. Sci. Rep. **3**(1), 1–6 (2013)
18. Park, S.H., Lee, P.J., Jeong, J.H.: Effects of noise sensitivity on psychophysiological responses to building noise. Build. Environ. **136**, 302–311 (2018)
19. Arezes, P.M., Barbosa, S., Miguel, A.S.: Noise as a cognitive impairment factor: a case study amongst teachers. In: 20th International Congress on Acoustics, ICA, vol. 2010, pp. 1–5 (2010)
20. Ho, T.K.K., Gwak, J., Park, C.M., Song, J.I.: Discrimination of mental workload levels from multi-channel fNIRS using deep leaning-based approaches. IEEE Access **7**, 24392–24403 (2019)
21. Thompson, W.F., Schellenberg, E.G., Husain, G.: Arousal, mood, and the Mozart effect. Psychol. Sci. **12**(3), 248–251 (2001)

22. Oswald, C. J., Tremblay, S., Jones, D.M.: Disruption of comprehension by the meaning of irrelevant sound. Memory (Hove, England) **8**(5), 345–350 (2000). https://doi.org/10.1080/09658210050117762
23. Omata, M., Nakazawa, K.: Regression analyses between physiological indexes and level of understanding with VAS of a listening task. In: PhyCS, pp. 21–29 (2018)
24. Omata, M., Kanuka, D., Mao, X.: Emotion estimation from biological signals and its application to an emotional painting tool. In: 2013 International Conference on Cyberworlds, pp. 240–246 (2013)

Author Index

A
Abam, Edwina Borteley I-3
Ad-Din Al Youbi, Salah I-25
Adrianzén Guerrero, Orestes Daniel I-297, III-151
Ahmed, Istiaq III-3
Alassaf, Hussain Assaf III-193
Aleixo, Everton III-30
Alenzi, Munira I-229
Alhedaithy, Lian Zeyad II-81
Alshammari, Saif I-229
Alsharif, Yasmin Fahad II-81
Alvarez, Alejandra III-111
Alyahya, Mashael Sulaiman II-81
Amaral, Ângelo III-119
Amin, M. Ashraful III-3
Andagama, José II-108
Andrade, Renato A. O. I-177
Antonaros, Peter I-253
Aparecida Paris Baston, Camila III-119
Apostolakis, Konstantinos C. III-239
Arevalo, Osvaldo II-305
Arpita, Faiza Omar III-3
Arsenopoulou, Natalia III-265
Aşcı, Melisa III-14

B
Bae, ISol I-157
Bahatheq, Nuha III-204
Bahloul, Mohamed II-81
Barbara, Nathaniel I-25
Baş, Ahmet Burhan III-14
Behravan, Majid I-198
Bhatt, Aakash I-14
Bijo, Kunnumpurath III-47
Blažica, Bojan I-292
Borges, Marcos Augusto Francisco III-119
Bouloukakis, Manousos II-124
Brandt, Thorben II-115
Bravo, Heidy I-237

C
Camilleri, Kenneth I-25
Camilleri, Tracey I-25
Castañeda, Harold III-111
Chang, Cailin III-182
Chatzakis, Ioannis III-239
Chen, Karen B. II-54
Chen, Yingyu II-91
Chen, Yunjia II-69
Chen, Yun-Ju III-285
Cheon, Soojin II-244
Choi, Bogyu I-157, II-100
Choi, HeeSun II-34
Choi, Mu Seong II-3
Cleger Tamayo, Sergio III-30
Correa, Hanah I. S. I-165, I-177
Croft, Bryan L. II-177

D
da Costa, Jeferson B. I-188
Dai, Yihang III-72
de Oliveira, Anderson V. C. I-177, I-188, I-244
Díaz, Agustín Alejandro Ortiz I-188, III-30
Doll, Jacky III-165
Domingos, Emerson S. I-188, I-244
dos Santos, Lillian Cristina I-322
Dowthwaite, Liz I-3
Doxastaki, Maria II-124
Duruaku, Fiona I-35

E
Edil, Arda III-14
Edwards, April I-253
Elsadouni, Eyad Raed III-193

C. Stephanidis et al. (Eds.): HCII 2024, CCIS 2319, pp. 355–358, 2025.
https://doi.org/10.1007/978-3-031-78516-0

Elsayed, Hoda II-81, III-193, III-204
Espejo-Viñán, Hernán II-108
Estrada L., Roberto G. I-188
Evdaimon, Theodoros II-124

F
Fan, Ling II-202, II-212, II-295
Faria, Juliana G. I-322
Farias, Paulo S. S. I-244
Felix, Juliana Paula I-322
Filho, Francisco III-30
Fiore, Stephen M. I-35
Fonseca, Afonso U. I-322
Franke, Ute II-263
Frempong, George II-186
Fujii, Ayaka II-194
Fukuda, Ken II-194

G
Gao, Xijie III-279
Gao, Xuan I-51
Garcia-Hernandez, Mariel III-25
Gaspar-López, Jose III-157
Ge, Jingbo III-72
Goh, Dion Hoe-Lian I-206, III-128
Gökgöz, Zeynep İrem III-14
Goram, Mandy I-60
Gračanin, Denis I-198

H
Hallmann, Michelle II-263
He, Yihao II-10
He, Ziming II-202, II-212, II-295
He, Ziqiang II-17
Heo, Eun II-244
Heredia Pérez, Grimaldo I-297, III-151
Hong, SungHee I-263
Hsieh, Tsuei-Ju III-285
Hu, Siqi III-215
Hu, Xiaoping III-339
Huaman Llanos, Alex Alfredo III-151
Huaman Monteza, Alexander I-297, III-151
Huang, Chenxin III-291
Huang, Liuyu III-128
Huang, Shunda II-23
Huang, Shuting II-161
Hub, Fabian II-115

I
Ishido, Hitoshi I-303
Islam, Ashraful III-3
Iza, Christian II-143, II-152

J
Jentsch, Florian G. I-35
Ji, Qian I-51
Jiang, Ke II-17
Jin, Shiming I-206
Jin, Shua-Hua I-70
Jones, Brooke III-40
Jung, SunOk I-263
Jurado, Matthew I-14

K
Kadam, Raavee II-186
Kapnas, George II-124
Kasote, Sparshad I-215
Khan, Muhammed Umair III-193
Kim, Hyun Seon I-272
Kim, Jiyoung III-301
Korozi, Maria II-124
Kuo, Shih-Mou III-339
Kwon, Jae-Hwi I-276

L
Lee, Hyebin II-257
Leonidis, Asterios II-124
Levy, Meyer I-253
Li, Dan III-138
Li, Jing III-72
Li, Jinling II-202, II-212
Li, Li I-86
Li, Ning II-273
Li, Xiaomei II-202, II-212, II-295
Li, Yi II-91
Lim, Chang Joo I-276, II-3
Lim, Jihee II-244
Lim, Yangkyu II-244, II-257, III-301
Lin, Yang-cheng II-221
Lin, Yun I-138
Ling, Jie I-86, I-281, II-23, III-138
Liu, Bo II-221
Liu, Rui II-23
Liu, Xiang I-70
Liu, Yang II-133

Liu, Yuanyuan I-97
Liu, Zixiao III-308
Lopes, Mariana I-165
Lowry, Jessica I-102
Lozano, Christian III-111
Luna, Mateus M. I-322
Luo, Qiguang II-23
Luo, Yinshan III-229

M
Maguire, Martin III-249
Margetis, George III-239
Markopoulos, Ioannis III-239
Marques, Joao III-30
Martin, Beth A. I-113
Martínez Garcés, Josnel II-305
Martín-Peña, Rosa E. II-233
Mifsud, Matthew I-25
Modic, Robert I-292
Moffis, Katlin T. II-34
Mohammadrezaei, Elham I-198
Mohtasim, Syed Niaz III-3
Molina, Lloyd II-108
Mondragon Regalado, Jose Ricardo I-297, III-151
Montenegro Juarez, Jannier Alberto III-151
Montenegro Juárez, Julio César III-151
Mundaca Araujo, Jaime I-297, III-151

N
Na, Kayoung III-301
Namgyu, Kang I-128, III-62
Naranjo-Pullupaxi, David II-143
Narváez, Jairo I-237
Nascimento, Thamer Horbylon I-322
Neto, Joao Soares de Oliveira I-322
Nogueira, Emilia A. I-322
Ntoa, Stavroula III-239

O
Oehl, Michael II-115
Ogrinc, Matevž I-292
Oh, David III-40
Oh, Seohyun II-244
Ohshima, Hiroyuki I-303
Olano Chuquihuanga, Wesley I-297
Ong, Albert I-206
Ordozgoith F. S., Pio H. I-177
Ostertag, Thomas II-263
Ou Yang, Li I-86, I-281, II-23, III-138
Özkurt, Arda III-14

P
Paixão, Najara II-43
Panyawanich, Kwan III-249
Paparoulis, George III-239
Park, Heehyeon II-249
Park, Juha II-257
Park, SunHee I-263
Phillips, Alison L. I-272
Polo Carrillo, Emilia María II-305
Poupou, Anna III-265
Pozo, Israel II-143
Pradel, Patrick III-249
Puentes, Sandra I-341

Q
Qiu, Haoran I-206

R
Rahman, Afnan Hafiz II-81
Ramírez, Carlos II-108
Rao, Santhosh I-215
Rashid, Hassan Harun ur III-193
Reddy, Pavan III-319
Ren, Jue I-118
Rizopoulos, Charalampos III-265
Roa, Jorge II-305
Rodríguez Estacio, John Smith I-297, III-151
Rodríguez-Villamizar, Mary Yaneth II-305

S
Salavarrieta, Oscar III-111
Saldaña Mendoza, Nancy I-297, III-151
Sanghi, Vanshika I-215
Santos, Alef II-43
Sarmiento, Fabian II-143
Sarmiento-Ortiz, Fabian II-152
Sarshartehrani, Fatemeh I-198
Sasaki, Akinori I-303
Schlüter, Benjamin II-263
Şeker, Sedef III-14
Sfakaki, Artemis III-239
Sharma, Abhishek III-47
Sharma, Lakshmi III-47
Sheng, Victor I-332
Shim, Bokwang II-257

Shimada, Shigenobu I-303
Si, Mei I-312, III-165
Sidhu, Amandeep III-47
Silbermann, Marcos I-165, II-43
Simčič, Andraž I-292
Singh, Aditya III-319
Siqueira, Joyce I-322
Soares, Fabrizzio I-322
Stephanidis, Constantine II-124, III-239
Stern, Michael II-263
Stivaktakis, Nikolaos Menelaos II-124
Stratakis, Christos II-124
Stuebe, Alison III-40
Suárez Peña, Willam I-297, III-151
Sufiyan Shoukat Ali, Muhammad III-193
Sykianaki, Eirini III-239

T
Tai, Chenxi II-69
Tanaka, Haruki I-128
Tarigonda, Amith I-14
Tayeb, Abdulaziz Mohammed III-193
Teofilo, Mauro III-30
Tong, Mu I-138
Topon - Visarrea, Blanca II-143, II-152
Torkar, Drago I-292
Traquair, Jason I-113
Triguero, Isaac I-3

U
Uenoya, Yuki III-62
Umejiaku, Afamefuna P. I-332

V
Valentin, Yves II-34
Varela, Carlos III-111
Vélez-Langs, Oswaldo III-157
Villamizar, Victor Hugo III-111
Voigt-Antons, Jan-Niklas II-263
Vona, Francesco II-263

W
Wang, Leirah I-118
Wang, Ran I-281
Wang, Runxin II-273
Wang, Shuyu I-206
Wang, Tianze III-72
Wang, Weirui III-331
Wang, Yan III-291
Webb, Helena I-3
Wei, Wenxi II-23
Weinberg, Dana I-253
White, Basil I-113
Williams, Florence I-145
Wu, Jiang III-72
Wu, Linfeng II-54
Wu, Peize III-72
Wu, Pengfei II-202, II-212, II-295
Wu, Zihong II-23

X
Xia, Ying I-97
Xiao, Qi III-80
Xu, Wangxuyu II-60
Xue, Yanmin II-161

Y
Yalçın, Sedat III-14
Yang, Ji Hyun I-157, II-100
Yepes, Isabel II-305
Yin, Stella Xin III-128
Yokoyama, Kota I-341
Yu, Dehua III-173
Yu, Xinyang III-215
Yuan, Jingyi III-96

Z
Zempo, Keiichi I-341
Zhang, Jiawen III-339
Zhang, Junjie II-69
Zhang, Lin II-273
Zhou, Longfei II-69
Zhou, Yalun III-165
Zhu, Fangzhou III-173
Zhu, Jin II-69
Zhuang, Li III-182
Zhuang, Yunyi III-138

The manufacturer's authorised representative in the EU is Springer Nature Customer Service Centre GmbH, Europaplatz 3, 69115 Heidelberg, Germany. If you have any concerns regarding our products, please contact ProductSafety@springernature.com

Printed and bound by CPI Group (UK) Ltd, Croydon, CR0 4YY
30/09/2026
02225597-0016